MUSIC FOR A CITY, MUSIC FOR THE WORLD

MUSIC FOR A CITY, MUSIC FOR THE WORLD

100 YEARS
WITH
THE
SAN FRANCISCO
SYMPHONY

LARRY ROTHE

ISBN 978-0-8118-7601-8

LIBRARY OF CONGRESS CATALOGING-IN-PUBLICATION DATA AVAILABLE
UNDER ISBN 978-0-8118-7600-1

MANUFACTURED IN CHINA.

DESIGN BY NOON.

JACKET PHOTOS: GOLDEN GATE BRIDGE, COURTESY OF THE SAN FRANCISCO
HISTORY CENTER AT THE SAN FRANCISCO PUBLIC LIBRARY; DOROTHY,
SUZANNE, AND MARY PASMORE, COURTESY OF MUSEUM OF PERFORMANCE
& DESIGN (SAN FRANCISCO); ALL OTHERS COURTESY OF THE SAN FRANCISCO
SYMPHONY.

ALL OTHER PHOTO CREDITS CAN BE FOUND ON PAGE 265.

10 9 8 7 6 5 4 3 2 1

CHRONICLE BOOKS LLC
680 SECOND STREET
SAN FRANCISCO, CALIFORNIA 94107

WWW.CHRONICLEBOOKS.COM/CUSTOM

FOR MORE INFORMATION ON THE HISTORY OF THE SAN FRANCISCO
SYMPHONY, AND TO HEAR HISTORIC AUDIO RECORDINGS FROM THE
SYMPHONY'S ARCHIVES, VISIT WWW.SFSYMPHONY.ORG.

To the artists and listeners, onstage and offstage,
whose love of music is the heart of the San Francisco Symphony.

CONTENTS

CHAPTER I

CHAPTER II

CHAPTER III

CHAPTER IV

CHAPTER V

CHAPTER VI

CHAPTER VII

CHAPTER VIII

CHAPTER IX

CHAPTER X

CHAPTER XI

8   INTRODUCTION

13   PRELIMINARIES: ON CIVILIZATION'S FRONTIER

20   A QUICK-START GUIDE TO MAKING AN ORCHESTRA
         The Henry Hadley Years (1911–1915)

39   PERSONAL STRUGGLES AND MUSICAL TRIUMPHS
         The Alfred Hertz Years (1915–1930)

60   CRISIS AND RESCUE
         The Basil Cameron/Issay Dobrowen Years (1930–1935)

81   SAN FRANCISCO'S FAVORITE SPORT
         The Pierre Monteux Years (1935–1952)

114   AN ENIGMA AND A TRAGEDY
         The Enrique Jordá Years (1954–1963)

137   MUSICAL BODY-BUILDING
         The Josef Krips Years (1963–1970)

154   A NEW KIND OF GLAMOUR
         The Seiji Ozawa Years (1970–1977)

177   A WEST COAST SUCCESS STORY
         The Edo de Waart Years (1977–1985)

196   MANDATE FOR CHANGE
         The Herbert Blomstedt Years (1985–1995)

221   ON THE FUTURE'S FRONTIER
         The Michael Tilson Thomas Years (1995–present)

253   ENDNOTES

265   PHOTO CREDITS

266   INDEX

It started with the end of a world. The earth-quake of 1906 destroyed one San Francisco and gave birth to another, also to a new orchestra —aimed at revitalizing the city's cultural life. Packed into that simple statement of ambition is a century-long story.

That story is a tale of transformation and evolution, about how people who understood music's power began with an idea, then shaped it into a cultural institution. Today we call the San Francisco Symphony *great*. That reputation was not conferred at birth. Such enterprises are always works in progress. We tend to see the progress thus far—the path that has led to this point a hundred years later—as a con-stant trajectory, proceeding at a single speed, the target in sight and the movement sure. Closer examination always reveals starts and stops, periods of relative stasis and exhilarat-ing times of rapid acceleration. Closer exami-nation reveals the dramas that emerge as obstacles are recognized and surmounted.

This story of the San Francisco Symphony is such an examination. As anyone who has climbed a trail to the summit knows, some parts of the ground are easier to cover than others. History is about stubborn movement forward, the different velocities that press against the wall of a future that is yielding in some places and resistant in others.

Symphony history is populated by men and women and the music they loved and continue to love. Some of the characters are outmatched by circumstances. Others wrestle circumstances to the floor. Some are simply well-intentioned. Others are visionary. Because music never exists apart from the larger and smaller universes in which it is born, this is also a story of an organization whose own history is interwoven with the histories of city, state, country, world. And while every orchestra in the United States can tell its own saga of public support, in San Francisco, the city's music lovers have been crucial to the Symphony's very existence.

Music, for its listeners, is something that exists not on the page, but in performance. Every performance is a transformation, too, one that brings music to life and to our lives. This alchemy, when the score becomes sound, demands powers of imagination and execution that seek to match the music's stature. Those who make music have no choice *but* to strive for greatness. Over the course of a century, the San Francisco Symphony has defined itself as an ensemble equal to those demands— more equal to them at some times than at others, although the mission has always been to bring music, and all that music means, to those hungry for it and to those for whom a first taste might lead to a second. Music is a gift for everyone, not just for select provinces of society. From the start, the Symphony made performances affordable and widely available. And as technologies developed, new audiences were reached in new ways. All this is part of the story, and part of the continuing story.

For the story continues, and whoever documents the Symphony's bicentenary will have a richer tale to tell. I tell of the San Francisco Symphony's birth, struggles, and achievements beginning with pre-earthquake San Francisco, to the orchestra's first performance in 1911, and through its first hundred years. I have attempted to be objective but not dispassionate, have tried not to overlook drama where it

10

exists nor create drama where it is absent. For helping me tell this story I am indebted to many, beginning with the musicians of the San Francisco Symphony (current and former), specifically (in alphabetical order): Alexander Barantschik, Chris Bogios, Charles Burrell, Stuart Canin, Don Carroll, Don Ehrlich, Jorja Fleezanis, Detlev Olshausen, Stephen Paulson, Scott Pingel, Paul Renzi, Peter Shelton, Robin Sutherland, and Jack Van Geem. For taking time from all-but-impossible schedules to speak with me, I thank the Symphony's current music director, Michael Tilson Thomas, and his two immediate predecessors, Herbert Blomstedt and Edo de Waart. Symphony President John D. Goldman and Executive Director Brent Assink supported this project from conception to completion. Among board members (current and former) who shared recollections were Ava Jean Brumbaum, Katherine Buchanan, Ellen Magnin Newman, and Genelle Relfe. I am grateful also to Joseph A. Scafidi, who joined the Symphony as jack-of-all-trades in 1939 and left as executive director in 1978, and to former executive director Peter Pastreich, who served in that post for twenty years. Both offered their reminiscences with wonderful generosity and candor; in addition, Pastreich made valuable suggestions on the manuscript. Director of Marketing, Communications and External Affairs Nan Keeton provided the experience, expertise, and direction that helped transform the project from idea into finished product. Along with Brent Assink, she also offered invaluable input on the manuscript, as did these other insightful readers: Caroline Colburn, Scott Foglesong, John Goldman, Gregg Gleasner, Polly Ikonen, John Kieser, Ellen Magnin Newman, and Oliver Theil. Kathy Brown, Katherine Cummins, Marie Dalby, and Jeanette Yu—my colleagues in the Symphony's Publications Department—ensured seamless department operations throughout the year in which I focused my concentration on this book. Music critic and writer Allan Ulrich conducted oral history interviews with former concertmaster Stuart Canin and violist Detlev Olshausen. Jason Gibbs of the San Francisco Public Library provided access to the library's rich collection of Alfred Hertz materials. Leta Miller of the University of California at Santa Cruz is probably the world's leading authority on Hertz and generously made her own original research available. Symphony Archivist Joe Evans and his associate, Kelly Chatain, have been crucial to this project from the start. Joe was a never-ending source of guidance, stimulation, knowledge, and moral support; he and Kelly also spent hours assembling the many images, with which the book's designer, Cinthia Wen, and her associate, Ed Ng, have illustrated the Symphony's history. My editor at Chronicle Books, Micaela Heekin, was tough, thorough, and inspiring; she possesses an editor's most essential asset, the rare power to be at once firm and unobtrusive. I am grateful also to Jeff Campbell, an extraordinarily scrupulous copy editor. Finally, I thank my wife, Karen Borst-Rothe, for the tough love with which she reviewed each chapter as it emerged and reemerged, and for the reassurance and good humor with which she bolstered me throughout.

No writer can produce a history such as this alone, but every writer knows that the final job of creating a felicitous and accurate account belongs only to one person. And so, having offered thanks to those who have helped along the way, I take sole responsibility for any infelicities or inaccuracies in what follows.

11

PRELIMINARIES: ON CIVILIZATION'S FRONTIER

In April 1905, the conductor of New York's Metropolitan Opera, happy to have arrived in San Francisco with the company's touring ensemble, reflected on the trials of a cross-country journey. From his suite in the Palace Hotel on lower Market Street, he wrote to an East Coast associate telling what he had encountered once he had left New York civilization. In Cincinnati, a bellboy greeted his complaint about poor service with an invective against "this damned opera company." In Minneapolis, the hotel restaurant shut its doors by nine in the evening. In Kansas City, a municipal ordinance forbade sale of mineral water on Sundays. A neighborhood church there offered a special twenty-five-cent "*Parsifal* Dinner" in honor of the opera the Met had presented in a local auditorium, a place whose fifteen-thousand-seat vastness defeated even an orchestra of Wagnerian size, and where a shouting spectator interrupted the performance, demanding a refund because he could not see the stage. In San Francisco, the maestro concluded, "everything is more Bohemian and a good deal like Paris."

When he wrote those words, Alfred Hertz had no clue that, ten years later, San Francisco would be his home. The city in 1905 did not even host a permanent orchestra. Yet symphonic music had long flourished in San Francisco, as had opera and song. Almost from the start, it was a city of music-makers. And although a professional orchestra of San Francisco's own seemed to elude music lovers intent on creating one, the "more bohemian" San Francisco of 1905 was a cultured place and clearly a relief, a haven after the distances Hertz had spanned on his way west from New York. From the window of his train compartment on the Santa Fe line he marveled at prairie fires that lit the evening clouds. As the engine labored across New Mexico and Arizona, wide-spaced

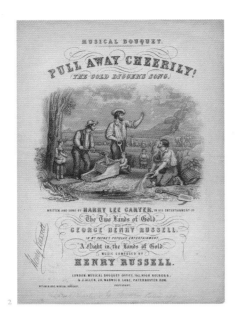

territories not destined to become states for another seven years, he gazed out at reservations corralling those who until recently had enjoyed unhindered passage over the plains and deserts. Geronimo was still alive. The massacre at Wounded Knee, South Dakota, was only fifteen years in the past. When Hertz arrived in San Francisco, he was back in a cosmopolitan world, a world that reminded him of Paris.

No longer did it suggest the town called Yerba Buena, settled in 1835 and renamed San Francisco in 1847. The story of the city's growth during the Gold Rush that commenced two years later is well known, with the population shooting from a thousand in 1848 to twenty-five thousand the next year.

With the discovery of gold, the history of music in San Francisco begins. The prospectors and fortune hunters who swarmed into the harbor town starting in February 1849 were as tough as they come. Living conditions were deplorable and costs were high. A night on a rooming-house cot could run fifteen dollars, and commodities and services were just as expensive. Life was as unstable

as the fault lines bisecting this virgin territory, where the possibilities for great gain and great loss turned some new arrivals generous and others mean, and made all of them wary. Most were men. Whether gearing up to head for the mountains or just returned from the gold fields, they longed for civilization. In this atmosphere, music and civilization were interchangeable terms. "The first grand concert of vocal and instrumental music," reported the critic for the *Alta California* on December 23, 1850, "was given yesterday afternoon at the California Exchange. Some forty musicians performed many of the most popular and grand overtures, symphonies, and variations of the composers." Just what kind of music was made on that afternoon before Christmas in 1850 isn't clear. It may have been a mixed bag. One number, reported the *Alta*, was an aria from Handel's opera *Attila*, performed by the trombonist "Signor Lobero." Especially enchanting was the singer: "What most particularly struck our fancy, ear and heart," the reviewer confessed, "was the Cavatina from *La sonnambula*, sung by Señora Abalos." As the audience of lonely, tired men headed home that evening—home through muddy streets to shacks and tents and boardinghouses— Bellini and beauty, thanks to the talented Señora Abalos, would have been synonymous, and in such synonyms lay reassurance.

Fortunes in gold came and went. So did musical ensembles. The Willis Brass Band. The Young Ladies Silver Cornet Band. The Mexican Philharmonic Society Band. The Russian Symphony Orchestra of New York. These were some of the groups that visited San Francisco as it grew from boomtown into one of the world's great cities, and as the completion

2
_____

"While tilting his dish up, / We merrily fish up, / Another supply of the glittering sand." Such lines, from British composer Henry Russell's "Pull Away Cheerily!" (aka "The Gold Digger's Song"), ignored gold field realities while conveying California's allure.

3

3
_____

San Francisco cityscape, 1905. After the frustrations of cross-country train travel, Alfred Hertz found everything here "more Bohemian and a good deal like Paris."

PLATT'S HALL,

San Francisco

PHILHARMONIC

SOCIETY.

THIRD CONCERT.

FIRST SEASON.

Friday Evening, Feb. 3rd, 1882.

Gustav Hinrichs,

Conductor.

Begins precisely at 8 P. M.
Carriages at 10 P. M.

Rosenthal & Roesch, Printers, Cal'a St.

4

4

As a viable city, San Francisco was barely thirty years old in 1882. Already it boasted a Philharmonic Society whose elegant printed materials suggest a lofty purpose.

Fritz Scheels Orchestra
SAN FRANCISCO. 1894

5

MONSTER

CONCERT,

In aid of the Family of the late EDW. BUECHEL
and A. PONCINI, an invalid Musician,

THURSDAY AFTERNOON,...... JUNE 23,

AT

PLATT'S NEW MUSIC HALL

The following distinguished Artists have in the
kindest way volunteered their services:

PAUL JULIEN,
SIGNORA GHIONI,
SIGNORA BIANCHI,
SIGNOR BIANCHI,
ERNST HARTMANN
THE S. F. HARMONIE, S. F. MAENNERCHOR,
THE TWELVE, AND A

Grand Orchestra of 80 Musicians

The whole under the direction of
PROF. R. HEROLD.

PROGRAMME.

PART I.

1—Marche du Sacre, from The Prophet—Meyerber
2—Grand Overture, Merry Wives of Windsor—Ni-
colai.
3—Romanza, nell'Opera Luisa Muller...........Verdi
SIGNOR EUGENIO BIANCHI.
4—Solo Violin...Capriccio............................Julien
MONS. PAUL JULIEN.
5—Cavatina nell'Opera Ernani............Verdi
SIGNORA GHIONI.

PART II.

6—Grand Overture Robespierre..................Littolf
7—Romanza nell'Opera I due Foscari..........Verdi
SIGNORA BIANCHI.
8—Piano Solo—Tannhauser March.................Liszt
HERR ERNST HARTMANN.
9—Grand Pilgrim Chorus from Tannhauser—Wagner......by the S. F. Harmonie, S. F. Maennerchor, The Twelve, etc., and Grand Orchestral
Accompaniment.
10—Pony Express Gallop.........................Buechel

☞ The Piano used on this occasion is furnished
by the kindness of A. Kuhne, Esq.

6

ADMISSION,................ONE DOLLAR.

☞ Concert to commence at 2 o'clock; Doors
open at 1 P. M.
☞ Seats may be secured at Fifty Cents extra, on
WEDNESDAY and THURSDAY, from 10 to 1
o'clock.

5

Fritz Scheel led one of the city's foremost ensembles. Returning to the East Coast, he founded the Philadelphia Orchestra.

6

As early as 1864, San Francisco had enough musical talent to present concerts of monster proportions: five vocal soloists, three choruses, and an orchestra of eighty.

of the railway from east to west in 1869 linked it to the rest of the country. The musical groups formed in the city itself were pulled together early. The first opera produced in San Francisco was *La sonnambula*—perhaps Señora Abalos had started something—staged in 1851 by Alfred Roncovieri, a French bass who raised his stock in the musical world of the frontier when he convinced people to start calling him "Count." The Count of San Francisco became a city fixture, and over the years he presented much of the now-standard nineteenth-century French and Italian repertory. Opera thrived. Adelina Patti, Luisa Tetrazzini—many of the legendary singers of the nineteenth century visited, and those visits became a tradition that continued to the eve of the 1906 earthquake. Legendary instrumentalists appeared as well: pianists Henri Herz and Ignace Jan Paderewski, violinists Mischa Elman and Eugène Ysaÿe. But despite these riches, the city's musical world was embarrassingly poor in one respect. San Francisco had no symphony orchestra.

Time and again, courageous musicians tried to fill the need for a symphonic ensemble. In 1854, a Germania Concert Society was organized. Rudolf Herold presented performances with the group for twenty-five years. A San Francisco Musical Institute was founded in 1869, and though what this was is unclear, a program broadside describes one of its 1871 concerts as a performance "With Grand Orchestra." The Orchestral Union was organized in 1879. J. B. Levison, destined to become a board president

of the San Francisco Symphony, joined as flutist in 1883. Fifty years later he recalled how the ensemble attacked the opening of the Overture to *The Merry Wives of Windsor*, causing the conductor to drop his baton and cover his ears. In 1880, Louis Homeier organized a forty-member orchestra that remained active "for several years," according to one source; another claims it lasted until 1894. Gustav Hinrichs, a German who came to San Francisco in 1870, founded the Philharmonic Society Orchestra in 1881 and conducted it for six seasons. He left the city in 1885 for the East Coast, where he went on to champion Italian romantic opera and conducted the first North American performances of *Cavalleria Rusticana*, *I Pagliacci*, and *Manon Lescaut*.

Though the Homeier and Hinrichs ensembles were active throughout the better part of the 1880s, existing records suggest that no one took them seriously as permanent music-making bodies. In 1883, fired with enthusiasm by the visiting Theodore Thomas Orchestra, which through its tours carried music across the country, Frederick Zech organized a group of rough-and-tumble musicians. The enterprise was short-lived, its accomplished players outnumbered by the less adept. Zech's podium theatrics offered little reassurance. Reported one observer: "His mere presence was exhausting."

In 1894, Fritz Scheel brought the Imperial Vienna Prater Orchestra to the Midwinter Fair. Scheel's concerts were tremendously popular, and when he returned the following year, a crowd of twenty-five hundred is reported to have packed the Mechanics Institute Pavilion (a building located essentially where the Bill Graham Civic Auditorium now stands). Scheel soon decided to

call San Francisco home. Before long he organized an ensemble he called the San Francisco Symphony Orchestra, his goal to present at least fifteen concerts each season. By 1898 the fifty-member orchestra was still intact, but a year later, when Scheel went east to found the Philadelphia Orchestra, his San Francisco group foundered, struggling until 1906, when the earthquake and the fire it spawned delivered the *coup de grace*.

Tracing the history of symphony orchestras in late nineteenth-century San Francisco is confusing. From Philharmonic Society Orchestra to San Francisco Symphony Orchestra (also called the San Francisco Symphony Society), from San Francisco Musical Institute to Frederick Zech's Orchestra, from Louis Homeier to Rudolf Herold: names, dates, and ensembles are often difficult to place. What is not difficult to ascertain is the *amount* of music being made. In her 1946 history of the San Francisco Symphony's first decade, the organization's then-president, Leonora Wood Armsby, claimed to have enumerated the concerts and recitals offered in the city between 1849 and 1906 and compiled a list covering seventeen pages, closely spaced. "San Francisco is naturally and temperamentally a *musical* city," said the New York conductor Walter Damrosch in 1901, while serving a stint at a local opera house. "What it needs is a good orchestra."

Such an ambition was nothing new. But it was put on hold starting at 5:12 on the morning of April 18, 1906. About fifteen miles from San Francisco, off the coast near Daly City in San Mateo County, the Pacific and North American tectonic plates slipped past each other. In the forty-two seconds that followed, San Francisco was torn open. The

17

Richter scale suppresses horror by assigning it a number: 7.8, in this case. That number translated into shock waves traveling through the earth at seven thousand miles per hour and an explosion of energy equal to a million tons of TNT, almost seventy times the equivalent of the atomic bomb that would detonate over Hiroshima four decades later. Once again, Alfred Hertz and the Metropolitan Opera Company were in San Francisco. Enrico Caruso had appeared as Don José in *Carmen* at the Grand Opera House (on Mission Street, between 3rd and 4th Streets) the evening before. Moments after the quake, Caruso was in the Palace Hotel lobby, treading across a floor littered with smashed glass. Spotting Hertz, the singer rushed to embrace him, "crying like a child," as Hertz recalled, certain of the doom they faced.

A new San Francisco appeared with unnerving speed after the earthquake, confounding the plan that architect and city planner Daniel Burnham had proposed in 1904. As historical geographer Gray Brechin writes, Burnham convinced business leaders that San Francisco "offered tremendous possibilities for creating a city worthy of an ocean as big as the Pacific." Burnham, architect of Chicago's great Columbian Exposition of 1893, envisioned a San Francisco of parks and boulevards, modeled on Imperial Rome and Belle Époque Paris, with a civic center fashioned after Paris's Place de la Concorde and targeted for the intersection of Market Street and Van Ness Avenue. But the natural disaster that razed San Francisco offered no tabula rasa on which Burnham's grandiose ideas could become real. As Brechin explains, the scope of destruction was met by a "frenzy to rebuild." In their haste to resurrect the city, developers had no patience for innovative plans.

San Francisco's rebuilding was accompanied by a deeper ambition. A city was by definition a place of culture. Great cities supported orchestras, and not only the cities east of the Mississippi. Minneapolis supported an orchestra and so did Seattle. The time had come for San Francisco to do likewise.

The genesis of the San Francisco Symphony was part of the city's rebirth. It grew from an ideal. You will find no references to this ideal in the minutes of board meetings or in newspaper clippings. But historian Kevin Starr identified it in his story of Josiah Royce, the California-born (in 1855) Harvard philosopher who wrote that "the 'winning of the West' . . . has been a spiritual much more than a merely physical conquest. And the spiritual history of the West has been the history of the formation of local institutions." Those institutions, Royce believed, helped pull life's jigsaw-puzzle pieces into place, helped shape societies, which is what the "winning of the West" was all about.

In the American saga, *West* has been any untamed territory that lies under the setting sun, as beckoning and threatening as the dark forests of fairy legends. To the Founding Fathers, *West* meant the Appalachians. To those who settled those mountains, it meant the Mississippi River. The history of the late nineteenth and early twentieth centuries in the United States is a history of the frontier's closing, of a narrowing definition of *West*, an increasing consolidation of business and government, the founding of cultural organizations, often supported by the frontier-taming wealth of the industries transforming America from a rural to an urban nation. If California during this time gave birth to the University of California

and Stanford University, older parts of the nation were no less culturally active. In Chicago alone, an orchestra and a university sprang up in these years.

The San Francisco Symphony's founding was part of a national trend, but it was also different, a specific response to a specific need in a particular place. A community defines its institutions and is defined by them. Those institutions also bind the community to the wider world. Music, we like to say, is universal, not tied to locale or time. We believe in its power to revitalize lives and to help focus energies and aspirations. That belief becomes a fact for those with first-hand experience of music—the kind of music with which Señora Abalos enchanted her audience of Forty-Niners, the kind that the San Francisco Symphony's founders were determined to present and to keep presenting, by an organization anchored in the community, resistant to the pressures and challenges that had wiped out so many organizations before it.

Unlike orchestras in New York or Philadelphia or Chicago, the San Francisco Symphony was conceived not just as a jewel in the municipal crown. It would become such a jewel, but from the beginning it was envisioned as more. For its foundation was poured along with that of a new San Francisco, and it was built to appeal even at the grassroots level to men and women eager for beauty and affirmation and fun, to this community of music lovers. Organizing concerts and performing music: that is the simplest way to describe the work of an institution that supports and presents an orchestra. But think of what concerts mean to those who create and perform and love music—those who believe that music can route us through the hazards of our own inner West as we negotiate the valleys and barely perceived trails, as we master our responses to the personal earthquakes apt to shake each day.

To San Francisco, which had come so close to world's end, the world that remained was dearer and more beautiful, and no time could be lost in shaping it.

8

7

9

7

Enrico Caruso as he appeared in Carmen. *He is outfitted here as Don José, the role he sang at San Francisco's Grand Opera House on the eve of the 1906 earthquake.*

8

Looking northeast from Gough Street after the earthquake. In the background are the ruins of City Hall. In the foreground, what was left of St. Ignatius School. The land where St. Ignatius stood would become the site of Davies Symphony Hall.

9

Architect Daniel Burnham imagined remaking San Francisco in the image of ancient Rome. His colleague Willis Polk's conception of Nob Hill and the urban tapestry below was part of the Burnham Plan. (Illustration from the San Francisco Bulletin, *1904.)*

II.

A QUICK-START GUIDE TO MAKING AN ORCHESTRA
The Henry Hadley Years (1911-1915)

A NEW CENTURY, AND OTHER BEGINNINGS

Early in the twentieth century, technology shifted into overdrive. In 1903, the Wright brothers proved that a flying machine was more than a dream. The next year America's decade-long effort to build the Panama Canal commenced. Even before construction began, its promoters envisioned a great world's fair to celebrate the project's completion. San Francisco, then one of the world's busiest seaports, was a natural locale for such festivities, but in 1906 the earthquake doomed that possibility. Or seemed to doom it. The city rebuilt at a phenomenal pace. By 1909 its population was

roughly what it had been three years earlier, about 417,000, and most of the Financial District was standing again. That October, civic boosterism was reignited in the first Portola Festival. The five days of parades and festivities ostensibly celebrated Gaspar de Portolá's sighting of San Francisco Bay in 1769, but in fact the pageant heralded San Francisco's rebirth. On December 7, 1909, the city launched a public relations campaign that culminated early in 1911, when San Francisco was announced as the site of the fair that so recently had seemed out of reach. The Panama-Pacific International

Exposition, whose scale would be comparable to Chicago's Columbian Exposition of 1893, was to open in 1915.

In this world of confidence and promise, the idea of the San Francisco Symphony took shape. On the afternoon of December 20, 1909, two weeks after efforts commenced to bring the world's fair to San Francisco, ten businessmen gathered in the Assembly Room of the Mercantile Trust Company of San Francisco, at 464 California Street. They too had rebuilding on their minds. Their purpose was to help reconstruct the

2

city's cultural life by organizing a permanent symphony orchestra.

In 1909, Boston offered the model for such an ensemble. For almost thirty years, Henry Lee Higginson's Boston Symphony had been the envy of cities across the United States, proof that orchestras could be viable civic assets in this country, as they were abroad. Higginson made it clear that he wanted to give Boston the kind of orchestra found in European cities. "The essential condition of such orchestras is their stability, whereas ours are necessarily shifting and uncertain, because we are dependent upon musicians whose work and time are largely pledged elsewhere"—*elsewhere* meaning theaters or dance halls or restaurants or cafes. Higginson proposed to pay the musicians himself, and he worded contracts in such a way as to guarantee the undivided service of his players. He would also make up any deficit the orchestra

might encounter. In a sense, Higginson was emulating old models from Europe, where orchestras associated with royal courts were supported by aristocrats.

If you were searching for musicians in San Francisco, you would find them in the kinds of places from which Higginson had lured them in Boston, baiting his offers nicely and making an exclusive Boston Symphony commitment worth a player's while. Higginson's idea was simple, but at the time it was an innovation: offered a living wage, the best musicians in theaters and cafes would migrate to a symphony orchestra.

Not every city boasted such a generous patron as Higginson. Clearly, however, any orchestral undertaking depended on musicians, and securing them depended on capital. San Francisco's financial model was more democratic than Boston's, and based on the belief that music

was essential not just for the civic good but also for its life-enriching potential. Music was for the people. So it was to the people that the San Francisco Symphony's founders turned. They began their search among those they knew best, who also happened to be those with means to help.

The December 20 meeting that laid the groundwork for an orchestra had been called by three men: T. B. Berry (the T. B. for Tiernan Brien), E. S. Heller (the E. S. for Emanuel Siegfried), and John Rothschild. Berry was a Maryland native who had headed west at age twenty, gone into real estate, divided a portion of Berkeley into building lots, and converted a block of San Francisco's wholesale district into warehouse and factory space; he also owned a coal mine and a cattle company. Heller, born in San Francisco, was an attorney whose name still heads the list of names associated with the law firm

4

2-4

*A trio of remarkable self-made men laid the
foundation of the Musical Association of San
Francisco: E. S. Heller (2), T. B. Berry, who
also served as first Association president (3),
and John Rothschild (4).*

5

*The Mercantile Trust Company, 464
California Street. In a conference room
here, on December 20, 1909, a plan was
introduced to form an orchestra.*

3

5

Heller, Ehrman, White, and McAuliffe. Rothschild grew up in Germany, emigrated when he was eighteen, and by age thirty-two had established the San Francisco export-import firm of John Rothschild & Co., with branches around the world. Berry, Heller, and Rothschild were self-made men. They loved the city that had given them opportunities, and they loved music.

On that winter afternoon in 1909, they were joined by seven of the twenty-five prominent citizens they had invited to participate in their venture. Another eleven had indicated interest. And so, with a total of twenty-one names on record, the Musical Association of San Francisco was organized. Berry was named chairman. A month later, the Association put its purpose in writing: "to foster Musical Art in all its forms, and particularly to establish a Symphony Orchestra in San

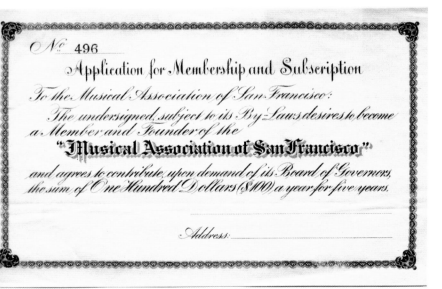

Nᵒ 496
Application for Membership and Subscription

To the Musical Association of San Francisco:
The undersigned, subject to its By-Laws desires to become a Member and Founder of the

"Musical Association of San Francisco"

and agrees to contribute, upon demand of its Board of Governors, the sum of One Hundred Dollars ($100) a year for five years.

Address: _____

6

Francisco" and "the building of a great opera house." In February, the group of twenty-one was formally declared the Association's Board of Governors. Now that they had committed themselves, they began grassroots work. They had no manual to work from, only business experience, intuition, and ideals. Those three

assets helped them learn as they worked. Had they looked back in years to come, they could have written a set of instructions: steps for assembling an orchestra, based on what they had learned.

THE SAN FRANCISCO MODEL: STEPS FOR ASSEMBLY

1. RAISE MONEY

Berry, Heller, and Rothschild began by approaching twelve hundred funding prospects. By March, fifty-eight had pledged a hundred dollars annually for five years. After five years the enterprise would be reassessed. The goal was three hundred guarantors and a total contribution of thirty thousand dollars. By October they were halfway there. Between October 1910 and mid-August 1911, board members wrote letters, knocked on doors, made calls.

2. HIRE A CONDUCTOR

On August 18, 1911, the board considered three conductors. Two were German: Philipp Wolfrum and Fritz Stein. One was homegrown: Henry Hadley. Hadley, then music director of the fledgling Seattle Symphony, had conducted orchestras in Europe and was a composer of considerable renown whose portfolio included symphonies, tone poems, songs, and oratorios.

The safest route might have been to hire one of the German maestros. Whatever Hadley's reputation, American conductors simply did not enjoy the prestige of their Teutonic counterparts. But the board performed its due diligence. Their inquiries

about the candidates extended as far as England and Germany itself. Wherever they turned, the promoters of what was then called the "San Francisco Orchestra" encountered the same advice: *Get Hadley. Do whatever you need to do, just get him. Hadley is the man for San Francisco.* Board member Frank Deering explained all this to a Chamber of Commerce meeting in November 1911. When Deering announced Hadley's acceptance, he was greeted with cheers.

Obtaining Hadley's services was a coup. Besides his musical talents, he came with collateral assets. He was handsome, had a reputation as a genuinely good fellow, and could mingle easily with the class of society on whose support the new organization would depend. Soon he became a member of the Bohemian Club, the exclusive fraternity that in 1912 produced his theatrical extravaganza *The Atonement of Pan* at its annual retreat in the redwoods north of the city. Hadley was diplomatic and a born organizer. He was, as Frank Deering had been assured, the man for San Francisco.

3. HIRE A CONCERTMASTER

Eduard Tak was Dutch by birth. He had studied with Joseph Joachim, a great violinist in his own right and an intimate of Johannes Brahms. Tak had played under such maestros as Felix Weingartner and the composer-conductors Richard Strauss and Max Bruch. Tak came from the great nineteenth-century Romantic tradition. He had the makings of a superb concertmaster. *Hire him,* Hadley directed.

4. HIRE MUSICIANS

This, the crucial step, was the hardest. Henry Hadley arrived in San Francisco in October 1911, and on the 30th of that month he told the board

7

what he had discovered as he took stock of the city's musical resources in ten days of exploration. By now he knew that San Francisco was home to many good musicians. He doubted, however, that many would be free to devote themselves to an orchestra. Somehow, arrangements would have to be made with their current employers.

The following week, Berry, Rothschild, and Hadley hit the streets. They went to hotels, to restaurants, to theaters, searching for the best musicians they could find. Four years later, as the *San Francisco Chronicle* looked back on this recruitment, the paper's editors reminded readers that standards of popular music in the city were high, and the musicians who worked in cafes and bars were professionals of the first order. But the opportunity to play Mozart and Beethoven was not enough for them to forsake well-paying positions

in hotel or restaurant bands. The Association simply could not afford to offer the kind of money to tempt them from their current jobs. This meant the players who agreed to join the Symphony would not be available for evening concerts. All performances would be matinees.

5. FIND A CONCERT HALL
Hadley was enthusiastic. He had persuaded many musicians to join the Symphony camp. In early November, he reported his success at a board meeting, but his optimism was questioned. Time was running out. Association Vice President Richard Tobin asked whether an ensemble "of proper character" could be assembled within a month. Inclined to churn the options out loud, Tobin had barely voiced his reservations before revealing that the Association was guaranteed use of the Cort Theatre, at 64 Ellis Street, for twelve performances at $150 each, with

6
_____
To make membership official: A variety of typefaces from the worlds of stock certificates and real estate underscore a serious commitment.

7
_____
Henry Hadley: composer, conductor, matinee idol.

25

INTRODUCING HENRY HADLEY

Henry Hadley, perhaps as Alfred Metzger saw him.

In 1911, every podium of every major orchestra in the United States was occupied by leaders from the far side of the Atlantic. All the more extraordinary that Henry Hadley, the San Francisco Symphony's first music director, was an American. Not until Michael Tilson Thomas assumed the orchestra's leadership in 1995, eighty years after Hadley's departure, would another American occupy the post.

Henry Kimball Hadley was born in 1871 in Somerville, Massachusetts, just outside Boston. His father taught music in the city schools, and his mother sang and played piano. Hadley was a blueblood. His father's family had settled in Massachusetts in 1714, and his maternal forebears included Roger Conant, founder of Salem. In the annals of American history, Somerville itself is hallowed ground, along the route Paul Revere rode as he called out the militias.

By the time he was twelve, Henry was composing. He studied in Boston with George Chadwick—another American composer whose music is rarely heard today—and before he was twenty-one he had written songs, chamber music, and an orchestral overture. He studied in Vienna, where he often encountered Brahms in cafes and on the street. In 1904, after a stateside stint, he was off to Europe again—Paris, Egypt, Italy, and finally Munich, where he continued his training. He guest-conducted the Berlin Philharmonic in his Third Symphony and took a permanent post as conductor at the opera house in Mainz, outside Frankfurt, then returned to the United States in 1909 to become music director of the Seattle Symphony. Two years later he accepted the invitation to lead a new orchestra in San Francisco.

Music critics in the Bay city greeted the news gladly. The *Chronicle*'s Harvey Wickham was star-struck. Meeting Hadley for a late-night interview in the conductor's hotel suite, he was awed by the dashing figure cloaked in a flowing dressing gown. In a gesture of manly camaraderie, Hadley offered a cigarette. "The Hadley smile is magnetic," Wickham reported. "With a baton in his hand he must be absolutely compelling."

Even Alfred Metzger lauded Hadley's appointment. Metzger, founder and editor of the *Pacific Coast Musical Review*, was a prolific writer whose roughly eloquent sentences sometimes offered more rhythm than sense or tact. Metzger had a knack for public sentiments that most writers prefer to consign to their diaries. "Honesty," he called this quirk. In the months of anticipation before the first concert, Metzger claimed he would take no interest in the orchestra until it achieved more permanent footing. When he learned that the orchestra's founders had not yet ensured the permanent status he advocated, he seems to have taken personal offense.

From that moment on, the only good thing Metzger could say about Hadley was that he was an expert composer. He deplored Hadley's technical skills and regretted that such fine musicians should be compelled to play under a leader "of such average ability." His viciousness verged on the comic.

All this was a surprising reaction to someone who had recently been lauded as a conductor in both the *New York Times* and the *Seattle Times*. To those who objected to his harsh treatment of Hadley, Metzger had an answer: they could not distinguish good from mediocre, or they refused to describe the emperor's nakedness. They lacked honesty.

In general, Metzger's displeasure seems to have rested mainly on what he claimed was Hadley's misjudgment of tempo relationships, his tendency to rush toward a climax, thus stripping it of its full effect—legitimate grounds for criticism; but Metzger went beyond music criticism to deeply personal attacks, suggesting what Hadley and the organization faced as they were trying to put down roots. Metzger was a man of his time, a time in which President William McKinley fell victim to an anarchist assassin in 1901, and a time that welcomed the publication in 1906 of Upton Sinclair's *The Jungle*, set among poor immigrants who toiled in Chicago stockyards. Metzger detested upper-crust society. His diatribes against the wealthy reveal his delight in unloading abuse. Henry Hadley had great social credentials. Those, along with matinee-idol good looks, a style as smooth as the Lafitte-Rothschild that Metzger would never taste, and a salary that translated to $220,000 in 2011 dollars, must have magnified any artistic shortcoming Metzger perceived, not to mention any imagined slights by the Musical Association. All this drove him mad.

Hadley fared better with others. What is most telling is how musicians reacted to him. On December 20, 1912, Henry Hadley's forty-first birthday, the San Francisco Symphony followed a performance of his Symphony No. 4 with an onstage ceremony in his honor. Concertmaster Adolph Rosenbecker praised Hadley's "great merit as a conductor," echoing the Seattle Symphony's musicians.

Whatever Hadley's podium talents, his first love remained composing. He wrote five symphonies and five operas, choral works, and tone poems. In 1920, when *Cleopatra's Night* premiered at the Met, *New York Times* critic Richard Aldrich called it "the best of the ten American operas produced in the Metropolitan." His lush, extravagantly colored Romantic style suggests Richard Strauss, who identified Hadley as the only American composer who really understood the orchestra.

Hadley kept abreast of what was happening in music, returning from a European summer in 1913 with a steamer trunk filled with scores by Debussy, Ravel, Reger, Rachmaninoff, and Stravinsky. Nothing in his own compositions suggests "American music" as we have come to think of it, listening to the work of composers such as Aaron Copland or Roy Harris or William Schuman, who were beginning their careers as Hadley was ending his. Possibly Hadley's music is heard so infrequently today because it relies so heavily on European models. Some believed he wrote too much, and even an early biographer inclined to hagiography spoke of his "fatal facility." Yet Hadley could write music of real quality. Listen to his 1921 tone poem *The Ocean* and you hear harmonic daring, themes with sharp jaw lines, dramatic tension, and gripping emotion. This is the real thing.

Hadley left San Francisco in 1915, three years later married soprano Inez Barbour, and suddenly went into high gear. In 1921 he was appointed associate conductor of the New York Philharmonic. Determined to bring music to a broad audience, he conducted the Philharmonic's low-priced concerts at Lewisohn Stadium. His score for the 1926 film *Don Juan* marked the first time music and sound effects were synchronized with a feature film, and in 1927 he scored the movie *When a Man Loves*, starring John Barrymore. He was a hit in Buenos Aires when he conducted that city's orchestra in 1927, and in 1928 he and the New York Philharmonic recorded a set of disks for a music-appreciation course. In his concerts with the Manhattan Symphony Orchestra, whose members invited him to become their conductor in 1929, he included American music on every program. In 1930 he conducted a series of concerts in Tokyo, and in 1933 he founded the National Association of American Composers and Conductors, dedicated to fostering American music and helping its creators. As the catalogue of his achievements suggests, Hadley possessed huge energy. In 1934 he made his final contribution to American culture, founding the Berkshire Music Festival, known around the world today as the Tanglewood Festival.

At Hadley's funeral, on September 8, 1937, notables from the music world served as honorary pallbearers, among them baritone Lawrence Tibbett, pianist Josef Lhevinne, violinist Efrem Zimbalist, and composer Deems Taylor. The American Academy of Arts and Letters, in a telegram of condolence to Hadley's widow, wrote that "he was greatly beloved for his kindness and sweetness. His generous services to the members of the musical profession was [sic] only second to his untiring service to American music, of which he was a gallant champion."

Seven years later, a Liberty Ship was christened the SS *Henry Hadley*. One might wonder how Alfred Metzger would have reacted, but by then, no one remembered to ask.

EDWARD TAK

8

9

rehearsals four mornings a week. He then tempered this good news with three big *ifs*: the season would be a financial success only if the "proper orchestra" could be organized, and if the season tickets sold well, and if the general public patronized the concerts and bought single tickets. He then backtracked from his original position and praised Hadley for forming an orchestra, although he continued to fret over just how good an orchestra it would be.

6. PUBLICIZE THE EFFORT

Six days after Tobin offered his tentative remarks, Hadley was in top form, addressing a luncheon audience of the Downtown Association, emphasizing how important a city's arts scene is to its business climate and pledging to do for San Francisco what Theodore Thomas had done for Chicago in founding that city's symphony orchestra.

Hadley had selected sixty-one players for an ensemble whose quality would, after all, reflect on him. "I came here expecting to find good, capable musicians," he told the *Chronicle* two weeks before the inaugural concert. "With such competent and earnest men as we have chosen I can safely assure the San Francisco public that it will hear a performance on December 8th which will compare favorably with the work of any symphony orchestra in the United States."

DOWNBEAT

Behind the scenes, the board encountered and addressed the innumerable details of concert production. After sixteen rehearsals, the big

event was about to take place. The orchestra in which Hadley had such confidence was ready to meet critics and audience on December 8. Packing the Cort Theatre that Friday afternoon were fourteen hundred people—one of the most fashionable audiences, according to the *Chronicle*, ever assembled for a matinee in San Francisco.

At 3:15, Hadley stepped onto the podium. He brought down his baton and launched Wagner's Prelude to *Die Meistersinger*. It was the start of quite a program, especially considering that most of these musicians were not used to performing classical music. Besides the Wagner, the orchestra played Tchaikovsky's *Pathétique* Symphony, an orchestration of the Theme and Variations from Haydn's *Emperor* Quartet, and Liszt's *Les Preludes*. This was big stuff, meant to dazzle, and Hadley and the musicians did their job well. The audience was there to listen, not just to be seen, reported the *Chronicle*'s Harvey Wickham. At *pianissimos*, the house seemed to hold its breath, and when the music ended the Cort was filled with "bravos, cheering and the sound of handclapping." San Francisco, Wickham concluded, "has had a great symphony orchestra lying around loose for a long time without knowing it."

Will L. Greenbaum, the orchestra's manager and a local impresario with a long history of success, proclaimed that, while other orchestras might be luxuries for the rich, the San Francisco Orchestra was for everyone. Already a series of popular concerts for students and "wage-earners" had been planned, and at affordable prices. And as early as December 29, schoolchildren enjoyed the first program designed especially for them. In January, the orchestra

SABOTEUR WITHIN, UNREASONABLE LADIES WITHOUT

When impresario Will L. Greenbaum was hired as the Symphony's first business manager, he had been bringing orchestras, singers, chamber ensembles, and instrumental soloists to San Francisco for sixteen years. He controlled the city's musical life and was someone to reckon with.

Greenbaum sponsored a Sunday afternoon concert series that conflicted with the popular concerts the Musical Association intended to present, and among the reasons for hiring Greenbaum was an effort to bring a competitor into the camp. Whatever Greenbaum's early efforts on behalf of the orchestra, they ended soon. As early as February 1912, Richard Tobin reported that Greenbaum had problems with conductor Henry Hadley, with the orchestra, the board, and "the whole enterprise." Critics and the public were getting an earful, none of it good. Tobin recommended Greenbaum's dismissal.

Whether from inside or outside the organization, Greenbaum knew how to do damage. A month after Tobin's report, board President T. B. Berry reported that Greenbaum was pocketing part of the fees the Association paid its soloists. The ex-manager was still up to his tricks in August 1912, when his replacement, Frank Healy, reported that Greenbaum was telling East Coast agents not to book artists for the orchestra without his permission.

Then came the final insult. Charter subscribers were to have their same seats for the orchestra's second season. But Greenbaum refused to turn over seating records, forcing Association Secretary John Rothschild to request that subscribers return a postcard, telling him which Cort Theatre seats they had occupied. Not everyone complied.

Rothschild found himself in an impossible position, sometimes facing as many as eight individuals vying for the same seat. He left no record of how he dealt with patrons, and insults he may have received are only hinted at by his dignified language: "Adverse criticism has been made by rival claimants for certain seats, and more or less ill feeling arose in a few instances, but these dissatisfied persons have been met in a spirit of courtesy and fairness, . . . and in almost every case a satisfactory conclusion has been reached." What Rothschild could not understand was why the women were causing him such grief. They fumed when they were denied seats others had occupied in season one. Why, they demanded, were no seating records available? At last Rothschild vented his exasperation. "Strange to say, the most unreasonable persons are ladies."

10

29

8
_____

The Symphony's first concertmaster, Eduard Tak.

9
_____

The Symphony's first home, the Cort Theatre.

10
_____

Will Greenbaum, an impresario who had already brought countless artists and ensembles to San Francisco when he began his short term as the Symphony's first manager. A mover and shaker, and someone to reckon with.

Special Concert

For the Library Fund

THE

San Francisco Orchestra

HENRY HADLEY, Conductor

SOLOIST

TETRAZZINI

(Courtesy of Tivoli Opera Co., W. H. Leahy, Manager)

Cort Theater

FRIDAY AFTERNOON · · MARCH 22, AT 3:15

MANAGER : WILL L. GREENBAUM

11

Musical Association of San Francisco

MAINTAINING THE

SAN FRANCISCO ORCHESTRA

HENRY HADLEY, Conductor

SEASON 1911-1912

First Concert Friday Afternoon, December 8, at 3:15

PROGRAM

1. RICHARD WAGNER .... "The Mastersingers."
2. PETER TSCHAIKOWSKY .... Symphony No. 6, B Minor
   - I.   Adagio (4-4) Allegro non troppo, B Minor.
   - II. Allegro Con Grazia (5-4) D Major.
   - III. Allegro Molto Vivace (12-8) G Major.
   - IV. Adagio Lamentoso (3-4) B Minor.

PAUSE

3. JOSEF HAYDN .... "Theme and Variations" from the "Emperor Quartette."
4. FRANZ LISZT .... Symphonic Poem "Les Preludes."

12

11

Soprano Luisa Tetrazzini starred in a benefit performance, helping the San Francisco Symphony purchase the Pittsburgh Symphony Orchestra's music library.

12

December 8, 1911. Not a holiday program, but a gift to San Francisco music lovers.

played on a Sunday afternoon for those whose jobs kept them from Friday matinees. Ticket prices started at fifteen cents and topped out at a dollar. In all, that first season consisted of thirteen performances: six "symphony" concerts of weighty fare and seven pops concerts (including two in Oakland) of lighter repertory. Three soloists were featured: concertmaster Eduard Tak in Lalo's *Symphonie espagnole*, pianist Vladimir de Pachmann ("Of all Great Pianists, the most unique," according to the program book) in Chopin's E minor Concerto, and Efrem Zimbalist in the Tchaikovsky Violin Concerto.

The organization was on its way, its mission clear: to serve music and the people. The Cort continued to be filled to capacity. Even Richard Tobin was encouraged. Now hyperbole replaced his earlier misgivings. Never, he said, had he encountered such enthusiastic audiences, and he claimed that no orchestra, local or

foreign, had drawn such crowds. He recommended Hadley's reengagement for three more years.

CONFIDENCE GROWS

In early 1912, as the first season drew to a close, a move toward professionalism began. The opportunity arose to purchase the music library of the Pittsburgh Symphony Orchestra, which had encountered hard times and disbanded, not to be resurrected until 1926. Now, liquidating its assets, it offered its ten-thousand-dollar collection of scores and parts at half price, a deal the Association finally sealed for four thousand dollars. Superstar soprano Luisa Tetrazzini appeared in a benefit concert whose proceeds helped acquire the library, which Hadley urged as a prerequisite to good programming. Hadley was growing restless, too, with the conditions under which he was compelled to prepare the orchestra. The Cort management refused to raise

13

14

13

Henry Hadley and the San Francisco Symphony: the first group of musicians in the first official portrait, at the Cort Theatre.

14

Luisa Tetrazzini.

the stage curtain at rehearsals, making it almost impossible to calculate if a soft *pianissimo* could be heard in the hall's far reaches, or what made for a house-filling *fortissimo*. Eventually, the orchestra would need a home of its own. Musicians would have to be secured for full-time employment. All that, however, would have to wait.

Conditions may not have been ideal, but Hadley and the orchestra made their music, and San Francisco liked them. The initial season was a success, artistically and financially: completed with a hefty surplus of $4,743.87, with a roster of guarantors totaling 293, and with contributed income of $28,500, short of Berry's $30,000 goal by only $1,500. The report in which the good financial news was delivered was dated April 17, 1912, just a day shy of six years since the earthquake that had threatened to doom the city.

Two days earlier, technological progress had been dealt a blow when the *Titanic* slipped under the waves, but technology also enabled news of the disaster to reach San Francisco almost immediately, and it was a front-page *Chronicle* story hours after the event. On April 17, world news notwithstanding, Association spirits were high. At a Chamber of Commerce luncheon that afternoon, Joseph D. Redding reported on negotiations with the city to build an opera house in the Civic Center. Target date of completion: 1915, to coincide with the opening of the Panama-Pacific International Exposition. Ticket prices would enable everyone entrée into what was expected to be a vast palace of music, seating between four and five thousand people. In fact, two decades would pass before a hall was built to house both the orchestra and an opera company. But at the moment optimism dominated.

T. B. Berry must have taken pleasure in the Symphony's successful first season and the excitement it generated. He would not take part in the struggles or triumphs of the coming years. On May 21, he succumbed to pneumonia at fifty-two—hardly a senior age even in those days before longevity was considered an entitlement, but enough time, in his case, to have helped ground an enterprise that would long outlive him.

FEELING THE WAY
TOWARD THE FUTURE
Less than a year after the San Francisco Symphony's first concert, critic Harvey Wickham wrote, "The orchestra, which was then [1911] a novelty, has become an institution."

Institutions need homes. In November 1912, the day after Woodrow Wilson pummeled William Howard Taft in the presidential election, board member William H. Crocker—the magnate responsible for construction of the Palace Hotel, Olympic Club, Masonic Temple, and the headquarters of the Bohemian and Pacific Union clubs—arrived at a meeting with news that opera house construction was practically assured. The City of San Francisco would donate the land; the Association would raise construction funds. Already $750,000 was guaranteed by subscription. The resolution to build an opera house, entered into board minutes, reveals the already close relationship between Symphony and city. The logic behind the legalese: The Musical Association's duty is to offer music and music education to "all the inhabitants of the City and County of San Francisco." The city's duty is to provide for the "public welfare, entertainment, benefit and education of its citizens and inhabitants." Musical Association and city share a common goal. Both wish to benefit the people. An opera house is necessary to enable city and Association to realize their mission. Therefore city and Association should cooperate in its construction. Once the opera house was completed, title would be vested in the city. Although this plan would bear no immediate fruit—a ruling from the California Supreme Court barred the municipality from donating property to a private organization for such a project—the goal would not disappear. San Francisco was determined to have a home for an orchestra and an opera company.

By February 1913, the board's new president, W. B. Bourn, predicted an end-of-season deficit of six thousand dollars and suggested that the directors pledge special guarantees to cover losses. He would start the emergency fund with a thousand dollars of his own money. The season actually concluded with a small surplus, $84.87. Press enthusiasm continued. Less than two years after the first concerts, *Chronicle* critic Harvey Wickham had one word to describe what the San Francisco Symphony had become: *necessary*. "One can't think of what the old town would now do without it."

Yet the board's ambition, which had helped create this necessity, had also made the Association less cautious, and although the deficit projected at the end of season two never materialized, John Rothschild counseled a more deliberate approach. Attempting too much, too quickly, had left too little in reserve. The Association had to move more carefully, he said. Its members had to be sure of their ground.

Proceeding more carefully, the Symphony fared better financially in its scaled-back season of 1913–14. But friction was developing between

15

Hadley and his employers. In October, the conductor voiced his frustration. Unable to offer an adequate salary, he had failed to persuade two local players to accept the post of principal horn. The only harpist available to the orchestra would not be able to handle a work Hadley was intent on performing, Reger's *Suite Romantique*. "This matter [of inadequate musicians] was presented to your notice last April," he wrote the Music Committee, "but it was the policy of the Committee to get along as best we could."

Although the orchestra's personnel remained constant from concert to concert, most musicians continued to be hired on a per-performance basis. Hadley might have disagreed, but his board worked to ensure a balance between what they could afford and what art demanded. That was the magic equilibrium, and the struggle to maintain it would rob generations of future administrators of countless hours of sleep. As early

as March 1914, Bourn saw a way of surmounting such struggles when he urged that a thirty-five-hundred-dollar anticipated surplus go toward an endowment fund. Only that, he maintained, would ensure the organization's permanence.

War erupted in Europe in August 1914. Soloists from abroad were denied passage, and music normally shipped from across the Atlantic could not be guaranteed. As war consequences go, such things hardly merit mention. But as constant reminders of a conflict in which America was not yet engaged, they were among the pressures that together would be translated into the nation's awakening sense of moral necessity. At the Symphony, this was most evident in a concert to benefit the Belgian Relief Fund: a statement, in other words, that the arts cannot pretend to exist in isolation, as America was attempting to exist apart from the European war.

15

W. B. Bourn, Association president from 1912 to 1916.

PROGRAMS NEXT WEEK'S CONCERTS

SAN FRANCISCO
ORCHESTRA
HENRY HADLEY-CONDUCTOR
VICTORY THEATRE
SAN JOSE, CAL.
TUESDAY NIGHT, NOVEMBER 26, 1912

PROGRAM

Beethoven	Overture, "Lenore" No. 3
Dvorak	Symphony, "From The New World"
Rimsky-Korsakow	"Spanish Caprice" (New)

CORT THEATRE
FOURTH SYMPHONY CONCERT

Friday Afternoon, November 29, 1912, at 3:15 o'clock

Soloist: TINA LERNER, Pianist

Beethoven	Symphony No. 3
I. Allegro con brio	III. Allegro, C minor
II. Andante, con motor	IV. Allegro, C major
Tschaikowsky	Concerto
	TINA LERNER
Wagner	Overture, "Tannhauser"

FOURTH POPULAR CONCERT

Sunday Afternoon, December 1, 1912
(Note Change in Date)

Soloist: TINA LERNER, Pianist

Mendelssohn	Overture, Ruy Blas
Grieg	Heart Wounds / Last Spring
	(For String Orchestra
Chopin	F. minor, Concerto
	TINA LERNER
Liszt	Liebestraum
R. Strauss	Tone Poem : Death and Transfiguration

FIFTH SYMPHONY CONCERT, FRIDAY, DECEMBER 6th

16

34

16

From the early years of its history, the San Francisco Symphony served music lovers throughout the Bay Area. A year after its founding, the orchestra was also performing in San Jose.

An international vision was a luxury, however, for an organization with immediate concerns about its survival. The Symphony's founders had agreed to reassess their enterprise after five seasons. Four seasons had come and passed, and the Association was not on solid ground. Rumor spread among the musicians that the 1915–16 season would be canceled. The most Richard Tobin could do was authorize the orchestra's new manager, Frank Healy, to assure players of the hope for another season, longer if possible. Lacking a promise, let alone a clear plan, the orchestra nevertheless responded with what is surely a tribute to music itself. In a letter to the board, this band of players from cafes, restaurants, hotels, and theaters—musicians who could not have been envisioned in a symphony orchestra until Henry Hadley and his determined board had gone searching for them and secured their commitment to give Beethoven and Brahms a try—these musicians now expressed their appreciation for "the opportunity we have had . . . to develop the Symphony Orchestra in San Francisco." They thanked Association members for their generosity. They spoke with gratification of their artistic strides. They pledged cooperation and envisioned a future when they would take their place among the country's leading ensembles. Their sincerity and determination were good enough for the board, which resolved to guarantee a 1915–16 season of ten concerts, with a budget of fifty thousand dollars.

A STANDARD OF COMPARISON

In 1915, the long-awaited Panama-Pacific International Exposition opened in San Francisco. Years before, when the fair was still an idea in the minds of its promoters, that idea had helped form the Musical Association. Now the fair joined forces with Henry Lee Higginson's original vision of orchestral glory. The San Francisco Symphony was about to be reborn.

This is what happened. The Boston Symphony Orchestra came to town. Beginning on May 15, it presented thirteen concerts under its music director, Karl Muck, in the architecturally splendid Festival Hall, modeled on the Petit Palais in Paris. For the Boston concerts, Festival Hall was rebuilt and its seating capacity nearly doubled, to eight thousand. Every performance sold out. Listeners experienced an epiphany.

The Boston Symphony Orchestra, wrote the *Chronicle*'s Walter Anthony, showed what was possible. At the first concert he overheard a woman sitting next to him. "It seems as though the orchestras we have had and heard have just been for the purpose of showing us how the tunes were supposed to 'go,'" she said. Boston's music-making was on a different plane. In print, Anthony had been friendly to Hadley and his orchestra, but now he laid out the facts as he saw them. The Boston Symphony revealed the need for a permanent orchestra, whose members were not compelled to divide their time between concert hall and cabaret. The Boston Symphony also revealed the need for "a director of genuine distinction." Hadley, for all his merits, seems to have lacked some essential ingredients, the kind that transform good meals into banquets.

17

18

17

Looking north on Van Ness Avenue from Grove Street. At left, the future site of the Opera House.

18

Symphony Manager Frank Healy.

The Board faced the obvious. Every maturing organization encounters the need to move to a new level, and that desire once unleashed lets no one rest. The Association had planned for an initial five years of concerts. As the fourth season ended, what had to happen was clear.

Association President Bourn tried to let Hadley down gently, praising his work in organizing the orchestra, and thanking him for what he had done for the city's cultural life, but ultimately telling him that the time for farewell had come. Not everyone was happy with the decision. Cecilia Casserly, wife of board member John Casserly, staked out a place in the camp of disgruntled Hadley supporters. A grande dame from the Peninsula south of San Francisco, she thought she knew what Bay Area music needed. If the San Francisco Symphony could no longer employ the dashing Henry Hadley, what about the dashing Nikolai

Sokoloff? Mrs. Casserly herself would guarantee Sokoloff's salary. Sokoloff was no lightweight, and he would go on to become the Cleveland Orchestra's founding music director. The temptation to accept Cecilia Casserly's offer must have been great, but acceptance would have meant relinquishing artistic control, and it was declined. She would not forget the slight.

Hadley, now out of a job, was resilient, and with little apparent regret he made way for his successor, Alfred Hertz. Hertz was everything Hadley was not, beginning with the way he looked, which was what central casting might deliver in response to a call for a troll. Hertz was German at a time when that nationality didn't win friends. He had spent a long stint at the Metropolitan Opera leading Wagner and Strauss, and he enjoyed a reputation as a take-no-prisoners conductor who demanded perfection and inspired players. On July 19, 1915,

his engagement as the Symphony's music director was approved.

"When the San Francisco Symphony occupies its proper position among the three or four great orchestral bodies of the country," the *San Francisco Examiner*'s Redfern Mason would eventually conclude, "the part played by Mr. Hadley in achieving that end will have to be recognized at its proper value." For now, musical San Francisco belonged to Alfred Hertz. Here, Mason believed, was a man who would lead the orchestra to artistic success and win the hearts of the city's music lovers for the San Francisco Symphony. Mason was right on both counts.

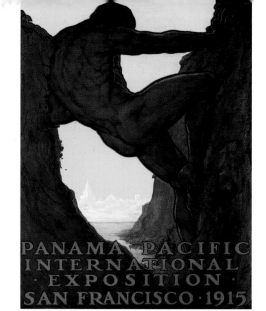

21

22

20

19

*Henry Hadley (left) and Alfred Hertz,
colleagues united by music.*

20

*Conductor Nikolai Sokoloff in his later
years. Peninsula grande dame Cecilia
Casserly lobbied for his appointment as
Hadley's successor.*

21

*Colossus straddles the isthmus. The Panama-
Pacific International Exposition celebrated
completion of the Panama Canal.*

22

*Festival Hall at the Panama-Pacific
International Exposition. Concertgoers
walked through its portals, heard the
visiting Boston Symphony Orchestra, and
encountered a standard of comparison.*

PERSONAL STRUGGLES AND MUSICAL TRIUMPHS

The Alfred Hertz Years (1915–1930)

A BAD TIME TO BE GERMAN, A GOOD TIME TO BE A MUSIC LOVER

Much of what we take for granted about San Francisco concert life today was introduced during Alfred Hertz's fifteen years as music director. Regular performances for young people, a summer series, radio broadcasts, recordings, even touring—they have changed shape over the years, but by Hertz's retirement in 1930, the San Francisco Symphony had embarked on all these activities and was moving into modern times. Hertz's tenure included countless musical triumphs and culminated in an orchestra with a national reputation, but it was marked by rivalries and animosities that threatened to derail him and the enterprise. Dedication to the music played the winning hand.

When he arrived in San Francisco in 1915, Alfred Hertz stepped into a world in transition. Nothing marked the shift from one century into another as indelibly as the ongoing war in Europe. In an age when hopes were high for the progress of humanity, the conflict abroad revealed the distance still to be traveled before optimism about the future could be more than a Pollyanna's dream.

Ever since August 1914, when the Prussian war machine flattened neutral Belgium on its march into France, anti-German sentiment had been building in the United States, and if you had ties to Germany—if you had relatives there, or maybe you'd been born there, or perhaps your name was Schmidt or Mueller or Schumacher—you had reason to worry. Bay Area Germans decided to remind the city that their native land had more to offer than trench warfare and the Schlieffen Plan. The Beethoven Choir of New York had presented San Francisco with a

2

2

Adolph Rosenbecker, concertmaster from 1912 to 1915.

3

In 1915, reminding San Francisco that their ancestral land was the birthplace not only of the Kaiser but also of great music, the city's German community erected a Beethoven monument in Golden Gate Park.

4

Program book cover from Alfred Hertz's first concerts as music director.

statue of the composer, and this the German community erected in Golden Gate Park, also putting forward twenty thousand dollars for concerts dedicated to Beethoven's music, to be the culmination of German-American Week at the Panama-Pacific International Exposition, which had opened in February 1915. Hertz was asked to conduct. And so that August, a month after joining the San Francisco Symphony, Hertz arrived for his first musical assignment in the city, leading the Beethoven Festival Orchestra.

At first, local Germans must have thought their strategy had succeeded. Under the headline "Thousands Pay Homage to Art of Beethoven," the *Examiner*'s Redfern Mason wrote on August 7 that "last night San Francisco did honor to the memory of Ludwig Van Beethoven. For the time being we were Teutons all in our love for the great man who, more than her militarists and equally with her poets and philosophers, has made famous the name of Germany wherever men and women love the good and the beautiful." *Teutons all.* Those were brave words in 1915. In May, German torpedoes had sent the *Lusitania* to the bottom of the ocean, taking twelve hundred lives, more than a hundred of them American. In July the *San Francisco Chronicle*

reported that the Wilson Administration, having appealed to Germany to protect US citizens on the high seas, was dissatisfied with the Kaiser's response.

Alfred Hertz believed that the opening concert of his Beethoven Festival was supposed to end with the Ninth Symphony. No one told him he was expected to lead "The Star-Spangled Banner" to conclude the performance, and his failure to do so became a problem. Hertz and the soloists took their bows and left the stage. The orchestra remained in place, awaiting the conductor's return during a silence that grew more awkward the longer Hertz remained absent. Finally, Concertmaster Adolph Rosenbecker took it upon himself to lead the patriotic song (it would not become the national anthem until 1931), raising the question of why the man who had led the concert was not out there now. The following night brought another faux pas. In place of Liszt's *Les Preludes*, which would have demanded unbudgeted rehearsal time, Hertz substituted Wagner's *Kaisermarch*. He did not know that Kaiser Wilhelm was at that moment contemplating a triumphal march into Warsaw.

Symphony board members Richard Tobin and Grant Selfridge had had enough. They resigned from the Musical Association. As part of a board faction devoted to Henry Hadley, they had protested Hertz's appointment. Now Hertz's nationality and blunders gave them the ammunition they needed. Selfridge was brusque: "A serious mistake was made in hiring a conductor so strongly pro-German in his sympathies." Hearsay stoked the flames. Hertz's former valet, Joseph Guttman, claimed his boss had given "many evidences of his joy" at the

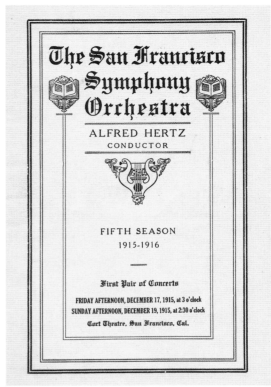

Lusitania's sinking. Here were two statements, one from a man angry at having been out-voted, the other from a former and possibly disgruntled employee. They didn't amount to evidence. But enemies are where you find them, especially in wartime.

Critic Alfred Metzger adored Hertz's music-making, and Hertz's three festival concerts were hugely successful, attracting a combined audience of twenty thousand. But the furor refused to dissipate. Finally the board passed a resolution stating it had investigated and found Hertz had no clue that "The Star-Spangled Banner" was to have been played. As late as December the issue remained alive, becoming a debate over whether such a work is even appropriate for concert performance. Incredibly, the noise was still going on three years later, when the Hertz crowd marveled at the conductor's inspired interpretation of "The Star-Spangled Banner." Whether the song

requires interpretation, or would receive it from a maestro more concerned with music of a different sort, is a concept from another era.

What kind of man stirs such passions in supporters and detractors? Alfred Hertz was born in Frankfurt in 1872. As did virtually all the great orchestra leaders of that time, he began as a conductor of opera, serving his apprenticeship in regional houses in Germany until he landed a major post in Breslau. In 1902 he came to the United States as head of German repertory at the Metropolitan Opera, where he remained for thirteen years, some of them spent working alongside Gustav Mahler. At the Met he led the first American performance of Wagner's *Parsifal*, infuriating the Wagner family, who insisted the work be performed exclusively in Bayreuth's Festspielhaus, the composer's shrine to himself. (Hertz would never again be engaged to conduct Wagner in Germany.)

In early 1915 he was in Los Angeles to conduct Horatio Parker's opera *Fairyland*. The conventional wisdom today is that LA loves glamour. Times were different then, or audiences were more inclined to look beyond surfaces. Hertz was short, bald, bespectacled, massively bearded, overweight, and with a limp left over from a childhood bout with polio. LA ignored this. Audiences there loved him and would love him more in years to come, for in 1922 he enjoyed spectacular acclaim when he inaugurated the Hollywood Bowl concerts. In 1915, the *Fairyland* raves brought him to the attention of the Musical Association of San Francisco. Having spent most of his career conducting opera, Hertz was eager to devote more time to concert music. Promised a permanent orchestra in San Francisco, and one that would be augmented to eighty players, he accepted a year's contract.

A LESSON WITH LOUIS PERSINGER

Young Yehudi Menuhin and his teacher,
Symphony Concertmaster Louis Persinger.

The San Francisco Symphony's first concertmaster, Eduard Tak, played with the orchestra for only one season. Tak yielded his place to Adolph Rosenbecker, then one of the most eminent concertmasters in America and former concertmaster with the Theodore Thomas Orchestra, forerunner of the Chicago Symphony. In 1915 Alfred Hertz invited Louis Persinger to become concertmaster. He served from 1916 until 1925.

Louis Persinger was born in Rochester, Illinois, in 1887, the son of a railway signalman. By the time he was thirteen, the boy's playing was so admired that he was given the chance to study at the Leipzig Conservatory, from which he graduated in 1904. He continued his studies with the great Belgian violinist Eugène Ysaÿe, made a two-year concert tour of Germany, Austria, and Denmark, and in 1914 became concertmaster of the Berlin Philharmonic. By the time Persinger came to San Francisco, he was a polished Amero-European, urbane, witty, as charming as they come. He held the sometimes irascible Hertz in his palm.

Persinger's son Rolf was himself a member of the San Francisco Symphony, joining during Josef Krips's tenure, then going on to many years with the San Francisco Opera Orchestra as principal violist. In 1986 he recalled his father's early years with the Symphony. At the family's Steiner Street house, the elder Persinger organized musicales and concerts of chamber music. "It was there that he began teaching. Teaching and performing—those were my father's favorite activities. He loved his work so much, and he was so grateful for the opportunities that he had as a young man, that most often he would teach the talented youngsters of San Francisco for free. . . . My father never took one cent from Yehudi Menuhin, for example. He thought it a privilege to help form such a great violinist."

Yehudi Menuhin was Louis Persinger's star pupil. In his autobiography, *Unfinished Journey*, Menuhin recalled going to San Francisco Symphony concerts as a child, sitting in the balcony on his mother's knee, and focusing on Persinger. He noticed that this man often played solo passages, and he learned to wait for those moments. After one such performance he asked his parents if he could have a violin for his fourth birthday—and Louis Persinger to teach him.

A year later, Menuhin got his wish. At his first lesson with Persinger, after the boy demonstrated what he could do, the teacher announced it was now his turn to play. Putting bow to strings, he introduced his pupil to the Adagio from Bach's Sonata in G minor for solo violin. "At the time, aged five, hearing the Adagio for the first time, I knew only that it was this sublimity that I must strive for. . . . In a single lesson, Persinger gave me what four years of college give so very few students: a sense of vocation."

Problems began almost at once. Manager Frank Healy estimated expenses for the coming season at sixty-seven thousand dollars and income at sixty thousand dollars if Hertz engaged the number of players he wanted, and he predicted disaster if the conductor failed to scale back his plans. At that point a clause was inserted into Hertz's contract, to protect the Musical Association if the season were canceled. Rather than the ten symphony concerts, ten popular concerts, and four additional concerts outlined originally, the board suggested cutting the number of concerts to ten and engaging a maximum of sixty-seven players. Hertz refused to budge. Almost all of October and most of November were spent in negotiations with the Musicians' Union. Full-time attention to Symphony work meant fewer chances of outside employment, so a player's contract had to promise a living wage. By November 23, eighty musicians were signed for ten pairs of regular concerts. Hertz had prevailed.

Vindication was immediate. Hertz's first concert that December—Beethoven's *Leonore* Overture No. 3, Brahms's Symphony No. 2, Wagner's *A Faust Overture*, and Berlioz's *Roman Carnival Overture*—simply blew away doubts. Redfern Mason led the charge in the *Examiner*: "On one previous occasion only have I seen a symphony audience in San Francisco wrought up to such a passion of enthusiasm as was manifested by the people who had gathered together in the Cort Theatre yesterday afternoon. That occasion was the final concert of the Boston Symphony in Festival Hall." The *Argonaut* noted a new tonal beauty and precision. The *Chronicle's* Walter Anthony compared Hertz with podium lions Karl Muck, Felix Weingartner, Artur Nikisch, and Anton Seidl. This orchestra, he said, was akin to the Boston Symphony so admired during the Panama-Pacific Exposition.

Such verdicts would not vary for the next fifteen years.

Programme

FIRST MUNICIPAL SYMPHONY CONCERT

SEASON 1925-1926

San Francisco Symphony Orchestra

ALFRED HERTZ, *Conductor*
EFREM ZIMBALIST, *Violinist* (GUEST ARTIST)

Exposition Auditorium, Tuesday Evening, November 17, 1925

Auspices MAYOR JAMES ROLPH, JR., AND BOARD OF SUPERVISORS

Direction Auditorium Committee

J. EMMET HAYDEN, *Chairman*   ANGELO J. ROSSI   EDWIN G. BATH

Alfred Hertz. In his appearance and as a conductor, he was Henry Hadley's opposite.

43

The People's Philharmonic's founder, Herman Perlet, never imagined his ensemble as a rival of the San Francisco Symphony.

William Sproule, Association president from 1916 to 1919.

ENEMIES AND RIVALRIES

In San Francisco, this was a new kind of music-making. But Hertz had enemies on the board, and the war in Europe continued to stoke anti-German sentiment. Since the conductor had been hired only for a year, some were interested in unseating him. As late as the end of February 1916, board President W. B. Bourn counseled patience on Hertz's reengagement. A few weeks later Bourn dropped a bombshell. Through William H. Crocker, he had learned that the great Arturo Toscanini would be happy to come to San Francisco and take over from Hertz at a salary of ten thousand dollars per season. Bourn had played his ace, and one imagines how satisfied he must have been with the probable reaction. Even in 1916, Toscanini was a confirmed superstar. Now he was available for the same price as Alfred Hertz. But a week later, a cable from Toscanini revealed a misunderstand-

ing. He expected a fee of ten thousand dollars per *month*, the first month's pay to be delivered to him in Rome before his departure. The board minutes report a sobering conclusion. "It was thought inadvisable to consider [Toscanini] for the conductorship."

Hertz had his own personal challenges. He detested manager Frank Healy, in his opinion an incapable and indifferent functionary. Hertz's assessment seemed borne out when Healy asked the orchestra to waive a week's salary after discovering he had miscalculated the payroll and owed the musicians for seventeen rather than sixteen weeks. John Rothschild shook his head and announced that the Association was honor-bound to pay for services rendered. The executive committee agreed, then passed a resolution abolishing the office of business manager and, with it, Frank Healy's job.

Then there was Cecilia Casserly, who, as Leta E. Miller has written, was still angry that the Musical Association had turned down her offer to underwrite Nikolai Sokoloff's salary, were he hired to replace Henry Hadley. Through the San Francisco People's Philharmonic, Casserly saw her chance for revenge.

Organized in 1913, and founded to make music widely available, the People's Philharmonic was originally supportive of the San Francisco Symphony, not a competitor. With ticket prices at 25¢, it brought many listeners their first contact with concert music. Of course the Symphony too had announced its intention to make music for all and offered its first popular concert, at popular prices, in January 1912. As late as the 1916–17 season, a subscription for a gallery seat to ten popular concerts totaled $2.50, and a subscription for a similar seat for twelve Sunday

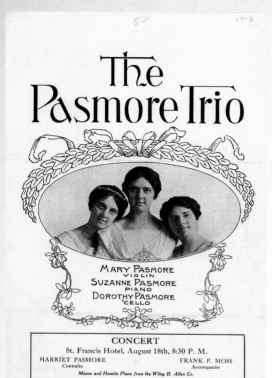

The Pasmore sisters in earlier and later years. The trio captivated Europe. Dorothy (below, left) and Mary (below, right) joined the San Francisco Symphony in 1925. Their sister Suzanne is shown at center, below.

For years, symphony orchestras were boys' clubs, and only the angelic harp seemed suited to a woman's touch. In bastions of what someone once called "old Europe," the Berlin Philharmonic did not admit women until 1982, the Vienna Philharmonic not until 1997. Sixty years before Berlin opened its ranks (grudgingly) to women, a fugitive from old Europe, Alfred Hertz, knocked down the gender barrier in San Francisco. During the 1923–24 season he hired violinist Helen Atkinson, the first woman (other than a harpist) to take membership in a major American orchestra. Violinists Eugenia Bem, Modesta Mortensen, and Frances Simonsen followed the next season, along with pianist Gyula Ormay. But two other women who also joined that year were more celebrated—not only in San Francisco's musical circles, but throughout the country and abroad. These were violinist Mary Pasmore and her cellist sister Dorothy.

The Pasmore sisters were the daughters of Henry Bickford Pasmore, a composer, an organist, and a choral director who was himself the son of an amateur flutist and cellist. Henry Pasmore had studied in London and in Leipzig, where he heard Brahms conduct Brahms. After his return to San Francisco in 1885, he held teaching posts at the College of the Pacific, Mills College, and Stanford. Of his six children, four daughters were musical. Besides Mary and Dorothy, Suzanne became a pianist and Harriet a singer. In 1905, Pasmore relocated his family to Europe for three years so his daughters could advance their music

studies in Berlin. There, he coached voice at the dance studio run by another San Franciscan, Isadora Duncan. Suzanne worked there, too, as keyboard accompanist to the young women known as the "Isadorables."

In 1908, Mary, Dorothy, and Suzanne formed the Pasmore Trio. They shocked an audience in Berlin when they played chamber music from memory, not a sheet of music in front of them, nor a stand. They toured Europe for three seasons, then the United States. They charmed even crusty Alfred Metzger, who in a 1915 issue of the *Pacific Coast Musical Review* wrote that they were "the only American Trio which has achieved the distinction of having appeared in public in Berlin thirty-four times in the three seasons they were there." Their ensemble playing, he said, was "as nearly perfect" as could be.

When Hertz hired Mary and Dorothy Pasmore, he was simply hiring the best musicians he could find. His disregard for boys' club rules paid off. Mary Pasmore was with the San Francisco Symphony until 1957, contributing the wealth of experience she had accrued since the early years of the twentieth century—which were really the final years of the nineteenth century, the culmination of that era's great musical tradition. She brought a sense of old Europe to the American West, where a groundbreaking orchestra had hired her when, across the Atlantic, women were still confined to the harpists' chairs.

symphony concerts was $5. This isn't quite the steal it seems to be: $5 in 1917 equaled about $85 in today's currency. But even if these prices are calculated in 2011 dollars, they make for a good deal—as good a deal in its own way as that found at the San Francisco People's Philharmonic. For the Symphony offered more complete and more sophisticated programs. Ideally, these would attract those who had come to music through the People's Philharmonic.

But the People's Philharmonic was short-lived and effectively came to an end in January 1916, when its conductor died. Two months later, it was reorganized—under the leadership of Cecilia Casserly. As a Hadley supporter, Casserly was by definition a Hertz foe, as was her husband John, an Association board member who sat on its powerful music committee. John Casserly was blunt in his appraisal of the music director. "I do not consider Hertz a good musician," he told the *Chronicle*. This may have been a hasty response to an unexpected question, or it may have been Casserly's honest opinion. In any case, it was an assessment of Hertz shared by virtually no one, not critics or audiences, nor conducting colleagues such as Bruno Walter and Otto Klemperer nor artists such as Yehudi Menuhin and Louis Persinger. If the Casserlys seemed unable to embrace popular opinion regarding Hertz, they seemed equally unequipped to present popularly priced concerts. Cecilia Casserly's reconstituted People's Philharmonic was a different kind of orchestra from the original. Tickets were more expensive, and her unspoken business plan included competition with the San Francisco Symphony. It was rumored that an overture had been made to Henry Hadley to assume the directorship; when he declined, Casserly

chose Nikolai Sokoloff as her conductor. The manager of the People's Philharmonic was Frank Healy, determined to get back at Hertz and the Symphony that had sacked him. The word *chutzpah* is not likely to have been in the Casserly vocabulary, but it is defined by their efforts on behalf of one organization that threatened another on whose board J. B. Casserly served. Their efforts finally came to nothing. The Casserly version of the People's Philharmonic disbanded after a year, probably due to expenses, but also because it had strayed from its mission and catered less to the "people" than did the San Francisco Symphony.

While the press loved the intrigues, the Musical Association was more united than anyone might have guessed from the daily papers. Hertz enjoyed considerable if not unanimous board support. Although Association President Bourn never claimed to have left in protest over Hertz, Bourn's resignation removed a powerful opponent, and his successor, the Southern Pacific's William Sproule, was clearly in the Hertz camp. For the moment disagreements were put aside. The focus had to be on guaranteeing a coming season. As Redfern Mason phrased it, "The San Francisco Symphony is more important than any individual conductor whatsoever."

ENSURING THE SEASONS
Alfred Hertz was a complicated man. He inspired love in audiences and in musicians he valued, such as his great concertmaster Louis Persinger, but along with wit and generosity he seems to have possessed an irascible streak. Years later, Winthrop Sargeant, by then the *New Yorker*'s music critic, recalled his days as a violinist in Hertz's San Francisco

8

Cecilia Casserly.

9
____

*Preparedness Day, 1916, minutes before a
bomb killed ten spectators.*

Symphony. Rarely, he wrote, had he met anyone so unwilling to court popularity. Hertz preferred respect—and that, Sargeant continued, he won through single-minded dedication to the music.

Conductor, orchestra, and board continued their good work. Faced with an Association deficit of thirty-five hundred dollars at the end of the 1915–16 season, seven members pledged to cover it with a contribution of five hundred dollars each. In the coming weeks a tentative plan to reengage Hertz was suggested, subject to raising a guarantee fund for another five years. It was proposed that the fund be doubled, from thirty thousand to sixty thousand dollars annually, at last enabling musicians to be engaged exclusively for the Symphony. The news was welcome. "We owe it to the community . . . to put the San Francisco Symphony on such a footing that

its director and individual players may do the best that in them lies," critic Redfern Mason urged in March. "If we do that, the Symphony will be a civic asset; it will carry the fame of San Francisco far and wide." The prediction might be thought premature, if not farfetched, but the organization was moving in that direction.

Two days before Hertz was rehired in late July, San Francisco was tense. On July 22, a massive civic parade had celebrated Preparedness Day, signaling America's intention to enter the Great War. Labor leaders had announced their opposition to the occasion, which glorified what they labeled needless militarism—a militarism whose flames, they believed, were fanned by captains of industry and would consume the masses forced to do the dirty work. That afternoon, as bands played and thousands marched, a bomb placed

in a suitcase left unattended at curbside on Steuart Street, just south of Market, killed ten and injured forty.

Art occupies a plane parallel to a world of such anxieties and tragedies, but it is also interwoven with that world and offers a place in which to reflect, in which to reconsider fundamentals. Great art is what Alfred Hertz stood for. In the midst of social turmoil, music lovers rejoiced at the news that concerts would continue under his direction. His salary was raised, but his contract extended only for a year. In fact, despite the critical and audience acclaim he enjoyed throughout his tenure, he would never have job security. He continued to be rehired on a yearly basis, and almost every one of those contracts included a clause that would release the Musical Association of its responsibilities if the season were canceled.

48

Harold Bauer, heard in San Francisco while he was in New York.

The concert hall is the last place where machines might be expected to displace humans, but had you attended the San Francisco Symphony's concert on January 31, 1919, you might have thought otherwise. British virtuoso Harold Bauer was due to play the Saint-Saëns G minor Piano Concerto. There on stage were Alfred Hertz, and the orchestra, and a piano. Harold Bauer was playing. But Harold Bauer was in New York.

The piano on stage was a Duo-Art concert grand, a "reproducing piano." Player pianos had been around since the 1890s. Reproducing pianos captured nuances that eluded those early models and offered more sophisticated playback, and as a result many famous musicians recorded rolls. The Duo-Art, a latecomer to the field, was introduced by the Aeolian Company of New York City in 1914. Four years later, interested in building an audience for its still-new instrument, Aeolian persuaded the Musical Association of San Francisco to use the Duo-Art as "soloist" for a pair of concerts. Helping seal the deal was a proposed payment to the cash-strapped arts organization—fifteen hundred dollars, about twenty-two thousand dollars in 2011 currency.

The Duo-Art had, in fact, already been used as a solo instrument with the New York Symphony and the Philadelphia Orchestra. W. V. Swords, vice-president of the Aeolian Company, assured the Musical Association's secretary, A. W. Widenham, that his firm's intentions were not commercial but purely artistic. He hoped San Francisco's music critics would agree.

The critics obliged. Yet as the *Examiner*'s Ray C. B. Brown wrote, a player piano substituting for a live soloist seemed to make more sense in the abstract than in the actual performance, which possessed "a tinge of the bizarre and the preternatural"—as though, he suggested, a chair were to slide across the room and offer itself to someone in need of a seat.

Brown wondered if machines were taking over but concluded that what was really on display was human intelligence—the skill with which Hertz and the orchestra kept the music synchronized. Brown understood the possibilities of documenting great artists, and he could not help but be impressed by Bauer's stand-in: "The performance was one of superlatively brilliant technique, if one may be allowed to compliment the Duo-Art as one would an artist, and was remarkable both for its record of achievement and its rich promise of what may be accomplished in the way of storing permanent records of artistry."

Bauer himself, telegraphing Alfred Hertz from Manhattan the evening before the San Francisco concert, was dumbfounded that, at the very moment he would be playing Tchaikovsky with the New York Philharmonic, he would also be playing Saint-Saëns in San Francisco. "Musical History contains no marvel to be compared with this."

In those days when sound recording failed to capture anything remotely like a full sonic spectrum, Alfred Hertz considered the Duo-Art a blessing to the future. Imagine, he said, what it would have meant to his generation if technology had enabled Franz Liszt or Anton Rubinstein to record their playing for those who came after them.

Duo-Art and its competitors, the Ampico and the Welte-Mignon companies, did indeed capture the work of great instrumental artists on piano rolls. As for a reproducing piano playing soloist with a live orchestra, it seems to have been done mainly because it *could* be done. Pianists would never be replaced by poltergeists at the keyboard.

The final word on the Duo-Art at the San Francisco Symphony came some months later. Aeolian's Mr. Swords had sent Alfred Hertz a token of the firm's appreciation. In thanking Swords for the "beautiful cigarette case," Hertz was expansive. "I will be immensely pleased to be reminded of these concerts every time I take a smoke, which is not daily but hourly with me." Some habits, like oddball performances, would eventually go out of style.

In the later years of his tenure, Hertz's correspondence with Association Secretary A. W. Widenham is a record of conditional terms and tentative steps forward. The conductor's frustration is evident, arising less from worry over his own employment as from concern about the music. He was solely responsible for hiring the musicians he wanted, and he was desperate not to lose players to the uncertainty of the entire venture. As one season ended, he needed the Musical Association's commitment to the next so he could get his players in place before they found other employment. Somehow, and even at the eleventh hour, Hertz managed to find the best musicians available.

Because some musicians felt secure in their jobs and others made do with less certainty, rehearsals could draw bad behavior both from the podium and the orchestra. While Hertz was apt to aim withering comments at those he believed he could replace easily, he was forced to endure equal disrespect from those on whose artistry he relied—a disdainful first oboist ("That man . . . knows how to wave a stick, but I know how to play the oboe"), or a harpist with the irritating habit of crunching on apples.

Hertz and those who governed the Musical Association could be annoyed with each other, but their story is simply the tale of two parties taking different paths toward a single goal. Both wanted to present fine concerts. Both adhered to their responsibilities. Hertz's were artistic, as were the board's, with fiscal responsibility added to the board's necessities. The formation in May 1917 of a Women's Auxiliary harnessed the power of a group of brilliant volunteers. Within six months, the women raised pledges of fifty thousand dollars.

Despite the unpleasantness in which financial uncertainties were bound to culminate—and which would clear the air for Hertz and the board—the San Francisco Symphony of this period would go on to acclaim that extended well beyond the Bay Area.

By the time the People's Philharmonic folded, in 1917, the United States was at war with Germany. The formal declaration was made in Congress on April 6. Hertz's nationality became an issue again. After war was declared, German aliens were not allowed to apply for US citizenship, and Hertz's application was denied. Yet Hertz had already filed for citizenship in February 1916 and submitted his final bid for naturalization *before* formal hostilities with Germany began. He fought the case and threatened to take it to the US Supreme Court if necessary, but the issue was settled in his favor in the San Francisco District Court.

Board member William Crocker objected to rehiring Hertz for the 1918–19 season, since anti-German feeling was bound to intensify. Against the evidence, Cecilia Casserly refused to believe Hertz was a citizen and suggested his presence called San Francisco's music scene into disrepute. Eventually the war took its toll even on programming, although not until August 1918 did the San Francisco Symphony follow the lead of Eastern orchestras in banning the music of living German composers (and of Wagner).

Three months later an armistice was signed. The war was over, but now a new enemy circled the globe. As thirty thousand San Franciscans took to the streets in November 1918 to celebrate the war's end, all wore

10

10

The 1918 influenza epidemic killed millions around the world and afflicted thousands in San Francisco. Face masks were essential although meager protection.

11

Alfred Hertz and his permanent orchestra, 1924.

face masks. Autumn had seen a deadly resurgence of the "Spanish Flu," which had appeared in milder form that spring. By late November, even after city residents were assured the danger had passed, more than twenty-one hundred deaths were reported in the Bay Area, and the following month, in contradiction to official assurances, five thousand new cases were diagnosed in San Francisco. Estimates of the number of lives claimed by the disease worldwide go as high as 50 million. The epidemic abated as suddenly as it had appeared, but theaters and other public gathering places were closed by health department order, and the beginning of the 1918–19 Symphony season was delayed. Three pairs of classical concerts and two popular concerts were cancelled and refunds made. Despite this, the ninth season ended with a balanced budget.

TOWARD A MID-TENURE CRISIS

In November 1919, composer Howard Hanson arrived in California from the East Coast for a year's stint as dean

of the College of the Pacific's Conservatory of Music, then based in San Jose. Logically, Hanson initiated contact with a conductor who might be interested in performing his music. When he sent his Symphonic Rhapsody to Alfred Hertz in hopes it might find its way onto a Symphony program, Hanson included these words: "I understand from some of my friends that you are especially interested in American composition, and as I have heard you conduct Wagner and Strauss in New York a good many times I would consider it a great privilege to have you read through this composition."

As an American, and as a member of the community, Hertz felt a responsibility to local composers. He maintained an extended, supportive, and occasionally scolding correspondence with Hanson. Hertz was also the idol of a struggling college student in Berkeley. Writing to Hertz in October 1921, Roy Harris thought of himself only as a young musician who dreamed of composing, and he referred to an earlier meeting in which the con-

13

ductor had expressed his encouragement. Hertz knew how to spot talent. In 1939, Harris would write what many still think of as the Great American Symphony (his Third).

Earlier in 1921, Hanson had expressed relief that the San Francisco Symphony was not disbanding and that Hertz had not accepted a European post. How such rumors may have started is easy enough to understand. Season-to-season financial troubles had everyone on edge—musicians, board, and conductor. In 1921, Hertz let his anger loose. He had built a fine orchestra, but as each season concluded he went begging to learn if he could expect another to commence. Humiliated, he wrote to the Association's new president, John D. McKee: "The Orchestra must either progress or go back; a stand-still is not possible. But it cannot progress if I am not put in a position to make arrangements with certain musicians ahead of time." The previous year, while awaiting the go-ahead to begin hiring for a new season, he had lost his first trumpet and third horn players. Replacing them with musicians of comparable talents had proved impossible.

At last, in 1922, he had had enough. He submitted his resignation. It was announced in the press. His final concerts were scheduled for March 31 and April 2. Before intermission at the March 31 concert, Hertz bade farewell. He praised the musicians. He thanked the audience. This day, he said, was both the saddest and happiest of his life.

Then something extraordinary happened. From the wings, a young woman appeared on stage. She was a graduate student from Berkeley, where she studied music at the University of California. Her name was Kathryn Roberts. She was not accustomed to speaking to large gatherings and her voice trembled. She fought tears. But she made herself heard.

"I don't know how you feel about this," she called out. "But if you feel as I do, you do not want to let Alfred Hertz go. They tell us that we are to have the orchestra, but what good is an orchestra without a conductor? They say that they could not offer him a contract for another year because they have not the money to pay his salary. There must be 1,500 of us here today. If each of us gives $10 or less, we can raise the $10,000 now. Are you with me?"

The theater erupted. People began shouting amounts. The first was an offer of $100. Then came one for $200. Then another, for $50. Noting the figures, Roberts asked the ushers to help her collect pledges.

She herself went into the audience with a pencil and pad to take pledges. Reporters surrounded her. They wanted to know who she was.

She refused at first to identify herself. "I'm Eleanor Smith," she snapped. "It doesn't matter who I am. I'm nobody."

After intermission, Hertz and the musicians played Richard Strauss's *Don Juan*, and when it was over Kathryn Roberts reappeared, this time to announce the pledge total: $10,489. More pledges were turned in after the concert, and the final tally was $11,000.

The case was not closed. Despite the audience's support, Hertz was not asked to reconsider his resignation. In May, he learned that Eugène Ysaÿe was about to leave his post as conductor of the Cincinnati Symphony, and in a confidential telegram to the orchestra there, Hertz expressed interest in the job. Three days later he wrote to Mrs. Charles P. Taft, president of the Cincinnati Symphony. He told her about the spontaneous collection of $11,000 at a concert but maintained nevertheless that he wished to be considered for the Cincinnati post. He never received a reply.

A few weeks later, having withdrawn his resignation, Hertz wrote a friend that he had considered rejecting a new contract, but he believed this would have meant the Symphony's death. That, he said, would have been a calamity. He ended the letter with that word, *calamity*, and added an exclamation mark.

Better days were ahead.

REACHING MORE WITH MUSIC
Alfred Hertz understood music's broad appeal. He was about to realize his dream of reaching huge audiences. As partners in music-making, and in making music widely available, he and the San Francisco Symphony were ideally matched. The coming years would see a regular popular series presented in tandem with the city, a youth series, a gigantic choral festival, recordings, broadcasts, and summer concerts.

Howard Hanson, composer and conductor, whose music Hertz championed.

John D. McKee, Association president from 1919 to 1927.

Civic Auditorium, packed with ten thousand listeners for the 1928 world premiere of Ernest Bloch's cantata America. *Hertz conducted an augmented orchestra, the Municipal Chorus, and three vocal soloists in this "Epic Rhapsody," celebrating US history from the Pilgrims' landing to the machine age.*

14

As early as 1918 Hertz had conducted the San Francisco Symphony in a "Grand Popular Concert" at the Exposition Auditorium (now the Bill Graham Civic Auditorium), attracting an audience of ten thousand. Similar events followed until, in 1923, a five-concert series of such performances was offered, presented by the City of San Francisco, meaning that the city purchased concerts from the Musical Association and presented them at prices subsidized by the city and available to the many. Forerunner to concerts that would be presented in cooperation with the San Francisco Arts Commission into the twenty-first century, these Municipal Concerts—the name became official in 1925—attracted thousands, and Hertz seems to have enjoyed them thoroughly. Hertz also established series of concerts in Oakland, Berkeley, and at Stanford University. And while concerts for schoolchildren had been given as early as

December 1911, a Young People's series was officially launched in 1922—conducted by Hertz himself.

Other notable events put San Francisco in the news. On August 2, 1923, President Warren G. Harding, having checked in at the Palace Hotel on his cross-country journey to meet with citizens and explain his policies, was talking to his wife when, in mid-sentence, he dropped dead. That same year—three years after the Nineteenth Amendment guaranteed them the right to vote—Alfred Hertz extended to women a privilege that, although never expressly denied, had never been offered actively. No major orchestra had hired a woman for a post other than harpist until Helen Atkinson joined the San Francisco Symphony violins in 1923. The next year, violinist Mary Pasmore was hired, along with her cellist sister, Dorothy, and violinists Eugenia Bem and Modesta Mortensen. The

San Francisco Opera also gave its first performance in 1923, with Symphony musicians forming the main contingent in the Opera orchestra, as they would for the next fifty-seven years.

The Young People's series, offered at the Civic Auditorium, was the setting in 1924 for the San Francisco Symphony debut of a remarkable seven-year-old violinist, Yehudi Menuhin. Menuhin was no stranger to the Symphony. Growing up in San Francisco, he was a regular at concerts. He was mesmerized by the playing of concertmaster Louis Persinger and went on to study with him. Hertz was serving as a competition judge when he first encountered the boy, and he became a staunch supporter. An artist as prodigiously gifted as Yehudi Menuhin may well have enjoyed success anywhere, but the fact that his first acclaim came in San Francisco, and with the instruction

53

15

Original stamping of RCA's first San Francisco Symphony recording, made in 1925 at the Victor Talking Machine studio in Oakland. Handwritten note by Association Secretary A. W. Widenham certifies disk's authenticity.

16

Programs for children had been introduced in the Symphony's first season. In 1922, a special three-concert series was launched, with the promise that programs would be "equally enjoyed" by adults. Hertz believed in outreach. He himself conducted.

17

Antonia Brico, who grew up in Oakland, studied at UC Berkeley, and in 1930 became the first woman to conduct the San Francisco Symphony, shortly after her debut with the Berlin Philharmonic.

and encouragement of two such key Symphony figures as Hertz and Persinger, was something Menuhin never forgot. He would go on to worldwide fame but would always hold the San Francisco Symphony dear, and he remained a friend throughout his life, performing as soloist with the orchestra and conducting it until 1993.

Big plans were realized in March 1924, with the four-day Spring Music Festival. Presented under the joint auspices of the City of San Francisco and the Musical Association, the popular-priced concerts attracted thousands to Civic Auditorium for mammoth performances of mammoth works. The orchestra was augmented to 125, and a Municipal Chorus of 500 recruited, along with conductor Hans Leschke, brought from Europe to direct it. The music-loving J. Emmet Hayden of the Board of Supervisors, who had already led the city's efforts on behalf of the orchestra in founding what would become the Municipal Concerts, spearheaded city support.

The Municipal Chorus mirrored the universal vision Beethoven had expressed in his Ninth Symphony, that great hymn to human fraternity. Society women were driven four times a week from the Peninsula to attend choral rehearsals. "Men of means would rehearse diligently, side by side with the man or woman who after punching the clock in the morning trotted forward to these evening hours of heart-stirring work with Alfred Hertz." A hundred soldiers from the Ninth Corps answered the call to volunteer for the festival chorus after Supervisor Hayden called on the US Army for aid. Programs included Liszt's *Faust Symphony*, the Beethoven Ninth, and the first complete performance in San Francisco of Mahler's *Resurrection Symphony*. The noise must have been sublime. The festival attracted an audience of more than thirty-four thousand and turned a profit of almost eleven thousand dollars. Alfred Metzger maintained that never before in America had a musical organization and a municipality joined in presenting such a festival.

The country was beginning to understand that extraordinary music-making was taking place in San Francisco. Nothing announced this as conclusively as an overture from the Victor Talking Machine Company of Camden, New Jersey, ancestor of RCA Victor. The company had already recorded the Boston Symphony, Philadelphia Orchestra, and New York Philharmonic. Now it wanted to add Hertz and the San Francisco Symphony to its artistic roster. The first recordings, made in the fall of 1925, were of Auber's *Fra Diavolo* Overture, and the Prelude and Good Friday Spell from Wagner's *Parsifal*.

Despite the constrictions that early recording technology placed on art-ists, the results that Hertz and the musicians achieved were extraordinary. Listening to their performance of Beethoven's *Leonore* Overture No. 3 or Mendelssohn's Incidental Music for *A Midsummer Night's Dream*, one senses what the excitement was about. The playing, heavy on string portamento (slides), radiates a quality whose antique nature may be startling to a present-day listener. The musicians heard on these recordings were trained by teachers who went back well into the nineteenth century, who taught a style of music-making different than today's. A fifty-year-old orchestra member would have been born in 1875; that musician's teacher could have heard Mendelssohn himself conduct his *Midsummer Night's Dream* Overture. One of Hertz's own major teachers, Anton Urspruch, had been born in 1850 and studied with Liszt. This was an orchestra with traditions rooted in what many considered—and what some still consider—music's most glorious period.

As Victor recordings carried the music across the country, broadcasts via the new medium of radio famil-iarized the West Coast with the San Francisco Symphony. In September 1926, a plan was announced to broadcast the Symphony on Sun-day afternoons, an entire season of twenty-one concerts. Nothing of this scope had been done before. Stations KGO and KPO agreed to broadcast the concerts free, donating technical services. Expenses, however, would still be steep. The Standard Oil Company of California became the White Knight that made broadcasts possible with a ten-thousand-dollar donation. Corporate support for the arts in America was a novelty in those days, and this was surely among the first such contributions. The broad-casts, inaugurated on October 31, 1926, would become known as *The Standard Symphony Hour*. They were tailored for radio and produced si-multaneously by KPO–San Francisco, KGO–Oakland, and KFI–Los Angeles. Never before had a radio series in the United States been devoted to symphonic music.

A few months earlier, the orchestra was featured at Civic Auditorium in a Summer Symphony concert series, organized to capitalize on the out-door performances presented on the Peninsula in the Woodland Amphithe-atre, a kind of miniature Hollywood Bowl. The eight-concert Woodland series featured the San Francisco Symphony and was managed by the Philharmonic Society of San Mateo County. The society's president was a grande dame, Mrs. George N. Armsby. With a name like that, she could have been anyone. But since George N. had long since vanished from her life, she dispensed with that part of her identity and began calling herself Leonora Wood Armsby. Of all those who would play key roles in the San Francisco Symphony's history, her role would be paramount.

Mrs. Armsby's first vice-president of the Philharmonic Society was none other than Cecilia Casserly, who had brought in her protégé Nikolai Sokoloff to lead the bulk of the concerts, other performances being led by guests including Ossip Gabrilowitsch—great pianist, mas-terful conductor, and son-in-law of Mark Twain—Hertz, and Henry Hadley. Because they were already in the area to lead concerts at Woodland, the conductors traveled north a day or two later and repeated their Woodland programs for San Francisco in the Summer Symphony series, under-written by the city. It was in that series that the first woman to con-duct the San Francisco Symphony,

SAN FRANCISCO SYMPHONY
ORCHESTRA CONCERT
PROGRAM

San Francisco
Sunday, October 31, 1926
2:45 O'Clock P. M.

Broadcast simultaneously by
KPO, San Francisco
KGO, Oakland
KFI, Los Angeles

This is the first of a series of programs of the concerts by the San Francisco Symphony Orchestra. It is suggested that if the programs are preserved they will comprise, at the end of the season of twenty-one concerts, a valuable collection of interpretative and descriptive notes on a great number of the world's musical masterpieces.

The broadcasting of these concerts has been made possible through popular public subscription and the
STANDARD OIL COMPANY OF CALIFORNIA

The radio show would come to be called The Standard Hour, *but when it was introduced in October 1926 it was simply a series of "concert programs"—the most extensive series yet to be carried on the air waves.*

On October 31, 1926, at 2:45 on a Sunday afternoon, the San Francisco Symphony embraced new technology to bring music to many. The orchestra was heard in a live radio broadcast carried simultaneously by KPO–San Francisco, KGO–Oakland, and KFI–Los Angeles. Alfred Hertz conducted Beethoven's Symphony No. 3—the *Eroica*—and Richard Strauss's *Ein Heldenleben*. Richard Strauss had composed his "Hero's Life" as a companion piece to Beethoven's groundbreaking symphony. Little did he know that, together with the *Eroica*, it would fit perfectly into the radio format, as would all the Sunday afternoon programs that season, which were designed for broadcast.

The first commercial radio broadcasts had been heard only six years earlier, and on July 2, 1921, radio came into its own, when Jack Dempsey and Georges Carpentier's heavyweight championship fight brought the new medium into the national consciousness. By 1930, radios would be in 12 million homes across the United States. But in the mid-1920s, broadcasters were still trying to determine what programming the public wanted. Nothing like a full season of concert performances had been attempted. Occasional concerts had been broadcast in other

communities, but not on this scale. When that scale proved prohibitively expensive, a local firm, the Standard Oil Company of California, offered ten thousand dollars. This contribution made possible the first network radio show in the country to feature symphonic music. In appreciation, the Symphony offered broadcasting rights to Standard. None of the programs carried a word of advertising for the firm. The title of the show, however, was a tribute to the generosity that made it happen: *The Standard Symphony Hour*, which later became simply *The Standard Hour*.

Standard Oil had expected to lend its aid to music's cause only for one season, but thousands of cards, letters, and telegrams, not to mention praise from the press, convinced Standard to continue its sponsorship, and a tradition was born. The "Standard Symphony Orchestra," organized in 1927 to broadcast from the Bay Area up and down the West Coast ("from Mexico to the Far North"), was made up essentially of San Francisco Symphony musicians. Eventually, broadcasts by the Los Angeles Philharmonic, the Portland Symphony, and the Seattle Symphony became part of the series, but San Franciscans thought of

The orchestra at San Francisco's NBC studio, 1942.

The Standard Hour as theirs. In fact the program's theme song, adopted in 1943, was called "This Hour Is Yours," and it was composed by the Symphony's orchestra personnel manager, violinist Julius Haug.

A *Standard School Broadcast* was launched in 1928 as a companion to the concert program and introduced the music to be heard in *The Standard Symphony Hour*. The first of these educational efforts reached only seventy-two schools, which happened to be the only schools on the West Coast that owned radios. Eventually, more than fourteen thousand schools tuned in. Even after *The Standard Hour* went off the air in 1955, the school broadcasts continued as an independent program until 1970.

Some worried that the broadcasts would make for smaller audiences at concerts. Alfred Hertz disagreed. He expressed enthusiasm for technological advances and felt radio was egalitarian in both the size and scope of the audience it reached. "Tonight," he told *The Radio Guide* in 1934, "we'll play to more listeners than we played to during the entire season before going on the air." Among Hertz's most cherished mementos

were letters from those who listened from their farms, and in small communities. ("In one little town a whole population is grateful for your gift," came a note from Palm Springs, California. "Away out here in the wilderness I have just enjoyed your concert, especially the 'Parsifal,'" wrote an admirer in Rimrock, Arizona.) And in 1937, in celebration of *The Standard Symphony Hour*'s five-hundredth consecutive program, which Hertz conducted, the *Call-Bulletin* noted that thousands of schoolchildren listened each week and that four West Coast colleges awarded degrees based on "radio lectures."

By 1942, when *The Standard Symphony Hour* won broadcasting's equivalent of an Oscar, the Peabody Medal, Standard Oil of California realized that its program, though broadcast only in the West, had achieved a national reputation. But within thirteen years the long-playing record, to say nothing of television, would take its toll on the audience. When *The Standard Hour* signed off at the close of its 1,456th regular Sunday evening program, nearly three decades of West Coast radio became history.

San Francisco Symphony Orchestra

- - -

IN A FAREWELL CONCERT

TO

ALFRED HERTZ

EXPOSITION AUDITORIUM
TUESDAY, APRIL 15, 1930
8:30 o'clock

Soloist: **YEHUDI MENUHIN**, Violinist

Arranged by
MAYOR JAMES ROLPH, Jr.
AND BOARD OF SAN FRANCISCO SUPERVISORS

Direction of AUDITORIUM COMMITTEE
J. EMMET HAYDEN, Chairman
VICTOR J. CANEPA   JESSE C. COLMAN

Thomas F. Boyle in charge of Ticket Sales

Antonia Brico, made her debut with the orchestra in 1930. Cecilia Casserly, incidentally, was herself soon to make a bid for a broader kind of public service. In 1928, she mounted an unsuccessful campaign to unseat four-term congressman Arthur M. Free as US representative from the Eighth District of California. She ran as a Democrat.

DENOUEMENT AND FINALE FOR HERTZ

The sheer amount of music being made outstripped anything the Bay Area had known. Alfred Hertz was a different man than the one who five years earlier had agonized over his resignation. On October 31, 1927, he found himself, of all places, on the cover of *Time* magazine. This was the year that Charles Lindbergh made his famous solo flight nonstop from New York to Paris. On a more

18

Alfred Hertz drew an audience of twelve thousand to his farewell concert.

somber note, it was the year Nicola Sacco and Bartolomeo Vanzetti, Italian immigrants and members of an anarchist organization, having been charged on flimsy evidence with armed robbery and murder, were sent to the electric chair, anti-immigrant sentiment having played a part in determining their fate. In this year of big news stories, and when distrust of the foreign-born still ran deep, Alfred Hertz's appearance on *Time*'s cover was quite an accomplishment. The San Francisco Symphony had arrived in the national consciousness.

Soloists the equal of any to be found in the world's greatest orchestras appeared in San Francisco during these years, among them pianists Artur Rubinstein, Alfred Cortot, and Vladimir Horowitz, and violinists Nathan Milstein and Mischa Elman. In what would become a Symphony tradition, composers conducted their own works. Georges Enesco, Howard Hanson, Ernst von Dohnányi, Maurice Ravel, and Ottorino Respighi all led the orchestra. Sergei Prokofiev was soloist in his Piano Concerto No. 3.

"Our future has never looked so bright as now," Hertz told critic Alexander Fried in 1927. "Not only have we solidified our popular backing and perfected the routine of our personnel during the past decade, but we are at last actually flying under the encouraging banner of financial solvency. Long may it wave."

In January 1928, Hertz led the San Francisco Symphony's first extended tour. The journey was only as far as Los Angeles, but it was notable for being what the LA press described as the country's first orchestra exchange—because the Los Angeles Philharmonic at the same time was on its way to San Francisco, and each orchestra gave three concerts in the other's home town. As the Symphony's train pulled in at the Southern Pacific station, a crowd gathered to welcome the orchestra. More than forty decorated cars were waiting, ready to transport the

musicians to the Biltmore Hotel, and as wailing sirens cleared the way for the convoy proceeding up Fifth Street behind motorcycle police, watchers gathered along the route.

Herbert Hoover was elected president in November 1928. The first television transmission was broadcast from a San Francisco laboratory. The country appeared to be moving forward, but for Hertz the denouement of his San Francisco years had begun. At the beginning of October 1929 he announced that, after fifteen years in one post, he was ready for a change. "I am now at my zenith. I have brought the orchestra about as far as I can, and I want to leave while San Francisco still loves me." By the end of the month, the stock market would crash and plunge the country into its darkest economic period.

An audience of twelve thousand heard Hertz's last performance as music director, at a pops concert at Civic Auditorium in the spring of 1930.

Just seven years earlier, San Francisco had been reminded of another bearded émigré who had dug in for his beliefs. As John Muir had fought to preserve natural beauties for posterity, Hertz had championed music in San Francisco. Muir had opposed the water project that would flood Hetch Hetchy Valley in Yosemite National Park, and although the 1923 completion of O'Shaughnessy Dam marked that struggle's loss, the defeat did nothing to diminish Muir's legacy as curator of the American landscape. Like Muir, Hertz had fought his battles, had won some and lost others, but had held firm as guardian of a heritage. He may never have gone out of his way to be liked, but the tribute that greeted him as he took his final bows at the Symphony's helm spoke of love. "Not the least significant portion of these ovations," observed a *Chronicle* editorial writer, "has been the persistent applause given him by the members of the orchestra. These men know, none better."

1

Basil Cameron, "The Quiet Maestro."

2

*Issay Dobrowen, reportedly one of the best young
conductors then on the international scene.*

IV.

CRISIS AND RESCUE

The Basil Cameron/Issay Dobrowen Years (1930–1935)

1

NO MATCH MADE IN HEAVEN

Arts organizations are businesses, and like other American businesses in the 1930s they suffered the pains of the Great Depression. Alfred Hertz had shown how a strong personality could catapult the orchestra to national prominence. In the years after his departure, San Francisco would discover how such a sharply etched profile could sag in the absence of managerial and artistic leadership. For the San Francisco Symphony, the years between 1930 and 1935 witnessed a perfect storm. No one individual was responsible for its troubles. Instead, executive miscalculation joined forces with

ineffectual music directors, not a winning formula to find the way through an economic malaise that paralyzed the country, that defeated Herbert Hoover in 1932, and that would bring Franklin D. Roosevelt to the White House.

J. B. Levison, the Association's president, did not reveal his reasoning, but at a board meeting in April 1930 he said he felt strongly that, to replace Hertz, "we should not engage any one man for the full season, but rather two or three." A less likely pair could hardly have been found than the ones hired, Basil Cameron

and Issay Dobrowen. The best that can be said of Cameron is that he had no effect on either orchestra or organization. Dobrowen helped send the Symphony on the road to bankruptcy.

Cameron was chosen in May 1930 to lead the first half of the 1930–31 season. Born in 1884 to a German father and a British mother in Reading, England, Basil George Cameron Hindenberg had a distinguished musical pedigree that included violin studies with Joseph Joachim and composition studies with Max Bruch. During the Great War, fearing the sort of anti-German sentiment that

3

had made life miserable for Alfred Hertz, he dropped the Hindenberg surname and became the thoroughly English Basil Cameron. Although he would become associated with such major-league ensembles as the London Philharmonic and London Symphony Orchestra after the Second World War, when he came to San Francisco he had led only regional orchestras in England. He did, however, come with the recommendations of composer Percy Grainger and conductor Thomas Beecham. "The Quiet Maestro," an article on Cameron in the *BBC Guide*, describes him: "An archetypal English gentleman, never assertive, Cameron was sometimes given a hard time at rehearsals by the London Philharmonic Orchestra, even to the point where he would leave the podium and lock himself in his dressing room." Cameron lived until 1975, minus the knighthood conferred upon virtually all British conductors of any renown.

Issay Dobrowen, hired along with Cameron, would conduct the second half of the 1930–31 season. He was born in 1891 in Nizhniy Novgorod, Russia, to parents so poor that they were forced to give him up for adoption. His birth name, Itschok Zorachovich Barabeitchik, went through several permutations before assuming the form by which Western audiences came to know him. He was a wunderkind, graduating with a gold medal in piano from the Moscow Conservatory, where he also studied composition with Sergei Taneyev. From Moscow he went to Vienna and then Paris, becoming part of a volatile, ferociously intellectual Russian expatriate community. He appeared as piano soloist with orchestras throughout Europe, and he composed. His conducting career took off brilliantly when, in 1919, he led a performance of *Boris Godunov* at the Bolshoi Theater, with

the great bass Feodor Chaliapin in the title role. Destined to become known especially for his work in the opera house, Dobrowen was on his way up after staging and conducting *Boris* in Dresden. In the concert hall he guest-conducted such ensembles as the Berlin Philharmonic, the Vienna Philharmonic, and the Leipzig Gewandhaus Orchestra. In his post–San Francisco period Dobrowen settled with his family first in Norway, then Sweden, where he directed operas and conducted at Stockholm's Royal Theater. Dobrowen was actively involved in recording with the Philharmonia Orchestra after its founding in London in the wake of World War II. He continued his opera work at places such as Covent Garden and La Scala. He seems to have moved in a fever, driving himself from project to project. Victim of a nervous breakdown during his San Francisco years, he died in Oslo in 1953 at the relatively early age of sixty-two, burned out.

Between Dobrowen's combustible energy and Cameron's glacial personality, San Francisco had harnessed fire and ice. When the time came to choose between them, the Symphony opted for fire. For by February 1931 it was apparent that audiences favored Dobrowen. Box office receipts for his concerts outstripped those for Cameron's performances, although Cameron presented by far the more interesting programs, leading such local premieres as Elgar's Introduction and Allegro and the US premiere of Sibelius's *The Tempest*. Yet he was not the one to enrapture the ladies of the Women's Auxiliary, who cited reports from abroad that, among young conductors then active on the international scene, Dobrowen was the best. Dobrowen possessed an undeniable magnetism. In an interview three years later, he would admit, "shyly," that he received

SAN FRANCISCO

BASIL CAMERON

ISSAY DOBROWEN

SYMPHONY ORCHESTRA

Twentieth Season
1930-1931

CURRAN THEATRE

Opening October 10, 1930

MARKING a new departure of outstanding importance to local music lovers, the San Francisco Symphony Orchestra has engaged two distinguished guest conductors for the twentieth season opening Friday, October 10.

Basil Cameron, the noted English conductor, and Issay Dobrowen, the dynamic Russian leader, will make their first American appearances here under the auspices of the Musical Association of San Francisco, the supporting organization of the Symphony.

The first portion of the season will be conducted by Mr. Cameron and the latter portion by Mr. Dobrowen.

The season promises to be unusually rich in its offerings, as both of these conductors from abroad are bringing with them a number of new scores, including novelties, detailed announcement of which is to be made later. In addition, the management is arranging for a number of guest artists, announcement of which will be made as soon as arrangements are concluded.

Once more the Symphony will be heard in the Curran Theatre. The regular season will be divided into three separate series of:

Thirteen Friday Afternoon Symphony Concerts
(Given fortnightly)

Thirteen Sunday Afternoon Symphony Concerts
(At which the Friday programmes will be repeated)

Eleven Sunday Afternoon Popular Concerts
(Alternating with the Sunday Symphonies)

Season tickets are sold separately for each series, for which order card is enclosed herewith. Reservations should be sent in at once so that the work of allotting locations may be made without delay. The customary method of allotting locations will be followed: (1) Members of the Musical Association according to the amount of their subscription; (2) Other subscribers to the symphony supporting fund; (3) Former season ticket holders; (4) New orders.

File order at once in order to avoid disappointment. Tickets will be mailed immediately after allotment, which will be about September 20.

GUEST CONDUCTORS

4

"scores of 'mash notes,' on perfumed, pink and orange paper, from women admirers after every concert."

Youthful fire, however, came at a price. Invited to assume the San Francisco post full-time for the 1931–32 season, Dobrowen countered that he would be available only for the first half and that he could not come for less than fifteen thousand dollars. Further demands followed: if he were reengaged for another season, he wanted a minimum of thirty thousand dollars. If he proved a hit, he would expect more. With an odd sense of diplomacy he disclosed that what most ingratiated San Francisco to him was his wife's fondness for the city. Dobrowen was engaged for half of the 1931–32 season at his stipulated figure. The other half of the season would again go to Basil Cameron, but at a fee far less than Dobrowen's. Beginning with the 1932–33 season, Dobrowen

would be engaged for three years, again at the minimum he had named. While Cameron eventually faded from view, the Association, in agreeing to Dobrowen's terms, bound itself to someone more intent on his career than on serving the cause of music in San Francisco.

As the country's economy seemed increasingly resistant to repair, exactly where Dobrowen's fee would come from was anyone's guess. In June, J. B. Levison actually reported increased concert revenue and reduced operating expenses, but a corresponding decline in contributions.

Levison knew the stakes were high. In June 1931 he told his fellow board members that the Symphony had to increase its "activity and community interest" or face a substantial deficit at the end of the coming season, though he failed to clarify what he meant by activity and community

---

SAN FRANCISCO SYMPHONY ORCHESTRA

BASIL CAMERON, Conductor

A. W. WIDENHAM, *Manager*

PROGRAMME
SECOND MUNICIPAL SYMPHONY CONCERT
SEASON 1930-31

SOLOIST

HEIFETZ

EXPOSITION AUDITORIUM
SATURDAY EVENING, NOVEMBER 29, 1930

Auspices MAYOR JAMES ROLPH, JR., AND BOARD OF SUPERVISORS
Direction AUDITORIUM COMMITTEE—J. EMMET HAYDEN, *Chairman*
VICTOR J. CANEPA   JESSE COLMAN
BENNING WENTWORTH, *In Charge of Ticket Sales and Accounts*

5

6

interest. He admitted he was at his wits' end. One cost-cutting measure, he thought, might be to scale back the orchestra's size. But such a move would contradict Dobrowen, among whose goals was an expanded orchestra, and a week later Dobrowen got his way. The budget finally agreed upon, $236,600, showed a projected deficit of $45,000—about $640,000 in 2011 currency and large by any measure. But while financial problems demanded attention, San Francisco music lovers continued to enjoy such soloists as Jascha Heifetz and Vladimir Horowitz, who were featured in the Municipal Concerts sponsored by the city. The Summer Symphony continued to present the orchestra in San Francisco concerts paralleling those at the Woodland Theatre in Hillsborough. Performances such as these may have given the impression that all was well. Levison knew otherwise.

RALLYING TO THE CAUSE

In the face of its president's ominous prediction, the Musical Association also had cause to celebrate, for the concert that opened the 1931–32 season would be the one thousandth performance since Henry Hadley and his band had launched things in 1911. Dobrowen suggested the Beethoven Ninth Symphony as a gala season opener. That plan was nixed. This was the last season the orchestra would have to make do with inadequate performance venues before moving into the War Memorial Opera House, then nearing completion (see "A Home for Music (*Finalmente!*)," page 67). The decision to present the 1931–32 season in the Tivoli Opera House would save six thousand dollars and make evening concerts possible, but those benefits came at the cost of a stage too small to accommodate the forces that the Beethoven symphony required. Instead of the Ninth, the works performed at the 1911 inaugural concert would be repeated—almost. Added to the program, in a salute to the Symphony's founding music director, was the Intermezzo from Henry Hadley's Bohemian Grove extravaganza *The Atonement of Pan*. Substituted for Tchaikovsky's *Pathétique* Symphony was Issay Dobrowen's Piano Concerto, a work already five years old but which was the most recent music he had composed and the last music he would compose, ever. Dobrowen himself would be soloist.

Everywhere in the country, orchestras labored under financial pressure, and the San Francisco orchestra had a smaller budget to work with than did other leading ensembles. The *Chronicle*'s Alexander Fried reported figures he had received from Association President Levison. In the year just past, the Boston Symphony's budget had been $960,000, the New York Philharmonic-Symphony's $900,000, and San Francisco's $224,000. Incredibly, given the financial climate, box office receipts for 1931–32 were equal to those of the previous season, although contributions were down from the record $155,000 of 1928–29 to $75,000.

As the first full year of the Great Depression came to an end, Issay Dobrowen conducted a San Francisco Symphony augmented to two hundred players in a benefit concert for unemployed musicians. Levison attacked financial problems with force and speed, naming a city-wide committee to help raise funds. Within a

7

*The San Francisco Symphony in the first
concert at Stern Grove, June 19, 1932.*

Opera House courtyard and City Hall by night.

The War Memorial Opera House under construction. 1932

A HOME FOR MUSIC (*FINALMENTE!*)

At the beginning, the San Francisco Symphony was forced to make do, playing in theaters that had not been designed for orchestral concerts. Early plans for a new home were derailed, but interest revived in 1919. Alfred Hertz was the spur. He believed such a venue "would crown the work of the Musical Association and begin a new epoch in the musical life of San Francisco." The board listened to him and resolved that a "Symphony Hall Committee" of twenty be appointed, ten of its members to come from the Association. E. S. Heller was assigned to draft a financing plan. That was in April. Things moved quickly. By August, Association trustee William H. Crocker suggested that "the Art Association, the Symphony Orchestra, and a Grand Opera House be included in the undertaking." He believed a Van Ness Avenue lot owned by St. Ignatius School—a lot that would become the site of Davies Symphony Hall—could accommodate a structure housing the three organizations. The following month, the Association took an option on this property. But the fund-raising target was $2 million, and at year's end contributions stalled at less than half that amount. At this point, Major Charles Kendrick entered the picture. Recently returned from the war and active in the American Legion, he suggested that, if the opera house project became a memorial to those who had served in the European conflict, he could raise support from veterans.

Plans for the War Memorial cultural complex were unveiled in a mass meeting at the Civic Auditorium in May 1920. Fund-raising reignited, and at meeting's end pledges stood at $1.65 million, including a $100,000 pledge from the city. The campaign then took to the streets. Pup tents were set up on corners, hats passed in theaters. By the funding drive's conclusion, $2.15 million was raised. The planned structure for the people would genuinely have been made possible by the people.

In 1921 the city accepted transfer of what had been the St. Ignatius property, but it became apparent that that plot of land was too small for the proposed complex, so the trustees of the War Memorial began acquiring the two blocks north of Grove Street, along Van Ness Avenue, opposite City Hall. An advisory committee chaired by Bernard Maybeck included other local architectural stars, among them Arthur Brown, Jr., and G. Albert Lansburgh, who collaborated on the design that proved most feasible. But plans stalled for almost a decade, and not until 1927 would funding for the project be complete. That May, a bond issue was structured to raise the needed $4 million for the War Memorial. Keeping in mind a California

Supreme Court ruling that determined the city could not maintain a joint venture with the Musical Association of San Francisco, the bond issue avoided mention of the proposed opera house and museum facilities and referred only to the construction of a "permanent building in or adjacent to the Civic Center to be used as a memorial hall for War Veterans and for educational, recreational, entertainments and other municipal purposes." A two-thirds majority was required for the measure to pass. That figure was exceeded by more than two thousand votes, the first but not the only time the citizens came through for the music.

Construction began at last on January 2, 1931, and proceeded rapidly. On September 9, 1932, eighty-two years to the day after California had entered the Union, the War Memorial Opera House was dedicated.

In early October, an acoustic test found Wallace Alexander, president of the San Francisco Opera Association, offering an onstage speech while Opera Association members scattered throughout the hall to listen. No matter where they were, they heard him perfectly. Critic Alexander Fried pronounced the acoustics "absolutely impeccable." Architect Albert Lansburgh was relieved. "Last night I couldn't sleep," he admitted. "Now I feel better. There is no severer test of a theater than the audibility of the speaking voice."

The first public performance, on October 15, 1932, was sold out. Puccini's *Tosca* was staged, with Opera General Director Gaetano Merola in the pit, leading musicians who doubled as members of the San Francisco Symphony. "*Ah! Finalmente!*" sings the character Angelotti to open the work. The audience, well aware how long this moment had been postponed, erupted in cheers.

While that *Tosca* performance marked the first time the public had heard the San Francisco Symphony in the Opera House—Opera orchestra and Symphony being essentially the same ensemble—the first orchestral concert was heard on November 4, when Alfred Hertz conducted a *Standard Hour* broadcast for NBC radio. The *San Francisco News* viewed this with satisfaction: "It was fitting that the first symphonic program in the new building should be directed by the man who devoted fifteen years of his life to the development of our San Francisco Symphony."

month, on February 15, 1932, a public Symphony Fund Campaign opened. It was chaired by Robert Watt Miller, who would go on to serve the San Francisco Opera with distinction, and its goal was to meet the current season's deficit and make a new season possible. Mayor Angelo Rossi issued a statement characterizing the orchestra as "the symbol of the cultural life of our city." He urged music lovers to ensure the Symphony's survival.

The day after Rossi's proclamation, lest the significance of the Symphony's appeal to civic spirit be overlooked, Supervisor J. Emmet Hayden told the audience at a Municipal Concert, "The San Francisco Symphony Orchestra is an institution of the people and not the child of a limited number of wealthy music patrons." Hayden was sounding a theme dear to him, for he believed in making music available to all. The month before he had been instrumental, with input from the Commonwealth Club of California, in creating a city Art Commission that would supervise and control expenditures of arts appropriations made by the Board of Supervisors, but whose broader purpose was dedicated to public art.

The Symphony Fund Campaign emphasized how much the Bay Area loved its orchestra. The campaign's goal was $175,000. In pursuit of that amount, publicity blanketed the city for three weeks. The Chamber of Commerce solicited businesses and corporations. Sixteen thousand direct-mail appeals were made. Twenty-two thousand pledge cards went to selected lists of music lovers. Another twelve thousand pledge cards were distributed to clubs, at concerts, and in hotels and department stores. The clergy was enlisted, along with men's clubs,

women's clubs, fraternal organizations, private schools, and the PTA. Citizens encountered the appeal on billboards and on streetcar panels. They read supporting stories in the newspapers, and the *Examiner* each day printed a clip-out "Save the Symphony" coupon that invited readers to pledge their support. Daily radio spots carried the message. Duke Ellington and his band, about to make their local debut, made it ahead of schedule on February 19, when they donated their services in a performance on KFRC radio hosted by Captain Dobbsie—Hugh Barrett Dobbs—who converted his "Happy Times Hour" into a program to support the Symphony. The Musicians' Union pledged three hundred dollars. A special Symphony broadcast on the eve of the campaign's launch brought responses from fans throughout the state, and from Nevada, Washington, Oregon, and Canada. When the campaign ended on March 7, all but $275 had been pledged. Almost three thousand people had responded. Most had never contributed to the Symphony before, and of the sixteen hundred who pledged less than ten dollars, more than half pledged less than five dollars. The campaign's success displayed the power of effective messaging. It also testified to how completely people embraced music in dark times. A few days earlier, the kidnapping of aviation hero Charles Lindbergh's infant son reminded America that tragedy makes its home in mansions as well as tenements, and what began as one couple's personal catastrophe became a story that in its sad way drew the attention of the country. Dark times, it seemed, could assume many forms.

And dark times refused to depart. To honor pledges offered in the enthusiasm of the moment took more than

good intentions. A month after the campaign closed, only fifty thousand dollars of the promised money had been collected, and any increase in that amount seemed in doubt. Levison advised drastic steps. He considered asking the musicians to accept a reduction in the minimum pay scale, perhaps even fewer weeks of concerts. At the same time, Dobrowen had received an offer to conduct the New York Philharmonic-Symphony Orchestra and requested a month's leave to accept that engagement. The Music Committee rationalized their unwillingness to cross their young star and concluded that this invitation from an elite East Coast ensemble would reflect well on San Francisco itself. Therefore the committee would comply with Dobrowen's request. In fact, compliance was moot. Dobrowen's divided loyalties were sanctioned by his contract, which included a clause granting him leave of absence during the season to conduct on the East Coast, specifically the New York Philharmonic. When Dobrowen followed up with a request to lead eight weeks with the Philadelphia Orchestra, "the committee concurred that in view of the uncertainty of the outlook for the local 1932–33 season Mr. Dobrowen should be given liberty to make his own arrangements at his own pleasure."

Summer was a particularly trying time for musicians. The Summer Symphony season was short, and short of funds. In June 1932, the great philanthropist Rosalie Meyer Stern, also a Symphony board member, organized the first orchestral concert at the grove she had dedicated to her husband's memory and where she planned to give free concerts for the city's music lovers. On June 19, 1932, beneath the pavilion designed by architect Bernard Maybeck in

San Francisco Symphony Orchestra

ISSAY DOBROWEN, Conductor

1932 - Season - 1933

FIRST PAIR OF SYMPHONY CONCERTS
1080th and 1081st Concerts

Friday, November 11, 3:00 P.M.
Saturday, November 12, 8:30 P. M.

WAR MEMORIAL OPERA HOUSE

Soloist: EFREM ZIMBALIST, *Violinist*

P R O G R A M M E

Overture, "Leonore" No. 3.................*Beethoven*
Concerto for Violin, in D major..........*Beethoven*
    Allegro ma non troppo
    Larghetto—
    Rondo

EFREM ZIMBALIST

I N T E R M I S S I O N

Symphony No. 2, in D major.................*Brahms*
    Allegro non troppo
    Adagio non troppo
    Allegretto grazioso
    Allegro con spirito

N O T I C E !

'our attention is called to the fact that the first two pair of
oncerts will be held on consecutive weeks: the second pair
'ill be given November 18 and 19. Thereafter the pairs will
be given fortnightly as usual.

8

Program for the first concerts in the War Memorial Opera House, November 11 and 12, 1932.

Sigmund Stern Grove, sixty San Francisco Symphony musicians gathered to present a performance that Mrs. Stern had organized as a benefit. Admission was twenty-five cents, and the proceeds went to the players. The Stern Grove Midsummer Music Festival was still years from conception. Once it began, in 1937, the San Francisco Symphony would be a regular feature every year. For the present, the summer outlook was bleak.

Matters were also bleak at the Symphony, an organization twelve thousand dollars in immediate arrears, with thirty-five hundred dollars in pledged contributions still uncollected from the previous season, and with a thirty-five-thousand-dollar bank loan past due. Manager Peter Conley, planning a 1932–33 season, compared expenses and revenues for prospective seasons of three different lengths: ten, twelve, and twenty-five weeks. Projections for a ten-week season actually pointed to a modest positive balance, but so short a season would reduce musicians' earnings significantly. The section players proposed that the season begin after the Christmas holidays and continue as long as possible into the new year, hoping for improvements in the economy that could help lengthen the season. But the first-chair players, unwilling to commit to a season starting as late as January, preferred to seek other employment. They proposed a short season that would open in November, assuring them continuous employment through the fall and into the winter. A short season of ten weeks was scheduled. The balancing act had begun.

FALSE STARTS IN A NEW HOME

In those days the start of a season was determined more by circumstances than it is today. President Levison wanted to comply with the principals' wishes and open in November. He urged Dobrowen to be in San Francisco. This would, after all, be the Symphony's first season in the home it had waited so long to call its own, the War Memorial Opera House. Dobrowen, however, would not be persuaded. So Plan B was adopted: a January opening with Basil Cameron, the season to conclude in March with Dobrowen, whose expected—but as yet unproven— successes in New York and Philadelphia could be touted to attract the audience at home. Unfortunately, the musicians were not consulted about Plan B, and none showed enthusiasm for it. Dobrowen then managed to rearrange his schedule. He opened the season with two pairs of November concerts, after which he promptly left town.

The 1932–33 season continued with guest conductors, primarily Alfred Hertz and the Italian Bernardino Molinari, director of Rome's Augusteo Orchestra, today known as the Orchestra of Santa Cecilia. With all of his out-of-town work, Dobrowen was becoming less of a local presence, and public attention began to focus on those who led the orchestra regularly, especially Bernardino Molinari. Molinari, whose relationship with musicians was by turns caustic and charming, possessed musical instincts as exciting and deep as his political views were naïve. He admired Mussolini, not as a dictator but as an efficient manager who would make Italy prosper and transform the country's traditionally chaotic society into an orderly whole, just as he himself managed orchestras from the podium. By February 1933, Molinari was stealing the show. He had led the orchestra throughout January, and his engagement had proven so popular that the board feared

9

Dobrowen's scheduled season-ending performances would appear anticlimactic. Talk turned to bringing Dobrowen back immediately for a single concert. The musicians held out instead for a full week of performances—their livelihood depended on playing, and two or three concerts paid better than one. Clearly, future changes were necessary. The answer seemed to be a 1933–34 season minus any guest conductors who might dim the music director's luster—a season, that is, under Dobrowen's exclusive direction.

Critic Alexander Fried went to the heart of the matter, reporting on a letter he claimed to have received from a member of the orchestra. Identified only as "An Orchestral Player," Fried's correspondent objected to the shortened season. Cutting twenty-six weeks of concerts to ten weeks, said the anonymous musician, undermined the orchestra's morale. He feared the financial deficit would turn into an artistic shortcoming.

Then Fried—or his typesetter—fell into a slip. Obviously wishing to treat Dobrowen fairly, Fried intended to write that the conductor "could not be expected to sacrifice splendid Eastern opportunities for us." But the word "not" was omitted, and in thus maintaining that Dobrowen "could be expected" to make sacrifices, the audience's expectations were voiced. Typographical gaffes aside, Fried's exasperation was apparent:

Mr. Dobrowen was here for so limited a period that all he was able to undertake was the successful launching of the season simply through the means of the energetic promotion of his own concerts. He is gone before he could make a lasting impression on the playing of his ensemble. He is gone without having left any personal mark on the orchestra's repertory or on the taste of the public.

Fried feared that, as a brief season ended, some of the city's finest players would compete for jobs in theaters or with radio orchestras and, once settled, would stay in their new positions, robbing the Symphony of their talents. What the Musical Association needed, wrote Fried, was money. This year the Association had scheduled only as many concerts as it could pay for. Next season it was bound to do the same.

The Association's meeting of March 9, 1933, tells much about Dobrowen's relationship with his board. It reveals a thinker of little substance who seemed to improvise from a cache of clichés. The New York Philharmonic and Philadelphia Orchestra, he said, also had their share of financial difficulties, but those organizations possessed a cooperative spirit he felt San Francisco lacked. He recommended that somehow the board figure out how to generate such spirit. The most necessary thing was to support the orchestra.

Unfortunately, such vagueness was allowed to pass. All present approved of Dobrowen's words, then decided to shelve the matter for future discussion.

Dobrowen did make one concrete suggestion. He recommended everyone on the payroll make a sacrifice and included himself in that plan, though he failed to name the figure he was willing to forfeit. Before anyone could ask him to elaborate, he revealed a new offer that had come his way: a proposal to conduct twenty concerts in Philadelphia, requiring that he be there for six weeks, starting in January 1934. Seeming to dispense with its hope to keep Dobrowen in San Francisco throughout the next season, the board approved.

"THE SYMPHONY SHALL GO ON"

As the Depression deepened, the board declared unanimously on March 23, 1933, that "the Symphony shall go on." Back on the table was a 1933–34 season under Dobrowen's sole direction—always a challenge, and now complicated by his Philadelphia engagement.

Trying times such as these forced an obvious conclusion. The Symphony needed professional direction. Some thought the board should be headed by two leaders, one devoted to artistic matters and the other to finance—a plan put on hold but which would reemerge two years later, with results that were to prove the concept's simple brilliance. At the moment, planning was an unaffordable luxury. J. B. Levison, eager to devote himself to his own business, resigned the board presidency. His successor was Richard Tobin, who had once left to protest Alfred Hertz's appointment but whose love of music and sense of civic duty eventually brought him back. As Tobin assumed his post at the board's head, membership increased gradually from thirty to sixty. A hardheaded banker, Tobin believed in rigid budgets and insisted that the Association avoid activities it could not afford.

By May 1933, Tobin was laying plans for a new season and wrestling with the difficulties posed by Dobrowen's schedule, coupled with the logistical necessities of the Symphony and Opera seasons. The two organizations were compelled to coordinate their performance runs, not just because the Symphony and Opera shared the War Memorial Opera House, but because the Symphony essentially *was* the Opera orchestra: most of those in the pit for *La Traviata* would be onstage when the Symphony played Beethoven and Brahms. Rather than

11

9

Agnes Clark with conductor Bernardino Molinari, July 1932, Woodland Theatre, Hillsborough, after she appeared as piano soloist with the orchestra in Franck's Symphonic Variations. Under her married name, Agnes Albert, she would become one of the most influential board members in Symphony history.

10

Issay Dobrowen and the San Francisco Symphony in early 1932, on stage at the Tivoli Opera House.

11

Richard Tobin, Association president from 1933 to 1935.

PETER CONLEY

presents

R U T H
Slenczynski

•

WAR MEMORIAL OPERA HOUSE
SUNDAY AFTERNOON, DECEMBER 13, 1936

Ruth Slenczynski, determined to give listeners
their money's worth, and more. Program is from
late in her career as a child prodigy.

ALL FOR THE SYMPHONY, AND THEN SOME

Ruth Slenczynski's violinist father was determined to raise a piano prodigy. Born in Sacramento in 1925, Ruth was subjected to a militaristic regime of lessons from the age of three. A year later she went to Europe, where she studied with such greats as Artur Schnabel, Egon Petri, Alfred Cortot, and Josef Hofmann. At five she presented a recital in San Francisco, and at six she made her Berlin debut. On January 18, 1934, a few days after her ninth birthday, she appeared in the War Memorial Opera House with conductor Bernardino Molinari and the San Francisco Symphony. The Musical Association was facing hard times, and the generous girl donated her services—and then some. The audience that heard her got much more than the music in which she was billed as soloist, the Beethoven Piano Concerto No. 1. For starters, they heard her play her own first-movement cadenza. Then, responding to the applause at the work's end, young Ruth asked Molinari if she could offer an encore. "He told me to play all the encores I wanted," she told an Associated Press reporter a few days later, when she arrived in New York. The New York reporter was interested in her story, for her encores had made national news.

As critic Alexander Fried described the evening in the *San Francisco Chronicle*, "First she played a Beethoven 'Rondo.' Then she played a 'Prelude and Fugue' of Bach. Then she played another 'Prelude and Fugue,' and another. At the end of each she bowed deep in all directions without leaving her seat. Then she played a Chopin 'Etude.' Then a 'Waltz.'" The hearty applause that had greeted her first encore became lighter. Backstage, Molinari was beside himself. "Can't someone pry her loose from that stool?" he demanded. "It's an insult to the orchestra . . . wonder child! And how! It's an endurance test, not a concert!" He donned his hat and coat, set to leave, although the concert was just half over. Association President Richard Tobin rushed out from the wings and tried to stop Ruth. She glared at him. "You're not Charley Wagner," she snapped, and continued to play. Wagner, her manager, was nowhere to be found that evening. The only one who could manage the girl was her father, who at last came out and persuaded her to exit the stage. "And then I went backstage and Mr. Molinari called me names—all kinds of names in Italian," she said. The verbal tirade helped him calm down. Off came the hat and overcoat, and the concert continued.

While words did little to stop her that evening, the stress of practice and touring effectively brought her career to a halt when she was fifteen. Not until fourteen years later, in 1954, would she return to playing. In 1957, she described her ordeal as a prodigy in a book, *Forbidden Childhood*. She went on to teach piano at Southern Illinois University, and as recently as 2002 she served as artist-in-residence at Soochow University in Taipei, also performing frequently in Japan.

In 2005, now billing herself (as she had already for many years) as Ruth Slenczynska, she celebrated her eightieth birthday by playing three concertos with the Huntsville Symphony Orchestra, one work each by Liszt, Chopin, and Tchaikovsky. She seemed still to possess the kind of energy that had propelled her through her encores that January evening seven decades earlier. As she told the Associated Press in 1934, "I like to play for people."

open the Symphony season in the fall, before the Opera season began, and then resume once the Opera had concluded, Tobin proposed a mid-January Symphony opening. But because Dobrowen was due to leave for Philadelphia on January 10 and would not return until the end of February, the alternatives were to engage a guest in his absence or suspend the season until his return. Tobin also proposed a reduction in Dobrowen's salary, applying his Philadelphia fees against his San Francisco contract.

Dobrowen's reply to this suggested pay cut was confusing. For the Symphony's sake, he would comply, but he then countered Tobin's offer with a higher figure. Tobin agreed, on condition that the musicians also accept reductions and a shortened season. His goal, he maintained, was to be free from debt. His determination could be energizing. Three days later, the board that was so pledged to a stable financial future looked toward a future audience. They outlined a series of Young People's Concerts. Such concerts, offered since the Symphony was born, had developed into a series under Hertz but had become more haphazard since his departure. With the Young People's series launched in 1933, concerts for children became permanent, and a great Symphony tradition was born—the more remarkable for being inaugurated in the midst of the Great Depression, when so many financial questions demanded attention.

One of those questions was just how long a season was possible, given the Association's resources. By the middle of 1933, the Association and the Musicians' Union, Local 6, were negotiating minimum fees that would apply to seasons of varying lengths, anywhere from ten to twenty-four weeks. Tentative budgets prepared at the time projected deficits ranging from $76,000 to $141,000, minus any contributed income. But now an exciting prospect arose. The San Francisco Opera's director, Gaetano Merola, was traveling to Italy, where he planned to meet with Arturo Toscanini and invite him to conduct the San Francisco Symphony. Tobin would have recalled that Toscanini, now music director of the New York Philharmonic, had once been rumored to be interested in coming to San Francisco as music director. This latest plan seemed more certain: a special series of concerts with Toscanini on the podium as guest. Alternatively, Toscanini might be part of a regular season in which conducting duties would be divided among Dobrowen, Molinari, and him. Considered from any angle, the Toscanini plan seemed a winner. Association members agreed to underwrite any unlikely loss up to ten thousand dollars.

As of the summer, thirteen thousand dollars was still needed to finance a ten-week season. Various proposals were floated: open in December with Toscanini for two weeks, continue with Molinari for five weeks, conclude with Dobrowen for three. Levison, still a board member, feared this would further diminish Dobrowen's standing in the city—that a brief appearance at season's end would be anti-climactic. He prevailed. The ten-week season would open not in December but in the fall, first with Dobrowen, followed by Toscanini, then Molinari. Of course this was all contrary to the original plan of a season with no guest conductors. But who wouldn't bend for Toscanini? Especially when, as Tobin told orchestra members, a visit by Toscanini would be "an event in the musical history of San Francisco of unprecedented importance."

Nice words, but they convinced no one. A day later, the union rejected Tobin's proposed reduction of minimum scale and season. After more offers and counters, a fifteen-week season was settled upon, with the option of canceling the last three weeks. The union accepted the offer.

With this agreement and escape hatch in place, the Symphony seemed set to go on.

THE TOSCANINI PLAN

So much was riding on Toscanini's appearance with the orchestra that fate could hardly allow it to happen. The first sign of trouble came when Merola claimed he had been misunderstood. His intention, he said, was never to contract with Toscanini but simply to sound him out, to invite him to San Francisco.

Tobin had, however, managed to negotiate a Toscanini engagement for December, working with the conductor's personal representative, Bruno Zirato, who also happened to be assistant manager of the New York Philharmonic, Toscanini's orchestra. Tobin had no signed contract but believed that, on the basis of discussions, Toscanini was morally obligated to come to San Francisco.

Neither Toscanini nor his manager felt bound by any obligations in the absence of a contract. In October 1933, Zirato proposed instead that Toscanini appear in San Francisco the following May, after his Philharmonic commitments. That was a long time off, and a long time after Symphony seasons typically concluded in San Francisco. Plans changed again: a season shared by Dobrowen and Molinari would run from December to February. As a concession to the musicians, who would not be pleased with the

12

Arturo Toscanini, the Symphony's great hope in 1933.

75

lengthy lapse between February and May, four weeks with Toscanini would be offered as a spring festival. The orchestra rejected this plan. It was too uncertain, they said.

They were right. Hopes for a Toscanini engagement were soon dashed. No reason was recorded. Toscanini did not need to provide reasons. His cancellation necessitated a revised plan and budget for the 1933–34 season. Adding to the embarrassment, Toscanini's engagement had been announced as a fait accompli. The orchestra's personnel manager, Walter Oesterreicher, told the *Chronicle* that "the great Italian maestro is as sorry about [the cancellation] as San Francisco is," and the report went on to say that "Affairs of the San Francisco Symphony are in such an unsettled state now that the Musical Association has put off the Toscanini visit indefinitely."

It was early 1934 and the Depression was eroding box office receipts. The situation was dire. Cash reserves

would be exhausted at the end of ten weeks. To finance the remaining two weeks of 1933–34, an additional fourteen thousand dollars would be necessary. Tobin proposed to raise this by asking thirty members each to contribute five hundred dollars. He also planned a public appeal, for subscriptions in any amount.

Why was so much allowed to rest on the Toscanini concerts, which were always uncertain? Determined not to incur further debt, Tobin is likely to have seen Toscanini not just as a deus ex machina. Toscanini's agreement to conduct in San Francisco would have been public proof that all was well, the sort of event that sends stock soaring. His withdrawal was an equally convincing indication of how uncertain the Association's future was.

If it appeared that the Association hit bottom, with the music library mortgaged to cover the projected deficit plus an outstanding bank debt, concerts continued bravely.

Audiences heard such soloists as the great Josef Lhevinne in Beethoven's *Emperor* Concerto, and they were treated to performances by the nine-year-old piano prodigy Ruth Slenczynski, who donated her services. But something had to change.

WILL THE SYMPHONY GO ON?
In early 1934, another prodigy reappeared on the scene as a savior. Yehudi Menuhin, San Francisco's favorite son, by now more virtuoso than prodigy, had agreed to perform an April benefit concert in Civic Auditorium. But funds to stage the concert might not even be available. Tobin proposed that ten signers already pledged to underwrite the concert at five hundred dollars each double their commitment, and they agreed.

Whether a 1934–35 season would materialize was uncertain. Tobin was reluctant to discuss it until money was in hand. Assuming the season extended for fifteen weeks and the

13

13

Joseph S. Thompson, Association president from 1935 to 1936.

14

Prodigy Yehudi Menuhin had grown into a young virtuoso by the time he appeared in a benefit performance for the Symphony, shortly before his eighteenth birthday.

SAN FRANCISCO SYMPHONY ORCHESTRA
ALFRED HERTZ, Conducting
WITH
YEHUDI MENUHIN
EXPOSITION AUDITORIUM ◆ SUN. APRIL 8, 1934
Benefit of the Symphony Sustaining Fund

14

musicians accepted a sixty-dollar minimum, expenses were estimated at $163,500. Minus projected receipts of $79,500, the amount required to guarantee the season was $84,000. Dobrowen himself had agreed to drop his fee from $30,000 to $18,000. Then, in a board meeting, in front of Tobin's colleagues, Dobrowen demanded an answer. He needed to know before his imminent departure from San Francisco (for another guest engagement) if a season were possible. Tobin must have been exhausted by this point. Looking at $84,000 in contributions needed to close the gap between income and expenses— $20,000 more than the previous season's gap—he could not answer.

It may have been such an exchange that prompted board member R. C. Newell to propose a radical idea. He suggested "there would be a certain moral effect to the announcement of

no season." Former board president John D. McKee agreed. He believed a lapse of a season would have a refreshing effect and spur the Symphony's revival. McKee suggested the musicians were to blame for the present problems.

Tobin begged to differ. He was on the musicians' side and advocated budgeting for a new fifteen-week season. This would be costly, and he issued a warning. Promise a season, he told his colleagues, and you must be prepared to make up any deficit from your own pockets. He failed to see how promises could be made to either Dobrowen or the orchestra without the necessary funds in hand.

Tobin was a man of principle, and not inclined to bend. He would commit to no performances the Association was unable to afford. That attitude, in an economic climate that allowed

little room for creative budgeting, practically ensured that the San Francisco Symphony's activities would be put on hold.

A SHOCK DOCTRINE
John McKee knew how to navigate through tight budgets. As president of the Musical Association from 1919 to 1927, he enjoyed the esteem that Bay Area music lovers bestowed upon Alfred Hertz's superb orchestra, and while McKee advised careful money management, he also had the good fortune to preside over the Association during the flush years of the Roaring Twenties. What he saw now exasperated him, and he was not one to hold his opinions close.

McKee was convinced the Association's finances needed to be more broadly based. Instead of a few hundred contributors giving thousands of dollars, thousands of contributors should give hundreds. And he reiterated the point he had made some weeks earlier: the opportunity had come, he believed, to administer a sort of defibrillating shock by canceling a season. Interest in reviving the orchestra would be immediate.

The recorded reaction at first tells little. Such a plan must have seemed shocking in ways other than those McKee intended, for his fellow board members appear not to have taken him seriously. The months that followed witnessed an excruciating exchange of proposals and counterproposals between Association and musicians—length of season, minimum scale: all went back and forth in a nightmarish tennis match that threatened never to end. Meanwhile, city funding was scaled back and donors claimed exhaustion.

Despite everything, Tobin was able to report at the June 5 annual meeting that austerity measures, general sacrifice, and generosity had enabled the Association to climb almost entirely out of debt. Then he looked to the future: "To now abandon an enterprise which has been productive of so much good, which has added enormously to the cultural character of this city, which has been a source of pleasure and elevation in mind and taste to the citizens of our city and which has distributed annually a large sum among the members of the musical profession—this would indeed be regrettable."

A few days later, Tobin announced he would not continue as president beyond another year. The following month must have confirmed him in the wisdom of that decision, as the labor climate turned ugly with a general strike marked by rioting and hatred that brought the city to the brink of open war (see "Bloody Thursday: Civil War Comes to San Francisco," page 78). By October only half the funds for Tobin's proposed season were in hand. The situation had barely improved a month later. Funding was available for eight or nine weeks. Perhaps an agreement could be made to pay the musicians on a per-concert basis. Perhaps a season should be abandoned. Torn between loyalty to the organization and to the musicians, recognizing that this crisis was not a question of "sides," and that no concerts could be given without the participation of either the musicians or those who presented them, Tobin must have wondered what circle of hell he had entered.

In December, he concluded that a season of even twelve weeks would be impossible to mount, except on a week-to-week basis, and with an option to cancel when funds were exhausted. But after moving in one direction, he felt pulled in another. In last-ditch attempts to salvage something—anything—he proposed budgeting for twelve weeks of twenty-four concerts at a per-concert minimum of forty dollars, meaning only sixty-nine hundred dollars more needed to be raised. The union essentially accepted the length of the season but requested a fifty-dollar minimum, to which the board assented, but not without a cancellation clause. Given a minimum that must have seemed a frustrating compromise, the musicians rejected the cancellation clause, which undermined guaranteed employment. The parties had reached an impasse.

EPILOGUE:
DISASTER AND REBIRTH

A bout of soul-searching followed. How could Dobrowen have been engaged in the first place? In a classic example of damning with faint praise, Tobin went on record as stating that Dobrowen had endured too much unfair criticism. He was a very satisfactory conductor, Tobin said, and while "perhaps not of the greatest, should be ranked as a good conductor." A week later, an editorial entitled "Save the Symphony!" ran in the *San Francisco News* and nailed the problem, which was not whether the conductor was competent. The problem was that "we have lacked . . . a leader whose heart and soul were in the success of this particular orchestra."

In the end, the best spirits prevailed, and no blame was assigned. The Association admitted that the musicians' demands were reasonable. The money was simply not available to meet those demands. Tobin knew that to continue with concerts under present conditions was to court bankruptcy. "The season of 1934–35 must be abandoned," he urged. And that was that. The season's cancellation was less a shock than an inevitability.

Inevitabilities need not be finales. In March 1935, City Supervisor J. Emmet Hayden, chair of the Art Commission's Music Committee, joined forces with the Musicians' Union and conceived exactly the kind of creative financing that had eluded everyone. The plan was radical, and its success would depend on San Francisco voters. They were offered the opportunity to prove that all the talk about the city's commitment to the arts was more than bluster, that San Francisco could well claim to be the nation's most musical community. Hayden had succeeded in placing an initiative on the ballot for the May 2 municipal elections. Amendment 3, one of nine Charter Amendments

In April 1935, the Municipal Symphony Orchestra performed at Civic Auditorium, generating support for Charter Amendment 3.

On May 9, 1934, longshoremen along the West Coast stopped working. At issue was the right of labor to organize and bargain collectively. In San Francisco, things came to a head on Tuesday, July 3. Hired strikebreakers loaded trucks with goods that had been sitting on the piers. When the trucks drove through picket lines, rioting broke out.

The police swung their clubs and mounted officers rode into the crowds. The strikers fought back, throwing boards and bricks. On Wednesday, Independence Day, all remained quiet. Then came Bloody Thursday. Again the strikebreakers' trucks rolled. Police shot tear gas into the crowds of workers and sympathizers. That afternoon, when an angry mob surrounded a police car and began rocking it, the police opened fire, killing a seaman and a sympathizer.

The California National Guard was called out. Two thousand troops armed with machine guns patrolled the waterfront. Many citizens advocated wider imposition of martial law. Construction of the San Francisco–Oakland Bay Bridge was halted for a day. Labor leader Harry Bridges called for a general strike, and on July 14 the San Francisco Labor Council authorized it. Mayor Angelo Rossi declared a state of emergency.

While the Longshoremen's Strike itself continued for nearly three months, all of San Francisco was on strike for four turbulent days. The city seemed on the verge of civil war.

Five Musicians' Union members were delegates to the General Strike Committee, and Union Secretary Eddie Love served on the strike's Executive Committee. The twenty-five hundred members of Local 6 expressed sympathy with the longshoremen as the state National Guard raided workers' meeting places and headquarters of the Communist party.

In the end, strikers and employers alike claimed victory. Labor had undoubtedly been empowered. A statement published that fall in the Local 6 newsletter and broadcast throughout the country summed up members' commitment to free enterprise and offered assurance that they endorsed no Communist sympathies: "The Musicians' Union, Local Six, is proud to have taken its place in the great sympathetic strike and demonstration in San Francisco and the Bay Cities, in a successful endeavor to bring order out of chaos, and lend its support to the constructive solution of these controversies."

Noble ideals. But in an atmosphere of struggle, murder, and class war, the Musicians' Union and the Musical Association of San Francisco had much to contend with as they sought to resolve differences and keep the Symphony afloat. In those bad days of the Great Depression, the cards were stacked against them both.

During the 1934 longshoremen's labor dispute, violence erupted in San Francisco, leading to a general strike.

voted on that day, would rewrite the City Charter to set aside half a cent per one hundred dollars of assessed property taxes to support a symphony orchestra. Hayden estimated this could raise thirty-five thousand to fifty thousand dollars in support of the orchestra.

Plans were afoot to work up enthusiasm for the amendment. On March 28, the city-sponsored "Municipal Symphony Orchestra," which included eighty members of the San Francisco Symphony, gave the first in a series of five concerts sponsored by the Art Commission and presented at the cavernous Civic Auditorium. The program: Beethoven's Ninth. The conductor: Alfred Hertz. An audience of sixty-five hundred gave Concertmaster Naoum Blinder an ovation and rose to its feet when Hertz entered. "Here," wrote Alexander Fried, "was the answer to the question what does San Francisco think about the decline of its regular orchestra."

Crowds continued to pack the Civic Auditorium throughout the concert series. As the May 2 election day approached, excitement rose. April 29 was declared Symphony Perpetuation Day. Thousands heard programs in stores, hotels, and on the street. A story in one of the city's papers announced that the amendment would not only make music available to everyone, at prices all could afford, but would also provide work for musicians.

When the polls closed on May 2 and the votes were tallied, San Francisco had again proved itself a city of music lovers. Amendment 3 passed by a margin of nearly two to one. Against 47,071 dissenting votes, 83,455 citizens had opted to tax themselves and guarantee their city a symphony orchestra.

In bidding farewell as Association president, Richard Tobin noted that the board now included three members of the Art Commission, Edgar Walter, J. Emmet Hayden, and Joseph Dyer, Jr., "City, Symphony Unite on Plan" was the title of the *Examiner* story announcing this new relationship. With the influx of Amendment 3 funds, a 1935–36 season would be possible. New Association officers were elected on July 22. Joseph S. Thompson took the office of president. Leonora Wood Armsby was elected first vice-president and also assumed a newly created post, that of managing director. Armsby would direct musical matters. Thompson would devote himself to financial issues. The dual board leadership envisioned two years earlier had been realized, with fiscal and artistic affairs each governed by a separate leader. Recognizing the need for such leadership was one of the lessons of the Dobrowen years. Putting such leadership in place was the great vindication of this period.

Almost immediately, Thompson organized a financial campaign and formulated plans for a season whose standards would be high (nothing mediocre or pennywise, he urged), to begin in January 1936. He had in mind a season led by a world-renowned conductor, with top soloists, and the best musicians he could find. All this, he said, would be announced with a vigorous public relations campaign.

Armsby would chair the Music Committee. Soon she would succeed Thompson as president. She would guide the organization for the next two decades. Together with the conductor on whom she had already set her sights, she would lead the orchestra back to greatness.

v.

SAN FRANCISCO'S FAVORITE SPORT

The Pierre Monteux Years (1935–1952)

A JOB OFFER

As Leonora Wood Armsby tells the story, Pierre Monteux—the great Pierre Monteux—was an easy catch.

In August 1935 the San Francisco Symphony's business manager, Peter Conley, was accompanying the orchestra on its trip to San Diego, where it was featured at the California Pacific Exposition. With help from Charter Amendment 3, the Association had managed to keep the orchestra together. Now the orchestra needed a leader. Conley had been in touch with Pierre Monteux, who was guest-conducting the Los Angeles Philharmonic and staying at the Hollywood Hotel. Learning that San Francisco was seeking a conductor, Monteux wanted some idea of what he might be getting into. He had asked to hear the Symphony's first-chair players. Over the years audition practices have evolved, but in those days the music director alone chose his players—his "men," they were called, even though women accounted for a fair proportion of the San Francisco Symphony's members. So Conley had arranged for the orchestra's section principals to play for Monteux. The great Pierre Monteux liked what he heard.

Armsby followed up. Not much intimidated Leonora Wood Armsby. The great Pierre Monteux did. *Awed* is how she describes herself. She had met him four years earlier, when he was conducting the San Francisco Symphony at a Woodland Concert in Hillsborough. She knew his quality. Her friend the *New York Times* critic Olin Downes had described Monteux as "every bit as gifted as Toscanini"—only, Downes added, with a "larger waistline."

As she met with Monteux at eleven in the morning, in a suite that overlooked a dahlia-filled garden, Armsby

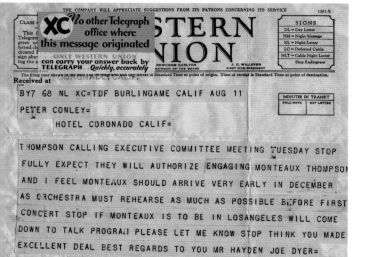

overcame her awe. "He listened intently to what I had to say to him about a wrecked orchestra and its problems." She knew her timing was right. Monteux was between jobs. He also wanted to stay in California since his daughter Nancie hoped to make a name for herself in the movies.

Always straightforward, Armsby laid out negatives and positives. She could offer a salary of only twelve thousand dollars, for the Musical Association was short on funds. On the plus side, the people of San Francisco had voted to tax themselves to help save the Symphony. "That is very fine, and makes me think very highly of your community," Monteux said.

The next day, he accepted her offer. The great Pierre Monteux assured Armsby that the music world would soon be talking about the San Francisco Symphony's astonishing recovery.

THE GREAT PIERRE MONTEUX

Leonora Wood Armsby had reason to be awed when she visited Pierre Monteux that August morning. Born in Paris in 1875, Monteux had become identified with the music of the twentieth century—even though no composer inspired his love as did Brahms, whom Monteux had met and even played for. In 1902 Monteux had been principal violist in the pit orchestra when Debussy's opera *Pelléas et Mélisande* was premiered. He was on the podium when Camille Saint-Saëns made his farewell appearance as piano soloist, in 1913. That same year he initiated a new era in music when he led the first performance of Stravinsky's *Le Sacre du printemps* in Paris. As conductor for Diaghilev's Ballets Russes, he had already

led the premiere of another groundbreaking Stravinsky score, *Petrushka*. Monteux had held posts as music director of the Boston Symphony Orchestra and the Concertgebouw Orchestra of Amsterdam and had founded the Orchestre Symphonique de Paris. In 1961, at age eighty-six, he would sign a twenty-five-year contract as principal conductor of the London Symphony Orchestra, a prospective tenure ended by his death in 1964. Always grounded in the world art seeks to reflect, Monteux served his country in World War I at the Battle of Verdun and at Argonne, and in the Second World War he would contribute his musical services to the US war effort.

Monteux left a rich legacy of recordings with many different orchestras. Those accounts reveal musicmaking of clear textures, tight ensemble, and rhythmic vitality—this last quality was something likely learned in the ballet theater, or in the Folies Bergère, where he conducted as a young man. "You couldn't be fooled by his baton technique. It was very efficient, very clear and very visible." As that statement by a Symphony musician who performed with him from 1940 until 1952 suggests, Monteux was undemonstrative on the podium. Yet he could inspire orchestras. Whether in San Francisco or Boston or London, the ensembles he conducted produced a bright, singing tone. "He never cued entrances by jabbing his finger at a musician," recalls Joseph Scafidi, who joined the San Francisco Symphony as a clerical worker in 1939 and left as executive director in 1978. "It was always through the eyes or through a beckoning gesture with the hand, as though he were inviting someone to play."

4

2
_____

Leonora Wood Armsby announces a mission accomplished.

3
_____

Pierre Monteux in the 1920s.

4
_____

Monteux and the orchestra in rehearsal.

Monteux had an enormous repertory and rarely hesitated to take on new scores. Under him, the San Francisco Symphony developed its reputation as an orchestra dedicated to contemporary music. Roger Sessions's Second Symphony, Walter Piston's *Incredible Flutist*, Vaughan Williams's Fourth Symphony, Bloch's Concerto Grosso—he introduced all those and more to San Francisco. He invited Paul Hindemith to conduct his Concert Music for Strings and Brass and asked Alexandre Tansman to lead his Fifth Symphony.

He refused to take himself too seriously. How many maestros would suit up as Santa Claus for a Christmas concert, as he did? Even in his seventies his voice, medium- to high-pitched, had the clear and steady tone of someone half his age. His excellent English was masked by an accent that required his auditors to fine-tune their ears.

A month before Monteux was due in San Francisco, the *Chronicle* was optimistic. Advance ticket sales were brisk. A sixteen-week season was planned, in which almost fifty concerts were scheduled. Local 6 and the Musical Association of San Francisco were working together as old friends might. When Peter Conley reported on how harmonious negotiations had been, Association members invited a committee of four members of the orchestra, along with the union president, to sit with the board at its meetings.

Monteux arrived on December 30 to begin rehearsals for a January 10 opening, a take-no-prisoners program that included Respighi's orchestration of Bach's Passacaglia in C minor, Beethoven's Symphony No. 7, Richard Strauss's *Till Eulenspiegel*, and the first San Francisco Symphony performance of Debussy's *Nocturnes*.

5

A dream about to come true: spanning San Francisco Bay from the city to Marin County via the Golden Gate Bridge, which would be completed in 1937.

6

Paris, 1915: Monteux was on the podium for Camille Saint-Saëns's farewell concert.

84

5

The conductor had estimated he would need five years to bring the music-making back to its former glory. But already the first pair of concerts convinced at least one critic that a new era had begun.

"Let's go to the symphony for the fun of it!" wrote Marjory M. Fisher in the *San Francisco News*. She described an audience that stomped and shouted approval. "We have watched the rise, decline and fall of the San Francisco Symphony. Its renascence is at hand. We have a good orchestra once more: one that merits support. But hearing good performances of good music is not a duty; it is fun. Symphony-going, thanks to Pierre Monteux, now seems destined to become San Francisco's favorite sport."

RENAISSANCE

By February, Leonora Wood Armsby already knew what San Francisco had in its new conductor. The music-making, she told her board, exceeded her highest hopes.

The San Francisco Symphony had embarked on a renaissance season, the kind of ambitious undertaking that Joseph Thompson had outlined upon assuming the Association's presidency, led by a star conductor and featuring such soloists as pianists José Iturbi and Myra Hess, and violinists Jascha Heifetz and Mischa Elman. Stravinsky himself would perform as piano soloist at a Municipal Concert—when someone of Monteux's caliber and experience called in favors, the returns were high—and the legendary soprano Lotte Lehmann appeared in a Wagner program. Soon Sergei Rachmaninoff would appear with the orchestra, playing his Rhapsody on a Theme of Paganini and the first three of his four piano concertos. Wasting no time, Armsby reengaged Monteux for three seasons.

By April, when the 1936 season closed, the story of the San Francisco Symphony's comeback made it into the pages of *Time*. "With its head held high for the first time in years the San Francisco Symphony this week ends its season. There has been talk all over the city of the reborn orchestra." *Time* also reported on a new work that closed the season, Meredith Willson's *A Symphony of San Francisco*, whose finale was intended to depict a great new bridge spanning San Francisco Bay.

Time should have used the plural, bridges. The city itself was about to experience a kind of rebirth, its geographical isolation surmounted by two massive spans on which construction had been proceeding for the past three years, although neither was yet complete. The San Francisco–Oakland Bay Bridge, to give the structure its full and formal name, had opened to the first vehicles in November 1936. Six months later traffic would begin to move between the city and Marin County via the Golden Gate Bridge, about to become one of the world's most recognized landmarks. As for the man who set the bridges to music, Meredith Willson would go on to fame two decades later as composer and author of *The Music Man* and *The Unsinkable Molly Brown*.

Unsinkable was the operative word, for the orchestra as for San Francisco. In February, Joseph Thompson reminded the board that any success

now was due to Richard Tobin's valiant effort to clear the Association of debt. Soon Thompson saw the path to more success and understood he could with clear conscience relinquish the presidency, for at his right hand was someone who could give the Association more: Leonora Wood Armsby. On June 2, 1936, Armsby became president and managing director. When she and Monteux joined purposes, they were unstoppable.

The first sign of that was the cash balance with which the season closed—modest, but positive. When Armsby announced that the coming season's budget would grow by thirty thousand dollars, mainly to increase the size of the orchestra, she knew that more than ninety thousand dollars in contributions would have to be raised. Given the Symphony's new popularity, she believed she could generate even more.

Franklin Roosevelt had given the country a New Deal, and voters responded by giving him a second term in 1936. San Francisco voters had given the Symphony a similar deal when they passed Charter Amendment 3 in 1935. As the bridges spanning San Francisco Bay opened—both projects of the WPA national workforce—they symbolized determination in the midst of continuing economic depression. They promised better times, as did other technological feats of the era—the recently operational Boulder Dam, for instance, which sent electricity flowing through the West, and a new aircraft about to revolutionize air travel, the Douglas DC-3.

San Francisco music lovers had also ensured better times, supporting an orchestra at their ballot boxes.

85

6

SILVER JUBILEE SEASON

WE CELEBRATE this year the Silver Jubilee of the San Francisco Symphony Orchestra. This important Anniversary represents not only a quarter of a century of notable achievement by the Orchestra but it also commemorates a long list of distinguished Sponsors and Patrons whose interest has carried the Symphony forward to this milestone.

To look back over the road the Orchestra has traveled with the idea of pointing out even the highlights in its history is beyond the province of this message.

It is the future which now engrosses us, bright as it is, with exceptional prospects.

In our leader, Pierre Monteux, we have an artist noted for his singularly balanced and appreciative point of view of the music of all schools. Monteux has a technical knowledge of everything pertaining to the instruments of the Orchestra, and of conducting. Under his direction our Orchestra is becoming an unrivaled symphonic body.

Spurred by these facts the Musical Association of San Francisco is working to increase its personnel to ninety players. An ensemble of this size would be adequate to any project entrusted to it. Such an objective seems particularly appropriate in view of the coming Golden Gate International Exposition when San Francisco can show the world what she is doing for music.

Confident of the merit of our plans we earnestly appeal to our Contributors and Patrons to assist in achieving the goal.

We are moving toward other eventful Anniversaries. The Orchestra we sponsor today is to bridge the gap between our time and coming generations. May we pass on to our successors a wonderful reminder of the 1936 Jubilee.

LEONORA WOOD ARMSBY,
President and Managing Director

The Symphony's ambitious 1936–37 season celebrated the orchestra's twenty-fifth anniversary and opened with a concert featuring George Gershwin in his *Rhapsody in Blue*. African-American contralto Marian Anderson, whose skin color would lead the Daughters of the American Revolution to bar her from singing at Washington DC's Constitution Hall three years later, was due to make her Symphony debut. And one of San Francisco's own would begin a long-term relationship with the orchestra: fifteen-year-old violinist Isaac Stern, a student of concertmaster Naoum Blinder, played the Brahms Concerto in March 1937, his first appearance on the Symphony's regular series, following his debut in the Saint-Saëns B minor Concerto a year earlier, in a special Municipal Concert. (A footnote to Stern's performance is that Monteux especially encouraged young local talent. In 1943, the fourteen-year-old San Franciscan Leon Fleisher appeared as soloist in Liszt's Piano Concerto No. 2.) Four Young People's Concerts were scheduled for Saturday mornings. The board grew from sixty to seventy-five members, primarily to expand its sphere of influence. As the season ended, Leonora Wood Armsby reported an increase in box office receipts of 28 percent over the previous year.

MUSIC AND MANAGEMENT IN THE GREAT DEPRESSION

The Monteux years have entered San Francisco Symphony legend as an era of great artistic accomplishment, and that is true. But those triumphs, along with recordings that document an orchestra of amazing fire and flexibility, and the genial figure of Pierre Monteux himself—*Maître*—obscure harder financial realities. The season of

1938 was the best-selling year ever, with almost four thousand season tickets sold. Interesting programs attracted interested listeners, such as a March 1938 performance in which Viennese dancer Tilly Losch offered her interpretation of the *Blue Danube* waltz. The next month, a Shakespearean evening featured actor Brian Aherne reading from the plays, while the orchestra offered Beethoven's response to *Coriolanus*, Mendelssohn's to *A Midsummer Night's Dream*, Tchaikovsky's to *Hamlet*, and Berlioz's to *Romeo and Juliet*.

But the country still labored in the grip of the Great Depression. Looking ahead to the season of 1938–39, the Finance Committee projected a deficit of thirty thousand dollars. Musicians had no easy time, either. Then as now, classically trained players coveted employment in major orchestras. "If I could one day just become a member of my favorite orchestra, that would be glory enough," recalled David Schneider, a violinist who joined the orchestra in 1936 and performed with the San Francisco Symphony for the next fifty years. With a season of only sixteen weeks— increased to eighteen weeks in 1938—musicians, even those who also played for the San Francisco Opera, were forced to earn their livelihoods from other sources in the off-season, often in other professions. As late as the 1950s, long-time Symphony violinist Verne Sellin sold insurance. Another member of his section, Florence Zamora, appeared in hotels and nightclubs in a Spanish dance routine. In 1938 Alfred Hertz came out of retirement to direct the Northern California component of the Federal Music Project and organized the Bay Region Symphony Orchestra, as much to offer work to struggling musicians as to entertain the community. Hertz

8

originated the "Dime Symphony," whose first ten-cent program that August drew an audience of ten thousand to the Civic Auditorium.

Generally barred by the Musicians' Union from recruiting orchestra members from outside the Bay Area—job security was especially important in those tough times—Monteux was a champion of his players, and if occasionally he would have preferred greater flexibility in hiring, he did not grumble in public and knew how to get results from a group of fine musicians. Early in 1938, Symphony players attempted to organize a pension fund. Because they were employed by a nonprofit organization, they were not covered by the Social Security Act of 1935 and would not be covered until 1950. This early pension fund was not the carefully structured vehicle it would eventually become, nor the permanent vehicle

Monteux would one day advocate. For now, musicians contributed fifty cents each week from their salaries. A special performance of Beethoven's Ninth was arranged to aid the fund, with expenses paid out of an Art Commission surplus, and with musicians, Monteux, and the Municipal Chorus contributing their services. The Musical Association supplied management and publicity, and sold tickets.

This collaboration of Association and musicians is significant. Musicians and management: described like that, the two groups seem opposites, and for years that is how each group's members saw themselves, especially when the time for contract negotiation arrived. Most musicians and managers would have it otherwise, preferring not to occupy different corners, but to engage in the single purpose of offering music to the public. Rocky

7
_____

A roster of stellar guests, to help celebrate twenty-five years of the Symphony.

8
_____

Contralto Marian Anderson meets with Monteux backstage at the Opera House, 1937.

LEONORA WOOD ARMSBY:
LEADER FROM THE LAND OF LINCOLN

Leonora Wood Armsby and Symphony Forum members at a pool party, at her Hillsborough home. Rarely was she photographed without a hat.

First you encounter the name. Leonora Wood Armsby. The syllables rise and fall in the rhythms of parlor music, evoking the delicate scents of rosewater and dusting powder. The name seems to have been created for a lady as fragile as porcelain, of transparent skin, a character encountered at high tea, the only meal she would have taken in a day begun with effort in mid-morning and drawn to an exhausted close by dusk.

The name says nothing about the woman Pierre Monteux called "the soul of the San Francisco Symphony." The name she was born with says more. *Leonora Wood*. Much tougher. More suited to her. The daughter of mining engineer Tingley Sylvanus Wood, Leonora grew up a tomboy in Springfield, Illinois—the center of the Golden Prairie Country, she called it, where in the 1880s she listened to stories about Lincoln from those who had known him. Her family's next-door neighbor, Ninian Edwards, was Lincoln's brother-in-law, and it was in the Edwards drawing room that Abraham Lincoln had been wed to Mary Todd. State capital and Smalltown USA, Springfield offered Leonora summer processions of political rallies and parades with marching bands. Looking back on this scene seventy years later in her 1952 memoir *So Near to My Heart*, she describes the kind of childhood that Charles Ives set to music in his *Holidays* Symphony.

Among the closest family friends was Illinois governor Richard Oglesby. "Uncle Dick," she called him, though no blood relationship existed. Oglesby was a Lincoln associate, and so close to the president that he was among the few admitted to the hotel room across from Ford's Theatre as his friend lay dying. From Uncle Dick, Leonora absorbed her love of Lincoln and his ideals. The strength of character and the determination her later-life associates would so admire—these had their roots in Heartland soil, were absorbed in an all-but-direct lineage from her presidential hero. Her sense of her capacities was well-developed by the time she went to work at full throttle for the San Francisco Symphony, in 1935. Had the Musical Association specified what kind of leader it needed in its darkest hour, no one better equipped could have answered the call than Leonora Wood Armsby.

The *Armsby* was added to her name on December 29, 1898, when she married George Newell Armsby, a captain of industry who pioneered the tactic of the corporate merger. He united four California canning companies into the California Packing Corporation, giving the world the Del Monte label, and he went on to head the investment banking firm of Bancamerica-Blair Corporation. He and Leonora divided their time between New York City and Hillsborough, California, where she gave birth to a daughter and a son. In 1929, Leonora claimed that Armsby had deserted her five years earlier, and she won a divorce settlement of $1 million, substantial for the time. The postscript that was George Armsby's subsequent life began a year after his divorce, when the fifty-four-year-old tycoon took a trophy wife eighteen years his junior, a woman with the exotic name Colette Touzeau, "said to be a former New York show girl" according to the *New York Times*, and described in *Time* magazine as "beauteous." They spent their honeymoon in a mountain cabin owned by Hollywood magnate Cecil B. DeMille. Armsby's death twelve years later was reported as having taken place "suddenly."

Always a lover of music, Leonora studied during her New York years at the Walter Damrosch Institute, where she began to compose. The Boston publisher C. W. Thompson, looking for exercises to teach children musical phrasing, discovered a collection of her tunes and asked her to supply words. She wrote a set of verses inspired by ornithology. Thompson published the words and music as *Birdland Melodies*, which went into service at the Damrosch school and which, in an orchestration by the San Francisco Symphony's Emanuel Leplin, Pierre Monteux would conduct in a radio broadcast in 1949.

She taught in the Settlement Schools of Manhattan, then displayed her administrative skills as treasurer of the Greenwich School, where she also discovered a talent for raising funds. She became first vice-president of New York's Schola Cantorum choral society. From New York, she went on to study in Paris, then returned to California in 1926 to check into matters at Hillsborough, after which she planned to continue her music training at Oxford University. But just then a Peninsula neighbor, Cecilia Casserly, was organizing a summer series of Sunday afternoon concerts in the outdoors, at the Woodland Theatre, featuring the San Francisco Symphony. It is to Mrs. Casserly, who a decade earlier had done so much to harass Alfred Hertz and who was determined to compete with the Musical Association of San Francisco, that a debt of gratitude is owed. Casserly convinced Leonora to stay in California, and to assume the leadership of the Philharmonic Society of San Mateo County, which presented the Woodland concerts. Had Cecilia Casserly been less persuasive, the San Francisco Symphony might never have enjoyed the Armsby brand of leadership—might, in fact, have been silenced after 1934.

The Woodland Theatre was Northern California's scaled-back version of the Hollywood Bowl. To Leonora fell the responsibility of engaging conductors of the first rank—a formidable task since the journey from East Coast to West was so lengthy in those days. She addressed the problem with her colleagues in Los Angeles and with New York impresario Arthur Judson, devising a system for multiple engagements at various stops along the way, bundling performances and thus providing the financial incentive to make the long cross-country trip.

At ease with musicians and with those who could support cultural causes, Leonora Wood Armsby did not confine her artistic endeavors to music. She authored two books. *Musicians Talk*,

from 1935, is best approached as a period piece. The tone changes dramatically in her 1960 account of her years at the San Francisco Symphony, *We Shall Have Music*. This is a vivid story of the trials through which she led the Musical Association, and a tribute to the artistry of Pierre Monteux and the orchestra. Her literary production is rounded out by a privately published poetry chapbook, *As Heaven Sings*, whose contents, though not those of a major poetic talent, charm with a radiant sensibility.

In poolside photos at her Hillsborough home, she poses in a full-length coat next to the young set clad in bathing suits: college men and nubile coeds, members of the Symphony's Student Forum. Rarely was she photographed minus a hat. The coat, the hat—those suggest a certain cultivated formality. But remember that, as a girl living with her family in Leadville, Colorado, where her father supervised a mine, she delighted in being lowered into the shaft in a bucket. And when claim jumpers set fire to the Leadville compound on a Christmas Eve, she braved the flames and winter weather as she made her escape. Small wonder at how completely she maintained her presence of mind on a midnight drive in 1920. She had just left a Long Island party and her chauffeured car wound down a country road when she spotted a vehicle in pursuit. Two masked escapees from the local jail were closing in. Eight shots were fired. "Don't mind the shooting," she told her driver. "Put on all the speed the engine is capable of making." Others might have chosen words more elemental to issue such a command. The chauffeur took the lady's advice, and they outpaced the bandits.

It was not the only time that weapons would be part of a story about Leonora Wood Armsby. Before an afternoon concert at the Woodland Theatre, conductor Artur Rodzinski sat in his dressing room, all nerves. Rodzinski, a great conductor, was among music's less predictable personalities. Now he showed Leonora a revolver and told her he was going to kill himself. She stayed calm. "No you're not," she said. She took the gun from him and dropped it into her purse. After the concert, she complimented Rodzinski on the performance. Then she handed him his gun.

Mrs. Armsby and friend.

9

10

relations existed in the last years of the Dobrowen era, while in the 1940s relations improved dramatically. "There was a great deal of camaraderie in those days," Joe Scafidi says, "between the musicians themselves, and between the musicians and management." In the late 1930s and early 1940s, professional administrative management was just starting at the San Francisco Symphony. Until then, much of the administration had been left to the board and to the music director. In her dual roles as board president and managing director, Leonora Wood Armsby was both the philanthropist determined to bring art to the community and the organization's managerial head—occupying the post that would now be called "executive director." Think of her as the complete CEO. In 1939, when Howard Skinner became the Associa-

tion's secretary-manager, he brought enthusiasm and charisma to his post as Armsby's lieutenant.

A common goal now seemed to unite those on stage and those behind the scenes, and perhaps as a result fund-raising became at once more aggressive and more sophisticated. New energy was apparent in all quarters, unleashed by Monteux and his team. In November 1938 the new position of the San Francisco Symphony among North American orchestras was confirmed when Olin Downes, *New York Times* music critic and director of music at the New York World's Fair, invited Monteux and the orchestra to perform there. "We are very eager to hear this orchestra as it has developed under [Monteux's] leadership," Downes wrote to Armsby. "I know so well his capacities as an interpreter, a musician and an orchestra

builder, that I would be certain, even if I had not heard reliable reports, that this orchestra was now one of the most important symphony orchestras of the country."

But the Symphony could not afford to travel to New York. The day Armsby shared Downes's flattering invitation with the board, she also disclosed that, despite intensified efforts to raise money, contributions to the Association's supporting fund were down considerably from a year earlier, dropping to $45,000 from $66,000 in 1937. To present the coming season of eighteen weeks would require additional contributions of $70,000.

The months ahead were both discouraging and hopeful. Monteux, in demand from the Opéra Comique in Paris, was asking for a raise.

Denied that increase because the Association was not in a financial position to offer it, he accepted a renewal of his contract for the three coming seasons, through 1943, with no changes in its terms. "I loved this city," he would write years later, "its style, its lavish way of life, its unique situation on seven hills overlooking the Bay, one of the most beautiful in the world." Leaving at this point was not an option. And he was doing great things with the orchestra. That February, guest conductor Leopold Stokowski turned to address the audience. In the San Francisco Symphony, he said, he found an ensemble of sensitivity and finesse. "I congratulate my colleague, M[onsieur] Monteux, upon its excellence and for its musicianship."

In September 1939, Hitler's forces invaded Poland, igniting World War II. The same year witnessed happier events closer to home—the publication of *The Grapes of Wrath*, California author John Steinbeck's quintessential story of the Great Depression, and, on February 18, the opening of the Golden Gate International Exposition.

The Golden Gate Expo, a world's fair celebrating the new bay-spanning bridges, sported elegant art deco structures lining the concourses of Treasure Island, a plot of land

91

9

Monteux's friendship with Stravinsky went back to 1911, when the conductor had led the premiere of Petrushka.

10

At the Golden Gate International Exposition, on Treasure Island, 1939–40. The midway shown here was called the Court of the Moon, and at its far end stands the Tower of the Sun.

11

Howard Skinner, Symphony manager throughout the tenures of Pierre Monteux and Enrique Jordá.

12

The orchestra with Monteux, five years after his arrival. It was a revitalized ensemble, offering San Francisco its favorite sport.

13

Stars of the Bay Area music community, 1944.
From left: Pierre Monteux, Darius Milhaud
(back to camera), Alfred Hertz.

14

Symphony Forum members meet with pianist
Artur Schnabel.

14

reclaimed from Yerba Buena Shoals and adjacent to Yerba Buena Island in San Francisco Bay. Originally scheduled to extend only through October, the fair reopened for an encore run through the summer of 1940. In 1915, in the last world's fair the city had hosted, the Boston Symphony had outshone the hometown orchestra. Now, in 1939, the San Francisco Symphony had the opportunity to lay the ghosts of 1915 to rest. Unfortunately, and although Leonora Wood Armsby served as the fair's director of music, the exposition's organizers had budgeted insufficiently to support much Symphony participation—except for a May 18 concert sponsored by IBM, significant for being broadcast nationally and, via shortwave radio, around the world. The Symphony fared better in the expo's second year, when the orchestra was a more central attraction and gave concerts with such guest conductors as Bruno Walter, André Kostelanetz, and the San Francisco Opera's Gaetano Merola.

Everywhere, however, economic realities continued to threaten. To combat them, a special Women's Committee of volunteers spread the word about the Symphony to musical clubs, private and parochial schools, neighborhood stores, the University of California, Stanford, Mills College, downtown shops. And at around this time, on the Berkeley campus of the University of California, a group of students began to give concrete form to their love of music.

THE FORUM

In 1937, one of Philip Boone's fraternity brothers at the University of California, in Berkeley, suggested they buy season tickets to the Symphony. Boone had little exposure to concert music but was willing to give it a try. He liked what he heard—especially the concert in which George Gershwin played his *Rhapsody in Blue*. A year later, Boone gathered a group of friends, and together they purchased a box in the Opera House for the season. Symphony manager Howard Skinner heard about this young man and his interest in the Symphony, and in 1939 Skinner sought him out at the Golden Gate International Exposition. Boone was working at the DuPont exhibit, one of whose highlights was a display of a new fashion accessory for women, nylon stockings. Skinner introduced himself. Quickly he steered their conversation from hosiery and turbines to music and what Boone was doing on its behalf. Skinner suggested that other student groups at Cal might be interested in purchasing boxes for the coming season. Boone knocked off work at five o'clock that evening. Three hours later he had sold eleven boxes to fellow students.

Looking back in 1973, Boone recalled Howard Skinner as "a great friend, supporter and teacher. His influence on a whole generation of young music lovers is probably unparalleled in this country and their affection for him, universal."

Together, Skinner and Leonora Wood Armsby saw what students could do for the Symphony and what it could do for them. Tickets for students were offered at half price. Soon crowds of young people were jamming the Opera House on Saturday nights. When Boone realized that, for all their enjoyment of the music, few students knew much about it, he convinced the university to let his group of friends use a room in the student union. Skinner negotiated

with Sherman-Clay, the San Francisco music store, which donated a record player and $250 worth of records. The students built a library of music reference books. They adopted an official name: the University of California San Francisco Symphony Forum—because they all felt *part of* the San Francisco Symphony, as Boone would recall. Every Wednesday night before the Saturday concerts, Forum members met and discussed the music they would be hearing. Skinner and Armsby, delighted at all this, arranged for the Symphony's visiting artists to attend these sessions. Thomas Beecham spoke about musical life in England. Yehudi Menuhin shared the experiences of a wunderkind-turned-mature virtuoso. One evening, when *Chronicle* critic Alfred Frankenstein failed to draw more than a handful of students, Boone got on the phone with all the friends he could contact, telling them to get over to Stephens Union and offering a free beer in return for their presence. Soon a respectable crowd had gathered, beer having an appeal to college men almost as universal as music's appeal to more tutored palates.

Monteux, of course, was involved in the Forum. He and his wife, Doris, met with students after concerts to continue the evening, generally at Lupo's Pizzeria in North Beach. Already sixty-four in an era when that age was considered advanced, Monteux might have pioneered the slogan that sixty is the new forty. This was, after all, the man who had played a defining role in the history of modernism when he introduced Stravinsky to the world. He continued to champion new music, maintained an active working relationship with composer Darius Milhaud at Mills College and Roger Sessions at Berkeley, and in

1940 celebrated Sibelius's seventy-fifth birthday with a festival of the composer's music. Being at the center of a group of young people just beginning to discover music—nothing could have been more exhilarating or satisfying to Pierre Monteux.

The Forum idea spread. By 1946, when the general public's demand for Saturday evening tickets became so great that the Association could no longer afford to offer students half-price tickets for that series, a Thursday-night concert series was added, expressly for a student audience.

"I have been told that many of the young ladies of the Thursday evening audience called me 'Twinkle Toes,'" Monteux wrote years later.

That pleased me no end, as I did not want those concerts to be austere and too formal. From the very beginning, a relaxed rapport was established between the orchestra, the young people, and myself. I must say, it was very pleasant to receive all of the very pretty girls in my room after each concert. All in all, this Forum was perhaps the most outstanding effort of my seventeen years in San Francisco.

The Forum continues today, offering half-price tickets to more than a thousand students each year, from more than thirty Bay Area campuses. In 1989, its fiftieth anniversary, it was renamed the Howard Skinner Student Forum, honoring the man whose brainchild it was. Of course, Skinner would have been the first to acknowledge that, minus the efforts of those like Boone, the Forum idea would not have flown. Skinner had the satisfaction of seeing the Forum flourish, and of welcoming Phil Boone to the Symphony's board in

1941. He also lived long enough to see the Forum pay other dividends. It had nurtured a generation of music lovers, committed to the San Francisco Symphony. Philip Boone became Symphony president in 1963 and served in that office for nine years. Lawrence Metcalf, another original Forum member, was president from 1974 until 1980. And Ava Jean Brumbaum, who as Ava Jean Barber was a Forum organizer in 1939, became the longest serving member of the Symphony's Board of Governors, joining the board in 1946 and continuing until this day. All were members of the Greatest Generation—those children of the Depression who knew the value of a dollar, stood by their neighbors, and fought a war to defeat the forces of darkness. All of them put that generation's best qualities to work for the music.

THE SYMPHONY FOREVER

Leonora Wood Armsby was happy to report at the end of summer 1940 that Symphony affairs had improved dramatically from the preceding year. Ticket sales had increased by

nineteen thousand dollars. All debts were paid. This came at a certain price, meaning that she and Howard Skinner had combed the budget and eliminated overhead wherever possible. And although the United States had not yet entered the European war, war charities and Allied relief funds sought stateside donations, with the result that contributions to the Symphony had fallen off. Incredibly, income from the 1939–40 season had grown by eleven thousand dollars, despite an eight-thousand-dollar drop in contributions. Ticket sales had made the difference, and students accounted for many of those sales. "We travel a long road when we are identified with organizations such as the Musical Association," Armsby told the board, "and at times our task seems burdensome, therefore the excellent report of our past season's achievements is welcome news and helps us face the future with better hearts." A year later, Armsby could offer a similar report. The 1940–41 season closed with a balanced budget.

At last, this was momentum, and it was headed in the right direction.

Hattie Sloss, a board member who also headed the Symphony's publicity team—she virtually constituted that team herself—suggested a new slogan: The Symphony Forever. It seems never to have caught on, perhaps because those who had been around in leaner times were reluctant to tempt the fates with so hubristic a statement, but the optimism it suggests was real and long in coming.

Slogans were not the only things Hattie Sloss suggested. A public relations powerhouse with a consuming love of music, she was determined to establish the Symphony as an organization for all. Every Saturday throughout the season she was heard on KNBC radio in a fifteen-minute segment, *Know Your Symphony*, talking about music, interviewing artists, and taking listeners behind the scenes. She spearheaded the development of three Symphony-related broadcasts in addition to her own, and when attendance at Friday afternoon concerts dropped because so many erstwhile audience members were employed in defense work, she coordinated a campaign with hotels, encouraging visitors to attend concerts.

The immediate publicity plan was to celebrate the Symphony's thirtieth anniversary, honoring the orchestra, Monteux, and the Musical Association itself. Festivities, set for December 2, 1941, would be held at Civic Auditorium, open to the public—because, as board member Mabel Coghlan explained, the orchestra belonged to everyone. Actor Brian Aherne emceed the event, and from loudspeakers through which radio lines were channeled came the voices of luminaries who had led the Symphony—Leopold Stokowski, John Barbirolli, Igor Stravinsky, Thomas Beecham—all offering congratula-

16

tions. Hearts were light that evening. No one knew the world was about to break.

IN A CITY IN A WAR

Shortly before eight o'clock on the morning of December 7, 1941, a Japanese bomber squadron descended on the US Naval Base at Pearl Harbor on the island of Oahu, unleashing the first wave of an attack whose second surge, an hour later, completed the task: 2,403 dead, almost two hundred planes destroyed, the Pacific Fleet hobbled. On December 8, Congress declared war.

The Symphony had been through one world war. This was different. In the months that followed, the West Coast would fall victim to war hysteria. Paranoia and rumor took complex shapes. Even Japanese-American farmers were imagined to be potential saboteurs and were

said to have planted tomatoes such that their stems, seen from the air, would point enemy bombers toward their prey. In February 1942, Executive Order 9066 authorized the deportation and internment of 120,000 Japanese and Japanese-American citizens from West Coast cities to camps in the desert interior.

Reality also played its part in war-time fears. Almost seven decades since the end of World War II, it may be difficult to grasp how vulnerable to attack the West Coast felt. Joe Scafidi remembers the war years. As a Civil Defense warden in the neighborhood near his home in San Francisco's Marina District, he conducted nightly patrols of the blocks under his supervision, making sure blackout shades were drawn. The streets were dark. When drivers heard siren alerts, they pulled over and killed their headlights. "It was horrible. . . . The war didn't come to

15

Surrounded by Forum admirers, Monteux receives a handshake along with the title "Fellow of Stanford University" from Stanford President Ray Lyman Wilbur. To Monteux's immediate right, eyes to camera, is Leonora Wood Armsby. Directly behind Monteux is Phil Boone.

16

Opening night, 1943. Military personnel hear the orchestra at the War Memorial Opera House, where throughout the war they attended concerts free of charge.

A late-night/early morning recording session for RCA, 1941.

96

RECORDING WITH MONTEUX

Monteux and RCA Victor personnel listen to a playback of Ibert's Escales, *1946. Seated next to Monteux is orchestra personnel manager Julius Haug; to Haug's left is* Chronicle *critic and Symphony program annotator Alfred Frankenstein.*

After eleven years in which no commercial recording had documented the orchestra's sound, the San Francisco Symphony and RCA Victor reached an agreement in January 1941 to record two three-hour sessions. They took place on April 21 and 22 and resulted in four albums of records with the orchestra under Pierre Monteux's direction: Ravel's *La Valse*, the March from Rimsky's *Coq d'Or* Suite, Vincent d'Indy's *Symphony on a French Mountain Air*, and Franck's Symphony in D minor and *Pièce heroique*. Thus began a recording relationship that would continue until 1952.

In those days even a symphony of average length covered many sides of the heavy black platters that spun on turntables at 78 revolutions per minute—ten sides, in the case of the Franck Symphony. Disks were enclosed in paper sleeves and bound like an oversized book, the album covers adorned with lavish artwork. Victor's confidence in its San Francisco Symphony investment was well-placed. Demand for the Franck Symphony alone was so great that the master disks wore out, so the work was re-recorded in 1950.

Those RCA recordings relied on unorthodox methods. The most suitable recording apparatus was in Los Angeles, but it could

Monteux introduced the world to
Le Sacre du printemps *in 1913
and recorded it with the San
Francisco Symphony in 1945.*

*Monteux's 1941 San Francisco
recording of Franck's Symphony
was among RCA's top sellers.*

not be transported to the Bay Area, nor could the orchestra travel to LA. So, using the NBC network lines installed at the Opera House for *Standard Hour* broadcasts, the signal was relayed by telephone line to Los Angeles. Because the lines had to be completely open, recording started only at midnight—not that that guaranteed an open line. Once, after the orchestra had labored over a passage in *La Valse* until it was just what Monteux wanted, the conductor signaled the microphones to be turned on. As the segment was about to end, the operator's voice intruded. "What number, please?" The late-night sessions were scheduled after concerts—usually on Saturdays, guaranteeing a day off after the grueling labor. Starting at midnight, conductor and orchestra would work until three or four in the morning.

Monteux believed that recordings should convey a sense of an orchestra's sound, as a concert should: no less and no more, and that if mistakes occurred—as they are apt to happen in concert—they shouldn't be taken too seriously in recordings. Charles Bubb, a fine player who would go on to become the orchestra's principal trumpet, was substituting on the *La Valse* recording for Benjamin Klatzkin, the regular first trumpet at the time. Bubb cracked on a high note of a tricky passage. After

a few more tries, Monteux concluded that his favorite was the take with the blooper. That is what went onto the pressing. Some time later, *La Valse* was programmed again, and at the first rehearsal Klatzkin, playing principal this time, missed the same note. "Oh, you want to sound just like the record," Monteux quipped.

Cavalier style and all, Monteux's San Francisco Symphony recordings are classics. First on 78-rpm platters, then on RCA's short-lived 45-rpm "extended play" disks, finally on 33-1/3-rpm long-playing records, Monteux continued to record with the orchestra until his final year as music director. And when he returned to guest-conduct in 1960, he took advantage of the occasion to make his last recording with the orchestra, of one of his favorite works, Richard Strauss's *Death and Transfiguration.* By then, the days of recording via telephone line were long past.

our hills, thank God—but it damn near did. It came close. And we were aware of that." For West Coast residents, who believed that only inadequate carrier and fuel support had kept the Pearl Harbor attackers from continuing their flight eastward to California, imminent attack was a specter that Allied victory alone would dispel.

Symphony administrators foresaw a decline in the audience, especially for concerts subject to blackout regulations. But when Armsby visited Mayor Angelo Rossi at City Hall, Rossi insisted that concerts continue as usual. The city would install a blackout system in the Opera House, and air raid wardens would be on hand in case of panic. Anticipating the first

17

evening concert of the war, Armsby wondered how large an audience would appear. She feared that sitting quietly for two hours in a public building in San Francisco would be too dire a test of nerves and was amazed when a crowd began to pour into the Opera House.

When the lights were dimmed for the first bars of music, the audience turned to look at the exit signs, then settled slowly to listen to their favorite

masterpieces. Pierre Monteux gave the signal for the opening bars of music. His listeners, magnetized by his calm and strong approach to his work, relaxed under his influence and remained in this mood to the end.

More evidence of Monteux's calm approach was soon apparent. During the First World War, music by living German composers had been banned from Symphony programs. Now, just ten days after Pearl Harbor and not quite a week after Germany had declared war on the United States, Monteux lobbied to continue playing works of composers such as Richard Strauss and others living in Germany. In his opinion, "when a piece of music is finished, it no longer belongs to the composer or his country, but to the people throughout the world." The Music Committee agreed. Its members did, however, consider Strauss's *Death and Transfiguration* and *Ein Heldenleben* too somber. *Death and Transfiguration*, scheduled for an early program, was replaced by the composer's *Don Juan*.

With the war's onset, military personnel due to ship overseas swelled San Francisco's population. Almost immediately, the Symphony invited soldiers and sailors to concerts— for free—and a box was set aside on Friday afternoons for convalescent soldiers from Letterman Hospital at the Presidio.

Among the letters of thanks the Association received, one was entered into the minutes. In April 1942, this came from Private William G. Faulkner, stationed at Fort McDowell and due to ship out to the Philippines:

It may not be many days before it would be impossible for me to write this letter. It's just a letter of thanks from one who has enjoyed the wonderful

18

entertainment of your fine orchestra and the gracious hospitality of your Association.

Let me do more than express the thanks of one soldier and extend the thanks and best wishes of the hundreds of men in uniform enabled to partake of some of the things we used to enjoy in civilian life.

If our good wishes mean anything, your orchestra will live a long and bright life. Of that I am certain.

Sentiments such as these would enable Leonora Wood Armsby to speak, toward war's end, of the Musical Association's role in maintaining morale— not just while the troops were in the Bay Area and able to hear the orchestra, but after they had mustered out, their spirits buoyed by memories.

Treasure Island, so recently the site of the great World's Fair, had become a naval base. On Christmas Eve 1942, Monteux and the orchestra joined members of the San Francisco Ballet, the Katherine Dunham dancers, and a chorus in a performance for the enlisted men there. Outfitted as Santa Claus, Monteux displayed a commitment to the troops that had assumed an added dimension, for he was now an American citizen, having been naturalized the previous spring in a City Hall ceremony that ended with him leading his fellow class members in the Pledge of Allegiance. In every performance Monteux and the musicians gave for the military— at army and navy posts, at the Presidio, at Mare Island—they always donated their services. The Treasure Island party was repeated every year until the war's end. War efforts also continued on the civilian front. In 1944, in a concert supporting the sixth of eight World War II US war bond drives, the orchestra raised more than $1 million toward the bond quota San Francisco had been assigned.

From the Office of War Information in New York, the Symphony received a request to record a program for broadcast on more than sixty stations, from Iceland to Australia, for the entertainment of the military and to position the United States as a bastion of civilization by displaying the country's thriving musical culture. Already the New York Philharmonic and Boston Symphony had been enlisted in such programs. Now it was San Francisco's turn. Monteux and the orchestra delivered what the War Information Office concluded was the finest contribution it had received.

San Francisco's concert attendance increased while, overseas, the conflicts continued. If the public craved reassurance that humanity had not gone insane, so did the artists on stage. The beginning of the war's end was in sight in March 1945, when Soviet forces were amassing for the Battle of Berlin. In San Francisco, Artur Schnabel joined with Monteux and the orchestra as soloist in Beethoven's Piano Concerto No. 4. Pianist and conductor alike were products of a European civilization that was being torn asunder. Now

they collaborated in one of the greatest works of Beethoven, a composer who represented the individuality and integrity that the present rulers of his birth-land detested. Elegance, reconciliation, elation—few compositions embody those qualities as does this Beethoven concerto, recreated that evening in San Francisco like a message from a lost world. At the end, Schnabel took his bow and turned to Monteux, taking him by the hands. Both fought back tears. To their art, these two brought experiences going back to Brahms and the tradition Brahms stood for, but nothing had prepared them for this moment, and they remained speechless until Schnabel found the words. "We are two old fools who love music very much, Monteux."

Not long after that evening, Beethoven again proved his power to guide listeners into inner spaces for reflection. Franklin Roosevelt died on April 12. The next day, in tribute to the president, Monteux opened the last Friday afternoon concert of the season with the slow movement of the *Eroica* Symphony, the funeral march. The audience stood in tribute throughout the music's fifteen-minute duration.

In May, Berlin fell and the war in Europe was over. Three months later, atom bombs exploded over Hiroshima and Nagasaki, and the war in the Pacific came to an end.

READY FOR PRIME TIME

"Last year was an enjoyable season as it was our first since peace was declared," Leonora Wood Armsby announced in 1946. "This return to our atmosphere of a little more serenity than we have enjoyed during the years of war, gave the concerts their old note of happiness and well-

Thirty-third Season
1944 - 45
SAN FRANCISCO SYMPHONY ORCHESTRA
PIERRE MONTEUX, *Conductor*

NINTH PAIR OF SYMPHONY CONCERTS

THURSDAY, MARCH 22, AT 8:30
SATURDAY, MARCH 24, AT 8:30

ARTUR SCHNABEL, *Guest Artist*

Program

OLD SONGS AND AIRS FOR THE LUTE,
FIRST SERIES . . . . *Arr. Respighi*
   Galliard, by Vincenzo Galilei
   Villanella, by an unknown composer
   Passamezzo and Mascherada, by an unknown composer

CONCERTO FOR PIANO AND ORCHESTRA,
NO. 4, IN G MAJOR, OPUS 58 . . . . *Beethoven*
   Allegro moderato
   Andante con moto
   Vivace
        MR. SCHNABEL

INTERMISSION

FOLK RHYTHMS OF TODAY . . . . *Harris*
   (First Performance in San Francisco)

SYMPHONY NO. 3, IN E FLAT MAJOR,
OPUS 97 *(RHENISH)* . . . . *Schumann*
   Lebhaft
   Scherzo: Sehr mässig
   Nicht schnell
   Feierlich
   Lebhaft

It is requested that subscribers who are unable to use their tickets kindly phone the Symphony Office—UNderhill 4008—giving location of their seats that they may be assigned to uniformed men and women. This courtesy will be deeply appreciated.

19

17

Monteux as Santa, conducting the orchestra in a Christmas Eve concert for enlisted men and women at Treasure Island.

18

Five days before the attack on Pearl Harbor, the Symphony celebrated its thirtieth anniversary in a lavish Civic Auditorium program.

19

Toward the end of the war in Europe, Artur Schnabel joined Monteux and the orchestra in emotion-packed performances of Beethoven's Fourth Piano Concerto.

99

being." Even before the war ended, the United Nations Conference on International Organization opened in San Francisco in April 1945, not quite two weeks after Franklin Roosevelt's death. The UN Conference led to the adoption that June of the UN Charter, signed at the War Memorial Opera House.

So yes to happiness and yes to well-being. For Monteux and the musicians, musical life went into overdrive. A new series of summer concerts had been inaugurated in 1945, and 1946 saw a Bruno Walter festival, three performances, with a program each devoted to Beethoven, Brahms, and Richard Strauss and Wagner. But that was nothing compared to what lay ahead.

In January 1946 Pierre Monteux proposed something that no West Coast orchestra had ever undertaken: a transcontinental tour. He envisioned a wide-ranging journey of broad artistic reach. As he addressed board members he began confidently. The San Francisco Symphony, he said, had taken a place among the greatest orchestras of North America, and it was certainly the greatest orchestra of the West. The Symphony had a cultural responsibility: to offer the nation's music lovers the chance to hear the orchestra in person. He outlined a tour that would proceed from Central and Southern California to New York, Boston, and as far north as Quebec.

Why not? Audiences were virtually guaranteed. According to Armsby, soldiers and sailors who had heard the orchestra in San Francisco had carried word of it back to their home-

towns. RCA, whose recordings had won the Symphony listeners throughout the country, would help promote the tour. Major financing would come from Standard Oil of California. "Your Orchestra," Armsby said, "is carrying the banner of San Francisco's cultural achievements in a manner never before even dreamed of by the people of the Pacific Coast." In its own way, the tour promised to fulfill the goals that the original Musical Association had envisioned. The orchestra's national reputation would be sealed.

The tour was a high point in the history of American orchestras. It proved that the United States had made the concert hall its own. For this journey was about more than showing the East Coast what the West Coast could do. The postwar years were not just a bobby sox-crewcut-Frank Sinatra-Rita Hayworth idyll. Servicemen and servicewomen often sought in vain for the civilian life they remembered, as even Hollywood acknowledged in William Wyler's now-classic 1946 film *The Best Years of Our Lives*. But this was also a period of elation following victories abroad, and as the United States rose to accept the mantle of world dominance, the Symphony tour signaled national optimism. Plotted on a map of the continent, the itinerary would show a network of cities large and small, knit together by the railroad lines that carried Monteux and the musicians from place to place, a national tapestry extending from coast to coast and from north to south, covering nine thousand miles: fifty-six concerts in fifty-seven days, a journey such as Jack Kerouac might have celebrated, had he been an orchestra musician. For eight weeks in 1947, the San Francisco Symphony became America's orchestra.

20

The Musical Association of San Francisco

Presents

San Francisco Symphony Orchestra

in a

BRUNO WALTER FESTIVAL

CIVIC AUDITORIUM
THURSDAY EVENING
AUGUST 29, AT 8:30

LEONORA WOOD ARMSBY   CHARLES PAGE   HOWARD K. SKINNER
President   Chairman   Manager

100

21

20

A Bruno Walter Festival in late summer 1946 brought the famed conductor—protégé, colleague, and champion of Mahler—to San Francisco for three concerts, devoted to music of Beethoven, Brahms, Wagner, and Richard Strauss.

21

Harpist Virginia Morgan helps hoist her instrument aboard. In the doorway is stage manager Jack Heavey, who had been with the orchestra since Henry Hadley's days.

22

The tour offered little time for sightseeing, but this group of musicians had cameras at the ready. From left: William Sabatini (horn), Merrill Jordan (flute), Joe Sinai (percussion), Mafalda Guaraldi (violin), Orlando Giosi (trombone), Anne Everingham (later Anne Adams, harp)

23

With a schedule of fifty-six concerts in fifty-seven days, musicians required a detailed itinerary to determine where they were along the route of the 1947 national tour.

23

Itinerary . . .

TRANSCONTINENTAL TOUR
1947

San Francisco Symphony Orchestra
MONTEUX · Conductor

JAMES SAMPLE, Associate Conductor

●

TOUR UNDER THE AUSPICES OF THE

MUSICAL ASSOCIATION of SAN FRANCISCO

LEONORA WOOD ARMSBY
President

HOWARD K. SKINNER
Manager

Tour Management
NATIONAL CONCERT AND ARTISTS CORP.
and
S. HUROK ATTRACTIONS, INC.

————◄●►————

THE SAN FRANCISCO
SYMPHONY ORCHESTRA
RECORDS EXCLUSIVELY
WITH RCA VICTOR

24

Toast of the tour:
Marcia Van Dyke, bound for Hollywood.

25

San Francisco welcomed the orchestra home in
May 1947.

26

Along with big cities, smaller communities across
the country enjoyed the orchestra's concerts on the
1947 tour. This is the program book cover from
the Galveston concert.

24

102

ON THE ROAD

Tour repertory was large and broad, far more extensive than the scaled-back tour programming of later years: twenty-seven works in all, including two Brahms symphonies, four works by Wagner, two tone poems by Richard Strauss, and three works by Bay Area composers—two of those composers being orchestra members to whom Monteux ceded the podium so they could lead their own music. Given the strenuous schedule, Associate Conductor James Sample relieved Monteux of some conducting duties, but never for an entire program. Monteux was well aware that he himself was among the box office draws.

On March 16, 1947, a party of 150 gathered at the Oakland depot: 95 musicians, along with press personnel, a doctor and a nurse, staff members, the Symphony librarian, and a group of stagehands supervised by the revered Jack Heavey, who had been

with the orchestra since the days of Henry Hadley and who had never expected to witness a moment like this. They boarded what would be their home for the next two months, a special Symphony train of twelve cars, including two offices, cargo cars for instruments, and sleeper coaches accommodating two people each, with single suites for principals. At 12:30 in the morning, the train pulled out of the station, bound for its first stop, Visalia.

City after city had invited the orchestra, and besides concerts at such obvious stops as Los Angeles, Washington, DC, Boston, New York, and Chicago, the itinerary tells the story of a country in love with music. Urbanites, blinded by their own brand of insularism, might not have expected to find that love deep in the heart of Texas, in places like Wichita Falls and Galveston, nor in Spartanburg, South Carolina; Newcastle, Pennsylvania; Lima, Ohio;

or Ottumwa, Iowa. Urbanites would have been wrong.

Cramped quarters and long days are part of the tour story. Flutist Paul Renzi had a fine time. He was twenty, determined to enjoy himself, and as a section principal had a private suite. Violinist David Schneider, on the other hand, described his two-berth roomette as "smaller than a prison cell," with no bath or toilet.

Except for hotel stays in Los Angeles and New York, the train was home. Every night was a travel night. After a concert, the train departed the station at 12:01 in the morning. Laundry was picked up once a week in the morning and returned by evening. Manager Joe Scafidi prepared tour manifests. "The only time I thought the musicians were set to kill me," he recalls, "was when we crossed the border into Canada one morning at about two. The Canadian authorities wanted to account for each person on the manifest, and I went with them from compartment to compartment, waking people. At the end, they couldn't account for one person. After trying to figure this out for a while, we realized it was I."

Pierre Monteux was not the only celebrity on board. Marcia Van Dyke was there. A violinist with the orchestra since 1943, Van Dyke was a budding starlet. Between 1932 and 1942 a cousin, W. S. Van Dyke, had directed such hits as *Tarzan the Ape Man*, *San Francisco*, a series of Nelson Eddy/Jeanette MacDonald vehicles, and three of the *Thin Man* movies, among them the original *Thin Man* of 1934. By 1948 Marcia had made the cover of *Life*, and in the years that followed she appeared in the only two movies of her career, 1949's *In the Good Old Summertime*, with Judy Garland and Van Johnson, and *Shadow on the Wall* in 1950. With Hollywood still in her future, Marcia was now embarked on a not-so-glamorous road trip, but her resourceful agent was able to parlay anything into publicity. So many reporters at so many stops en route wanted to talk to Marcia that Howard Skinner feared she was distracting the press from Monteux, and he put a stop to further interviews with her. Nonetheless, the May 5 issue of *Life* devoted a posttour story not to the orchestra but to the woman described in its pages as "the prettiest first violinist now in the symphony big time." For a family magazine like *Life*, "pretty" was a euphemism. The local press commented more freely on Marcia's blue eyes and raven hair, on looks that were made for the movies. She had, *Life* reported, turned down a movie contract because she intended to concentrate on her playing and because she had just become engaged to the orchestra's principal horn player, William Sabatini. Accompanying the story is a photo of Marcia

and Bill walking out on stage at Carnegie Hall: "Mere acquaintances in San Francisco," the caption reads, "couple became engaged in Wichita Falls, Texas, after 10 days on tour." Everything moves faster on a train.

By the time the orchestra arrived to play in Los Angeles, the Symphony had already given concerts in Visalia, Ontario, Pasadena, and San Diego. After LA the grind began. Fifty-six concerts in fifty-seven days is a marathon, and to complete such a run is a feat of stamina and athleticism such as no professional sports team is likely to have accomplished. Nothing can evoke the effort that went into this tour, nor the moments of exhilaration it could bring. Phoenix. El Paso. At every stop, audiences were enthusiastic and the press was delighted—even when the audiences were minimal. "The San Francisco Symphony orchestra . . . gave the few San Antonians present the musical treat of the season," wrote the critic of the *San Antonio Light*. In Houston, a Sunday matinee brought out scarcely four hundred music lovers, proving, as the *Houston Chronicle*'s reporter wrote, that the city's public preferred light entertainment to cultural uplift. But the Lone Star State had its enthusiasts too. Denton audiences cheered, the concert in Wichita Falls drew a record crowd, and the Fort Worth critic disclosed an all-but-forgotten musical fact, reminding readers that Monteux had already visited in 1916, conducting the Ballets Russes when Nijinsky danced the *Prelude to the Afternoon of a Faun*. Leonora Wood Armsby, recalling the tour in 1960, remembered crossing the vast spaces of Texas by train. She loved the nights, with sunsets that were "sparkling and had the radiance belonging to the color in precious stones," much as, so long before, Alfred Hertz

25

26

Isaac Stern and his teacher, Naoum Blinder.

NAOUM BLINDER AND HIS MOST FAMOUS STUDENT

Naoum Blinder, who joined the San Francisco Symphony as concertmaster in 1932, occupied that chair for twenty-five years, longer than anyone in the orchestra's history. But that was only one of his distinctions.

In 1931 concertmaster Mishel Piastro moved to the same post in Arturo Toscanini's New York Philharmonic. To find a replacement, music director Issay Dobrowen conducted a nationwide search. He found Naoum Blinder, then forty-three, teaching at New York's Institute of Musical Art (now the Juilliard School). Blinder was born in Lutzk, Russia, graduated from the Imperial Conservatory of Odessa at fourteen, and continued his studies in England. He returned to Odessa to teach at the conservatory, moved to the Moscow Conservatory in 1921, then in 1925 settled in New York. His tone and ear were superb, but his first years in San Francisco were difficult, for despite his expertise he had never been a concertmaster. A concertmaster is more than the first-chair violinist, more than the one who plays the solos in orchestral works. The concertmaster is leader of the violins, responsible for bowings and ensemble precision, responsible essentially for the sound at an orchestra's core.

Blinder was a quick study. When Pierre Monteux arrived in San Francisco, in late 1935, he decided quickly to give the concertmaster a long contract. "He was superb; I think him without a doubt one of the finest leaders I have ever encountered."

Teaching occupied a special place in Blinder's life. As Yehudi Menuhin had been Louis Persinger's most illustrious pupil, Isaac Stern was Blinder's. The concertmaster and his wife had lost their only child, and they came to look upon Stern as a son. Stern revered them both and over the years continued to visit whenever his concert schedule took him to San Francisco.

Stern was twelve when he became a student of Mr. Blinder— Stern never referred to him any other way—and he continued those studies for five years. He learned more than violin. He learned about music and about attitude and commitment. The Blinder home was the site of marathon chamber-music parties with members of the Symphony. Stern was part of all this— the playing, the enormous meals that followed the playing, and the playing that then followed the meals. Years later he spoke of how important those evenings were, how he learned by actually making music. "And these experienced musicians, with great love they didn't hesitate to give me hell."

Pierre Monteux came to the San Francisco Symphony when Stern was sixteen. The young man attended rehearsals whenever he could, watching his teacher closely. "I learned how to look. I learned how to know." And he became committed to the San Francisco Symphony. From his first performance with the orchestra in 1936 until his last, in 1997, and to his final San Francisco recital in 2000, the year before his death, Stern remained among the orchestra's closest friends.

Long before that, in 1986, the concertmaster's widow knew how important Stern was to her husband's legacy. "Mr. Blinder will never be forgotten now," she said, "because Isaac still brings his teacher's spirit into his music-making. I still can hear it."

had crossed the plains in the opposite direction and had seen the night skies illuminated by prairie fires.

Day after day, playing in different halls—not just bona fide concert halls but also high school auditoriums, gymnasiums, and skating rinks—acoustics varied from fine to horrible, and every new venue demanded new ways of playing the same music.

Montgomery. Birmingham. "We played in a lot of little towns," Paul Renzi recalls. "No building more than one story, a little barber shop, a little coffee shop." The train station at Spartanburg, South Carolina, was well outside the town limits. "It was very quiet. Our train was out in the fields." Out in the fields were hobos drinking Sterno. "Somebody— I think the first oboe player—gave them half a buck. Half a buck in those days was like $10 today."

"This was Jim Crow time." Violist Detlev Olshausen also recalled that Spartanburg stop. "We had a very nice African-American porter from Richmond, here in California, who was with the train the whole time. The orchestra liked him very much. He was one of us. He couldn't get anything to eat there. They wouldn't serve him in the station lunchroom. The orchestra fellows, they had to bring him food from town."

Atlanta. Norfolk. The Norfolk concert took place on April 4. Monteux turned seventy-two that day, and at intermission a cake was brought onto the stage and everyone, musicians and audience, sang "Happy Birthday" to him.

Richmond. Baltimore. In Washington, DC, President Truman, who professed to be one of Monteux's great fans,

attended the concert at Constitution Hall and greeted the conductor backstage before the concert.

Pittsburgh. New Brunswick. Then came New York City and Carnegie Hall. Nerves were taut. Monteux sensed this at the Carnegie rehearsal. "Tonight," he said, "we play the Brahms First as Brahms wrote it." The atmosphere calmed. That evening, before a packed house, some musicians spied Arturo Toscanini in the first box, looking down through binoculars. As applause rang out at the end of the Brahms First Symphony, Toscanini rushed onto the stage and embraced Monteux. Never, he assured his colleague, had he heard such an ovation—not even for himself and his orchestra. "Out of the West came Pierre Monteux and the San Francisco Symphony to Carnegie Hall last night," wrote critic Miles Kastendieck in the *New York Journal-American*. "They came, they played, they conquered."

With success in New York behind them, Monteux and the orchestra moved on to Worcester, Massachusetts, then to Boston, where the *Globe's* critic reported that the reserved Brahmin audience responded with stomping and cheers.

New London. Schenectady. Then into Canada: Ottawa. Quebec. Back into the United States. The train from Quebec, due to arrive in Jamestown, Ohio, at 7:30 that evening, was delayed and did not arrive until 8:15. By the time the cars were unloaded and the stage set, it was almost ten in the evening. The audience took it in stride and waited. They enjoyed an unexpected treat when the formidable Madame Maître, Doris Monteux, entertained them with a standup routine, telling stories about the tour, about the Monteux estate

27

Taking a break from the tour's rigors: Maître contemplates the sky, Madame tends to Fifi, and Howard Skinner assumes the classic pose of the onlooker.

in Maine, and about the San Francisco Symphony and its history.

Buffalo. Columbus. Newcastle. Dayton. In Lima, Ohio, Paul Renzi incurred the wrath of a native when he asked if he was in Lima, pronouncing the city's name like the Peruvian capital, not the bean. Other than big cities, the towns began to seem interchangeable to the weary travelers.

Chicago. The feared critic Claudia Cassidy, whose vitriol a few years later would cut short conductor Rafael Kubelík's music directorship of the Chicago Symphony, pronounced the San Francisco Symphony an orchestra of "extraordinary vitality."

St. Paul. Milwaukee. Across Iowa. Over the Continental Divide, then through the Pacific Northwest and back into Canada, at last heading south again for a last concert in Sacramento. On Sunday, May 11, at noon, Monteux and the Orchestra

arrived home. Members of the Art Commission, Junior Chamber of Commerce, and press greeted them at the Ferry Building. Mayor Roger Lapham proclaimed the next seven days San Francisco Symphony week, during which the National Association of American Composers and Conductors—the organization Henry Hadley had founded—awarded Pierre Monteux the medal named after the Symphony's first music director, declaring Monteux a representative of the best in American music. With the tour, the best in American music had been carried the length and breadth of the county.

Hard work had paid dividends, had carried music across the continent and alerted the musicians to how many music lovers in how many places appreciated their work. Orchestras had made long tours before. The Minneapolis Symphony had amassed an impressive road record, and in 1884 the pioneering conductor Theodore Thomas had

traversed the country with his orchestra, playing seventy-three concerts in as many days, in thirty cities. In duration and its fifty-three-city extent, the San Francisco Symphony's 1947 tour takes its place alongside such a marathon. A national profile had been established.

ENDING AN ERA

Miscalculations in the tour budget had resulted in a shortfall of almost forty thousand dollars. Members of the Musical Association worked hard to pool their resources and retire this amount themselves. Other financial news was better. Board vice-president Charles Blyth pointed out that, in comparison with other major orchestras, the San Francisco Symphony's earned income was high and its deficit low. In fact, among twenty-three orchestras, San Francisco was sixth in ticket sales, behind only Boston, New York, Philadelphia, Chicago, and Minneapolis. And only Cincinnati, Boston, Philadelphia, and

28

29

New York had posted lower deficits. But in the lives of US arts organizations, money and its sources are permanent concerns, and as late as 1951 the Association struggled to meet the weekly payroll. Philip Boone, back from military service and by now well beyond his student years, maintained his enthusiasm for the San Francisco Symphony. He organized a special events committee and formulated the idea of one such event that could raise money for a contingency fund. His goal was fifty thousand dollars. The event would be called a *tombola*, Italian for *raffle*, the foreign terminology meant to impart a touch of class. Boone's plan was to sell raffle tickets for almost three months prior to a grand celebratory concert at the Civic Auditorium, where prizes donated by local merchants would be awarded. That 1949 tombola was a success, ensuring that tombolas would be part of the next two seasons.

The 1950 tombola was a celebration of Pierre Monteux's seventy-fifth birthday. Arthur Fiedler conducted

the orchestra, beginning a long association with the San Francisco Symphony, and the party came complete with a huge cake mounted on rollers. Founding members of the Symphony Forum pushed it down the aisle, and Monteux was compelled to stand on a chair as he reached up to begin cutting at the top tier. The theme was "French café," and artist Antonio Sotomayor, whose caricatures of Monteux appeared in the San Francisco press throughout the concert season, painted a stage backdrop that depicted Monteux walking his poodle Fifi past the Eiffel Tower. The Civic Auditorium audience of nine thousand sang "Happy Birthday," and Boone presented Armsby with the money raised by the event, forty-four thousand dollars.

At seventy-five, Monteux felt he still had worlds to conquer. He had been with the San Francisco Symphony for fifteen years and was looking forward to a twilight career as a conductor who could accept whatever engagements he was offered, when

28

The Tombola of 1951. The theme, Show Boat, *was timed with the release later that year of a film version of Jerome Kern's 1927 Broadway hit.*

107

29

Leonora Wood Armsby at her desk, Hillsborough.

30

San Francisco artist Antonio Sotomayor created a series of caricatures that expressed the city's affection for the Symphony's music director.

30

31

32

he wanted to accept them, and be free of the duties a permanent post entailed. Already he had told Leonora Wood Armsby of his retirement plans, but she convinced him to stay. She herself, she said, planned to leave in two years. They would depart together. "I feel I should have relinquished my post at the end of the war," Monteux would write in his memoirs, "but there was no refusing Leonora Wood Armsby who was the soul of our organization."

One more thing Monteux wanted to ensure in San Francisco was on behalf of the musicians he had come to love. He urged a permanent pension plan. By the end of 1950, a change in federal law allowed non-profit organizations to waive their exemption from taxes under the Federal Insurance Contributions Act, making it possible for their employees to participate in the Social Security system, and the Musical Association promptly waived that right. Although Monteux's dream of a pension plan

would not be realized until 1956, a period of increasing respect for musicians had begun. As the cost of living rose, their salaries slowly adjusted to the pace of the times.

And times were changing, not all for the good. Attendance at Saturday concerts was decreasing. The financial burden, in part still related to tour indebtedness, was growing. Ticket sales for 1949–50 fell below the previous season by almost thirty thousand dollars, almost exactly the deficit the Musical Association was showing. The 1950–51 season would also close with a deficit. That season's tombola concerts—three of them, all conducted by Fiedler—would lose money rather than contribute to a contingency fund.

Throughout all this, Leonora Wood Armsby maintained her composure. The Association had survived many crises, she asserted, perhaps because it had been born of a crisis, had been established to help restore a city's

cultural life. The founders had believed in the Symphony and toiled on music's behalf. Their efforts had led to the present moment, when San Francisco was known worldwide as a destination for music lovers.

But Armsby also believed that the orchestra's modest beginnings were reflected in the vagueness of the parent organization's name. In 1951 she proposed a measure designed to link city, orchestra, and organization in the public's mind. From henceforth, the Musical Association of San Francisco would be known as the San Francisco Symphony Association. Measures such as this, so seemingly insignificant, can be critical steps in establishing identity, something beyond what twenty-first-century marketing teams call a brand.

That identity also resided in the person of Pierre Monteux, who was now prepared to leave San Francisco. In April 1951, when Monteux at last

THE MUSICAL ASSOCIATION OF SAN FRANCISCO maintaining

the san francisco symphony orchestra

PIERRE MONTEUX · Conductor and Musical Director

WAR MEMORIAL OPERA HOUSE
SAN FRANCISCO 2, CALIF.
PHONE UNDERHILL 1-4008
HOWARD K. SKINNER, Mgr.

OPERA SYMPHONY BOX OFFICE
SHERMAN, CLAY & COMPANY
SAN FRANCISCO 8, CALIF.
PHONE SUTTER 1-1331

—————————————————————— 1911 | 1951

April 25 1951

Leonora Wood Armsby
Forestview Avenue
Burlingame California.

Dear Leonora:

     This letter, my dear, and good friend, is to tell you that the season 1951 and '52, that is to say, the coming season will be my last as permanent conductor of the San Francisco Symphony Orchestra. I have come to this decision after deep thought and many hours of weighing the pro's and con's in regard to such a step.

     You know me, perhaps better than others as an artist and conductor and knowing me, you realize that when I tell you I must go on to other fields, it means that I have come to an impasse which can only be satisfied by new worlds of music, new public, and new work. I have long wanted to go to South America, where I have been asked every year; then to, I have many ties in Europe, such as the Concertgebouw, and the English Orchestras which I would like to conduct again. In other words, new horizons, new and old friends.

     Now I have set forth my personal reasons for resigning my post, but there is also in my mind that after my long and happy stay here in San Francisco, it would perhaps be advantageous to the Symphony Society to provide the public with another conductor which might serve as a stimulant for increasing attendance at concerts. Naturally you know it is my great desire to see the Association and the Orchestra have everything possible to assist in maintaining the high standards we have always aspired to, in the community. I shall always cherish these past years of work and attainment as something very rare and unforgettable. Will you kindly present my respect and sincere affection to our Board of Govenors and thank them for their invaluable aid to me in my work as Conductor of the San Francisco Symphony Orchestra. Without their comprehension and help many times, I would have found it difficult to continue.

     In closing my very dear friend, I wish to tell you that you have been the finest partner a musician could have wished for over the years. I shall always hold these years in a corner of my heart as a wonderful example of true and noble friendship.

     So, dear friend, unlike the General, I do not intend to 'fade away' I hope sincerely to make my beautiful music to the end of my days here on this old earth, which needs the harmony of true art more than ever.

Lovingly *Pierre Monteux*

31

Orchestra women donned can-can apparel and danced for Monteux at his farewell party.

32

Pierre Monteux, against the backdrop of his adopted city. "I loved this city, its style, its lavish way of life, its unique situation on seven hills overlooking the Bay, one of the most beautiful in the world."

33

Pierre Monteux formalizes his leave-taking.

33

announced his planned departure at the end of the 1951–52 season, he was touching in his tributes to Armsby and to his art: "I shall always cherish these past years of work and attainment as something very rare and unforgettable," he wrote to her. "You have been the finest partner a musician could have wished for over the years.... So, dear friend, unlike the General [Douglas MacArthur], I do not intend to 'fade away.' I hope sincerely to make my beautiful music to the end of my days here on this old earth, which needs the harmony of true art more than ever." The harmony Monteux spoke of was indeed in short supply. For almost a year, the United States had been involved in a new war, this time in Korea. At home, Senator Joseph McCarthy was beginning to exploit fears of Communism and had launched an attack on Secretary of State George Marshall, architect of the Marshall Plan, which helped rebuild Western Europe in the years after World War II. Monteux, true

to his nature, believed in music's power to help reestablish the balance that such events and actions upset. Everyone knew he would be a difficult act to follow.

As befitted a man of Monteux's high spirits, even the good-byes were ebullient. At a farewell party at the Fairmont Hotel, eleven of the orchestra's women danced a can-can. His final concerts opened with Franck's Symphonic Variations for piano and orchestra, and he invited a special soloist to perform that work: Agnes Albert, niece of Richard Tobin, who had served as board president in the dark years just before Monteux's arrival. Albert herself would go on to become one of the Symphony's most influential board members. Now here she was, with sold-out audiences guaranteed. "I don't think Monteux was thinking too much about me or the Franck," she said years later. "He was thinking about the rest of the program." The rest of the program was the Beethoven

Ninth Symphony, which Monteux had programmed ten times in his San Francisco years. At his final concert, when the last notes had sounded and he laid down his baton, he received an ovation that lasted ten minutes.

The San Francisco *Call-Bulletin* was straightforward in its farewell: "We'll leave all the fancy words about his greatness as a musician to the music critics and just say that he was an extraordinarily likable guy, and that San Francisco will miss him and Mme. Monteux very much."

"It was impossible to think of the gold curtain of the Opera House rolled back for any conductor but Pierre Monteux," wrote Leonora Wood Armsby, who kept her post as board president for a year after he left. Her words were prophetic.

AN AUDITION (THE WAY IT WAS)

Violist Detlev Olshausen joined the San Francisco Symphony in 1940, winning his place through an auditioning process long since abandoned, when prospects performed for the music director, who either accepted them or not. (For the way auditions work seventy years later, see page 226.) Olshausen made his initial Symphony contact through Albert Elkus, who chaired the music department at the University of California in Berkeley and was also a Symphony board member. Elkus had encouraged Olshausen to switch from violin to viola. The next step was to introduce him to Pierre Monteux.

In early 1940 I played for Monteux privately in his apartment up on Nob Hill. I didn't play well. . . . Of course, this was just an informal, private visit. He said, "Well, you know, there would have to be three openings for you to have a chance to get in to this orchestra because"—this would be impossible today—"one position"—and imagine telling me this, too, just in conversation—"one position has been promised to Walter Herbert." . . .

[This] was just an individual session, letting him hear me. And I thought, *Well, that finishes that.* . . . So the summer passed. To my utter surprise—I think it was a week before Thanksgiving in November—I was called by the personnel manager, Julius Haug, who asked if I would come for an audition on Saturday. So I auditioned in the personnel manager's residence, which was an old storefront on Sacramento Street.

I played the slow movement of the spurious Handel Viola Concerto by Henri Casadesus. I played it very cantabile, like "Where E'er You Walk," or Handel's Largo. And Monteux said, "I like your tone. But we have to hear some others." This was an audition. In Julius Haug's residence, on Sacramento Street in San Francisco. Haug and Monteux were the only two people present. There was no committee of any kind; it was just the conductor and the personnel manager. . . .

And I remember, he wanted to give me something to read and he had the wrong part, so what I read wasn't what he really wanted. So, on Thursday, Thanksgiving Day, I was having quartet rehearsal in my house on Hillegass Avenue in Berkeley. My sister was in the kitchen preparing the turkey. The phone rang in the middle of our rehearsal and who was it but Julius Haug, asking me to come to the rehearsal on Saturday morning. That was my first rehearsal with the San Francisco Symphony, the Saturday after Thanksgiving of 1940. . . .

I was the next-to-the-last stand. Nathan Firestone was the principal and a very nice gentleman. But it was explained to me—and I believed it—that Monteux was probably a little apprehensive about taking this green young fellow into the orchestra. It turned out that Al White, who had been a member of the viola section, . . . was planning to leave the orchestra for at least three years to go to [the NBC Symphony]. . . . Monteux wanted to keep the place open for him in case he wanted to come back. . . . Well, Al White didn't come back until much, much later. . . . So I was in that year without a contract. I could have been kicked out at any time, actually. . . .

I got a contract at the end of the season for the next season. At that time there was no tenure. I didn't have tenure for the first twenty-seven years I played in the Symphony, because there was no such thing. That came after the big strike [in 1967–68]. Four weeks before the end of the season, I think everybody was very apprehensive, waiting to get a notice that either Monteux wishes to have your services for the following season or we regret that we cannot renew your contract.

After joining in 1940, Olshausen went on to play with the orchestra for the next fifty years. He left in 1990, having served the last thirty-four years as associate principal of his section.

Members of the viola section join Detlev Olshausen (second from right) at his retirement party. Setting: a castle in France. Time: the 1990 European festival tour. Offering a toast is Leonid Gesin. Seated, from left, are Wayne Roden, Nancy Ellis, Olshausen, and Geraldine Walther.

Monteux takes his leave of San Francisco after a performance of the Beethoven Ninth: April 12, 1952.

VI.

AN ENIGMA AND A TRAGEDY

The Enrique Jordá Years (1954–1963)

DISCOVERIES AND DECISIONS

More than any music director in the San Francisco Symphony's history, Enrique Jordá embodies a question every listener asks sooner or later: *Can I trust my ears?* The acclaim with which Jordá's tenure began turned to dismay by its conclusion. As the years went on and questions arose over his suitability for the job, factions developed, pro and con. Neither side's position was unbiased or unassailable. As if no controversy existed, he was encouraged to continue in his post. He was thus positioned for a fall. Aristotle identified the decent man's plunge from the heights as an element of tragedy. Jordá, who knew his philosophers, might have agreed, but he was too dignified to say so.

An element of melodrama was also present. It began with the search for a successor to Pierre Monteux. The 1952–53 season was presented as the Season of Discovery. The 1953–54 season would be the Season of Decision. Throughout this time, a parade of guest conductors occupied the Symphony podium in what were essentially public auditions. Presumably, the discoveries of 1952–53 would help narrow the field, eventually leading in the following year to the choice of a music director.

As Monteux made his exit, having led the orchestra through wartime, the United States welcomed a war hero to the White House. It has been said that the San Francisco Symphony's ensemble playing during the last years of Monteux's tenure had grown ragged, but a *Standard Hour* recording made the night before Dwight Eisenhower's presidential inauguration reveals a tightly coordinated orchestra and brilliant sound,

all captured live by the Ampex Corporation in an early demonstration of stereo recording.

Alfred Wallenstein, who conducted that *Standard Hour* concert, was among those featured in the Season of Discovery. Others included Leopold Stokowski, Erich Leinsdorf, Victor de Sabata, George Szell, Bruno Walter, and Enrique Jordá, who was making his US debut.

Even by comparison with such legends-in-their-own-time as Stokowski, Szell, and Walter, Jordá was a favorite with audiences and critics. Marta Morgan, in the *San Jose Mercury-News*, described him as a conductor of "brilliance, sensitivity, and innate musical ability." He was, she said, "definitely the choice of [the] majority of symphony players. . . . It is my belief that if a vote were to be taken at this junction, Jordá would win hands down since he has emerged as the most popular contender to date." The *Examiner*'s Alexander Fried and the *Chronicle*'s Alfred Frankenstein both noted the conductor's tendency to shout at orchestral climaxes, claiming to have heard him even over the orchestra, and they advised him to rid himself of this habit, but that was the limit of their criticism. Frankenstein, the Symphony's program annotator as well as the morning paper's music critic, might have been suspected of divided loyalties, but in those days few perceived conflict of interest in such dual posts, and San Francisco was hardly the only city in which critics worked for the orchestras whose concerts they reviewed.

Leonora Wood Armsby was enthusiastic about Jordá. She believed the Symphony had found a major talent, had made a discovery. But even before the Season of Decision began, the day she had both looked forward to and dreaded arrived. She had told Monteux they would leave the Symphony together, but she had stayed after his departure. Yet not even she was immune to ill health and age. On July 24, 1953, she submitted her resignation as president and managing director, taking that action at her doctor's and her family's urging. A month later J. D. Zellerbach, head of the Crown-Zellerbach paper empire, was nominated to succeed her as president. Armsby was named the Symphony's Life Honorary Chairman.

Jordá, as expected, was invited back for the Season of Decision. Also heard were Stokowski, Walter, Ferenc Fricsay, William Steinberg, and, for the first time at Symphony concerts, Georg Solti. Again Jordá received a warm welcome. "No guest conductor . . . has produced such a wealth of glowing, sonorous tone from strings, brasses and woodwinds . . . as this Spaniard," wrote Marjory M. Fisher in the *San Francisco News*.

A few days after Fisher's review appeared, the board of the Symphony Association met to discuss the guests they had heard. Some members were disappointed that no one had measured up to Monteux. They wanted to postpone choosing for another year. But if you have called your series of concerts a Season of Decision, you are committing yourself to taking a stand. This story of the rise and fall of Enrique Jordá could be a casebook in management rules, the first of which would be: *Do not allow your public relations efforts to box you into a corner.*

Few board members seemed excited about any of the guests. Guido Musto

2

J. D. Zellerbach, two-term Symphony president: from 1953 to 1956, and again, after serving as US Ambassador to Italy, from 1961 to 1963.

3

Announcing the Season of Decision.

Leopold Stokowski

2 weeks — 6 concerts

This distinguished symphony conductor returns this season to conduct the opening concerts. A world traveler, he has conducted great orchestras everywhere. Long acknowledged a musical leader in the United States, he has built up many musical organizations and introduced many significant contemporary works.

Ferenc Fricsay

3 weeks — 8 concerts

Makes his American debut this Fall with the Boston Symphony. Born in Budapest, 1914. Studied with Bartok, Dohnanyi, Kodaly. Founder and present Conductor of Berlin's RIAS (Radio in American Section) Symphony. Regularly guest conductor at the Salzburg, Edinburgh, Rome, Zurich, and Firenze Festivals.

Georg Solti

3 weeks — 9 concerts

Now General Music Director and Opera Director of Frankfort-am-Main. Conducts the famous series of Museum Concerts in Frankfurt. Is still active as General Music Director of the State Opera in Munich as well as regular Guest Conductor of the Berlin and London Philharmonic and the Vienna State Opera and Symphony Orchestras.

Enrique Jorda

7 weeks — 18 concerts

Won the heart of San Francisco last year when he made his American debut here. Formerly Conductor of the Madrid Symphony Orchestra; presently Conductor of South Africa's Capetown Orchestra. Regularly guest conductor with the London Symphony, Halle Orchestra, Paris Conservatory, Liverpool Orchestra and the B. B. C. Orchestra.

William Steinberg

2 weeks — 6 concerts

Until 1952, Conductor of the Buffalo Philharmonic which he made one of the nation's major orchestras. He is now Conductor of the Pittsburgh Symphony. Although a longtime San Francisco favorite, he has not been heard in this city since the 1949 San Francisco Symphony Season.

Bruno Walter

2 weeks — 5 concerts

Returns to conduct the closing concerts. Founder of the Salzburg Festivals. Former Musical Advisor of the New York Philharmonic, Conductor of the Metropolitan Opera and musical leader in Munich, Berlin and Vienna. Renowned on two continents, he appears regularly with major orchestras in the United States and Europe.

Pianists

Violinists

Leon Fleisher

3 concerts

He won the coveted Queen Elizabeth of Belgium International Music Competition in 1952. Afterplay in nearly every country in a tour of 42 concerts in the capitals of the World, he will open his American Tour in his native San Francisco.

Artur Rubinstein

2 concerts

Since the age of 11 he has traveled more than 2 million miles to music. He has toured widely in the world. One of the last pianists in the Grand Manner, a true citizen of the world.

Michael Rabin

3 concerts

Born in New York City, 1936. He made his Carnegie Hall debut in

Isaac Stern

3 concerts

San Francisco's adopted son and gift to the musical world. He re-

Guiomar Novaes

3 concerts

This is San Francisco's first chance to hear this outstanding Brazilian artist. She has toured widely in the Americas and Europe, winning acclaim both as soloist and recitalist.

Gonzalo Soriano

3 concerts

Hailed in Europe, called the "greatest keyboard artist to come from Spain in the last 25 years," he makes his American debut this season. Studied with Cubiles and de Falla.

William Kapell

3 concerts

The young American who is famous far beyond his years. He has appeared with every top orchestra in the country. Studied with Olga Samaroff Stokowski.

SAN FRANCISCO SYMPHONY ASSOCIATION

3

---

suggested that any contract should be short-term, fearing the new leader might not be the next great star. Walter Heller advanced a proposal to consult the audience. And in fact management had already decided to take a vote from all season ticket holders and anyone else who had close ties with the orchestra. By the meeting's end, the search for a music director began to be referred to as "the conductor problem."

Almost two thousand season ticket holders and contributors received ballots, and more than eight hundred returned them. The results:

552 for Jordá
164 for Steinberg
83 for Solti
35 for Fricsay
27 for Szell
2 for Leinsdorf

J. D. Zellerbach claimed to have conferred personally with the critics and with "a cross section of the orchestra." A few board members continued to hold out, but the majority wanted to decide. Since Steinberg had removed himself from the running, the choice was between Solti and Jordá. The musicians, Zellerbach said, believed both conductors to be excellent and could work with either; although Jordá, the more sensitive of the two, was able to elicit more consistently beautiful playing. Zellerbach felt the critics favored Jordá, and Philip Boone reported that the Symphony Forum board shared the critics' opinion, as did members of the Symphony Foundation, a group of volunteers he had recently organized.

The time for decision had come. A motion was put forward to hire Jordá. Another was put forward to hire Solti. A show of hands yielded twenty-seven ayes for Jordá, six for Solti, and six abstentions. Jordá was offered a two-year contract with an option to renew for three years.

Enrique Jordá was about to enter a period that would be the zenith and nadir of his career. Georg Solti embarked on his own path, on the way to becoming one of the twentieth century's most illustrious conductors.

THE ENIGMA DEEPENS

Who was Enrique Jordá? He was born in 1911 in San Sebastián, Spain, and took pride in his Basque heritage. He trained at Madrid University and at the Sorbonne in Paris, and before he concentrated on music he was a serious student of medicine, philosophy, and theology, interests he followed for the rest of his life. He made his conducting debut in 1937, in Paris, where he chose to stay rather than return to his native country and the Franco dictatorship; although in 1940, when the Nazis invaded Paris, he did flee France for Spain, becoming music director of the politically independent Madrid Symphony Orchestra—he refused to conduct the Franco-backed Madrid National Orchestra. In 1947 he assumed leadership of the Cape Town Symphony

4
_____

Georg Solti, around the time he appeared in the Symphony's Season of Decision.

5
_____

Early reactions to Jordá gave no hint of the problems he would encounter.

4

in South Africa, yet his discomfort with apartheid soon led him to seek another post. He found it in San Francisco. One thing he had in common with Pierre Monteux was his openness to new repertory. Enrique Jordá's programming confirms his claim that he had no musical prejudices. In addition to the world premieres he led in San Francisco—including Rodrigo's *Fantasia para un Gentilhombre*, Roy Harris's *San Francisco Symphony*, Darius Milhaud's Symphonies No. 8 and No. 12, and Andrew Imbrie's *Legend*—he expanded the orchestra's repertory dramatically, introducing music by such composers as Paul Hindemith, Ralph Vaughan Williams, Leon Kirchner, and Hans Werner Henze, whose Symphony No. 2 had its US premiere in San Francisco under Jordá's direction. He gave established composers a fair shake, too, as when he conducted only the second San Francisco performance of a work Monteux might

have been expected to take on but never did, Berlioz's *L'Enfance du Christ*. His book on conducting, *El director de orquesta ante la partitura* (probably best translated, though not literally, as *The Conductor and the Score*), was published in 1969. In 1970 he assumed his last regular post, with the Antwerp Philharmonic, where he remained for six years. He spent the next two decades in retirement and died in Brussels in 1996 at age eighty-four.

Enrique Jordá was a man of culture, personal integrity, and charisma. To read his words about music and his profession is to be inspired. He possessed great social finish in an era that placed high value on such finish. Those who knew him off the podium grew to esteem him. J. D. Zellerbach thought him a fine gentleman. Violist Detlev Olshausen admired his erudition and his "beautiful sense of music." Charming and very gifted, said board member Agnes Albert.

But there was a problem.

"He didn't conduct," recalled former Principal Flutist Paul Renzi. "Whether we played together or not, Jordá was just as happy. And he didn't help."

"Jordá spent an enormous amount of time talking in rehearsal. . . . It got to the point where [the musicians] felt, 'My God, not another rehearsal.' And of course, this kind of feeling obviously made itself known through the performance. It had to." That is Joe Scafidi's recollection.

"People were saying the only way to stay together is not to look at the stick or the conductor," Olshausen remembered.

Agnes Albert summed up what was wrong. "He had no control over the orchestra at all. None."

Jorda Hailed at Concert As Permanent Conductor

By ALEXANDER FRIED

Enrique Jorda gave further clear proof, Thursday night at the Opera House, that the San Francisco Symphony has done well to pick him as its permanent conductor. A large audience seconded the choice all evening and by the pointed, lengthy applause with which it first greeted him.

He led a program full of interest and variety—from Rossini's witty, glinting "Italiana in Algeri" Overture and the exquisite French savors of Roussel's "Spider's Banquet" ballet music to the rapturous Lied and dance-like poetry of Schumann's "Spring" Symphony.

By the clock, the program was one number too long. But Jorda and the orchestra made it so alive with beautiful musical idea and delivery that it ended up by being refreshing, not tiring.

Any new conductor must gradually answer a number of questions. How will he conduct this style of work and that? How will he be as an orchestral accompanist?

In Jorda's case, there is an especial question. His musical concepts are so fastidious in detail; they penetrate the whole orchestral texture with such revelations of sound and phrasing, that one asks: "Will his style be short-breathed, or will it also sweep along over the big forms and masses of great masterworks?"

He certainly captured the large flow and spirit of the "Spring" Symphony. His performance was glowing and fluid and rich of heart, as well as delicate.

All this he accomplished with sufficient grandeur, but with characteristic restraint. He was never merely rhetorical—such as to drag out a final big chord to make sure to shake the rafters. In fact, a shade more of outgoing rhetoric, in the right spot, might not at all hurt his supreme artistic taste in the long run.

Alicia de Larrocha, a tiny lady from Spain, was successful piano soloist in Mozart's A major Concerto and Franck's "Symphonic Variations." Her Mozart was all excellent and accomplished, but slightly tame. In the Franck, she spoke out with greatly enjoyable accent and bravura.

In both the Mozart, on its apt small classic scale, and the Franck, Jorda's accompaniments were consummate. The concert will be repeated tonight.

Sentiments like these are puzzling, in light of the excitement Jordá generated at first. Hiring him had been a bold decision. He was untried, a genuine "discovery." The consensus —among audiences, critics, and musicians—was that he was brilliant: good for the orchestra, good for the music, good for San Francisco.

Jordá had several strong suits, among them his affinity for composers such as Berlioz, Falla, and Dvořák. Choral works came off well under his direction. He had a genuine sense of musical adventure. His predilection for contemporary works is thought to have hurt him with audiences, but it cannot have damaged him as much as his rehearsal talk did with the orchestra. One of the surest ways for a conductor to antagonize musicians is to waste rehearsal time. Once, a horn player kept track of how long the orchestra spent actually playing in a Jordá rehearsal. Eighteen minutes, out of three hours. Jordá regularly offered his philosophical take on the music, asking for sounds that were cosmic, tragic, or universal and using such terms to describe what he was after. A famed maestro once remarked that a conductor should limit spoken directions to *faster, slower, louder, softer.* For those eager to know how firmly to apply a bow to strings or how long to hold a fermata, Jordá's poetics meant nothing. He was not helping the musicians do their jobs. He also had a problem making his English understood. Exasperation grew in the orchestra. Often, not every work to be performed in concert was covered in rehearsal. Time simply ran out.

But opinions were divided. Detlev Olshausen harbored no ill will. "He got a very round, beautiful sound out of the orchestra," Olshausen says, phrasing his assessment in a way

119

*Enrique Jordá and the San Francisco
Symphony, 1957.*

that suggests Jordá was responsible for that sound—that he was, after all, helping the musicians do their jobs.

The sound of Jordá's orchestra can be heard on two commercial recordings that have continued to be readily available over the years. The orchestra is superb in Falla's *Nights in the Gardens of Spain*, recorded for RCA in 1957 with pianist Artur Rubinstein, and in Charles Cushing's *Cereus*, a twentieth-century work recorded in 1961 for CRI—Composers Recordings, dedicated to contemporary American music. Studio recordings, of course, can mask inadequacies, with takes and retakes assembled into a cohesive whole, yet the one Jordá/Symphony recording on which repeated takes have been documented, that of Rachmaninoff's Piano Concerto No. 2 with soloist Alexander Brailowsky, is a poor, enervated performance that argues against excessive tinkering.

So the question remains. Whose ears could be trusted?

CHANGING TIMES

The Jordá years show a musical organization in a changing society. In his classic study of the period, *The Fifties*, David Halberstam paints a panorama of the times. Housing developments modeled on an original planned suburb in Levittown, New York, made home ownership possible for the postwar generation. Automobile monstrosities abounded, such as the short-lived Ford Edsel. Now-classic Chevrolets and Pontiacs mimicked the design of spacecraft found in science-fiction comics, while the simpler reality of Russia's orbiting Sputnik satellite terrified Americans who believed the space race had already been forfeited to their Cold War foe. Halberstam's book is at once a trip into nostalgia and a fascinating social study. No one

paints a more vivid picture of an era when conformity was a virtue while juvenile discontent attained populist chic.

The age of consumerism was rising. Disneyland, the first theme park to capture the imaginations of children around the world, opened in 1955. That same year, in opposition to the staid safety they condemned in their elders, a group of young poets, Gary Snyder and Allen Ginsberg among them, inaugurated the San Francisco Renaissance with a reading at the Six Gallery. Jack Kerouac dispensed wine and led the crowd in a cheering section. A year later Ginsberg published *Howl* and the Beat movement had found its voice. Eisenhower was elected to a second term, and Elvis Presley rocked a TV audience of an estimated 60 million on the *Ed Sullivan Show*.

In San Francisco as in other major cities, people were leaving for the suburbs. San Francisco's population in 1950 was 775,360. In 1960, it was 740,300, a downward trend that would continue through the 1980s before reversing. (Los Angeles was a notable exception to the rule of shrinking urban populations.) Attendance at Saturday evening concerts dropped. Those who might once have been audience members now took off on weekend outings in their long, finned automobiles—1957, after all, saw the publication of Kerouac's *On the Road*. Others, comfortable in new suburban homes, proved reluctant to travel into the city. In response, the 1957 concert schedule changed from Thursday and Saturday evenings and Friday afternoons to Wednesday and Thursday evenings, and Friday afternoons.

In J. D. Zellerbach the Symphony had found another strong board leader, a man who once admitted

that the Symphony was his "favorite community interest." He was fair-minded and tried to give musicians an even shake, and it was he who at last, in late 1956, oversaw the start of a pension fund for the orchestra. Among major US ensembles, only Boston, Cleveland, New York, and Philadelphia had made similar provisions for players. The Association and musicians contributed equally, musicians donating their service in special pension fund concerts. The first of these, in March 1957, was billed as a Dixieland Ragtime Jamboree. In 1958 pianist Rudolf Serkin became the first artist to contribute his fee to the fund. The violin-playing comedian Jack Benny would do the same, giving a 1959 performance of the Mendelssohn Concerto that brought the fund fifty-one thousand dollars and earned him honorary membership in Local 6.

One of the board's rising stars, Philip Boone, who in 1939 had founded the Symphony Forum at the University of California, launched the San Francisco Symphony Foundation in 1953, aimed at generating interest in the Symphony and raising money in small amounts from a large number of people. The Foundation's ultimate purpose was to help build an endowment fund. As a *Chronicle* headline announced in January 1954, "The Era of the Big Symphony Angels is Over—You, Too, Can Help." Boone's plan was to recruit a battalion of smaller angels. Membership in the Foundation cost ten dollars. So successful was Boone that, by March 1954, he was able to deliver two checks, one for $24,342 to be applied to the endowment fund, the other for $17,002 for current season operations.

Zellerbach, like former board president Richard Tobin so many years before him, admired musicians. Unlike Tobin, Zellerbach understood fund-raising. When the May T. Morrison Trust Estate pledged to contribute two hundred thousand dollars to the endowment fund, contingent upon the Association raising three hundred thousand dollars from other sources, Zellerbach ensured that the Symphony upheld its end of the bargain within the year the Morrison Trust had stipulated, thus bringing the endowment a healthy influx of cash.

Zellerbach was a taskmaster. In 1955, observing that contributions had fallen below the preceding year by seven thousand dollars, he admonished his colleagues, noting that such a downturn pointed in the wrong direction, but he also took pride in the knowledge that the Symphony's

7

1954–55 gross ticket income of $351,300 placed San Francisco near the top of US orchestras with comparable annual budgets. Only four had earned more. He spoke of the need to erase deficits and not allow them to accumulate. The orchestra, he said, was "the cultural heritage of San Francisco." He was determined to lead it to even greater acclaim than that of the Monteux years.

Zellerbach was fortunate in the board colleagues who supported him in his efforts. Besides Boone, there was Charles Blyth, a man who knew his finances and who had been dedicated to the Symphony since the 1930s. And there was Anna-Logan Upton, a diminutive woman with a giant personality, and a gentility she had absorbed in her native South. Mrs. Upton, who enjoyed a good time and was sure others did too, felt responsible to the position she

occupied in the upper tiers of San Francisco society. She was the kind of person who said things like, "San Franciscans have champagne in their blood," and meant it. Acting on that belief, she organized what became and remains a Symphony tradition, the Black & White Ball, introduced to the city on April 19, 1956. One of the ball's goals was to help recoup the twenty-five thousand dollars in annual income lost when the *Standard Hour* radio broadcasts were canceled in 1955, victim of television and the long-playing record. The first Black & White Ball was a success. Conductor André Kostelanetz had so enjoyed performing there that he offered to fly from Paris at his own expense so he could participate again in 1957, when an encore of the event was planned.

When the Eisenhower Administration named Zellerbach Ambassador to Italy in 1956, to succeed playwright and former member of Congress Clare Boothe Luce, he resigned the Symphony presidency, confident in his board colleagues' continuing good stewardship. Replacing him was Kenneth Monteagle, scion of a civic-minded San Francisco family whose Symphony roots ran deep. Assisting Monteagle as executive vice-president was the redoubtable Anna-Logan Upton. Zellerbach had one more order of business before he left. He proposed approaching the Ford Foundation for a grant. He knew that corporate America would be a future source of funding.

As he embarked for Rome, Zellerbach must have felt he had left matters in good hands, starting with the man on the podium. Early in the year he had argued successfully for a full extension of Enrique Jordá's contract, on which the Association had a three-year option. But at the February meeting that ended with Jordá's

reengagement, signs of uncertainty had appeared. The question was whether the conductor should be offered a year's extension, or be hired for two more years, or for three. Zellerbach believed that to offer fewer than two years would suggest a lack of confidence in Jordá. He stressed that Jordá had exhibited enormous promise, and that he had earned the right to more time. Critics Frankenstein and Fried, he argued, were impressed. Letters to the Symphony were twenty to one in Jordá's favor.

Ava Jean Pischel and Phil Boone submitted a reasonable recommendation. Offer Jordá a three-year contract, they suggested, but also form a committee to examine other conductors during the next three years, so that Jordá could be evaluated more objectively. What was never said for the record, but what is clear from the amount of soul-searching that took place, is that most of those present harbored reservations about their music director. Zellerbach dismissed Pischel and Boone's suggestion. To form a committee such as they recommended, he said, would be tantamount to casting a vote of no confidence. After a motion to reengage Jordá for a full three years passed, Zellerbach congratulated his colleagues on their decision, then shared a letter from none other than Leonora Wood Armsby. In it, she shared her high opinion of Jordá. She counseled reengaging him, for such an extension would give him time to show all he could do, and enough time "to establish himself more firmly in the leadership of our great orchestra." Her words beg the question of why he needed more time, and suggest his leadership had been less than firm. Even she seemed uncertain of what he might offer. Perplexing and inspirational,

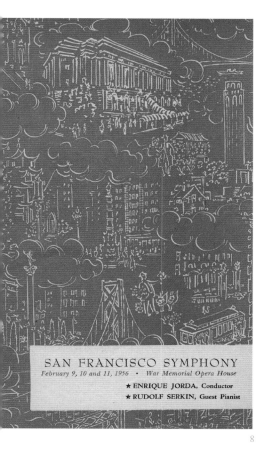

SAN FRANCISCO SYMPHONY
February 9, 10 and 11, 1956 • War Memorial Opera House
★ ENRIQUE JORDA, Conductor
★ RUDOLF SERKIN, Guest Pianist

8

membership concerts

SFSF 1954 SEASON

MARCH 17, 21 and 23, 1954
WAR MEMORIAL OPERA HOUSE

san francisco symphony foundation

9

7
—

Enrique Jordá and composer Ferde Grofé—of Grand Canyon Suite *fame—in April 1960, when Grofé led the orchestra in his* San Francisco Suite. *Between them is Anna-Logan Upton.*

8
—

The program book cover in 1956 depicted San Francisco as a destination city. This program featured pianist Rudolf Serkin, a regular guest between 1949 and 1986. In 1958 he would become the first artist to donate his services to the musicians' Pension Fund.

9
—

The San Francisco Symphony Foundation had no formal relationship with the Symphony Association but offered its members a way to get close to the music.

Jordá—the clear choice in 1954— had not become the music director everyone had hoped for.

SETTING THE SCENE
FOR TRAGEDY

"Little by little," Philip Boone recalled in 1973, "a rejection [of Jordá] began to set in." Jordá's problems with English, his inefficient rehearsal technique, and occasional memory lapses undermined the orchestra's respect for him. Little by little is how it happened, but eventually the trickle broke into a torrent.

All seemed calm through 1957, the year failing eyesight forced Naoum Blinder, concertmaster since the days of Issay Dobrowen, to yield his post to Frank Houser. The next year, local baseball fans rejoiced when the Giants moved from New York to San Francisco. The team opened the

season at Seals Stadium, treating the crowd to an 8-0 shutout over their old East Coast rivals the Dodgers, who were also playing their first year in a new California home.

Early in 1958, composer Virgil Thomson conducted the orchestra, and Stravinsky returned to lead his *Apollo* and his third version of the *Firebird* Suite. In May, Enrique Jordá's contract was once again the subject of a board meeting. The contract was due to expire at the end of the 1958–59 season, and now Kenneth Monteagle urged a five-year extension. Monteagle, Boone would later conclude, had yielded to pro-Jordá forces on the board, although at this point the conductor still enjoyed the support of critics Fried and Frankenstein. Zellerbach wrote from Rome, citing all he believed Jordá had done for the orchestra. He predicted a new period of progress, now about to commence. He thought

the wise move would be to tie Jordá to San Francisco by extending his employment. Backed by powerful advocates, Jordá received his contract renewal. Considered purely on a box-office basis, the move appeared smart. Ticket sales continued strong throughout the 1958–59 season, one of whose highlights was the local debut of the young Texas pianist Van Cliburn, who in 1958 had won the Gold Medal in Moscow's Tchaikovsky Competition and become an immediate Cold War culture hero, seeming to bridge Soviet and US differences through his art.

In retrospect, Jordá continues to puzzle. While the musicians he worked with could express misgivings, some podium colleagues had high praise. Conductor Leopold Ludwig, in town to conduct Strauss's *Die Frau ohne Schatten* and Berg's *Wozzeck* at the San Francisco Opera, was concerned that he might need

123

more rehearsal time with the orchestra for these difficult works, as he did in Vienna. Afterward, both he and the Opera's Kurt Herbert Adler marveled at the orchestra's first-rate performances. Adler maintained that five years ago this could not have happened, and that credit for the ensemble's flexibility was due solely to Jordá—a curious statement that discounts not only the musicians' contribution, but also Leopold Ludwig's. Besides, as Joe Scafidi has said, the orchestra was widely known for its agility, which it developed by playing not only for the Symphony but also for the Opera and the San Francisco Ballet.

"I think we can do better," said John F. Kennedy throughout the campaign that led him to the White House in the election of 1960. In San Francisco in this new era, a potential source of arts funding was in the offing, its source a proposed hotel tax that would funnel collected monies to arts organizations. The twentieth-century zeitgeist was evident in Symphony programming, which in 1960–61 included works by such celebrated modernists as Shostakovich, Schoenberg, Kirchner, Hindemith, Berio, Henze, Lutosławski,

10

and Milhaud, and by many lesser known names. The next year would see the establishment of a Symphony series on the Peninsula, south of San Francisco, in Los Altos. Over all this hovered the spirit of the early Kennedy era, the belief in doing better.

In San Francisco, that spirit became evident early in 1961. Some critics, notably Alexander Fried of the *Examiner* and

Jack Loghner of the *News Call-Bulletin*, were voicing displeasure with Jordá, and concert attendance was diminishing—although the amount of contemporary music Jordá programmed might have had something to do with that. Alfred Frankenstein, as a member of the Symphony staff, encouraged such programs. As a member of the press, he also supported Jordá in print. But to be championed by such a critic could hurt Jordá, for Frankenstein's Symphony ties undermined his credibility.

On the morning of February 16, 1961, the board's Executive Committee met to discuss the emerging bad press. Monteagle claimed the committee had studied the situation but did not elaborate. The conclusion was to go into denial—not to address complaints with action, but with a resolution: that the Symphony was committed to high standards, that Jordá's contributions had been magnificent, that ticket sales, while in decline, were still well above the national average, and that the board had complete faith in Jordá and the orchestra. After reading the resolution to his colleagues, Monteagle summoned Loghner and Fried, who had been waiting outside the room, and read them the statement.

Resolutions solved nothing. Soon the board convened in an attempt to determine if criticism was justified. As Philip Boone pointed out years later, someone with good musical instincts and experience and knowledge could have helped at this point, and that person would have been manager Howard Skinner. For whatever reason, Skinner avoided involvement. While praising Skinner for his commitment to the organization, Boone felt he had neglected his responsibility in failing to emphasize how serious matters stood. Now the board pondered asking members of the orchestra their opinions. Mrs. Upton fumed. Much of the harm, she said, came from the musicians themselves, who were open in their criticism of Jordá. She recommended reprimanding the whistle-blowers.

J. D. Zellerbach disagreed. Having left his ambassadorial post, he was back in San Francisco and would soon be reinstated as board president. Now he noted how many personnel changes Jordá had made—between thirty-five and forty members of the orchestra had come on board during his tenure—and change so drastic was never easy. Such an amount of new talent would also have called for clear and firm direction to help integrate it into the orchestra, and since such direction was exactly where Jordá was found wanting, ensemble problems may well have grown as more new players were recruited. This was not, however, raised as an issue. But Zellerbach did go on record for the first time with a criticism of Jordá, noting a stiff podium style that somehow distressed the audience. Despite his misgivings, Zellerbach concluded the problem was one of public relations, not artistic deficiencies.

But artistic shortcomings made for bad PR, and together they made for a Jordá Problem, which all through March and April a special committee investigated, with no clear result. Zellerbach was increasingly concerned. Contributions had been down since the 1959–60 season, from almost $256,000 to $208,000. Ticket sales for 1960–61 were $43,000 under budget. The Black & White Ball, which netted $35,000 in 1960, netted $27,000 in 1961. This was an organization in trouble.

With the Symphony's fiftieth anniversary season approaching in 1961–62, some board members wondered if one day Jordá would have to be bought out of his contract, especially if ticket sales continued to be poor—1960–61 posted a loss of a thousand season tickets. Zellerbach, determined to erase the writing from the wall and make the conductor a success, proposed welcoming Jordá publicly when he returned from Europe to start the Golden Season.

The Golden Season of 1961–62 was due to open on November 22. Phil Boone had devised a scheme to herald Jordá's arrival back in San Francisco on November 19. A reception would be held at the Ferry Building. From San Francisco International Airport, where Jordá was due to arrive from Europe via New York, a helicopter would transport him across the city and descend as the party began.

Everything hinged on Jordá making his New York connection. Boone had worked with American Airlines to ensure that all went smoothly. Jordá had adequate time to make his San Francisco flight from New York. Through some miscommunication, he missed it. Two hundred friends and board members were waiting at the Ferry Building when the helicopter arrived, minus the guest of honor. That evening Boone's board colleague Mortimer Fleishhacker took him aside. "I don't know what we can do," he said. "We just can't win with this man."

BELIEVING GEORGE SZELL'S EARS
Leonora Wood Armsby died on January 20, 1962, spared the final act of the Jordá drama. On March 14, George Szell arrived in San Francisco to conduct two weeks of concerts. Szell, music director since 1946 of the

11

125

10
_____

Kenneth Monteagle, Symphony president from 1956 to 1961.

11
_____

Frank Houser, concertmaster from 1957 to 1964.

Scene from the 2005 edition of the Black & White Ball.

GLITTER AND DO GOOD:
THE BLACK & WHITE BALL

The year was 1956, a half century since the city had been leveled by the great earthquake and fire. Five decades after that catastrophe, not one sign of its destruction was apparent. In the wake of the earthquake, San Francisco had turned crisis into opportunity. Now Symphony board President J. D. Zellerbach wanted to turn opportunity into an event, an event to commemorate the 1906 quake, to celebrate the city that had risen on its ruins, and most of all, to raise funds for the Symphony—which, like its thriving hometown, had been conceived in the civic response to the earthquake's devastation. From its inception, the Black & White Ball was an affair that rejoiced in San Francisco spirit: when things are rough, or when they're not, throw a party.

Zellerbach borrowed the black-and-white idea from Italy, where he had attended a grand ball whose dance floor was populated by guests clad in those colors. To board Vice-President Anna-Logan Upton he assigned the task of finding a suitable venue for such a ball. Diminutive, iron-willed, and canny, Anna-Logan Upton enjoyed challenges as much as she enjoyed her power to meet them. This time, however, she seemed puzzled. Civic Auditorium was insufficiently elegant. But no other place was large enough to contain the crowds she hoped to draw. Then came inspiration. The ball would be held in four of the city's top hotels, enabling her to stage not one ball but four parties: four, just as a symphony typically includes four movements. Each party would have its own theme and name. At the Sheraton-Palace, it was *Valse allegro brillante*. At the St. Francis, *Fandango vivace*. At the Fairmont, *Rondo con spirito*. At the Mark Hopkins, *Molto be bop*. (continued)

If *Molto be bop* seems a little square, remember that this was 1956. The generation that had endured the Great Depression and World War II now reveled in postwar prosperity and relative calm, but its members knew that some hipness was good for the soul. They were unaware of how wrenchingly their children would challenge their ideals of social stability. For 1956 was about more than good times as good times had come to be interpreted. It was the year of Allen Ginsberg's *Howl*, and the Beat era was dawning. Just a month before the Black & White Ball appeared on the scene, Elvis Presley's debut album had hit the record stores.

It began at ten on a Thursday evening, April 19, 1956. At the Sheraton-Palace, Admiral Chester Nimitz, commander of the Pacific Fleet during World War II, embraced Anna-Logan Upton and waltzed her across the floor as Enrique Jordá led members of the San Francisco Symphony in Strauss's *Tales from the Vienna Woods*. A crew of 473 volunteers had answered Mrs. Upton's call to help with the décor, and under the direction of professional designers they put their arts-and-crafts skills to work. The perimeter of the Palace ballroom was defined by fern-covered boxes that anchored trees topped by globes of flowers, all white and pink—gardenias, azaleas, stock, roses. At the Fairmont a twenty-three-foot obelisk peaked in a gold sunburst, décor was all gold and white, hedges were sprayed with copper-colored paint, tables were set with gold candelabra and black candles. The Mural Room of the St. Francis was flanked with white and black palms, "and the portrait of a gorgeous senorita filled the wall behind the band stand"—where Cal Tjader and his orchestra played a medley of Latin favorites. Afterward, décor was sold to partygoers as souvenirs. The Palace rose trees fetched twenty-five dollars a trunk, and a flock of stuffed parakeets five dollars each.

The four ball venues were spaced at considerable distances from each other. Guests shuttled between the hotels on a fleet of buses that departed at five-minute intervals and that were decorated, as the hyperbole of the era's social pages would have it, "to look like carriages for a queen." One wonders what sort of royalty would have entered coaches trimmed, as another columnist described them, "to the hub caps with streamers and banners." No matter. As the evening went on, the mood grew more festive—the ball's major sponsor, after all, was Black and White Scotch whisky—and the buses themselves became party vehicles, filled with laughter and song. One couple claimed to have had such a good time riding the streets that they had forgone the indoor pleasures.

The cost of admission was ten dollars per person, a sum that seems a remarkable bargain but which, fifty-five years later, translates to eighty dollars, minus drinks. Attendance tallied at four thousand, and the Symphony netted $24,000, more

ADMIT ONE
to the
BLACK AND WHITE
Symphony Ball
THURSDAY
APRIL 19, 1956
10 p.m. until 2 a.m. at all 4 hotels

3268 $10.00

Free transportation on special shuttle buses available at all 4 hotels.

Valse:
Allegro Brillante
The Sheraton-Palace

Fandango Vivace
The St. Francis

Rondo Con Spirito
The Fairmont

Molto Be Bop
The Mark Hopkins

The 1956 Black & White Ball, St. Francis Hotel.

than $187,000 in the currency of 2011. The Thursday night—chosen because the hotels and the orchestra were booked on weekends—was "too hard on the men," Mrs. Upton admitted, for of course the men were the ones who had to face work the next morning. But Anna-Logan Upton had no regrets. Years later she recalled how she was thrilled "to stand on Nob Hill and look down on what had once been charred ruins and think of how in 50 years the City had been so beautifully rebuilt and how it was now celebrating. It was like a miracle, a great romantic celebration."

It was a hit, and it was repeated in 1957, and again in 1959, 1960—when the theme honored two new states, Alaska and Hawaii—and 1962, when comedian Bob Hope was the headliner. By 1969, Mrs. Upton and her cadre of planners were searching the soul of the ball, and to some extent it became black and white in the racial mix of its guests as well as in its sartorial theme. The headliners that year: the Grateful Dead. They played at the Hilton Hotel, and they drew a younger crowd, which was really the point. But by 1969, those who had been youngsters in 1956 had grown into rebels. The mix of old and young turned sour. The Dead's Jerry Garcia had just finished a chat with columnist Herb Caen, and as Garcia walked away Caen was approached by a woman he described as a "society matron."

"Oh, it talks, does it?" she asked. "What in the world do you find to *say* to people like that?"

"I couldn't find anything to say to her so I left," Caen reported.

It would be his last Black & White Ball, or anyone's, for thirteen years. Mrs. Upton had not been happy with the ball's young guests. "It was the hippie era and these young people, some of them children of my good friends, behaved so badly," she recalled in 1987. "There was drunkenness, boorishness, dope and even vandalism." She was appalled when she discovered that seven murals created by artist Antonio Sotomayor,

paintings she had sold for $150 each to raise more money, had all been defaced. Under such a weight, the camel's back gave way. "Until people can behave like ladies and gentlemen," declared Anna-Logan Upton, "there will be no ball."

Her word was final. Until 1982. That was when board President Brayton Wilbur, Jr., asked Charlotte Mailliard what kind of Symphony benefit would be a good draw. Mailliard, then San Francisco's chief of protocol, knew her parties, and she told Wilbur that the Black & White Balls were the best parties the Symphony had ever given. She recommended reviving them—but not as they had been, for she believed that memory has a way of gilding the past, and any attempt at duplication was sure to fall short. She was intrigued by the architecture of San Francisco's Civic Center—the Opera House, the Veterans Building, City Hall, and the newly built Davies Symphony Hall—and she suggested using these buildings as ball venues. So it was proposed; and so—but for a few excursions to the Embarcadero in the 1990s—it was done.

In its later incarnations, the ball evolved into an extravaganza complete with light shows that swept the night clouds and pulsed across the façades of the Civic Center buildings. A special performance in Davies Symphony Hall preceded the ball proper. Singer Seal was featured there in 2008, Tony Bennett and k. d. lang in 2010. One constant over the years was the epic street scene, the cascading waves of black and white: men and women, handsome and gorgeous in evening dress, the duo-chrome vision surreal and memorable, the vast late-night crowd showered with fireworks heralding the Midnight Surprise.

The Black & White Ball seems a metaphor for pure pleasure, but this party bore a serious rationale, for the funds it raised were earmarked for Symphony education programs. Those who believe music celebrates life know that the ball, in its efforts on behalf of San Francisco schoolchildren, has celebrated music.

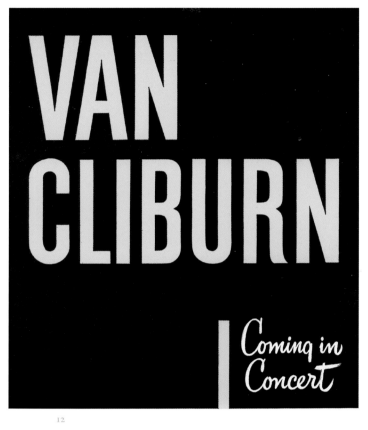

12

Cleveland Orchestra, had transformed that ensemble into one of the world's greatest orchestras. A wunderkind who had once been hailed as the next Mozart, Szell conducted the Berlin Philharmonic at seventeen and went on to become a protégé of Richard Strauss. An obsessive perfectionist, he was tyrannical on the podium, feared but also widely respected.

Szell conducted his first week in San Francisco, then departed, claiming illness. But people began talking. Was exhaustion truly the reason for his departure?

Alfred Frankenstein was a man whose sense of his own rectitude compelled him to press forward with arguments he would have done better to concede. In George Szell, he met his match. On March 24, he wrote to Szell:

Dear Mr. Szell:
Many thanks for your extremely kind and thoughtful letter. We were very much distressed, of course, to learn that you could not conduct here this week, and hope you had a good refreshing rest. We are all very sorry, also, that we could not hear you this week, and I personally also regret very much that we could not lunch together.

As the enclosed telegram indicates, there has been a grand crop of rumors all over the country about your withdrawal from the local scene, and this has not been at all good for the San Francisco Symphony. It would, therefore, be a just,

proper and pleasant gesture if Mr. Jordá could be invited to serve as guest conductor in Cleveland next season. I hastily add that I propose this entirely on my own, and that Jordá would be furious at me if he knew I was doing it.

Two days later, Szell replied:
Dear Mr. Frankenstein:
Up until this moment I have tried to be as polite and discreet as possible about my early departure from San Francisco. Your letter of March 24, however, contains a tactless provocation which compels me to step out of my reserve.

Since you presume to tell me what would be a "just, proper and pleasant" thing to do, I feel forced to say that your delicate dual position as Music Critic of the Chronicle and Program Annotator for the San Francisco Symphony, which in itself is liable to cast grave doubts upon your objectivity, should have prompted you to exercise particular restraint in this matter. It is entirely out of order for you to suggest my taking a step designed to be interpreted as implicit approval of what I found to be the saddest state of musical affairs I have encountered in any American or European city during the almost fifty years of my active conducting career.

Since you have reopened this question which I thought closed, and because it is a matter of public interest I reserve the right to make our correspondence accessible to other persons.

Szell forwarded a copy of his letter, along with one of Frankenstein's, to Alexander Fried, who knew a good story when he saw one and published both in the March 28 Examiner.

Exactly what Szell encountered at his concerts is unclear. Poet Kenneth Rexroth, then an *Examiner* columnist, used Szell's letter as the opportunity to launch a diatribe of his own,

---

12
———

Van Cliburn became a Cold War hero to Americans when he won the Soviet Union's International Tchaikovsky Competition in 1958. A year later, he made his debut with the San Francisco Symphony.

13
———

Enrique Jordá with Boston Pops conductor Arthur Fiedler, a San Francisco summer fixture from the 1950s to the 1970s, when he led Symphony pops concerts. At right: the San Francisco Opera's Kurt Herbert Adler.

claiming to have long wondered what was happening under Jordá's leadership. He agreed with Szell. Things were falling apart.

Zellerbach, asked to comment on Szell's letter when it became public, disputed Szell's assessment of the musical affairs in San Francisco. "I think the man is emotionally immature," he maintained. Zellerbach's read on Szell is less defensive than it may seem. George Szell was known not just for the perfection of his performances, but for his vicious tongue. And for all his dedication to artistic integrity, he enjoyed the attention of the press and liked to plant the seeds of scandal. When *Time* reported in 1963 on an altercation he was said to have had with pianist Glenn Gould, Szell professed shock at the story and pronounced it apocryphal, although Gould would learn that Szell himself had been its source. The *Time* article also suggested that Szell failed to take seriously the role he had played in Enrique Jordá's life. In his criticism he had only been trying, he said, to be "a good boy." A conducting colleague was blunt: "Szell is one of the world's great musicians and a cold, cold sonofabitch."

What was Enrique Jordá to do? A conducting god had damned him. At the rehearsal the morning after Szell's letter was published, the musicians made a point of applauding him, but how he managed to show up for work is anyone's guess. He was, as both Philip Boone and Agnes Albert would recall, in a situation he failed fully to comprehend.

Although Szell had so summarily dismissed Frankenstein's idea of a conductor exchange, board member Mary Faber found merit in it and suggested that Jordá might trade places with the conductors of other major US orchestras, as guest. But Jordá's manager already reported that he could not find guest engagements for his client anywhere in the country. Zellerbach had been attending rehearsals to determine how other conductors worked. He wanted musicians' opinions. Boone accused Fried of shirking responsibility to the orchestra and the best interests of the community.

But Boone was nearing a conclusion. Jordá's position had become impossible, yet Boone knew that if Zellerbach asked him to leave, pro-Jordá factions would revolt against the Association president. Boone himself was the only person who could do what needed doing, and in a meeting with Jordá one night, he asked him to resign. He told him he owed it to himself, his family, and his friends to take matters into his own hands. The next morning Jordá phoned Boone to say he agreed. On May 2, Zellerbach shared the conductor's letter of resignation with the board.

Jordá would remain for another season while his successor was sought. A Conductor Selection Committee organized to search for the new music director had already stipulated three criteria: that the candidate be of international stature, that he would have conducted American orchestras before American audiences, and that he be able to speak competent English. As insurance against making the same mistake twice, those were good starting points, and when the esteemed Viennese conductor Josef Krips was named to take over, future success was all but assured. Already Krips had made a decision that would determine the Symphony's course in coming years. Unable to appear with

131

13

SAN FRANCISCO SYMPHONY PREVIEW

A TIMELY RADIO SHOW

presented by

KNBC

AS A PUBLIC SERVICE

in cooperation with

THE SAN FRANCISCO SYMPHONY ASSOCIATION

Sundays 7:30 - 8:00 p.m.
680 AM and 99.7 FM

Featuring

ALEXANDER FRIED
HOST - MODERATOR

Mr. Fried, distinguished Music Critic of the San Francisco Examiner, is host-moderator of this series of radio shows geared to Symphony-goers, and will be heard every Sunday evening throughout the Symphony Season.

Highlights of forthcoming Symphony Concerts will be discussed and musically illustrated with excerpts from recordings; guest artists and members of the orchestra will be interviewed; and problems involved in the presentation of orchestral music will be analyzed.

14

the orchestra for a week of concerts in 1963, he suggested as his replacement a young Japanese conductor, Seiji Ozawa, who had made his Symphony debut the year before.

The debacle in which Jordá's tenure ended had cost the Symphony prestige, but the resilience of both the orchestra and the organization would soon be proven. Nor was all the news distressing. During the Jordá period, many new works entered the Symphony's logbook. Along with innovative fund-raising, dedicated volunteers assumed greater responsibility, not just in grassroots efforts such as the San Francisco Symphony Foundation, but also in spectacular events like the Black & White Ball, which proved that those who loved highbrow music also knew how to have fun. The musicians' Pension Fund, established at last, offered a measure of financial security to those who had devoted their lives to the Symphony. Businesses and corporations began contributing to the community good by helping music's cause. Incredibly, considering the preoccupation that the Jordá affair created, a plan to absorb the Oakland Symphony had been explored, Zellerbach's belief being that the Bay Area could support only a single major orchestra. (The merger seemed to have some chance of success until death claimed its main East Bay supporter, Oakland Symphony president Thomas Price.) Over the course of eight years, musicians' salaries increased 29 percent, outpacing the national rate of inflation by about 1 percent. And, awakening from the bad dream in which Enrique Jordá's term concluded, the board would become increasingly sensitive to the needs of the music and those who made the music. The organization as a whole had taken another step,

albeit a painful one, on the path to professional management.

Outside the concert hall in these early years of the new decade, US military involvement in Indochina increased, the country unaware of its implications, and unprepared for an imminent catastrophe that would establish the tone of the century's remaining decades. In the midst of this, the San Francisco Symphony was finding its place among the great arts organizations of the modern era. If growing pains were part of the process, so be it.

Although "so be it" is a heartless way to bid Enrique Jordá farewell. At the close of this drama, the stage was strewn with corpses, for Jordá was not the only one to depart. Alfred Frankenstein left the San Francisco Symphony after twenty-five years as program annotator. His friendship with Alexander Fried was at an end. Within a year J. D. Zellerbach would die suddenly, to be replaced as Symphony president by Philip Boone. Only George Szell, who had played Iago, seemed untouched by what he had set in motion. To the end of his days in San Francisco, Jordá retained loyalties. On a memo attached to Zellerbach's written acceptance of the conductor's resignation, the Symphony's public relations consultant, Vic Weston, scrawled a red-penciled comment in screaming bold letters: "God bless Jordá!!!" Whether he left San Francisco with or without blessing, Enrique Jordá would never head a major orchestra again.

SAN FRANCISCO SYMPHONY

Golden Season

Enrique Jordá, Conductor and Musical Director

GEORGE SZELL, *Guest Conductor*
March 14, March 15, March 16, 1962
War Memorial Opera House

15

16

17

14

San Francisco Examiner *music critic Alexander Fried, who published an unfortunate exchange of letters.*

15

Even in a formal portrait, the gaze is withering: George Szell, who triggered a chain of events that ended in Enrique Jordá's departure.

16

San Francisco Chronicle *music critic and Symphony program annotator Alfred Frankenstein, who made the mistake of offering George Szell a suggestion.*

17

The recording of Falla's Nights in the Gardens of Spain *reveals an orchestra that produces rich textures and luminous sound.*

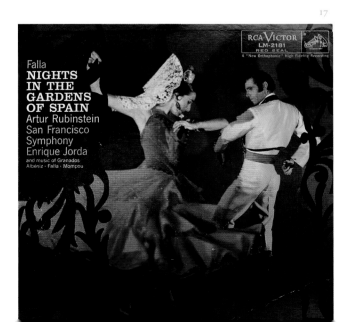

Falla
NIGHTS IN THE GARDENS OF SPAIN
Artur Rubinstein
San Francisco Symphony
Enrique Jorda
and music of Granados
Albéniz · Falla · Mompou

RCA VICTOR
LM-2181
RED SEAL
A "New Orthophonic" High Fidelity Recording

BREAKING THE COLOR BARRIER: CHARLES BURRELL JOINS THE SYMPHONY

Even before Charles Burrell joined the San Francisco Symphony in 1959, African-American musicians had been members of symphony orchestras in the United States, but none had yet found a post in so prominent an ensemble.

Burrell was born in Toledo, Ohio, in 1920 and grew up in Detroit. He started lessons on the string bass and tuba when he was twelve, and not long after that he tuned in his crystal radio set to a San Francisco Symphony broadcast. He remembered the conductor, Pierre Monteux. "That was the exact moment I determined that I wanted to become a professional musician," he said years later. His goal became more specific. He wanted to become the first black musician in the San Francisco Symphony.

He graduated from what was then a top music school, Cass-Technical High School in Detroit. Cass-Tech alumni were usually prime candidates for orchestra work. Charlie Burrell was not. He was black.

His first teacher, the Detroit Symphony's principal bass player, agreed to take him as a student, on condition he not play the classics. The classics were for white people. Charles Burrell was glad for the instruction and ignored the condition. Later, when he began studies with another Detroit Symphony musician, Oscar Legassey, he discovered he had been taught incorrect techniques, on purpose. Legassey was different. He encouraged him. He set standards. He demanded that Burrell study the

classics. But, as most bass players know, music is about more than the classics of the concert hall. Burrell also played jazz. He was sixteen when he began his lessons with the great Al McKibbon, who became a mentor and inspiration. Another jazz giant, Milt Hinton, also left his mark. "He gave me my first real lessons in jazz and also my first real lesson in life. I mean he taught me some things you don't learn in books. I mean how to be a person, how to take care of and respect yourself, and how to respect others."

Fats Waller, Lionel Hampton, Billie Holiday—Charlie Burrell played with them all. Then he enrolled at the New England Conservatory of Music. It was 1941, wartime, and soon he was in the US Navy, playing in the first-ever all-black Navy band. Stationed near Chicago, he continued his studies at Northwestern University, then completed his music degree at Wayne State. A teaching job in the Detroit schools was denied him because of his color. No matter. It was as a classical musician that Burrell wanted to make his mark. Milt Hinton told him to keep at it, told him he could do it.

He did. His first orchestra job was with the Denver Symphony. In 1959, visiting San Francisco, he parked near the War Memorial Opera House. As he was leaving his car, he noticed the bass case in the back seat of a vehicle just pulling up. He struck up a conversation with the driver: Philip Karp, the San Francisco Symphony's principal bass. Karp asked him if he was interested in auditioning for the orchestra. Fast forward to Burrell's first rehearsal as a member of the San Francisco Symphony. He was at his place in the section when the conductor walked on stage. A guest conductor. More than forty years later, Burrell recalled that day. "If there were one moment in my life as a musician that I consider my glory, it was showing up for that first rehearsal with the San Francisco Symphony when out walks Pierre Monteux. It was like the Messiah had walked in. There has never been a moment like that before or after. That was paradise."

Charles Burrell remained with the orchestra for five years. During that time he also taught at the San Francisco Conservatory of Music, where one of his students was George Duke—his cousin—destined to become a leading jazz pianist. Charlie spent summers with Earl "Fatha" Hines's big band. He left San Francisco, at last, for the reason many non-natives leave. Enrico Caruso had forsaken the city after the ground shook him awake in April 1906. Burrell felt the earth heave, concluded he needed none of that, and returned to Denver. There, he groomed his niece, Dianne Reeves, for a singing career in whose course she went on to win four Grammys. And he was back in the Denver Symphony, where he performed until 1999. "Music is my great love affair and, in fact, it is my first [love] and always has been my first." Besides, he had accomplished what he set out to do when he was twelve.

Charles Burrell during his San Francisco Symphony years, backstage at the War Memorial Opera House.

VII.

MUSICAL BODY-BUILDING

The Josef Krips Years (1963–1970)

"LET US CONTINUE"

The ensemble that Josef Krips encountered in his first rehearsal with the San Francisco Symphony in November 1963 was not the kind of "wrecked orchestra" Leonora Wood Armsby had described to Pierre Monteux when she hired him in 1935, after an earlier bad period in Symphony history. Krips found the morale of the orchestra good, and he had perhaps encouraged this himself with his opening words: "Ladies and gentlemen, let us begin to make music." Playing commenced. He liked what he heard.

The sound was new, and not only because the conductor was new. Krips had been unhappy with the existing acoustic shell used for the orchestra's Opera House performances. A new shell had been installed just before he arrived. Designed by acoustician Heinrich Keilholz, who created sonic modifications in such venues as the Vienna Musikverein and the Festspielhaus at Salzburg, the fiberglass structure that now lined the back and sides of the Opera House stage provided better musical communication and

a more focused and richer sound for the audience.

Musically, every reason existed to rejoice. Then America stopped. The grand reception planned to welcome Krips to San Francisco on November 25 was canceled. Three days earlier, John F. Kennedy had been assassinated in Dallas, and the country was in mourning. The tragedy would have far-reaching consequences, as yet unforeseeable. For all the distraught confusion now, everyone understood that life had to proceed.

On the Wednesday after Kennedy's death, Thanksgiving eve, the country's new president, Lyndon Johnson, addressed a joint session of Congress and delivered a message to the American public: "Let us continue."

2

3

4

The Symphony season opened November 29, according to schedule, with a gala concert. Phil Boone accompanied Krips to the podium. Boone's request for a moment of silence to honor the slain American president and also the recently deceased J. D. Zellerbach fused national tragedy with local loss. Then, as though to emphasize the urgency of going forward, Boone presented Krips with his baton. He predicted that a golden age of the Symphony was about to begin, and the concert suggested that those words might well be borne out. The orchestra was in fine shape. The program was pure Krips, and purely Viennese: Mozart's *Jupiter* Symphony, Richard Strauss's *Don Juan*, and Brahms's Symphony No. 1.

That evening's music was a sign of things to come. An orchestra hones its skills on core repertory, exactly the repertory of which Josef Krips was a master. Krips was a product of Vienna. Born there in 1902, he studied in his native city with Eusebius Mandyczewski, who had been a close friend of Brahms, and with the great conductor Felix Weingartner, whose assistant Krips became at age nineteen. He learned his trade in regional opera houses and returned to Vienna in 1933 as principal conductor of the State Opera. Forced from that position in 1938 upon the Nazi annexation of Austria, Krips was barred from working in the country of his birth; for although he had been raised a Catholic, his father was Jewish. He conducted in Belgrade for a year, until Yugoslavia fell to the Nazis,

then returned to Austria, working for the war's duration in a factory that canned pickles.

To say that Krips returned to music in 1945 is hardly to give him his due. What he did was rebuild Vienna's musical life. Gathering a group of singers and instrumentalists, he led a performance of Mozart's *Le nozze di Figaro* at the Volksoper in May 1945. He arranged for the Theater an der Wien to become temporary home to the Vienna State Opera while the opera house, destroyed in bombing raids, was restored. When the Musik-verein reopened and the Vienna Philharmonic returned to perform there, Krips was on the podium. Soon he was in demand throughout Europe, and he led all the continent's major orchestras. He spent five years at the head of the London Symphony Orchestra. In 1954 he secured his first US post, as music director of the Buffalo Philharmonic. (Another future San Francisco Symphony music director, Michael Tilson Thomas, would become one of Krips's Buffalo successors in 1971.) Krips first conducted the San Francisco Symphony in 1961. He enjoyed that round of performances and loved the city. In 1962, when he was approached

to take over the orchestra's leader-ship, he brought with him a lifetime of experience and total immersion in European tradition and the Viennese classical style. He was a genuine old-school maestro of an authoritarian mold, a type increasingly rare in 1963 and all but extinct today.

Krips also brought audiences back. Portly and balding, eyes bulging behind thick corrective lenses, he possessed the kind of plump-cheeked smile that sculptors had fashioned for cherubs in Vienna's Baroque churches. But he was more an aveng-ing angel who had winged in to the Bay Area to clean up the musical territory, and concertgoers were prepared to make him theirs. Even as the 1963–64 season opened, ticket sales were thirty-one thousand dol-lars in excess of what they had been in 1962–63.

A man of deep faith who spent time serving meals to the needy at Saint Anthony's kitchen, Krips had a massive appetite for good food and drink, and fine cigars. The illness and early death of his first wife, Mitzi, shrouded him with melan-choly. He moved into a room at the Bohemian Club, where his loneliness was assuaged by the camaraderie of its interesting members, whom he entertained at the piano. His spirit revived after his marriage to Harri-etta Procházka, a musicologist who had been a friend both to him and Mitzi, and who treated his foibles with adoring affection.

Within a few weeks of Krips's arrival, Alfred Frankenstein, who had kept his job as *Chronicle* music critic, would write that the conductor had led the greatest performance of Strauss's *Till Eulenspiegel* he had ever heard. Krips believed he had been hired to trans-form the San Francisco Symphony

7

Joseph A. Scafidi joined the Symphony in 1939 as jack-of-all-trades. He departed in 1978, having served for many years as manager and finally as executive director.

8

Jacob Krachmalnick (second from left), concertmaster from 1964 to 1970. His music-making was as impeccable as his personal style was abrasive.

8

into a great orchestra, the equal of any in the United States, and he was determined to do the job. This would come at a price. On the podium, Krips was an autocrat whose view of music-making was more dictatorial than collaborative.

But he could be a collaborator, too. Flutist Paul Renzi appreciated his honesty. If, in rehearsal, Krips concluded the orchestra was not playing to its potential, he would mince no words. *"That was terrible!"* He held no grudges. After Jordá's broken English, musicians also welcomed Krips's command of the language, although oddities crept in as he translated literally from German. He described sloppy ensemble as "a chicken stable" or, another time, as sounding like salad—a fairly apt rendition of *gemischter Salat*, mixed salad, meaning the ensemble was breaking into bits and pieces, a real mix, a sound-salad. He spent little rehearsal time

lecturing or explaining and maintained that almost everything a conductor communicates to an orchestra can be accomplished with the baton. The musicians were also grateful to be playing more of the meat-and-potatoes works whose repeated performances help perfect their skills: Mozart, Beethoven, Brahms, Bruckner, Mahler, Richard Strauss.

Krips worked on basics, critic Arthur Bloomfield would write years later, when in 1970 he bid the conductor farewell. "He got sections to come in together, without crunching attacks, and to end phrases together." The Krips years, Bloomfield asserted, included the greatest artistic successes in the orchestra's history. And while that statement reflects only the history of which the critic had personal knowledge, it supports the claim that, for the orchestra, Krips's tenure did encompass a kind of Golden Age.

INTO THE SIXTIES

A new music director, a new momentum—the formula seemed simple. But in 1960s America, nothing was simple. Beatlemania, which raised bubble-gum rock 'n' roll to a grander level, arrived in the United States in February 1964 when John Lennon, Paul McCartney, George Harrison, and Ringo Starr mesmerized a national TV audience on the *Ed Sullivan Show*, as Elvis Presley had done a decade before them. A month earlier, a darker and more serious brand of popular music was infused into the culture with the release of Bob Dylan's new album *The Times They Are A-Changin'*. Few musical events could have been so prophetic. On San Francisco's new-music scene, Terry Riley had introduced *In C* that May, heralding a stripped-down, hypnotic style that became known as minimalism. Times were changing, and those who thought change a good thing had only to point to the passage that year of the Civil Rights Act, which extended voting privileges and outlawed racial segregation, and which twelve months earlier had been heralded by a March on Washington in which Martin Luther King, Jr., had outlined his dream of national unity. But acts of Congress were slow in taking hold. As late as 1965, marchers who supported voting rights clashed with troopers at the Edmund Pettus Bridge in Selma, Alabama.

Change stirred at the Symphony as well. Some was unrelated to the times. In May 1964, Howard Skinner, a Symphony mainstay for three decades, retired from his post as manager, to be replaced in that position by his longtime assistant, Joseph Scafidi. William Bernell moved into a post that would come to be known as artistic administrator, hiring and contracting with soloists and guest conductors, and helping to plan programs. Other changes reflected the activism emblematic of the sixties. In 1962, unhappy with the support the American Federation of Musicians offered them, players in orchestras had taken their fate into their own hands when they founded the International Conference of Symphony and Opera Musicians: ICSOM. Musicians' contracts until then had been hammered out largely between boards and local unions. ICSOM opened the way for player involvement through committees of orchestra members and won them the right to ratify their own contracts. In San Francisco, a Symphony season that was short, relative to other major US orchestras, translated into lower annual wages even when the weekly minimum was comparable to wages at other major orchestras. Musicians in the fall of 1964 hoped to move from twenty-six- to thirty-week seasons within three years. Philip Boone discerned the direction in which this was leading. A longer season would demand a new performance space, one where the Symphony would no longer be compelled to share a stage with the Opera and Ballet and which would make possible a year-round Symphony season. San Francisco, Boone believed, had to keep pace with the changing arts scene, and he agreed with a proposal being floated to modernize the War Memorial arts complex with funding from a $29 million bond issue, although that funding would not be realized.

That same year, 1965, saw the founding of the National Endowment for the Arts, which gave the arts the new prestige of mandated government funding. Boone, however, was not optimistic. In his opinion, the time was coming when increased operating costs would soon reduce the number of US orchestras. All this was set in the context of a country seething with tension. In August 1965, the Los Angeles community of Watts exploded in six days of race riots that left thirty-four dead. A year earlier, the Gulf of Tonkin Resolution had led the way to a rapid increase of US troops in South Vietnam.

These were angry years, angry and combative, and those national maladies seemed to filter down right to the inner workings of an orchestra. Consider the San Francisco Symphony's new concertmaster, Jacob Krachmalnick. Krachmalnick's personality was the flint against which his colleagues' pent-up frustrations struck. Bitterness had built throughout the artistic struggles of the Jordá years, the arm-wrestling over contract terms, and the simple fact of knowing that audiences dispensed their affections not on musicians but on conductors, the only orchestra members who produce no sound. Krips understood such things, sympathized with musicians, and liked to think of himself as a colleague— a colleague, however, who never forgot who was boss. While he did not shy from confrontation, he did not enjoy it. In Krachmalnick, he found someone who could be confrontational for him. When dirty work was called for, Jake Krachmalnick was the man to do it.

"Jake's great problem," said Joe Scafidi, "was that he enjoyed insulting his co-musicians." Symphony violinist David Schneider took pride in having mastered the solo part of Roger Sessions's difficult and thorny Violin Concerto. When he invited Krachmalnick to his performance of the work with the San Francisco State University Orchestra, the concertmaster brushed him off. "Why do you play a piece like that? You

9

Krips and the orchestra in action.

10

*Formidable on stage, Krips could
be gregarious behind the scenes.
Here, he meets with members of
the Student Forum.*

11

*Musicians' union president Charles
"Pop" Kennedy.*

must get the same thrill playing the Sessions Concerto as you get from kissing your mother-in-law." (Krips attended the performance and programmed the work, with Schneider as soloist, for the coming season.) Some believed Krachmalnick's high standards were the source of his abrasiveness. Woe to those who failed to measure up! By 1968, when the union slapped Krachmalnick with a suspended fine for his treatment of his fellow musicians, the board promised to dismiss him if the antagonism continued. No one doubted Krachmalnick's dedication to the music. His playing style was so clear and demonstrative that the orchestra could, if necessary, simply follow his lead. But there was a major complication. The orchestra despised him.

Josef Krips felt otherwise. Impressed not only by Krachmalnick's prodigious skills as a violinist and concertmaster but also by his credentials—he had served as leader of the Concertgebouw Orchestra in Amsterdam and of the Philadelphia Chamber Orchestra—Krips relied on him. Before the opening of the 1965–66 season, Krachmalnick drew up a plan in which nearly all the strings were reseated. A conductor occasionally requests that a player be reseated to achieve a particular sonority in the section. Krachmalnick made a wholesale alteration of the seating plan. Some players believed it arbitrary. Many saw it as spelling demotion. String players are often hired for outside performances and teaching posts based on how far to the front of their sections they sit—and since no musician in the orchestra was employed throughout the year by the Symphony, outside job opportunities were crucial. Krachmalnick's plan bruised egos and attacked livelihoods. The musicians did not buy it. On November 29, at the season's

first rehearsal, they voted 60 to 26 to retain the preceding season's seating, or not play. Krips interpreted this as insubordination. He refused to conduct.

Boone and Scafidi had their work cut out. In a session that began that evening and continued into the early morning, years of long-submerged grievances surfaced. Board member Agnes Albert, Association attorney Philip Ehrlich, and a committee of musicians were present, as was the head of Local 6, Charles "Pop" Kennedy. The Association's representatives discovered dissatisfaction that extended back to the Monteux years, bred by minimal job security—an individual's contract could be renewed or denied at the conductor's discretion—inadequate retirement benefits, and health insurance that consisted essentially of a sick musician's colleagues taking up a collection to help cover the costs of illness. Boone, disturbed by the lack of communication between orchestra and Association, sympathized with the players and was intent on further talks, although he was determined to defend the music director's control of artistic issues, mindful of the strides made since Krips's arrival. He fastened especially on Claudio Arrau's words. Arrau, among the leading pianists of his time, had said, "What has happened in San Francisco since 1963 is a musical miracle." The San Francisco Symphony, he claimed, was on its way to becoming one of the nation's great orchestras.

Boone was convincing. For the present, the string players agreed to the new seating. Years later, Krips, still paternalistic and never the most sensitive of men, wrote that, because of the reseating, "our violins began to have a Viennese sound, which I

9

10

11

had not thought possible, and gradually they began to realize this themselves."

THE SCENE SHIFTS

Around the time that representatives of the orchestra and Association had their all-night meeting, the American orchestra scene was reinvented. The Ford Foundation, having listened to what orchestra musicians were saying, agreed that a living wage was a fair wage. The foundation also understood that demands for year-round employment and better living conditions cost money. To help orchestral associations across the United States meet such costs, the foundation devised a matching-grant endowment plan to distribute $80.2 million to sixty-one US orchestras. For the San Francisco Symphony, this meant a grant of $2 million, to be matched over five years with $3 million. An

outright gift of $100,000 per year for each of these five years would aid in meeting operating costs while the money was raised.

Had Symphony musicians needed justification in demanding better working conditions, they would have found it when, in April 1966, no less a national icon than *Time* had placed them in a special class, naming the San Francisco Symphony one of the nation's "Elite Eleven" orchestras. The next month, the *New York Times* wrote enthusiastically of rising contributions—$340,000 in the current year compared to $293,000 in the year immediately preceding—and both Boone and Krips knew that a fine orchestra translated into full houses at concerts and effective fund-raising.

Along with these positive signs, problems remained. Boone and a handpicked committee met every

two or three weeks with orchestra representatives. By late 1966, the issue of reseating remained open. And, in the opinion of the board and Krips, a longstanding issue threatened to keep the orchestra from realizing full potential. This was the issue of "imports"—musicians hired from outside the Bay Area, who were not members of Local 6. Stated briefly: When a vacancy in the orchestra occurred, any Local 6 members who wanted to audition would be heard. If the music director concluded no one was acceptable for the position, a request was made to import a musician from outside. The union would respond in one of two ways. Either it would propose an alternate player from within the local. Or it would grant the import, but bar that person from performing for any other musical organization within the union's jurisdiction for a stipulated period, thus making the Symphony position

An ebullient Josef Krips prepares to board a Cessna, enroute from Grass Valley back to San Francisco.

Eager to establish itself as an orchestra for all of Northern California, the San Francisco Symphony visited Grass Valley on April 23, 1966. This town in the Sierra foothills, founded during the Gold Rush, had its share of history. It had been home to singer Lotta Crabtree and was the birthplace of philosopher Josiah Royce. Now, in collaboration with its neighbor community Nevada City and with support from the California Arts Commission, it brought the orchestra to town.

Grass Valley lies 140 miles northeast of San Francisco, and travel time by automobile is almost three hours. To shorten the trip, a single-engine Cessna would transport Josef Krips, along with Symphony Manager Joseph Scafidi. Krips pressed Scafidi to be sure the pilot had no access to a bar while they were at the concert. The conductor was no stranger to air travel and had flown around the world, but a single-engine Cessna gave

him pause. He was used to being in charge, unaccustomed to confronting an array of aeronautical controls spread in plain sight before him, with no clue what all those knobs and levers meant. Scafidi reassured him. The pilot would be with them at the performance.

The concert: the Overture to Wagner's *Meistersinger*, Richard Strauss's *Don Juan*, and Tchaikovsky's *Pathétique* Symphony. The performance won Krips a new fan: the pilot. Soon they were airborne again, Krips happy his recruitment efforts had borne fruit. Then—*bang!*—the door next to him sprang open and he was looking down hundreds of feet onto Central Valley farmland. Scafidi, seated in back, threw his arms around Krips and held him in a bear hug. He shouted to turn around and get back to the airport.

The next morning, Mrs. Krips was in Scafidi's office. She demanded the pilot be fired. Clearly, he had left the door ajar because he was bent on murdering Josef Krips. From anyone else, the accusation would have been absurd. From Maria Krips—Mitzi—it was another reminder of a paranoia that had its seeds in the cruelties of World War II. She was convinced of a plot against her husband. She ordered the locks changed at their Huntington Hotel apartment. She believed a death ray aimed at their suite would strike him down. Eventually, when Mitzi could no longer travel with him, Krips took up solitary residence at the Bohemian Club. He was a lively bohemian, a card player and a cigar smoker, but he was lonely. He recalled one New Year's Eve, coming back to the club after conducting a concert of Viennese waltzes and polkas, sitting alone with half a bottle of rosé. "You know," he confessed, "I do my performance, and everybody is applauding, and then I go home and there's nothing."

Mitzi's illness was also physical. She soon succumbed to cancer. But this tale is not all unhappy. After Mitzi's death, Krips married the woman who had been her companion and to whom he too had grown close, musicologist Harrietta Procházka—Countess Procházka. Years later, the countess edited Krips's memoirs, *Without Love, You Can Make No Music*. On the ground as in the air, luck was with Josef Krips.

12

less attractive to outsiders. Unions were created to protect their members, and Boone had no problem with protection. But he believed that, when the question was one of optimum artistic excellence, musicians and Association shared a common goal. The best musicians meant better concerts, better concerts meant larger audiences, and larger audiences meant greater stability and better salaries. The talent pool, he believed, had to extend beyond the Bay Area. Simple logic led to the conclusion that the best players could not possibly be concentrated in a single geographical region. Both sides could make good arguments for issues such as these, and both sides did. And when smart and determined people are at odds, common goals become obscured and movement toward those goals stops.

On the morning of January 21, 1967, Philip Boone exercised the moral authority he had earned through his almost thirty-year history with the organization, going back to the first days of the Symphony Forum when he was a Berkeley undergraduate. In retrospect, what he did seems simple, but at the time it was an unprecedented step by the head of the Association. He spoke with the orchestra. He was concerned, he said, that no direct lines of communication existed between board and musicians. Under the current configuration, the board dealt with the union, the union dealt with the orchestra committee, and the committee dealt with the orchestra. He sought common ground. He admitted that, in the past, his Association colleagues had not always appeared sympathetic to the players' plight. Today, he said, "you have a board which thinks you ought to have what you want, that takes pride in you individually, in your families and in your achievements. I think we ought to be doing this thing together."

12
_____

Seiji Ozawa, Krips's handpicked successor, with board member Agnes Albert and Joe Scafidi in 1967, shortly after Ozawa was signed as music director. He assumed that post in 1970.

13

14

13

Symphony percussionist Peggy Cunningham Lucchesi backstage with two of her three young children.

14

Ronald Reagan with his wife, Nancy, their daughter, Patti, and comedian/violinist Jack Benny, after a concert by the San Francisco Symphony in Sacramento on January 4, 1967, in honor of Reagan's inauguration to his first term as California governor.

Today, Boone's call for a gentlemanly and reasonable approach seems timeless, but it was an anachronism in a period of US history when the entire country struggled for focus, when the currents of old and new repelled each other and little except Mozart and Beethoven and Brahms promised stability. On January 4, 1967, California took a turn to the political right when Ronald Reagan was inaugurated governor, in a ceremony at which Krips and the orchestra performed. Then, exactly one week before Boone met with the musicians, hippie culture entered the mainstream of the national consciousness when the first Human Be-In took place in Golden Gate Park. A crowd of thirty thousand gathered, hoping to foment a revolution: not an overthrow of the Johnson Administration, but what a local underground newspaper proclaimed would be "a renaissance of compassion, awareness, and love, and the revelation of unity for all mankind." For the next six months, heeding the call, thousands of young and would-be young streamed into the Haight, celebrating the culture of sex, drugs, and rock and roll, and initiating what would come to be known as the Summer of Love. In June, the Monterey Pop Festival drew even bigger crowds westward and propelled Janis Joplin, The Who, and Otis Redding into the movement's consciousness, with their soundtracks for the free spirit. Middle-class parents alternately wrung their hands and seethed as radios across the country tuned to the gossamer-voiced Scott McKenzie, who sang about going to San Francisco, admonished visitors to wear flowers in their hair, and predicted they would "meet some gentle people there."

In this atmosphere, contract negotiations between the orchestra and the Association began. Throughout the long period of give and take, Boone emphasized the importance of year-round employment to his board colleagues. It was important, he stressed, for the musicians to know that the Association wanted to find solutions.

Other changes were afoot that would affect the future. Josef Krips had long admired the work of the young Japanese conductor Seiji Ozawa, and when he mused about his successor at the San Francisco Symphony, he envisioned Ozawa taking his place. On July 31, the board took a step to ensure that would happen, resolving to open negotiations that would bring Ozawa to San Francisco as music director at the beginning of the 1970–71 season. On October 4, in a meeting in Chicago with Ozawa and his manager, Ronald Wilford, Boone, Scafidi, and Agnes Albert sealed the deal. That Krips had not yet announced his retirement and would learn of the Ozawa decision only a week later, in a letter from Boone, would be a sore point, although Krips was happy in his successor. In fact Boone had made good on his pledge to himself, never to allow a conductor to fall prey to the horrors with which Enrique Jordá had to deal. He had a strong leader in place while the current leader was still strong.

As he looked back on the 1966–67 season, Boone was able to report the kind of artistic successes that had drawn the attention of the national press, including a Beethoven cycle featuring pianist Rudolf Serkin, a youth concert series that had grown to seventeen performances, a series of ten in-school concerts offered to the city's public school children during the summer, and a new-music series, Musica Viva, directed by the dean of American composers, Aaron Copland. Yet Boone saw no way to meet demands for a forty-week season, or a weekly minimum of $225. In 1963–64, the beginning of Krips's tenure, the season had been twenty-four weeks long, the minimum $146.25. The Association proposal for 1967–68 was for thirty-five weeks at a $200 weekly minimum. Boone was not sure it would be enough.

It wasn't. For seven weeks the orchestra went on strike, the first in its history. When a deadlock seemed unbreakable, Mayor Joseph Alioto entered the picture. He invited musicians and Association members to talk. In the middle of an all-night session at his home he woke his sons and asked them to make sandwiches and coffee for everyone. Alioto had sequestered each group in a separate room, and as the parties munched salami and absorbed caffeine he mediated back and forth between them. By dawn, agreement had been reached.

In a sense, the resolution was good all around. The musicians won sick leave, medical insurance, better pay, and, for the first time, a multiyear contract. The Association won the right to bring in imports. The audition process was overhauled to allow musicians and music director substantial input over hiring. A ten-member musicians' committee would audition prospective members. A system was devised whereby a candidate would be required to score at least 200 points to be hired. Each committee member could award up to 10 points. The music director could award up to 150 points. Averaged, the committee could dispense 100 points, total. The musicians could not force their will, nor could the music director force his. The decision had to be mutual. The system worked.

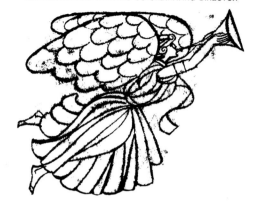

THE SAN FRANCISCO SYMPHONY ASSOCIATION PRESENTS

MUSICA VIVA

A FOUR-PART FESTIVAL OF CONTEMPORARY MUSIC
WITH AARON COPLAND AS CO-ORDINATING DIRECTOR

FOUR OUTSTANDING PROGRAMS - OPERA HOUSE - 8:30 P.M.

JANUARY 30, 31; FEBRUARY 2, 4
1967

GUEST ARTISTS ARE LISTED ON PAGES 9 AND 11

15

15

Aaron Copland, dean of American composers, led the Musica Viva new-music series throughout its three seasons, from 1966 to 1968.

16

Joseph Alioto, San Francisco mayor from 1968 to 1976, helped settle the orchestra's first strike.

147

16

148

17

Lawrence Metcalf. A founding member of the Symphony Forum in 1939, he served as board president from 1974 to 1980.

18

On tour in Japan, Josef Krips and Philip Boone lay a wreath at the memorial to the victims of Hiroshima.

COMPLETING A CIRCLE

As financial vice-president, Lawrence Metcalf saw columns of red ink in the years ahead but remained hopeful. Like Boone, Metcalf had been a founding member of the Symphony Forum in 1939. He was committed to the organization in its artistic and its business aspects. He was an advocate of careful planning, and of increasingly sophisticated predictors of financial performance, such as cost/benefit analyses of soloists' fees compared to the box office returns they brought, and programming effectiveness compared to dollar income. He emphasized the need for a continuing endowment drive and for an effective program of public relations. What Metcalf was describing, although he did not say so outright, was an increasingly professional Symphony management, one equipped with solid business expertise.

Phil Boone believed the orchestra required a home in which it could perform forty weeks each year. Mayor Alioto had pledged support for such a place, but Boone doubted that a bond measure would win much public enthusiasm if it exceeded $10 million, and in fact the project was put on hold. In many ways, a new home, devoted exclusively to the orchestra, would have closed the circle whose arc had been described since 1911. Boone knew other accomplishments had to precede that one. The orchestra was due to embark upon its first tour abroad. In April 1968, Japan would await the San Francisco Symphony. The 1947 transcontinental tour had encompassed fifty-three cities, when fifty-six concerts were played in fifty-seven days. This one would take the musicians to seven cities, for twelve concerts in seventeen days.

Excitement was growing over the Japanese adventure when, true to the spirit of the times, chaos erupted. On April 4, Martin Luther King, Jr., was assassinated in Memphis. African-American communities across the country exploded in outrage. The King murder was another grim marker in a year that had begun with North Vietnamese troops catching US forces off guard, leading to a request for 206,000 additional troops to be dispatched to Southeast Asia and increased anti-war activity at home. In the midst of this, Japan offered welcome relief.

The orchestra's Pacific crossing was troubled. After a stormy landing in Honolulu, low fuel forced an unscheduled stop at Wake Island. The weather at the final destination, Osaka, was so bad that the flight was diverted to Nagoya, after which the trip continued by car, a three-hour drive. Scheduled to arrive in Osaka at five in the evening, the orchestra pulled in at 1 A.M. and found a champagne reception waiting. Krips was dissuaded from scheduling a rehearsal for nine that morning.

The next evening, the orchestra opened the Osaka International Festival. The audience in San Francisco's sister city loved the performance, a reaction repeated along the way in Hiroshima, Nagoya, Nagano, and Chiba. Although Tokyo was more reserved, the tour was a great morale booster and gave the orchestra a sense of its artistic strengths. Krips was delighted. In his memoirs, he proudly quotes Hans Pringsheim, chief critic of Osaka's English-language press, who said that, of the many US orchestras that had visited Japan, he believed the San Francisco Symphony's sound closest to that of a European ensemble. Neither could Krips resist including the *Los Angeles Times* report that a noted Japanese conductor, Fuzo Sotoyama, had said, "Our ears have been accustomed to the best, but what we heard was even better." Programs included Viennese classics from Haydn to Bruckner, but also music of Copland, Stravinsky, and Tchaikovsky, and Japanese composer Tōru Takemitsu.

The tour was a respite from madness. In June, Robert Kennedy, senator from New York and candidate for the Democratic nomination in the 1968 presidential election, was assassinated in Los Angeles. In August, before an international television audience, the Chicago Police Department brutalized antiwar protestors who had arrived to disrupt the Democratic National Convention. President Johnson, commenting on the war in Vietnam, had warned that things would get worse before they got better, and it seemed his prediction applied to US society at large.

The Symphony responded to the times. The board's nominating committee was on the lookout for member prospects from the Japanese and African-American communities. Noting that the atmosphere in the neighborhoods was tense and in need of change, the Association distributed free tickets to community social-service agencies. Mayor Alioto supported this, cognizant that public support for performing arts funding depended on the Symphony reemphasizing its inclusive appeal. The appeal was apparent. During the past season, the number of in-school concerts had increased to thirty. As the year ended, the orchestra presented a concert at the Milton Meyer Recreation Center in the depressed Hunter's Point neighborhood.

The 1968–69 season now beginning would be the longest ever, thirty-six weeks. For Symphony musicians who also played in the San Francisco Opera Orchestra, this meant year-round employment. About thirty others who were not part of the smaller Opera Orchestra still faced three months without work. As the year continued, Larry Metcalf displayed a new kind of thinking at the Symphony, focusing on a longer-range future. Seiji Ozawa had not yet assumed his post at the orchestra's head, but already Metcalf urged that his colleagues begin considering the conductors who might replace him when eventually that time came.

The good news was that the Ford Foundation matching drive begun three years earlier, and whose goal was $3 million, already stood at fifty thousand dollars more than the targeted amount. The Ford money, however, was earmarked for endowment, not operating expenses, and operating expenses were creating financial problems for orchestras across the country. Metcalf distributed a series of graphs comparing the San Francisco Symphony's position with twenty-seven other major US orchestras, examining the years starting in 1963 and continuing to the present. In every case, expenses exceeded income. Deficits, which held steady through 1965–66, rose sharply between 1967 and 1969. From 1963 through 1968, the San Francisco Symphony presented fewer concerts than other major orchestras, and its season was in every case the shortest. Contributions in San Francisco, on the other hand, outpaced all the others. As in the past, the San Francisco public could be relied on. Projecting a deficit of $1.5 million at the close of the 1971–72 season, Metcalf recommended reconsidering the Association's investment policies. Boone recognized that more aid had to be forthcoming from local, state, and federal governments. The great irony of the Ford Foundation grants is that, in making lavish funding available, they immediately created expectations that, while justified, rose more quickly than arts organizations could address. Gifted musicians who had spent years of training had long been poorly compensated. Now that picture seemed possible to change. Arts organizations had been thrown a challenge to which they had to respond.

GOLDEN YEARS AT TWILIGHT
The summer of 1969 concluded one of the country's most turbulent decades in a way that characterized the exultant and disturbing sixties. On July 20, the United States landed men on the moon and a few days later brought them back to earth.

RELAXING WITH JOSEF KRIPS

After conducting his San Francisco concerts, Josef Krips loved to relax by dining at Trader Vic's. Joe Scafidi, Symphony manager in those days, accompanied him on many of these outings. "He had an *enormous* appetite, *enormous*. He used to start off by drinking what was known as a Fog Cutter. A Fog Cutter was made up of several types of rum and God knows what else, and it came in a very tall glass." Krips had just finished one of these drinks when he spotted the waiter. "Please—again. More fog!"

Trader Vic's had a novel way of signaling last call. "They had a gong," Scafidi recalls. "It was huge. And they'd give it a bang, and whoever was in the restaurant would understand that it was time to go. It never fazed Krips at all. They kept hitting that damned thing, and eventually they cracked it."

SAMOAN FOG CUTTER

2 ounces lemon juice
1 ounce orange juice
½ ounce orgeat syrup
1½ ounces light rum
½ ounce gin
½ ounce sherry wine
4 ounces ice cubes
4 ounces crushed ice

Fill half mug with ice cubes, flash blend all ingredients with crushed ice. Pour into mug. Float sherry wine. Garnish: mint sprig and long stirrer.

In mid-August, a crowd of four hundred thousand gathered in a field near Woodstock, New York, for a three-day high of music and other recreation, seemingly a culmination of what began with the Summer of Love. But earlier that month the Manson "family" had visited tragedy on a home in Los Angeles, leaving five people brutally murdered— bringing the sixties, as Joan Didion suggested, to an abrupt end. "The tension broke that day," she wrote in *The White Album*. "The paranoia was fulfilled."

At the San Francisco Symphony, Josef Krips's tenure was ending. Philip Boone, as Zellerbach before him, entertained dreams of merging the Symphony Association with the Oakland Symphony, eager for the increased support that could be diverted to the Symphony Association, were such a merger accomplished. The merger never happened, and although he denied wanting in any way to undercut a smaller arts organization, Boone planted a suspicion of the Symphony's motives that would persist for years. His goal, he said, was to serve all of Northern California. That, of course, would involve touring, and surely he knew the costs of even a West Coast tour, having just seen the orchestra through a summer 1969 journey with Arthur Fiedler, who led Symphony pops concerts in San Diego, Hollywood, Santa Barbara, and Fresno, and farther north, in Portland, Seattle, and Vancouver.

As 1970 opened, board member Agnes Albert donated a hundred thousand dollars to lay the groundwork for an in-depth music program that would take Symphony musicians to public schools throughout the city, eventually reaching thirty thousand children and, incidentally, offering work to Symphony musicians not employed by the Opera orchestra. By November, when Local 6 president Jerry Spain accepted the invitation to attend the board's annual meeting, the road ahead seemed happier, especially when Spain named Albert an honorary union member, pointing out that, in the hundred-year history of Local 6, only twelve such memberships had been extended.

Earlier that year, Krips had drawn a great ovation at his final concert as music director, which, like Monteux's farewell performance, had featured the Beethoven Ninth. May 29 was declared Josef Krips Day in San Francisco, Alioto named him an honorary citizen, and Boone read a list of his San Francisco Symphony accomplishments, which included conducting 700 concerts, 215 works, 91 of them from the twentieth century, and 13 of them world premieres. Then he announced that Krips would bear the title Conductor Emeritus and presented him with a solid gold baton, with the engraving "The Golden Years, Josef Krips, San Francisco Symphony Orchestra 1963–1970." Krips, the taskmaster who now displayed the sentimental Viennese side of his personality, was deeply touched. The decade had seen its share of the bizarre and the tragic. In the orchestra world, new stresses and outcroppings of old grievances had led to restructured relationships and better lives for musicians, with a longer season and better pay. In San Francisco, the outgoing music director had helped restore the orchestra's sense of self-respect and pride. Artistic and administrative heavy lifting had added muscle in the form of an excellence recognized nationally and abroad.

It was time to build on this.

19

Krips triumphant.

151

EDUCATION FOR A COMMUNITY

"Our San Francisco Orchestra will be used for the benefit of all classes," wrote Symphony manager Will Greenbaum in a *Chronicle* article the day of the orchestra's first performance, December 8, 1911. Making music available to all is one step. The other part of this equation is to stimulate appetites. The music itself can do that. But the music can be helped. To provide the extra impetus, the Symphony has assumed the role of educator. Here are some landmarks.

Violinist David Schneider, who would spend fifty years with the orchestra and write his own history of the Symphony, shown here in a 1970 school workshop.

1911
On December 29, three weeks after the Symphony's first concert, a "Young People's Program" is presented.

1922
Young People's Symphony Concerts are launched this year. These concerts for schoolchildren continue into the present as Concerts for Kids: special weekday performances at Davies Symphony Hall for nearly thirty thousand children throughout Northern California. Study materials and CDs are mailed to schools in advance.

1967–68
Thirty in-school concerts are presented throughout the city's neighborhoods, including student workshops with orchestra members.

1970
Board member Agnes Albert donates a hundred thousand dollars to support the Symphony In-School program, presented in two phases. In the first, a six-week summer course, orchestra members instruct four hundred students in grades five to twelve, with a concert by the full orchestra at the end. Phase two takes place in the fall, when forty musicians visit schools throughout the city, especially those in disadvantaged neighborhoods.

1971
The forty-member "Little Symphony" visits students in nineteen San Francisco Schools, gives forty-five demonstrations, and conducts more than three hundred workshops.

1972
Bay Area composers contribute to the summer music program. Students work with program composer-in-residence Javier Castillo, whose Symphony-commissioned *Sculptures for Orchestra* receives its world premiere during the workshop's final weeks, as does Darius Milhaud's *Music for San Francisco*, composed especially for the Symphony's educational programs.

1973
Eight hundred young musicians train with school-district teachers and orchestra members during the summer and work with program composer-in-residence Loren Rush to prepare the world premiere of his *I'll See You in My Dreams*.

A Youth Music Education Fund is founded to support Symphony education programs and provide concert tickets to students at the San Francisco Conservatory of Music.

1981

Inaugural season of the San Francisco Symphony Youth Orchestra, a pre-professional orchestral training program, tuition-free, serving talented young musicians between the ages of twelve and twenty. (See pages 192-193.)

1988

Adventures in Music, AIM, is launched. A music education program designed for San Francisco's public elementary schools, AIM has grown to serve every student in grades one to five in every classroom of the San Francisco Unified School District, as well as a number of the city's independent and parochial schools. (See "Heritage Transmission: Giving Children Adventures in Music," page 207.)

1990

Free "Inside Music" talks, inaugurated in 1987, are offered before concerts on the orchestra's regular series.

1993

California Arts Council cites AIM as a model arts education program.

Music for Families is inaugurated. Concerts showcase symphonic music and its elements. Free materials promote music appreciation at home.

1995

A Bass Training Program is established to address the scarcity of student bassists. The program recruits beginning players in San Francisco and at selected schools in the East Bay and assists them through coaching and workshops.

Symphony begins TicketReach, a free ticket program to support the music-education initiatives of selected local community organizations.

2002

SFSKids.com launches: a free website providing online learning for children, parents, teachers, and schools. Average daily visits are fifteen hundred to two thousand.

2006

Instrument Training and Support offers free coaching for instrumental programs in San Francisco's public middle schools and high schools. Professional musician-clinicians visit schools each week of the academic year. This program offers bows, reeds, mouthpieces, instrument repairs, music stands, and sheet music, as well as tickets to selected Symphony concerts.

MUSICAL ASSOCIATION OF SAN FRANCISCO
Maintaining the

San Francisco Orchestra

HENRY HADLEY, Conductor

First Popular Concert

A YOUNG PEOPLE'S PROGRAM

Cort Theater

FRIDAY AFTERNOON, DECEMBER 29, AT 3:15

SOLOIST

MME. MARTHA RICHARDSON

Prima Donna Soprano, "The Paris Grand Opera Co."
(By courtesy of M. Pierre Grazi)

MANAGER : WILL L. GREENBAUM

153

TOP: *The Symphony was mindful of young audiences from the start. The first program for young people was presented on December 29, 1911, three weeks after the inaugural concert.*

BOTTOM: *Violinist Verne Sellin was a member of the orchestra, conducted the Symphony in children's concerts, and served as orchestra personnel manager. Here he revels in his role as educator.*

SAN FRANCISCO SYMPHONY
Golden Season
Enrique Jordá, Conductor and Musical Director

SEIJI OZAWA, *Guest Conductor*
RUTH SLENCZYNSKA, *Guest Pianist*
January 10, January 13, 1962
War Memorial Opera House

The program book for Ozawa's debut concerts in 1962. Along with Ruth Slenczynska, an old Symphony friend, came a young conductor making his first North American appearances.

Seiji Ozawa. He brought love beads, turtlenecks, and style.

VIII.

A NEW KIND OF GLAMOUR

The Seiji Ozawa Years (1970–1977)

LOVE, AND LOVE BEADS

Everyone loved him. Everyone. Even eighteen-year-old girls in miniskirts. On the cover of a 1969 recording he had made with the Chicago Symphony Orchestra, of Mussorgsky's *Pictures at an Exhibition*, Seiji Ozawa stands in a gallery of the Chicago Art Institute, contemplating the masterpieces on the walls. He is dressed in a sharp black suit. His outfit, his Beatles haircut, his stance, his gaze—all these define *hip*, a concept then new to the world of classical music. The eighteen-year-old girl holding the album marveled. "He's so *cute!*" Never mind who she was. She was eighteen. The

walls of her small apartment were purple and the place was scented with patchouli. And her verdict was that Ozawa was cute.

Except employed as a weapon of irony, *cute* was not a word to be associated with Josef Krips, nor with any former music director of the San Francisco Symphony, nor with any music director of any major orchestra in America in 1970, when Seiji Ozawa assumed his post at the Symphony's helm. Cute, however, was just a fringe benefit. Krips himself, never content with skin-deep beauty, had once pronounced this

young Japanese conductor the future of the San Francisco Symphony, and he had envisioned Ozawa as his successor.

Ozawa had first come to the San Francisco Symphony in 1962, making his North American debut at the War Memorial Opera House as a last-minute substitute for Armenian composer-conductor Aram Khachaturian. Ozawa's turtlenecks and love beads, his trademark thick mane that hid his ears and draped over his collar—all these were in the future. In 1962, he looked like an exchange student just arrived on a

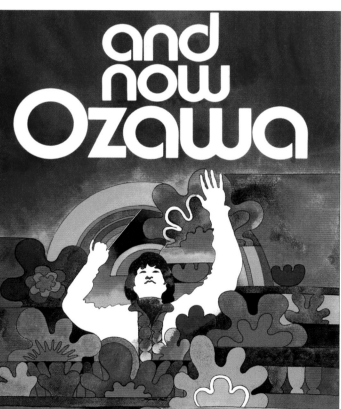

bargain flight from Tokyo, a diffident young man with close-cropped hair, perhaps marveling at how far he had come, and how quickly, which had nothing to do with jet travel. He made a sensation conducting Beethoven's Eighth Symphony and Berlioz's *Symphonie fantastique*, the same program he would lead in 2001 when he returned to San Francisco to celebrate the fortieth anniversary of his first US engagement, the start of a journey during which he would grow into a musical lion.

He was born in 1935 in Manchuria, to Japanese parents who had settled in that Chinese province after its invasion by Japan in 1931. His father was a dentist-turned-magazine publisher. His mother, a housewife who insisted that her sons be raised in her own Christian faith, made sure he was enrolled in Sunday school, where he sang in the choir and learned to play piano. In 1937, with the outbreak of the Second Sino-Japanese war, the family returned to Japan. There, Seiji continued piano studies despite wartime deprivations and his family's poverty. His father, ever-encouraging, having learned of an affordably priced piano for sale in Yokohama, rented a pushcart, trekked the twenty-five miles to the seaport, and hauled the instrument back home. Seiji studied for seven years at the Toho School of Music in Tokyo with the legendary professor Hideo Saito, who had trained in Europe. To pay tuition, the fledgling student became Saito's assistant, helping with everything from score preparation and stage-hand duties to mowing the professor's lawn. Next came a brief period in France, where Ozawa won the Besançon Conductors' Competition. Jury member Charles Munch, then music director of the Boston

Symphony Orchestra, invited him to take part in the Tanglewood Conductors' Competition, where he won the Koussevitzky Prize. A scholarship to Herbert von Karajan's conducting seminar followed, then an appointment as Leonard Bernstein's assistant conductor at the New York Philharmonic. It was with this resume that, at age twenty-seven, Ozawa made his first San Francisco Symphony appearance. When the Symphony Association asked him to take up permanent residence, he had been serving since 1964 as music director of the Ravinia Festival, summer home of the Chicago Symphony, and since 1965 as music director of the Toronto Symphony. Rumor had it that the New York Philharmonic wanted him as Bernstein's successor. San Francisco got him first.

And Now Ozawa. That was the slogan for Ozawa's first San Francisco Symphony season, and it was perfect. *Now* brought conductor and orchestra into the present moment. *Now* suggested a break with the past. *Now* meant the beginning of a new era for the San Francisco Symphony and the start of a new decade: 1970, a farewell and good riddance to the turmoil of the years just ended. Here was a conductor—the "Now Generation Conductor," the press called him—whose every movement on the podium was fluid, who danced with the music, who inspired the orchestra to performances more exciting than any heard in years. He was only thirty-five. He dressed in Nehru jackets and wore medallions and beads around his neck when he conducted. For street clothes, he chose jeans and sandals. *And Now Ozawa.* The phrase was the brainchild of the Symphony's then-artistic administrator, Bill Bernell. A corporation tends to adopt a slogan and stay with it, and for more

than two hundred years the US government has stuck with *E pluribus unum*. An orchestra invents a new slogan for each new season. In 2009 Bernell recalled the brainstorming session at which marketing phrases were tossed around. Only one stuck. *And Now Ozawa* went up on billboards around the city. It was spelled out in flowers in front of the Conservatory in Golden Gate Park. Manager Joe Scafidi ordered a new license plate for his Cadillac, a plate that bore only one word, OZAWA. All this was more than public relations. Looking back thirty years later, Scafidi summed up the feeling in town: "It was fun."

The differences between Krips and Ozawa went far beyond the way they looked. Krips would arrive for concerts an hour early and engage in an almost ritualistic mental preparation that included careful attention to his attire, down to brushing his

patent leather shoes. Ozawa would show up a minute or two early, greet everyone backstage with a hi-how-ya-doin', slip into his concert suit, turtleneck, and love beads, and stride onto stage with not a second to spare. The instant Ozawa stepped onto the podium, everything changed. Violinist David Schneider recalled his intensity, and the clarity of a beat with "not an inkling of flabbiness or indecisiveness" about it. Flutist Paul Renzi admired his complete control. Violist Detlev Olshausen remembered the close of Stravinsky's *Le Sacre du printemps*—famously difficult, especially if the rhythms are just counted out mechanically. Ozawa danced his directions. "You just went with it, and it was never so easy."

His ability to absorb music became legendary. Handed an unfamiliar score in the morning, he would know it by memory that night. Ozawa's

3

Stuart Canin, concertmaster from 1970 to 1980.

4

With Ozawa, the Symphony entered the psychedelic world of the seventies.

5

Even before he arrived in San Francisco, Seiji Ozawa defined "now," as this album cover from 1969 suggests.

6

And Now Ozawa: *A slogan so apt it could even be said with flowers. Here it is spelled out in front of the San Francisco Conservatory of Flowers in Golden Gate Park.*

7

7

With Ozawa, the orchestra returned to recording, this time (1972) with Deutsche Grammophon.

8

Symphony volunteers have staffed Repeat Performance, a high-end resale shop, since its opening in 1972.

San Francisco concertmaster, Stuart Canin, recalled a rehearsal of Messiaen's *Turangalîla,* a work well over an hour long, full of traps, written for an orchestra of massive proportions. On the podium was a thick score that Ozawa never opened. During a break Canin sneaked a peak at this tome. It was simply a book of blank pages—an artifact, Canin assumed, that Ozawa kept with him for some Zen-like purpose.

Ticket sales leapt. Concerts attracted younger listeners. Canin put it simply. "He just was perfect for San Francisco."

THE NEXT LEVEL

Seiji Ozawa's first season with the San Francisco Symphony could hardly have opened more auspiciously. In January 1971 sales of single tickets were already twenty thousand dollars greater than anticipated in the year's budget, and by the end of May sales had exceeded the preceding season's purchases by almost a hundred thousand dollars. For Ozawa's next season, 1971–72, sales almost immediately exceeded those of his first season by 18 percent. What's more, the Ford Foundation matching campaign had been completed. The goal of $3 million had been exceeded by almost an additional $2 million. A committee had been formed to explore plans for a new home for the orchestra, one in which it could perform throughout the year, and it was anticipated that by 1976 or 1977 that structure would be finished, although such dreams would take longer to realize. Ozawa wanted to take the orchestra to Europe. He wanted to record. His contract, due to expire in 1973, was extended for another three seasons. He had even declined an offer from the august Boston Symphony Orchestra to become its music director. The reason, said Phil Boone, was Ozawa's love of San Francisco. Boone expected Ozawa to stay for another ten or fifteen years. The San Francisco Symphony was headed for the next level: recognition around the world. For Bay Area music lovers, the times could hardly have been happier.

In late 1971, the San Francisco Symphony opened its sixtieth anniversary season. To celebrate, four works were commissioned with contributions from board member Dr. Ralph I. Dorfman and his wife, Peggy, who together in the coming years would prove themselves among new music's best friends by continuing to support those who curated it. Commissions for the sixtieth season would go to two local composers, Charles Boone and a former violinist with the orchestra, David Sheinfeld. Another would go to American composer Gunther Schuller, and a fourth to Hungarian composer György Ligeti,

whose music had recently been co-opted for the score of the psychedelic movie extravaganza 2001: A Space Odyssey. Soloists such as violinists Isaac Stern and Yehudi Menuhin would be part of the anniversary season, along with pianists Rudolf Serkin, André Watts, and Vladimir Ashkenazy. Pianists Garrick Ohlsson and Christoph Eschenbach would make their debuts with the orchestra. Among the guests on the podium would be Dean Dixon, an African-American maestro then making a sensation as he returned to the land of his birth after years abroad, racial prejudice in the United States having denied him the success he had enjoyed in Europe. The season would increase from thirty-seven to thirty-nine weeks. It seemed all was right with the Bay Area music world.

Then, at the end of January 1972, Philip Boone disclosed the disturbing information that the Boston Symphony Orchestra had again approached Ozawa, this time sweetening its offer by agreeing to share him with San Francisco. That was all it took. While retaining his San Francisco post, Ozawa would also become music director in Boston in 1973. Unfortunately, the musicians of the San Francisco Symphony learned the news through an item in the February 7 issue of *Newsweek*, which stated, incorrectly, that Ozawa intended to leave San Francisco when he went to Boston. Guest-conducting in Philadelphia when this news broke, Ozawa canceled a rehearsal and hopped a plane for a flight across the country to assure San Francisco's musicians that he had no intention of abandoning them. He pledged to divide his time in the United States only between San Francisco and Boston. He would accept no other North American

engagements. "We started work together only last year. . . . We have a long way to go with this work. . . . I am not going to change my job from one place to another." In reiterating Ozawa's commitment to the Bay Area, Boone reminded his board colleagues that the conductor owned a home on San Francisco's Twin Peaks. His first child had been born in the city. His ties to the area were strong.

And yes, there was work to be done. After twelve years, the orchestra was recording again, this time with Deutsche Grammophon, perhaps the world's most prestigious classical label. The sessions captured the new spirit that had taken hold, highlighted by an Ozawa specialty, William Russo's Three Pieces for Blues Band and Symphony Orchestra, featuring the Siegel-Schwall Blues Band. So popular was this recording that DG released a movement of the work as its first-ever 45-rpm disc.

159

8

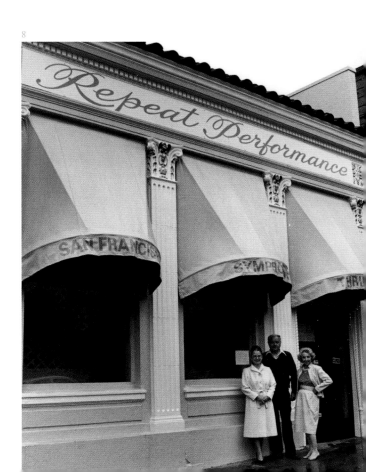

A CHORAL JOURNEY,
FROM *STAR TREK* TO STARDOM

In 1973, Seiji Ozawa decided the San Francisco Symphony should have a permanent chorus, an asset few orchestras enjoy. For performances of Verdi's Requiem, the Beethoven Ninth, or any of the other great works of the choral-orchestral repertory, he had been forced to rely on any or all of three different choruses, those of the Oakland Symphony, UC Berkeley, and Stanford University. Ozawa wanted a chorus that was a permanent part of the Symphony. To audition singers, he recruited Joseph Liebling of the Oakland Symphony Chorus and Niklaus Wyss, who for three seasons had served as the San Francisco Symphony's assistant conductor. Invitations were sent to every member of every Bay Area vocal group.

One of the 125 accepted was alto Sandy Sellin, who has been with the chorus ever since. The daughter of Verne Sellin, a Symphony violinist who performed with the orchestra for almost fifty years, she had been singing and playing piano since childhood. "It was a wild first year," she said of the 1973 inaugural season. "We did the *St. Matthew Passion*, the Berlioz *Te Deum*, *Gurrelieder*. Big stuff. Five different directors prepared us. They were all auditioning for a permanent job." The winner was Louis Magor, who went on to spend a decade as the chorus's first director. His departure brought Margaret Hillis to San Francisco for a year as interim director. Hillis, a legendary figure among choral conductors, had organized the great Chicago Symphony Chorus. Among her many talented students and protégés was Vance George, who succeeded her when her year was up and who held the job of chorus director until 2007. That

Dressed in their "Trekkie" uniforms, members of the San Francisco Symphony Chorus pose with founding director Louis Magor.

Ragnar Bohlin, who became director of the San Francisco Symphony Chorus in 2007, rehearses chorus sopranos and altos.

year, the post was filled by Ragnar Bohlin, a Swedish native whose artistry and sense of sound were formed by his country's great choral tradition.

Chorus membership in any given season stands at about 120 volunteer singers, with another 30 paid members of the American Guild of Musical Artists. Choristers rehearse one to three nights a week, for three hours a night. During performance weeks, they are on call six nights. Collectively, they commit roughly forty thousand hours a season to their Symphony singing. They come from all backgrounds. Membership is by rigorous auditions that test sight-reading as well as vocal skills.

Odd as it may seem, the increasing standard of professionalism is reflected in the singers' attire. During the first few seasons, they wore canary-yellow choir robes with two-tone satin collars, red and purple. In the late seventies, these gave way to what Sandy Sellin calls "Trekkie outfits": black slacks for the men, black skirts for the women; teal blue polyester tops—turtlenecks for the men, blouses for the women. Gradually, the sartorial code sobered up: the men wore black tuxedos; the women, black evening gowns.

In 1993 the Chorus helped the San Francisco Symphony capture its first Grammy award—for Best Choral Recording, no less—for Orff's *Carmina burana*. Since then the singers have been featured in additional Grammy winners, including recordings that took the awards for Best Classical Album.

Increasingly, the chorus has had a starring role. This is confirmed not only by awards but in concert: annual choral concerts, holiday concerts, and regular performances with the orchestra. A series of especially memorable concerts took place in 2009. A sixteenth-century antiphonal masterpiece by Gabrieli, meant to carry listeners to the edge of sonic heaven, was followed immediately by György Ligeti's 1965 Requiem, in which the composer confronts listeners with terrifying sounds not encountered in choral music before or since. To move from Gabrieli's paradise to Ligeti's inferno demanded skill and sensitivity few ensembles can muster, and risk-taking of a kind that few ensembles dare. Michael Tilson Thomas, who conducted those performances, believed they heralded the chorus's arrival on a new artistic plane.

"Song is the source of music," says Tilson Thomas. "Some of our greatest composers have enlisted human voices as essential components in their most ambitious orchestral works—Bach, Handel, Beethoven, Mahler, Ives. When we turn to the choral masterpieces, we are blessed in having magnificent singers to help us bring these works to life. These are men and women who give 100 percent, 100 percent of the time."

9

David Plant, Symphony president from 1972 to 1974.

In May 1972, the European tour taking shape for the spring of 1973 assumed an added dimension when the Soviet minister of culture, Madame Ekaterina Furtseva, visited San Francisco, attended a concert, and immediately invited the orchestra to perform in Russia. This was an era of thawing relations between the West and the Communist world. President Richard Nixon had visited China in February 1972. The Russians, no longer close friends with the Chinese, had their own Western overtures to make, and Furtseva's invitation came even before the US and USSR had signed a formal cultural-exchange agreement. The European portion of the tour was already long, with eighteen concerts scheduled. Visiting the Soviet Union would add twelve performances and extend the journey to seven weeks. The expense was also considerable, but in the early 1970s, arts organizations increasingly sought corporate support, and the San Francisco Symphony secured tour underwriting from the Bank of America and Standard Oil Corporation of California. Without that, the journey would not have been made.

The 1971–72 season closed with the association in the black. Ticket sales were up by 16 percent, contributions stood at a record $565,000, and a positive balance of $18,000 was posted on the books. Even Josef Krips was part of the good news. The Conductor Emeritus had returned to lead the orchestra, celebrating his seventieth birthday with a gala concert and the fiftieth anniversary of his performing career with a free performance of Mozart's *Coronation* Mass at Saint Ignatius Church. And fund-raising became increasingly creative. If corporations were the most obvious sources of major support, help also came from volunteers behind the scenes. At the beginning of the year, Symphony Foundation members opened Repeat Performance, a high-end resale shop on Fillmore Street, stocked with standard items alongside Gucci gowns. Proceeds were to benefit youth concerts, and in its first four months the store netted almost twelve thousand dollars. After ten years as board president, Philip Boone must have felt he was at the top of his game when he resigned that post in October 1972, turning over the responsibilities to David Plant.

Looking from the outside and listening, all was well. What refused to disperse was the worry that Ozawa would soon forsake San Francisco for the East Coast and one of the world's greatest orchestras. The specter of Boston, its traditions and its Brahmin culture, had long loomed over San Francisco. Almost from the start, the San Francisco Symphony had had to deal with unflattering comparisons when the Boston Symphony appeared at the Panama-Pacific Exposition in 1915, demonstrating the way an orchestra was *supposed* to sound. But the cultural jitters were about much more than music. The unspoken truth was that, when the West Coast contemplated the East Coast and found itself wanting, the place that triggered such anxieties was Boston. New York and Philadelphia, big-shouldered Chicago and gritty Cleveland—those places all had their own kinds of tough reality and could be dealt with on their terms. Boston owned mystique. "If West Coasters are generally hung up on the East Coast, well, all right," an irritated Ozawa told critic Heuwell Tircuit in 1972, insisting again that he planned to stay. "But that's their problem. Don't transpose your hang-ups to me."

9

Ozawa wanted a happy orchestra. Symphony musicians, he said, were like family to him. He wanted to take this family to wider artistic worlds. The imminent tour to Europe and the Soviet Union was one step toward such places. Another way of reaching them was more practical and potentially more painful. Ozawa felt he needed to assume greater control over tenure decisions and selection of principals. By the end of 1972, in ongoing contract negotiations with the musicians, these subjects became the source of disagreements. Perhaps hastily and somewhat undiplomatically, Ozawa had spoken with seven section principals in a way that made them feel their jobs were on the line. Under the contract then expiring, vacant principal chairs had to be filled from within the section—"an impossible situation," David Plant

pointed out, for principals had to be players of the highest caliber, and a section player was not necessarily of that rank. Ozawa wanted open auditions. While he believed he had to remain firm on the seating issue, he felt he could live with the musicians' proposal that they be given power to award tenure. By April 1973, a new contract was in place. The question of principals' seating would not become an issue during Ozawa's years with the Symphony. The question of tenure would.

CULTURAL AMBASSADORS

When the San Francisco Symphony gave the first concert of its first European tour, on May 15, 1973, it was in no remote outpost that allowed for warm-ups. It was in Paris, in the Théâtre des Champs-Elysées, where sixty years earlier

the orchestra's former music director, Pierre Monteux, had inaugurated the modern era of music when he conducted the premiere of *Le Sacre du printemps*.

Now an honor guard from the French navy was on hand. A brass contingent from the orchestra, posted at opposite sides of the stage, launched the tour with the antiphonal splendor of a Gabrieli canzon. The audience went wild, but not so wild as they did at the conclusion of the second work on the program, when André Watts was soloist in the Beethoven Fourth Piano Concerto. Rhythmic applause greeted him as he finished, dying down only long enough for him to play an encore, after which the clapping resumed.

The concert was transmitted live to San Francisco on KKHI-FM, the

10

10

At the orchestra's Vienna stop, Josef Krips threw a party for the musicians at a Heuriger *in the countryside outside the city. Flanking Krips are Ozawa and David Plant.*

11

The 1973 European tour began with a Paris performance.

12

Intermission at the opening concert of the 1973 tour, at the Théâtre du Champs-Elysées. Standing: David Plant and Phil Boone. Seated: Commentator Bill Agee and San Francisco Mayor Joseph Alioto. Plant, Boone, and the mayor were featured in an intermission segment beamed to San Francisco via satellite.

first stereo radio broadcast ever relayed via satellite, and through this technological miracle listeners at home heard what was happening in Paris, in real time. The intermission feature that originated in the Théâtre's broadcast booth, with commentator Bill Agee interviewing David Plant, Phil Boone, and San Francisco Mayor Joseph Alioto, is a case study in how to court public support. Plant, still somewhat tentative in his new role as president, talks about the new and challenging audiences the orchestra will face throughout the tour, and how the musicians will rise to this challenge, reaching new performance planes that will guarantee a great San Francisco season to come. Boone, gravelly voiced and assured, manages to be convincing even in an unrehearsed and less than coherent statement such as, "I trust everyone in San Francisco will appreciate that it is *their* orchestra, it

is *their* support, it has been *their* loyalty springing out of that great opera house of ours that has made [this tour] possible." Alioto, the consummate politician, congratulates the "men like Phil Boone and David Plant who were largely unknown throughout the city, who worked so hard to achieve a standard of excellence in music that now is being demonstrated in Paris tonight. There isn't enough we can say about San Francisco citizens like this." Warming to the task, he continues: "There isn't enough we can say about the foresight of those men who in the very midst of the Depression built that opera house of ours. What we have tonight is simply the culmination of the fact that we have that great musical facility there to develop the kind of an organization we have tonight." Reading between the lines, the mayor is pitching the idea of a new concert hall. He had promised Boone his support. Now he was in effect announcing his support to San Francisco.

The concert ended with Berlioz's *Symphonie fantastique*—music in which Ozawa always excelled, performed now in the city where it had first been heard 143 years before. The Parisians embraced the musicians with applause, demanded three encores, and kept everyone on stage for another half hour.

Similar experiences followed. From Paris, the orchestra traveled to Brussels, Brighton, London, Chartres (for an atmospheric but acoustically odd concert in the booming interior of the great cathedral), Zurich, Basel, Berne, Hannover, Berlin, Frankfurt, Linz, and Vienna. In the Vienna suburb of Grinzing, at a *Heuriger*—a restaurant offering traditional Austrian fare along with its house wine—an old friend, Josef Krips, threw a party for the musicians, revealing a jovial side few who had worked with him had encountered. Two concerts in Florence followed. From there, it was on to uncharted territory.

In 1973, St. Petersburg was still called Leningrad. By any name, the city's contrast with Florence could not have been more stark. Tour guides were rumored to be KGB operatives. Hotel facilities were basic. Agnes Albert, part of a contingent of board members accompanying the orchestra, once returned to her room to discover it had been painted while she was out, forcing her to deal with all but asphyxiating fumes. Corridor monitors insisted that guests coming and going check in with them, even when moving only from one floor to another. The food was unpalatable. Dark bread and cucumbers were culinary staples.

The flimsy window shades did little to block the sun, which, in this northern latitude, shone almost until midnight. One hot evening— this was early June—when the musicians could no longer bear to quench their thirst with the Georgian bottled water that tasted of iodine, Ozawa learned that a hotel across town sold Tuborg beer, from Denmark. He ordered two bottles delivered to each orchestra member—not to intoxicate them, but just so they could imbibe some palatable fluid. Tasks such as this were not part of his job description. He knew how to improvise.

The Soviet Union had not seen an American orchestra in eight years, and the Leningrad public welcomed the San Francisco Symphony like long-lost friends. After each of the four performances, fans greeted Ozawa and the musicians. Many players wore "Ozawa" buttons and traded them with the fans for Russian pins and medals. The scene then shifted to Vilnius, in Lithuania, where the orchestra played the most American of works, the Ives Fourth Symphony. But the high point of the Soviet visit was yet to come. In Moscow, the great Mstislav Rostropovich was scheduled as soloist in the Dvořák Cello Concerto. Rostropovich had been banned from performing in his homeland for his outspoken defense of dissident writer Aleksandr Solzhenitsyn. Ozawa insisted that Rostropovich appear with the orchestra, and the authorities had relented. Under the most emotionally neutral circumstances, the Dvořák Concerto is a charged work. Given the context of this performance in the Great Hall of the Moscow Conservatory—an American orchestra led by a Japanese conductor, featuring Russia's favorite son, who

11

165

12

15

ARTIST'S SKETCH OF NEW MUSICAL ARTS BUILDING

SAN FRANCISCO WAR MEMORIAL CENTER

14

was a champion of expressive freedom—the stage was set for a combustible performance. No one was disappointed. "The cellist played like a god," David Schneider recalled. "And in every nuance Ozawa was as if living in the skin of Rostropovich. For those forty minutes they were blood brothers." At the end, the faces of even the crustiest musicians were streaming with tears.

The tour was over. When the flight from Moscow touched down in Amsterdam, some musicians kissed the Western soil. The orchestra had accomplished what it set out to do. The musicians had planted the seeds of the San Francisco Symphony's international reputation. This chapter of Seiji Ozawa's tenure had a happy ending.

FOUNDATIONS FOR THE FUTURE
In his radio broadcast from Paris to San Francisco, Mayor Alioto had made little effort to mask his conviction that great concert halls were prerequisites for great orchestras. As early as 1971, a "Citizens Committee for a Center for Performing Arts" had been formed. In late 1973, the plan for a new hall was revived. Such a hall would be a foundation for the long term. Behind the boosterism Alioto had beamed back home through outer space was the fact that the Opera House had indeed nurtured the ensemble's artistic development—a development which, as the mayor said, culminated in a European tour that brought the Symphony and the city the recognition and respect of music lovers in Europe, the cultural validation for which every great American orchestra thirsted. The time had come for the orchestra to take the next step, to move into a concert hall of its

own, dedicated to the performance of symphonic music. The artistic value of that move would accrue over the long term. Of course funding and building a hall would take time. For the present, other artistic plans were more immediate.

One was the formation of a chorus: a *symphony* chorus, whose primary purpose would be to perform with the orchestra in works from Bach to Mahler and beyond. Not many orchestras were blessed with choral partners of their own; in the United States, only Chicago and Atlanta enjoyed such a benefit. More typically, choral performances required recruitment of independent singing groups, or choruses from local universities. In the Bay Area, the San Francisco Municipal Chorus and the Stanford Chorus had partnered with the San Francisco Symphony over the years. From its start in 1973, nothing was tentative about the San Francisco Symphony Chorus. Already in the group's first season the singers tackled large-scale works that included Stravinsky's *Les Noces* (a rhythmic minefield), Bach's *St. Matthew Passion* (almost four hours of emotionally committed singing in which the chorus becomes a primary actor), and Schoenberg's *Gurrelieder* (an outsize work in every way, not least in the hyper-Romantic atmosphere the chorus helps create).

Recording also called for immediate attention. Philips, a Dutch firm, had offered terms more attractive than Deutsche Grammophon, and Ozawa and the orchestra made their first recordings for that company in May 1974. The repertory was standard, Beethoven's *Eroica* Symphony and Dvořák's *New World*, reflecting the orchestra's increasing profile on the broader music scene. This was not simply an ensemble that recorded

novelties such as the Russo Concerto for Blues Band; this was an orchestra that could hold its own in the crowded field of the classics.

Philips's interest in the Symphony was certainly also spurred by Ozawa himself. Increasingly, he was a music celebrity, although not always a willing one. He valued his study time, rose each morning at four to peruse scores, disliked cocktail parties and the socializing to which every American music director must submit. Some conductors are temperamentally more suited than others to mingle with their fans, and with those potentially responsible for the next major contribution, personal or corporate. Ozawa, for all the glamour with which the press portrayed him, was a reluctant participant in the process that was turning him into a legend. He preferred his own society, and that of those close to him, partly because his English, while completely equal to the job of making music, was not practiced in the subtleties and nuance of the post-concert gathering. Yet no apparent communication difficulties could keep people from demanding his time and capitulating to his charm. After exchanging a few sentences with him, those gripping their napkin-wrapped highball glasses would themselves begin dropping articles and verbs, in unconscious emulation of the man they adored.

Two conductors who would become identified with the San Francisco Symphony made their debuts in 1974. In January, Michael Tilson Thomas, the brilliant young music director of the Buffalo Symphony Orchestra, made a powerful impression leading performances of Mahler's Symphony No. 9, a work he would record with the orchestra thirty years later as

16

13
—
Ozawa pins became a hot commodity in the Soviet Union, where Symphony musicians traded them for Russian trinkets.

14
—
Modeled on New York's Lincoln Center, a new performing arts complex for San Francisco was proposed in 1968 but failed to gain traction.

15
—
Cellist Mstislav Rostropovich and the orchestra in their Moscow rehearsal.

16
—
In the orchestra's recording of Russo's Three Pieces for Blues Band and Orchestra, Deutsche Grammophon found a surprise hit on its hands.

1967 SEASON

SAN FRANCISCO
SYMPHONY
"POPS"
ORCHESTRA

ARTHUR FIEDLER
Guest Conductor

POPULAR AND SERIOUS,
THIS MUSIC IS FOR EVERYONE

A few weeks after conducting the San Francisco Symphony's inaugural performance in December 1911, Henry Hadley led the orchestra in its first popular concert, with ticket prices low enough to appeal to a broad range of music lovers. Hadley was slammed for programming thought to be condescending, as though the San Francisco public needed to enter the concert hall by taking baby steps. Seven popular concerts were performed that first season, and by season two the number had increased to ten. Audiences heard opera overtures, suites from ballets like *Coppélia* and *The Nutcracker*, Strauss waltzes, even a tone poem by Hadley himself.

The next step: Municipal Concerts. They were not called Municipal Concerts until 1925, although the first of these was presented in 1923, when the City of San Francisco purchased the orchestra's services and offered popularly priced tickets to the public. In 1933, a year after the establishment of the Arts Commission, the relationship between city and Symphony became still closer. Arts Commission pops performances began as part of the annual schedule and were given at various times of the year. That changed in 1951, when pops concerts were focused into a summer series.

For most summers from the fifties until 1977, Arthur Fiedler was the San Francisco Symphony's pops conductor. Leader of the Boston Pops from 1930 until his death in 1979, this dean of America's pops maestros quickly became a much-loved part-time

Arthur Fiedler, longtime Symphony pops conductor, rehearses the orchestra for the 1950 Tombola.

San Franciscan, an antic presence whose trademark silver hair drew the eyes of spectators even from the farthest balconies.

Fiedler was only one among many pops celebrities, of course. The great Ella Fitzgerald made regular appearances with the orchestra from 1975 until 1991. Sarah Vaughan was soloist in a Gershwin concert with Michael Tilson Thomas conducting in 1976. That was not a "pops" concert technically, but it was pops in spirit, as were performances over the years by Garrison Keillor and Peter Schickele (aka P. D. Q. Bach). Rosemary Clooney, Patti Page, Skitch Henderson, Ray Charles, Bernadette Peters—some of the greatest artists in popular music have appeared with the San Francisco Symphony. Latin American music has been a staple of pops programs (Pete Escovedo, Los Lobos). The Colors of Christmas holiday concerts have featured Peabo Bryson, Sheena Easton, Dionne Warwick, and a host of artists from the worlds of rock and R&B. And when Michael Tilson Thomas reflects on the musical lessons he learned from James Brown, Godfather of Soul, the distinction between *popular* and *serious* music blurs. Even the American Mavericks festival of 2000 devoted an evening to the great Duke Ellington, a composer whose music is always popular and never less than serious, in the best sense of that word.

With Fiedler leading the way, the San Francisco Arts Commission and San Francisco Symphony collaborated in presenting pops at Civic Auditorium. The Arts Commission/Symphony collaboration continued but the venue changed in 1997—to Davies Symphony Hall. There, the series took a new name, Summer in the City, and programming ventured into a more classical domain, with evenings devoted to "greatest hits" of favorite composers. In 2009 the series assumed a new name again: Summer & the Symphony, with the spotlight trained on the featured orchestra.

By any name, popular concerts retain their traditional purpose: to bring music to a wide audience. For that reason also, the orchestra ventures beyond Davies Symphony Hall every summer, offering free outdoor performances in Stern Grove and Dolores Park, and opening the fall season with a free open-air concert, which for many years took place at Yerba Buena Gardens and then moved to Justin Herman Plaza, at the head of Market Street, near the Ferry Building. The symbolism is almost too obvious, but obviously too good to ignore. In the shadow of that 1898 landmark, which withstood the 1906 earthquake and continues to serve a vital purpose in the city's life, the orchestra that rose with a reborn city draws thousands of listeners.

its music director. And in April, Edo de Waart, who eventually would become Ozawa's immediate successor, was named principal guest conductor, a post he would assume in 1975.

THE SUBJECT WAS TENURE

Despite the affection that the orchestra's musicians felt for their conductor, anxieties continued to stem from Ozawa's professed aim to reach a new artistic peak. The problem now was that he wanted to dismiss the principal horn, Herman Dorfman, and reseat three other principals, violist Rolf Persinger, cellist Robert Sayre, and trumpet player Donald Reinberg. He also wanted to reseat the assistant principal of the cellos, Mary Claudio. Concerns over musicians' reseating and tenure had been addressed in recent contract negotiations. Musicians who objected to their reseating could initiate a multistep appeals process. Tenure, after a player had been with the orchestra for two preliminary seasons, would be determined by a committee of players in consultation with the music director. Both the committee and music director had to agree on granting tenure; through a scoring process in which the player under consideration was awarded points, either side, committee or music director, could override the other and deny tenure. Ozawa believed he could come to amicable agreement with a players' review committee. After all, this was family.

In 1974, eight musicians were up for tenure. The committee granted tenure to six, and Ozawa agreed. Then the committee denied tenure to principal bassoonist Ryohei Nakagawa and timpanist Elayne Jones. Ozawa never voted because no total

number of points that were his to award could have counterbalanced the committee's vote. Nakagawa and Jones would not receive tenure.

The case was not closed. Nakagawa accepted the committee's decision. Jones, faulted for her intonation and rhythm, was livid with personal and professional hurt. She was popular with the public, and she enjoyed the support of the city's major music critics.

US society today is said to be "post-racial," but that was unknown terminology in 1974. Elayne Jones was African-American. Her presence as one of the few African-American players in a US orchestra had evidenced San Francisco's progressive image. Suddenly the tables turned. Accusations of gender and racial discrimination grew ugly. Letters poured in to the Symphony offices. A group called Black Women Organized for Action urged the National Endowment for the Arts to investigate if Jones's tenure denial was discriminatory and, if it was, to withhold the Symphony's funding. Supervisor Terry Francois demanded a freeze on the Symphony's annual allotment from the city's Hotel Tax Fund.

Reports of this sad period focus on racial grievances and organizational distress. Jones's personal dismay has received less attention. Performing artists put themselves on the line each time they appear on stage. Every person in an orchestra, from conductor to timpanist, always aims for musical perfection and always copes with the specter of failure, which is defined as anything less than perfection. This was an especially sensitive issue for Jones. "I had to prove that music could be played by anyone who loves it," she

17

Timpanist Elayne Jones.

18

Seiji Ozawa with composer Elliott Carter. In the background are Mrs. Ozawa and the youngest Ozawa child.

17

18

said around this time. "I always felt I had to do better; that I wouldn't be allowed the lapses other musicians have." Now, feeling the affront, Elayne Jones hit back. She brought suit against the committee. She withdrew the suit when the Symphony offered her another provisional year with the orchestra. But at the end of that year the review committee's assessment of her playing remained unchanged, and the decision to deny tenure stood.

While some believed the Jones issue was based in racism and others agreed that it was an artistic question, still others saw the affair as a matter of the orchestra asserting its power. Reportedly, Ozawa was initially ready to live with the committee's decision on Jones but was dismayed by its ruling on Nakagawa. Shouldn't the music director have final say? Perhaps to press this question, Ozawa soon expressed sup-

port for Jones as well as Nakagawa. But the contract was clear. The music director did not have final say. When the time came once more to vote on Elayne Jones's tenure and the vote went against her, Ozawa concurred. Jones brought suit again. It was dismissed by the court in 1977. Late that year, in what she called "probably the most painful letter I have ever had to write," Jones informed her supporters of the judgment. Until 1997 she continued as timpanist with the San Francisco Opera Orchestra, having performed with that ensemble even before coming to the Symphony, and having been tenured at the Opera at the time she was denied Symphony tenure.

No one in 1974 and 1975 could have imagined that the decision to deny Jones tenure would have been popular, or that it would *not* be interpreted as racist or sexist or both.

19

20

173

19

*Seiji Ozawa and the San Francisco
Symphony: the official portrait.*

20

On tour in Japan in 1975.

Every musician, however, is evaluated on one basis only: performance, and other factors have no bearing on that. But although the committee concluded that Jones's playing presented problems of rhythm and pitch, the issue is broader. How could she have been denied a post by the Symphony after having found a position with an ensemble so closely aligned with the Symphony? Disagreements over what constitutes an ideal of playing are common. Before Jones arrived at the Symphony, Ozawa was dissatisfied with the playing of timpanist Roland Kohloff, who departed San Francisco for a distinguished career with the New York Philharmonic under Pierre Boulez, a conductor who could never be accused of tolerating less than precise rhythm or intonation. Naoum Blinder, the San Francisco Symphony's longtime concertmaster, a musician Pierre Monteux hailed as the greatest leader with whom he had ever worked, was at first considered unequal to the job, both by colleagues and by the conductor who hired him, Issay Dobrowen. Even legends such as violinist Jascha Heifetz and pianist Vladimir Horowitz have had their detractors.

Years later, Symphony manager Joe Scafidi recalled asking himself how, having wanted only to work on music's behalf, he had managed to find himself in such straits. Music-making is complex enough in itself. Then add the human dimension. Seiji Ozawa had led the San Francisco Symphony to a new place in the consciousness of the nation's music lovers. But a high profile attracts attention of all kinds. Just as the eyes of musical America were trained on the San Francisco Symphony and its glamorous music director, the national press also focused on the struggle over Elayne Jones's tenure. The episode was fraught with questions

that can stir passions almost four decades later. Whether it hastened Seiji Ozawa's departure from San Francisco is unclear, but it cannot have tempted him to stay.

END OF THE AFFAIR

In August 1974, Richard Nixon stopped fighting his long war against the obstruction-of-justice case Congress had brought against him, and he resigned as president of the United States. A departure closer to home came two months later, when David Plant left his post as president of the Symphony Association. Succeeding Plant was Lawrence Metcalf.

Plant had had his woes, for sure. He had seen the ongoing Elayne Jones case unfold, and he had watched helplessly as a strike by city employees kept the orchestra out of the Opera House, which was surrounded by picket lines the musicians could not cross. That resulted in canceled concerts and ticket refunds, and twenty-eight thousand dollars in lost income.

Metcalf could not promise happy times, although he was pleased to report that, as operating costs had risen, so had contributions, individual and corporate donors giving an all-time high of $642,000 in 1973–74, an increase of 2.7 percent over 1972–73.

A June 1975 tour of Japan repeated the European success of two years earlier. Even Tokyo, cool to the orchestra in 1968, was won over. "At the end of the concert," reported *The Daily Yomiuri*, "there was such a burst of shouting as might have greeted a new sumo wrestling champion. No one stirred from his seat for 10 minutes of thunderous

applause." Ozawa had played his cards wisely, programming chestnuts guaranteed to appeal to a public still acquainting itself with Western classical music, including Tchaikovsky's *Pathétique* Symphony, Leonard Bernstein's Serenade (with Concertmaster Stuart Canin), and two works that featured Peter Serkin, the Brahms Piano Concerto No. 2 and the Mozart Piano Concerto No. 27. Such works were a departure from Ozawa's San Francisco programming, which over the years had included such local firsts as George Crumb's *Echoes of Time and the River*, Ravel's *L'Enfant et les Sortileges*, and György Ligeti's *San Francisco Polyphony*, this last work a fulfillment of a commission that the composer accepted happily. In 1972 Ligeti had heard Ozawa and the orchestra play his *Melodien*. He had heard it played by other orchestras, but the rendition he heard in San Francisco, he claimed, was the work's first real *performance*.

Praise such as that was especially poignant now. The pervading sense was that this tour would be the last time Ozawa and the orchestra would travel together. Michael Steinberg, one of the country's foremost writers on music, would join the San Francisco Symphony in 1979 as artistic adviser and program annotator. But in 1975 he was still music critic for the *Boston Globe*, and that January the *Globe* published his telling profile of Seiji Ozawa. "Increasingly," Steinberg wrote, "San Francisco views its relationship with Ozawa with the melancholy of a lover who knows that the end of the affair is inevitable."

A month after the orchestra returned from Japan, Steinberg's prediction was fulfilled when Ozawa submitted his resignation. He would remain as music adviser through the 1976–77 season. This departure, this choice of Boston over San Francisco, had long been dreaded and was now a reality. To say that it cleared the air would be going too far. But by the following January, a new three-year contract with the musicians had resolved several issues. Each year would consist of forty-one weeks plus an eleven-week "supplemental season," amounting to year-round employment. Pension benefits increased. Reseating would require consultation with a review committee of orchestra members if the reseated musician refused to accept voluntary reseating. A major concession was that, if a vacancy occurred as the result of reseating a principal, an open audition would be called.

The year 1976 marked the United States bicentennial, and American music was a major part of the programming, including William Russo's *Street Music* and Loren Rush's *Song and Dance*, both of which had their world premieres, along with music by Barber, Copland, Gershwin, Hovhaness, Ives, Ruggles, Virgil Thomson, and Olly Wilson. Even as he prepared an exit, Ozawa was not one to settle for the tried-and-true.

Just as changes in artistic personnel were in the offing, administrative changes were afoot. In a gesture recognizing the need for increasingly professional staff leadership, Metcalf announced that Joseph Scafidi would henceforth be executive director, while Victor Wong would be manager, the position Scafidi had occupied until then.

Edo de Waart, who had shown much promise as principal guest conductor and had won the respect and goodwill of the musicians, would become

music director beginning with the 1977–78 season. He was young and energetic, and he carried impeccable musical credentials. De Waart himself attempted to keep hopes linked with realities. All he wanted to do, he said, was to make the best music that could be made.

Perhaps he did not want to raise expectations higher than they already were. For the possibilities of music-making in San Francisco were about to broaden dramatically. In late 1976, a design for a new concert hall was approved, and this time construction would go forward. With Seiji Ozawa's departure, the San Francisco Symphony lost a star. But that star had raised the city's consciousness of the orchestra to a peak unknown since the days of Monteux, and although Ozawa might be gone, awareness of the orchestra remained high. In fact, the transition of music directors and simultaneous commencement of the most important building project in Symphony history was a seismic concurrence—hugely challenging and, depending on how the challenge was met, filled with potential for equally huge triumph. The future was filled with uncertainties and opportunities. All of those were focused in the construction of the new concert hall, which Larry Metcalf predicted would be "the most important cultural step for the City since the building of the Opera House." The task of the orchestra and Edo de Waart would be to make good on that promise.

21

22

21

"Two for the Music": announcing the Ozawa–de Waart transition.

22

Ozawa meets with Student Forum members, 1971.

IX.

A WEST COAST SUCCESS STORY

The Edo de Waart Years (1977–1985)

A NEW TEAM FOR A NEW HOME

Edo de Waart's goal for the San Francisco Symphony was refreshingly realistic: to "make as good music as possible." In a world where more expansive words are often associated with stock phrases, reality carries its own excitement. A lot goes into good music-making, and "as good as possible" suggests wider vistas. *Possible* is the key word. Anticipating the newfound possibilities offered by its new home, Louise M. Davies Symphony Hall, the San Francisco Symphony was about to expand its sense of purpose.

Edo de Waart was familiar to San Francisco music lovers when he led his first concert as music director in December 1977. In the two years he had served as principal guest conductor, he had come to know the orchestra, and he tried to assess it honestly. Among its members were some of the finest musicians he had worked with, and others who were not. The battles of the Ozawa years had soured the mood. De Waart knew he faced challenges, but he found challenges enticing. Besides, a new concert hall would soon transform the San Francisco Symphony into a full-time orchestra. He wanted

to be part of all this. He did not know how large a task he had undertaken. More than three decades later, he still considered it the hardest job of his life.

De Waart was thirty-six when he became music director, just a year older than his predecessor had been when Ozawa assumed the post in 1970. Born in Amsterdam in 1941, Edo de Waart had studied at that city's Lyceum. He fell in love with America on his first visit to the country, when he was nineteen and spent three weeks touring the United States with a woodwind ensemble that had been awarded a Fulbright grant. At twenty-one he took a post as associate principal oboist with the great Royal Concertgebouw Orchestra. Two years later he won the Dimitri Mitropoulos Conducting Competition, and with that came the opportunity to work with Leonard Bernstein as the New York Philharmonic's assistant conductor, a post Ozawa had also held. After a season in New York de Waart returned to Holland, where he assisted Bernard Haitink at the Concertgebouw, then moved on to the Rotterdam Philharmonic, first as permanent guest conductor, then as chief conductor. In that post, and as founder and director of the Netherlands Wind Ensemble, he became a champion of new music. With a predilection for the contemporary that was reflected in his love for the latest electronic gadgetry, he was nevertheless also known as a maestro who valued substance over style. "I'm a stickler for playing the music as it was written," he said in later years. "I find . . . vanity in conductors and musicians very upsetting." Vanity may not have been de Waart's strong suit, but the camera and he were friends, and he was glamorous despite himself. With his restrained intensity and boyish charm, he attracted a legion of female admirers.

Having come up through the ranks of the orchestra himself, he understood musicians and their needs; he invited them to seek him out if they thought he could be helpful and maintained that his door was always open. This was not the way every music director operated, certainly not Josef Krips, nor even Ozawa.

This change in leadership style headed a list of other imminent changes. After forty years with the Symphony, the last fourteen of them

in the organization's top administrative position, Joseph Scafidi was ready to retire. Brayton Wilbur, Jr., who would take over from Larry Metcalf as board president in 1980, asked then-concertmaster Stuart Canin how to go about finding a new chief administrator. Canin's advice was simple. Go to the middle of the country, the region with the worst weather and some of the best orchestras. That, Canin maintained, was where the next manager would be found.

He was right, although the process was more complicated than Canin described. It began with an overture from Joe Scafidi, who in 1977 phoned his colleague Peter Pastreich, executive director of the St. Louis Symphony. Could Pastreich suggest someone who might step in when Scafidi left? Pastreich had someone in mind. On March 6, 1978, Pastreich himself was introduced to the board as the San Francisco Symphony's new executive director. During his twelve years in St. Louis, the orchestra there had risen from regional to national prominence. Now Pastreich—"the top orchestra manager in the country, by common consent," said Metcalf when he presented him to the board—was ready to go to work in San Francisco.

Pastreich wasted no time. Since the mid-1960s, orchestras in the United States were increasingly high-budget, big-business operations, and the moment was right to treat them as the professional organizations they had become. Within months, Pastreich identified strategic administrative needs and hired a management team to take them on.

The change was rapid. Among the reasons Pastreich was hired were his many national connections and a

2

2
_____

A scene from the first years of the de Waart tenure.

3
_____

Edo de Waart and the orchestra, 1978.

perspective that extended beyond the Bay Area. Over the past two decades, musicians had come to be recognized as artists and professionals rather than as instruments on which conductors played. Budgets grew as pay scales began to reflect that professionalism. Orchestras' activities expanded. New sources of income had to be sought, not only from individuals but also from private foundations, businesses, and government agencies such as the National Endowment for the Arts. Awareness of orchestras was growing. Television programs such as the Young People's Concerts that Leonard Bernstein led throughout the 1960s with the New York Philharmonic did more than excite a new generation of listeners. They brought a major orchestra and a charismatic conductor into living rooms across the land, into the lives of those who may never have thought of entering a concert hall.

Long-playing records had made a broad cross-section of the orchestral repertory widely available. Concert music, so often considered an art form for the privileged, was reaching a wider audience of the less well-to-do who understood that the real privilege was simply to be able to hear great music. Those lucky enough to encounter an orchestra in the flesh knew that the experience could never be duplicated by any recorded form. By the late 1970s, orchestras saw new possibilities for realizing their artistic potential and broadening their reach. The San Francisco Symphony had to seize those possibilities or be left behind. Pastreich, feeling a mandate to make such a move, became a partner with de Waart, backing artistic endeavor with administrative expertise.

For all his emphasis on management, Pastreich was no technocrat. He understood that music and mu-

sicians were the foundation of the San Francisco Symphony's artistic future—which is not the tautology it seems. He also knew that artists require support behind the scenes. He ramped up departments devoted to artistic administration, marketing, finance, operations, and public relations. "Staff recommendations" became increasingly frequent at board meetings, and soon staff liaisons were established with board committees.

The management consulting firm McKinsey & Co. joined the Association's Long-Range Planning Committee and developed a blueprint for coming years. Working closely with the committee was McKinsey's Robert H. Waterman, Jr., who in 1982 would publish the best-seller *In Search of Excellence* with coauthor Tom Peters. After hours of discussion, Waterman presented the board with three goals: to be a great

6

5

180

5

Peter Pastreich, executive director from 1978 to 1999.

6

Michael Steinberg offers an open-rehearsal audience some context for the music they are about to hear. Artistic adviser and program annotator, Steinberg loved to bring listeners closer to music and introduced Symphony audiences to regular preconcert talks.

7

Edo de Waart and Louise M. Davies assess progress on the new concert hall.

8

Brayton Wilbur, Jr., Symphony president from 1980 to 1987.

orchestra, to be recognized as great, and to serve the community—to which a postscript would be added: to do all this in a fiscally responsible way. Peters also mapped out tactics aimed at meeting those goals: to tour, to record, to broadcast, to fill the house, and to encourage a strong and involved board.

Pastreich himself preferred to keep a low profile, convinced that arts executives, for all their importance, held little interest for the music-loving public. One of Pastreich's appointments did, however, enjoy more visibility: artistic adviser and program annotator Michael Steinberg, who had served in a similar capacity at the Boston Symphony Orchestra after twelve years at the *Boston Globe*, where he developed a reputation as the country's most esteemed music critic. A writer of uncommon eloquence and an engaging speaker, Steinberg almost single-handedly

turned the genre of the program note into an art form. His prose style and his personal style were of a piece, combining erudition and accessibility. In his writing and his preconcert talks, he brought a new elegance to the Symphony. Through his counsel as artistic adviser—a post not commonly found at US orchestras—he advocated new music and offered insights about potential guests.

Excitement about the orchestra and the new home being built for it translated into ticket sales: by September 1979 they were 18 percent above 1978 sales. By September 1980, the beginning of the first season in the new concert hall, all series except Thursday matinees had sold out. A hundred seats for each concert had been held back for single-ticket sales. The subscriber renewal rate stood at 87 percent, about as high as renewal rates go. Change came in

USUALLY NEW, ALWAYS UNUSUAL

Even for a new-music mecca such as the Bay Area, the New and Unusual Music series was special. It brought artists to San Francisco who might not otherwise have performed there: Meredith Monk, Reinbert de Leeuw, Glenn Branca, Pierre Boulez and his Ensemble Intercontemporain, and the unforgettably named composer-pianist Charlemagne Palestine. Names less flamboyant, familiar and unfamiliar, also showed up on NUM programs (in no particular order): James Tenney, Dane Rudhyar, Lou Harrison, Diamanda Galas, Paul Dresher, Charles Amirkhanian, Bruno Maderna, Philip Glass, Aaron Copland, Ingram Marshall, Anton Webern. The series gave John Adams a platform, too. His *Grand Pianola Music* received its world premiere at a NUM concert. The NUM roster even included a work by the Symphony board member and composer Gordon Getty: the opera *Plump Jack*, based on Shakespeare's Falstaff.

7

8

all forms. A study was afoot to assess the relationship between the San Francisco Symphony Association and the San Francisco Symphony Foundation. By September 1980, the two entities would merge, the Foundation's historical reliance on volunteerism being taken up by a new Volunteer Council, the word "Association" being dropped from the title of the umbrella corporation. Pastreich knew the value of a name. No longer would there be either a Foundation or an Association. Now there was only the San Francisco Symphony.

A PLACE FOR MUSIC

With the move to Davies Symphony Hall, the San Francisco Symphony could no longer share personnel with the San Francisco Opera Orchestra, for their seasons would be concurrent. Some musicians remained with the Opera Orchestra, offering de Waart the chance to assemble an ensemble he believed would reflect his concept of good music-making. As the 1980 season opened, 20 percent of those onstage were new to the Symphony: twenty new musicians out of a hundred, including the concertmaster, Raymond Kobler. And now this new orchestra took up residence in a new home. To grasp the significance of this move, consider the path traveled to Davies Symphony Hall.

The Symphony spent its first decade in the Cort Theatre, where playing and listening conditions were little more than adequate. The year 1921 brought a move to the Columbia Theatre for a single season. Then the brand-new Curran Theater became home for nine years, followed by a season at the Tivoli Opera House and at last, in 1932, the first of forty-eight years at the War Memorial Opera House. Over time,

9

*The first performance in Davies
Symphony Hall was a concert for
those who had built it.*

10

*Conductor, orchestra, and audience
join in "The Star-Spangled Banner"
on opening night, September 16,
1980.*

11

Nearing completion on the outside.

12

Nearing completion within.

182

2957

LOUISE M. DAVIES SYMPHONY HALL

HARD HAT CONCERT

INAUGURAL WEEK

SEPTEMBER 13 1980
EIGHT PM

SAN FRANCISCO SYMPHONY
EDO DE WAART MUSIC DIRECTOR

COMPLIMENTARY

COMPLIMENTARY

2957

9

the Opera House's limitations had become more apparent. In the pit, an orchestra sounded fine; but acoustics were not the venue's strong suit for an orchestra on stage. And because the Symphony shared space with the San Francisco Opera and San Francisco Ballet, a fifty-two-week season was impossible. As costs everywhere rose, the possibilities of increasing income remained fixed, and equally fixed were the possibilities of artistic development. A plan for a new concert hall was envisioned in 1964, but a year later the bond issue intended to help fund it was defeated, opposed by those who saw such a venue as a project for the privileged few.

In the wake of the bond issue's defeat, Harold Zellerbach, president of the San Francisco Art Commission since 1948 and brother of former Symphony president J. D. Zellerbach, intensified his labors on behalf of a new performing arts center, an effort he maintained until his death in 1978. Ultimately, he would conclude that private funding was the surest route to a new performance space. But the doomed bond issue convinced him that only those whose lives had been nurtured by the arts would understand their value, and he came to envision city-wide cultural development. That vision helped birth the Neighborhood Arts Program, which was launched in 1967 and is known today as Community Arts and Education. Musicians, writers, actors, and visual artists across the city found encouragement. In the spirit of J. Emmet Hayden, his Art Commission predecessor from the 1930s, Zellerbach reaffirmed the fact that the arts were for all. He also believed San

Francisco needed an adequate space for visiting artists to perform, and thus to enrich the community. The Zellerbach Family Fund commissioned architects Vincent DeMars and John Wells to design a new performing arts center, initially planned for the area directly west of the Opera House.

Although that project gained no traction, the idea of a new hall never faded entirely. By 1973 it was decided that the Symphony itself would fund a new concert hall, although the site now earmarked, at Larkin and Grove Streets, had already been claimed by the San Francisco Public Library for a new main building of its own. In any case, this was an auspicious time to think about building in San Francisco, for the Transamerica Pyramid had opened just a year before. Love it or hate it, the Pyramid was destined to become a city landmark. A new place for music could become another architectural jewel, and the challenge of building one appealed to board member Samuel Stewart, who became president of the recently incorporated Sponsors of the Performing Arts Center. Sam Stewart had already played a crucial role in construction of San Francisco's Bank of America Building during his years as BofA senior vice-president. He was the ideal head of the Sponsors. For seven years, he raised funds for what would become a $27.5 million project. By November 1976 another design was revealed, this one by architect Pietro Belluschi, who had worked with such colleagues as Eero Saarinen, creator of St. Louis's Gateway Arch. With modifications by Skidmore, Owings and Merrill, Belluschi's design was adopted. The site would be the parking lot on the southwest corner of Van Ness Avenue and Grove Street, a parcel owned by the Board of Education, and yielded in return for land of equal value, guaranteed by the Board of Supervisors.

Louise M. Davies was a Symphony board member and a philanthropist whose community efforts included support of the San Francisco Opera, Stanford University, the Exploratorium, and the medical center named after her husband, Ralph K. Davies. In January 1977, she contributed $4 million to the project. "I had the money," she answered when asked why she gave so much, "and we certainly needed that hall." Within six months, only $5 million more was needed to bring funding to its goal before construction could begin. At last, on February 24, 1978, ground was broken for the building that would bear Louise Davies's name. Mayor George Moscone hoisted a gold-painted shovel and turned a pile of soil. Members of the San Francisco Mime Troupe, the theater of sixties counterculture, were on hand to protest what they believed would be a temple of elitism. "Those kids are wrong," Louise Davies said afterward. "This center will be for all the people."

Throughout the summer of 1980, work on the hall proceeded in preparation for a fall opening. The box office staff assigned seats whose locations conformed as closely as possible to those that season ticket holders had occupied in the Opera House. The music library moved cartload by cartload into its new space, two thousand cubic feet of scores and instrumental parts to be housed in custom-built steel shelves extending from two inches above floor level upward, a full fourteen feet to the room's ceiling. Seating charts and musical storage were in place by opening night, although

some walls still awaited paint. But the show went on.

The first listeners to hear a concert in the hall, on September 13, 1980, were familiar with it. They were the workers who had built the place, and the performance for them was billed as a "hard hat concert." The official opening came on September 16, 1980. Louise Davies was delighted when she took her seat. "It puts its arms around you!" she exclaimed about the auditorium.

Then the TV cameras went on—the entire opening concert was telecast live, across the country. Edo de Waart stepped onto the podium. And with the hall, the music extended its arms. Among the works performed that evening, along with Berlioz's *Roman Carnival* Overture, Mendelssohn's Piano Concerto No. 1 (with Rudolf Serkin), and Beethoven's Fifth Symphony, was new music that Louise Davies herself had commissioned: *Happy Voices* by David Del Tredici, a Northern California native who had made his San Francisco Symphony debut as soloist in Saint-Saëns's Piano Concerto No. 2 in 1955, shortly after his eighteenth birthday, and who in the years since had become one of America's foremost composers.

Balloons and confetti showered the audience at the end. Violinist Jorja Fleezanis would go on to become associate concertmaster, but she was new to the orchestra and a temporary player that season. Thirty years later, she recalled the excitement that night—"Ten billion times more excitement in a season opening than I've ever experienced." She sensed that the hall itself announced the Symphony's autonomy, representing one organization standing on its own feet, and housing an orchestra about to grow—about to *become* the

10

11

12

13

Builders: Louise Davies meets with construction workers.

14

A gala evening ends with a balloon drop.

15

Raymond Kobler, concertmaster from 1980 to 1998.

16

Annouuncing a new concert hall.

17

During opening week of Davies Symphony Hall, Yehudi Menuhin conducted Leopold Mozart's Toy Symphony *with a septet of special soloists. Starting behind Menuhin and proceeding counterclockwise: Brayton Wilbur, Jr., Larry Metcalf, Louise M. Davies, Edo de Waart, Agnes Albert, Peter Pastreich, and Sam Stewart.*

18

Davies Symphony Hall on a concert night. Anyone outside could look in and see crowds silhouetted against warm yellow light. As an invitation to join them, the image was more powerful than any spoken welcome.

184

13

14

15

San Francisco Symphony—as it fed on a continuous diet of the symphonic repertory. Sam Stewart and his team, and more than six thousand contributors, had managed to pull off what he described as "the greatest civic project constructed in San Francisco in the last fifty years."

Community groups from around the city filled the hall two nights later, having purchased tickets at special prices for an "All San Francisco Concert," which became an annual tradition. A September 21 concert benefited the musicians' Pension Fund, featuring a performance of Leopold Mozart's *Toy Symphony*. The soloists were a septet representing talents artistic, philanthropic, and managerial, the three sectors that form the foundation on which American orchestras stand. Louise M. Davies herself played triangle. Agnes Albert played the cuckoo, Sam Stewart banged the drum, former board president Larry Metcalf shook the rattle, and the current president, Brayton Wilbur, Jr., played the mechanical quail. Edo de Waart took the part of the nightingale. Peter Pastreich played trumpet. On the podium was the Symphony's old friend Yehudi Menuhin, whose performances to benefit the organization went back to 1934.

The air was filled with happy voices, but one problem was apparent. The acoustics were not what had been expected, something that was true of many American concert halls built in the second half of the century. "Where the Opera House is dull, dim and distant for symphonic music," critic Michael Walsh noted the day after the gala opening, "Davies Hall is alive, even noisy. Last night, in fact, it seemed from my seat in the middle of the main floor overly reverberant."

INAUGURAL WEEK

17

18

Those on stage noticed problems, too. "I remember it was a very confusing space to be in," Principal Percussionist Jack Van Geem recalled in 2005. "The acoustician was bragging about the fact that [the hall] had a seven-second decay. . . . No wonder we couldn't even understand what Edo was saying in rehearsal. When he spoke to us, it was garbled. His voice would just disappear." In concert, musicians strained to hear each other. From the perspective of the audience, sound varied from one part of the hall to another. Those in the center of the main floor who heard muddy textures might be apt to believe that others farther back on the orchestra level were less than candid when they described the splendid sound where they were sitting. But everyone was telling the truth. Just as Bay Area microclimates force residents to bundle up, shed wraps, and rebundle within the space of a few blocks as heat and

cold come and go, the sound in Davies Symphony Hall seemed distributed throughout its spaces in sonic pockets alternately brilliant and dull.

The War Memorial Opera House, as de Waart noted, is a good venue for opera, but not for an orchestra on stage. Having coped with the acoustics there, he and the Symphony musicians now faced new challenges. He maintained a brave attitude in discussing them. "The important thing to remember is that [Davies] is a very big hall—the biggest in the world in cubic feet—over a million cubic feet. So the amount of air . . . we have to make reverberate is a huge amount. . . . Some sounds will travel much better." One source of the acoustic problem was financial. To generate maximum ticket revenue, the hall had been built for maximum seating capacity. Although its 3,063 seats were outnumbered

by the Opera House's total of 3,300, it was still so large that, as de Waart said, some sounds traveled better than others, making some of the hall more congenial to good listening. By adjusting to the hall's environment, de Waart and the musicians worked as best they could, but a million-plus cubic feet of space imposed limits. Twelve years after Davies opened, an acoustic renovation would transform it at last into a performance partner.

Built by the Symphony, the hall is owned by the City of San Francisco, to which title was transferred, with the Symphony guaranteed first rights for the hall's use throughout the year. In 2005, as the Symphony celebrated the twenty-fifth anniversary of the hall's opening, Peter Pastreich reflected on what the hall had made possible. "San Francisco got a rejuvenated Civic Center with first-class restaurants, shops, apartments, and a hotel; three excellent performance venues; a new level of community pride and donor generosity that affected virtually every part of San Francisco; and a world-class orchestra. . . . Davies created the critical mass that enabled the arts in San Francisco to take off. Two orchestras where there had previously been one, more than seventy terrific musicians brought to San Francisco for the Symphony and Opera orchestras, twice the number of concertgoers in the area on most nights—all this transformed the cultural life of the [Bay Area] . . . and confirmed San Francisco's place among the great cities of the world."

MAKING MUSIC CONTEMPORARY
A new home signaled a new era. Davies Symphony Hall heralded a more contemporary mode. The Opera House had served the orchestra well since 1932. But over the years its stern gray façade and its formality had solidified into symbols of "high culture" that seemed exclusive. Now, across the street, stood a building that seemed built mainly of glass, its interior visible to all through massive windows. On concert nights, anyone outside could look in and see crowds silhouetted against warm yellow light. As an invitation to join them, the image was more powerful than any spoken welcome.

Yet the world in which Davies Symphony Hall opened demanded more than a stated commitment to contemporary culture. Just two years earlier, two events had shaken the Bay Area. On November 18, 1978, in an apocalyptic mass suicide, more than nine hundred followers of the Reverend Jim Jones died at the People's Temple complex in Jonestown, Guyana, on the northeast coast

of the South American continent. Jones, who was among the dead, had founded his cult in San Francisco. His victims came mainly from the Bay Area. Most were poor.

A week later, on the morning of November 27, San Francisco Mayor George Moscone and Supervisor Harvey Milk were shot and killed in their City Hall offices by a disgruntled colleague, former supervisor Dan White. Moscone was a popular mayor. Milk was the city's first openly gay supervisor. His assassination added a layer of personal hurt to those who believed him targeted because of his activism on behalf of the city's increasingly visible and vocal gay community. Coming so soon after Jonestown, the City Hall murders seemed somehow connected to the Guyana massacre. Although that suspicion was quickly discounted, San Francisco suffered, for while still trying to absorb the impact of one horror a second had descended.

The culture responds to history. Bach and Mozart speak the language of their times. A composer addressing contemporaries speaks the current language or looks ahead and imagines how it may someday be spoken. While the events of November 1978 never had a direct response in the concert hall—nothing would have been adequate—they were inescapable reminders of the world beyond the concert hall. The question, not uttered then but always on the minds of those who love classical music, was, *How to bridge those worlds? How to speak of contemporary things in a contemporary language?*

Contemporary music and the San Francisco Symphony had been synonymous since the days of Henry Hadley. Pierre Monteux, Enrique

Jordá, and Josef Krips had programmed it without apology. Seiji Ozawa took it further, even inviting shakuhachi flute players and a blues band to share the stage. In Edo de Waart, the Symphony found its most dedicated champion yet of contemporary works.

The Bay Area had long been home to adventurous composers. The composition department at the University of California in Berkeley had numbered Ernest Bloch among its members. It had invited Roger Sessions to encamp as guest faculty in the 1940s and again in the 1960s, and later it would do the same with another composer who became associated with the San Francisco Symphony, George Perle. Andrew Imbrie was a long-time Berkeley faculty member. But when people thought of composers on the cultural edge, they were more apt to look to Mills College in Oakland, where Darius Milhaud had been ensconced from the 1940s to 1971, and where Robert Ashley organized concerts that gave voice to groundbreakers who explored new modes of expression and pressed musical boundaries. Steve Reich, one of Milhaud's students at Mills, encountered a preacher sermonizing on a San Francisco street, recorded him, and used the tape in his first major work, *It's Gonna Rain*. Throughout the sixties, Pauline Oliveros, Terry Riley, and Morton Subotnick were working at the San Francisco Tape Music Center. At the San Francisco Conservatory of Music, the school's New Music Ensemble played works by John Cage, Pierre Boulez, and Morton Feldman. San Francisco was a new-music haven, and in this territory Edo de Waart wanted to stake a larger claim for the Symphony. As head of an American orchestra, he felt duty-bound to help the American musical

Gary Bukovnik

*Artist Gary Bukovnik's first
San Francisco Symphony poster.*

In late March and early April 1982, during the San Francisco Symphony's second season in its new concert hall, the orchestra presented Bach's *St. Matthew Passion*. To announce this special occasion, the Symphony adopted special means.

Earlier that season a local watercolor artist, Gary Bukovnik, had offered to contribute a painting that could be turned into a poster, something to herald upcoming concerts and, in their wake, commemorate them. Bukovnik was obsessed with flowers. They seemed to leap from every panel of paper he mounted on his easel. Music also consumed him. What could be more fulfilling than to nurture two passions at once? For his first Symphony painting, he depicted Easter lilies, flowers naturally associated with Bach's masterpiece and with spring, when the *St. Matthew Passion* was first heard in Davies Symphony Hall.

The poster was a hit. So the Symphony asked Bukovnik for artwork for its 1982–83 season poster. He donated another painting. Since then, the momentum has not stopped: 2011 marked the thirtieth year that Bukovnik donated his original art to the San Francisco Symphony for posters. No other visual artist and American musical organization have enjoyed so long a relationship.

Gary Bukovnik grew up in a Cleveland suburb and was not yet in high school when he discovered the Detroit broadcast *Adventures in Good Music*, and also the Metropolitan Opera's Saturday radio programs. During art school he worked in a record store in downtown Cleveland, just to keep in touch with music. He was twenty-seven when he moved to San Francisco in March 1976, having set his sights on the city's cultural scene. He celebrated his arrival with a night at the Symphony and still remembers what he heard: soprano Martina Arroyo singing the Four Last Songs of Richard Strauss.

Bukovnik's paintings have been shown around the world, from Japan and Australia to France and Spain, and they are on display in the collections of the Art Institute of Chicago, Brooklyn Museum, Library of Congress, and New York's Metropolitan Museum of Art and Museum of Modern Art. In 2005 his work was the subject of a retrospective, *Gary Bukovnik: Watercolors*, published by Hudson Hills Press. "I've been fortunate. Many wonderful artists get nothing. I've been lucky not only to live in San Francisco, but also to have a life in art, doing something I love. I was interested in finding a way that I could pay back San Francisco for giving me a life. I realized I could do that by giving something to an organization that's dear to me. I can't contribute huge amounts of money to the Symphony because I don't have huge amounts of money. But I can give of myself. I always wanted to belong to my community and to the city. In many ways, the Symphony has helped me become part of our cultural life."

19

19

The New and Unusual Music series expanded the Bay Area's contemporary musical vocabulary.

20

Members of the San Francisco Symphony outside Carnegie Hall in the fall of 1980, on the orchestra's first national tour since 1947.

21

During the 1983 New York visit, the orchestra's softball team took on the New York Philharmonic's nine. Final score: San Francisco Sympho-maniacs 11, New York Penguins 6. Edo de Waart hoists the trophy. Zubin Mehta, the Philharmonic's music director, plays the role of the good sport.

22

Philips recording engineers converted Davies Symphony Hall into a studio when the firm began recording the orchestra in 1981. At a break in the music, Edo de Waart confers with the recording producer, stationed in a sound booth.

23

Mayor Dianne Feinstein proclaimed October 13, 1982, "Symphony Recording Day" to celebrate the Philips release of Mahler's Fourth Symphony, which marked resumption of the orchestra's recording.

language, so he sought someone to help direct him to American composers.

As composers learned how receptive the Symphony might be, de Waart found himself inundated with scores. Around this time, the president of the San Francisco Conservatory of Music, Milton Salkind, recommended a member of the school's composition faculty who might be able to assist in reviewing and selecting works for performance. That is how John Adams and Edo de Waart met. Years later, de Waart recalled their first encounter. "John walked into my house and I thought, 'This is the guy I'm looking for.'" In 1978, Adams was added to the Symphony payroll as New Music Adviser. No major American orchestra had ever retained a composer in such a post. The relationship Adams and the Symphony enjoyed became the model for a program launched in 1982, when the New York-based enterprise Meet the Composer began underwriting composer residencies at orchestras throughout the country. Offered the opportunity to choose its own composer-in-residence, the San Francisco Symphony knew exactly whom to hire. Adams moved into the new post and held it for three years, until 1985.

De Waart aimed to create a series devoted to music of the twentieth century, not as a way of culling such music from regular subscription programs, which had always combined new offerings with appeals to more traditional tastes, but to spotlight a broader range of composers. Festivals devoted to Michael Tippett, Vivian Fine, Roger Sessions, and Ellen Taaffe Zwilich were part of subscription weeks during de Waart's tenure, as were a marathon birthday salute to Stravinsky and

a not-quite-so-marathon celebration of Elliott Carter's seventy-fifth birthday. A policy of annual commissions was instituted. One of the resultant works, the Symphony by Tobias Picker, was taken on national tour immediately after its 1983 world premiere during the regular season. De Waart conducted the world premieres of John Adams's *Harmonium* on the subscription series, as well as the first performances of Adams's *Harmonielehre*, perhaps the herald of tonal music's ongoing vitality and a work whose repercussions continue to be felt into the twenty-first century. Even music so confrontational as Louis Andriessen's *De Snelheid*, which elicited critical scorn and audience outrage, was performed as part of the Symphony's normal activities—activities that brought four awards for adventurous programming to the Symphony from the American Society of Composers, Authors and Publishers during Edo de Waart's tenure.

De Waart also envisioned a special series of music for ensembles smaller than a full symphony orchestra. That series, New and Unusual Music, launched in 1980 and was devoted to a spectrum of the century's music, lesser-known works of acknowledged masters standing side-by-side with music of the avant-garde. Even the first NUM concert illustrated this concept: Berg's Chamber Concerto of 1925 shared a program with Ivan Tcherepnin's 1979 *Flores musicales* for Instruments and Electronic Obbligato. The series featured members of the San Francisco Symphony, and also recruits from the broader musical community, such as the Conservatory's New Music Ensemble, Meredith Monk and her ensemble, and Reinbert de Leeuw's Schoenberg Ensemble.

Because the series was not expected to fill a large concert hall, and to emphasize its nontraditional thrust, NUM began in a smaller venue at the San Francisco Galleria, South of Market, moving eventually to the Kabuki Theatre in Japantown. At places like these, listeners could enjoy a drink along with the music when the lights went down. NUM invited concertgoers to dress as casually as they would for a jazz performance or a rock concert. And when the stage was occupied by performers such as the eleven guitarists and the percussionist who delivered Glenn Branca's ear-shattering "symphony" for guitars and drums, the decibels climbed to rock-concert levels.

ROAD TRIPS AND RECORDINGS
The San Francisco Symphony's new concert hall had attracted the eyes of the American music world.

Now the Symphony needed to hold that attention. Not since 1947 had a national tour been scheduled. But in November 1980, just two months after the first concerts in its new home, the orchestra hit the road, to perform first on college campuses across the country—Boulder, Madison, Champaign, Ann Arbor. The next three performances would be in Carnegie Hall, with the final concert at the Kennedy Center in Washington, DC.

The 1980 tour was a riskier undertaking than the marathon journey of 1947. The orchestra on that earlier tour had played together under Pierre Monteux for eleven years. The musicians were familiar with each other, with the conductor, and with the sound they created together. New members populated the orchestra of 1980. They had played together for fewer than eight weeks in an acoustic environment that left much

Volunteerism has long been standard operating procedure at the Symphony. A Women's Auxiliary was organized in 1917. The Women's Public Interest Committee, founded by Anna-Logan Upton, worked on epic fundraisers like the early Black & White Balls in the 1950s, as well as humbler efforts such as the 1961 Phonorama, when members set up shop in the windows of three downtown department stores (I. Magnin's, the White House, and Joseph Magnin's) and phoned ticket-buying prospects. (They sold six hundred subscriptions.)

In 1953, the Student Forum's first members, by now no longer students, formed the San Francisco Symphony Foundation to generate interest in the orchestra. As an organization named for the Symphony but not linked with it officially, the foundation had an identity problem by the late 1970s, its creators having long since moved to the Symphony board. For years, the Symphony had sought to coordinate foundation activities with its own. In 1980, the groups merged. From the foundation grew the Volunteer Council: the VC.

At its head was Kathy Buchanan. From her days as a student subscriber, starting in 1956, through a series of steps not even she recalls, Kathy sat on the foundation board. Now she would help coordinate all volunteers under one parent organization. Her work was cut out for her. Besides those in the foundation, music lovers across the Bay Area had formed working groups dedicated to the Symphony but (like the foundation) not technically part of it. These were the leagues. They became part of the VC structure.

Kathy Buchanan quickly built a fledgling VC of fifteen members into the most powerful band of volunteers at any American orchestra. The new look of the Symphony itself helped her recruit members. That new look—and new feeling—came with the opening of Davies Symphony Hall. A different kind of energy was pulsing through the organization, with an expanded season, an orchestra filled with new members, and a home that heralded a more contemporary mode. The VC grew quickly. In its first year, it realized 180 percent of its income goal. Within three years its membership was at the thousand-plus level it has maintained since.

Arts groups from as far away as England have studied the model of the Volunteer Council. It has won awards from the League of American Orchestras for the creativity of its programs. Its members are spread across the Bay Area, many allied in one of the regional leagues that carry the VC's mission of fundraising, audience development, and community service throughout San Francisco and as far south as San Jose, east to Pleasanton, and

to the northern edge of Marin County. Volunteers' dedication is expressed in many ways; numerically, their work translates into an annual net income of $1 million, vital nourishment for the Symphony operating budget. The VC is the force behind such fundraisers and events as the Black & White Ball and Opening Gala, and such ongoing projects as the Symphony Store and Repeat Performance thrift shop. Radio marathons and Fantasy Auctions have offered high-end prizes in return for dollars pledged or bid. The VC has even produced a cookbook: *A Taste of San Francisco*, published in 1990 by Doubleday, filled with recipes contributed by Bay Area culinary stars.

Symphony leagues have always had an appealing grassroots flavor, sponsoring auctions, art swaps, wine-tastings, domino tournaments, bridge tournaments, "and other happy activities," as a board report from 1972 described league events. Other happy activities are more far-reaching and have resulted from happy ideas. During opening week of Davies Symphony Hall, an exhausted foursome took a break from meet-and-greet duties. While the orchestra played to a packed house, Kathy Buchanan passed her time in the lobby with fellow volunteers Charlotte Mailliard and Genelle Relfe. Along with Deborah Borda, then the Symphony's manager, they reclined on the Grand Staircase and looked out across Van Ness Avenue, at the stately domed image of City Hall illuminated against the night sky, framed by Davies's floor-to-ceiling windows. In the suggestive play of light, they imagined tall evergreen trees decorated for the holidays, standing against those windows and that backdrop. Three months later, this vision grew into Deck the Hall, a holiday party for children. Louise M. Davies herself helped finance the event with a check for ten thousand dollars, which Kathy Buchanan had never requested. Louise Davies was simply a fan of the volunteers. At that first Deck the Hall, she donned a Santa cap, appeared as Mrs. Claus, and handed out toys. The party became an annual event. And each year since 2000, a special edition of Deck the Hall has welcomed children from local community organizations and underserved schools.

In 1990, another touch was added to Davies Symphony Hall's interior architecture when new Volunteer Council offices opened, bringing the volunteers into the Symphony's home, their home. The largest underwriters of the construction project, with a $1 million contribution, were the volunteers themselves, everyone from those who stuffed envelopes to Symphony board members. In those offices are women and men, some just out of college and others long retired, from across the social and ethnic strata. Music brings people together. And if solidarity can be visible, this is the place to see it.

to be desired. But this tour was designed to promote an orchestra still in its infancy. Audiences everywhere responded enthusiastically, although the coveted New York reviews were lukewarm.

From his seat in Carnegie Hall, however, an executive of Phonogram records liked what he heard. Among Phonogram's labels was Philips, with whom Edo de Waart was under contract and for which he had recorded extensively with the Rotterdam Philharmonic and the Netherlands Wind Ensemble. De Waart now insisted on recording only with his own orchestra. Negotiations were completed for ten discs. And so, after a six-year hiatus, the orchestra returned to the recording business on October 16, 1981, when Davies Symphony Hall was transformed into a studio. Three initial releases resulted from these first sessions, one disc devoted to

Mahler's Symphony No. 4 (with soprano Margaret Price), another to music of Respighi, and a third to vocal music of Ravel, DuParc, and Debussy (with soprano Elly Ameling and mezzo-soprano Janice Taylor). Philips had played a key role in developing the new digital technology enlisted to capture the orchestra's sound. When the recordings were released in 1982, they appeared as conventional long-playing records, for few music lovers owned the kind of equipment required to play a digital recording as it was meant to be heard, via a compact disc read by a laser beam. Few music lovers had ever seen a compact disc, let alone heard the sound of recorded music free of pops and crackles, which plagued the grooved platters that were the preferred way of distributing recorded music almost from the turn of the twentieth century.

24

Conductor Jahja Ling was the San Francisco Symphony Youth Orchestra's founding music director. Here he leads a Youth Orchestra rehearsal, 1981.

24

25

Not only recording, but touring was part of the plan for recognition. Although the San Francisco Symphony had not ventured across the country in more than three decades before 1980, another national tour was already underway by 1983, including stops in Chicago, New York City, Boston, and Washington, DC. Critics this time took notice. The *Chicago Tribune*'s John von Rhein wrote that "the San Francisco Symphony plays with an enthusiasm born of confidence." And Roy Guenther in the *Washington Post* praised a "performance of nobility, passion and grandeur." Two years before this journey the orchestra had toured the West Coast, and a year after that the musicians played throughout California. Now board president Brayton Wilbur suggested that a sponsor be sought for a tour of Europe, in celebration of the orchestra's seventy-fifth anniversary season in 1986–87.

NEW BLOOD AND FESTIVALS

In the spring of 1980, sixty members of the San Francisco Symphony attended a Board of Education meeting to voice their support of public school music programs, already suffering cutbacks since the passage of Proposition 13 in 1978. Soon orchestra members would put their advocacy to work in a new way. The opening of Davies Symphony Hall enabled board member Agnes Albert to realize a long-cherished dream, a youth orchestra. Opera House schedules had never allowed sufficient time or space for such an ensemble to rehearse or perform. With a home of its own, the Symphony was able to host an orchestra of young musicians.

Auditions for the San Francisco Symphony Youth Orchestra were held during the last week of May and first week of June 1981. Of the

25

In 1982, the Black & White Ball was reintroduced to San Francisco. Dormant since 1969, the revived ball occupied venues throughout the Civic Center. From left: Charlotte Mailliard, who conceived the new ball, Edo de Waart, and Judy and Brayton Wilbur.

26

Installing the Ruffatti organ's final set of pipes, 1984.

27

Among the recordings Edo de Waart and the orchestra made for Philips was a disc recorded shortly after the Ruffatti organ was installed in Davies Symphony Hall. This account of the Saint-Saëns Organ Symphony featured soloist Jean Guillou.

three hundred who auditioned, eighty-five musicians were selected, ranging in age from eleven to twenty and coming from as far away as Napa and Santa Cruz. In September, the ensemble met for its first rehearsals under San Francisco Symphony Assistant Conductor Jahja Ling, who served as Youth Orchestra music director. Rehearsals would take place every Saturday afternoon, preceded by hour-long sectional rehearsals coached by members of the San Francisco Symphony. The young musicians paid not a cent for this preprofessional training, but they were expected to work hard. They would present three full-length concerts in the course of the season. Repertory would be challenging. No concession would be made to inexperience.

At its first concert, on January 17, 1982, the Youth Orchestra offered what was undoubtedly a finer performance than the San Francisco Symphony itself had delivered at its debut some seventy years before. Youth Orchestra musicians were better-trained and more thoroughly rehearsed, and orchestra members were coached by skilled professionals. Guest artists performing with the San Francisco Symphony also worked with the Youth Orchestra in rehearsals. Kurt Masur, Isaac Stern, Yo-Yo Ma, Emanuel Ax—all contributed their expertise in its early years. By 1983, conductor Masur, not a man to dispense compliments easily, told Ling that the ensemble was the finest youth orchestra he had heard anywhere.

In its first two years the Youth Orchestra also proved itself a vital member of the community. The young musicians performed for Queen Elizabeth II of England when she visited the city, and also for the

California Music Education Convention, Laguna Honda Hospital, and at the grand opening of Opera Plaza. In years to come they would perform at Mayor Willie Brown's inauguration and for the opening of the San Francisco Public Library's new main building.

The full-length season made possible by Davies Symphony Hall ensured much more than a youth orchestra. Part of the year-round employment that Symphony players now enjoyed was devoted to annual festivals in June, starting with a Beethoven Festival that would be a feature of every season until 1995. Among the highlights of this yearly event were 1983 concerts in which Kurt Masur led the nine symphonies. Michael Tilson Thomas conducted a less traditional Beethoven Festival in 1989, re-creating the marathon concert of 1808 that saw the first performances of the Beethoven Fifth and *Pastoral* symphonies. Mostly Mozart festivals, patterned on those presented at Lincoln Center, were a feature of every season from 1979 to 1990. Autumn of 1984 saw a festival celebrating the music of Johann Sebastian Bach, commemorating the three hundredth anniversary of his birth.

FIGURES FOR SUCCESS

The excitement about this revitalized San Francisco Symphony translated into increased contributions. Just as money had become a more common topic of American conversation and contemplation in the early 1980s, funding told a story about the San Francisco Symphony's growth. By late fall 1980, $1.05 million had been raised for the fund that covered annual expenses, a 10 percent increase over the preceding year.

26

27

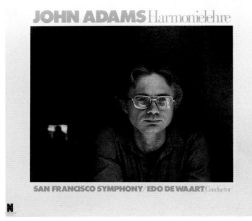

JOHN ADAMS Harmonielehre

SAN FRANCISCO SYMPHONY / EDO DE WAART Conductor

28

28

Among Edo de Waart's last projects as music director was a recording of John Adams's Harmonielehre, *made shortly after he led the San Francisco Symphony in the world premiere of this seminal work.*

29

At a press conference on March 27, 1984, Herbert Blomstedt was named Edo de Waart's successor.

Generosity came in many forms. Great instruments define an orchestra's sound but are prohibitively expensive. To help leap that hurdle, donor Pauline Chickering established a fund intended for the purchase of exceptional instruments.

Donations of every kind proved increasingly important as the National Endowment for the Arts slashed funding. The NEA appropriation totals for 1981 were scheduled to be lowered from $175 million to $159 million, the 1982 appropriation from $190 million to $119 million, and the 1983 appropriation from $207 million to $130 million. And every arts organization in the country wanted a piece of this.

In the climate of the early 1980s, every arts organization also had to use its own entrepreneurial expertise, creating not only new performance opportunities, but new ways to raise money. Americans of a conservative bent felt the country was getting its groove back. The Iran hostage crisis had been resolved and Jimmy Carter, who had chided the country for its "crisis of confidence," yielded the White House in 1980 to a former governor of California, Ronald Reagan. Dress-up parties came back in style. In 1982, the first Black & White Ball was held since 1969.

Even in the recessionary climate of 1982, and once the novelty of the new concert hall had passed, ticket sales remained strong, projected to end higher than the year before. Sound finances, never a Symphony strong suit in times past, had become the order of the day. By September 1983 a projected annual deficit of $219,000 had been eliminated, and a net operating surplus of $136,000 was posted, enabling the Symphony to capture a Mellon

Foundation challenge grant, conditional upon posting a positive operating balance for five consecutive years. And a year later, still another surplus was posted.

More needed to be done. In 1984 a campaign was launched to raise the current endowment of $13 million—low in the economy of the times—to $35 million within the next five years. That goal was expected to be reached by September 1986, the beginning of the Symphony's seventy-fifth anniversary season.

Sometimes, in discussing the finances of an arts organization, a sense of the art itself recedes. Yet financial stability and the music are always fused. A case in point was the construction of Davies Symphony Hall. Another was the installation of the element that completed the hall. Davies opened minus a concert hall organ, although an organ had always been part of the plan. The instrument commissioned from Fratelli Ruffatti of Padua, Italy, began to arrive in San Francisco in a series of shipments in the spring of 1983. Its $1-million-plus cost was underwritten with a donation of $350,000 from benefactor Frank Tack. Installation began in July 1983 and was complete the following March. Its inauguration, on April 7, 1984, was marked with a gala concert. Tickets were in such demand that a post-gala program of organ solos was scheduled for midnight.

A TRANSITION

In helping repopulate the orchestra and in leading it into Davies Symphony Hall, Edo de Waart had assumed an enormous job. The many new vacancies had been filled quickly, but not all were filled with permanent players, and establishing a

29

stable group took another three seasons. De Waart and the musicians worked hard. A fundamentally new orchestra had been formed. But for the conductor's critics, change had not come fast enough. "I had spent my capital," de Waart recalled in 2010. "I was exhausted." The musicians focused on his strengths, and they rallied around him. "That gave me a tremendous lift."

De Waart announced his departure in 1983. He planned to return to Holland in 1985, as music director and principal conductor of the Netherlands Opera. Familiar figures such as André Previn and Kurt Masur had been discussed as his replacement. But in February 1984, Herbert Blomstedt, then almost unknown in the United States, led two weeks of concerts that intrigued the audience, the press, and the musicians. Blomstedt, the dark-horse candidate for music director, was offered the post and accepted.

As Edo de Waart prepared to leave San Francisco during the 1984–85 season, the Symphony was able to sustain the increase in attendance that came with the move to Davies Symphony Hall. The Symphony's budget had more than tripled since 1974, but so had income from the regular subscription series. De Waart's last season was filled with his favorite works. He opened with the Mahler Eighth Symphony, and his final concert as music director, in March 1985, was another work by Mahler, the Symphony No. 5. As ever with de Waart, contemporary works played a prominent role in programming— among them was the Symphony-commissioned *Harmonielehre*, the last work John Adams would write for the orchestra while composer-in-residence and before he embarked on a career that would see him become America's highest-profile composer.

Looking back on his San Francisco years, Edo de Waart remained modest. "I was lucky in being able to lure excellent players who were approaching the top of their game. We got a lot of good depth in the strings. I felt quite proud that I left a very good orchestra."

De Waart in fact had been key in the Symphony's transformation. Spiritually and psychologically, the move to Davies Symphony Hall was the equivalent of staking out territory on a new planet. On this expedition, which de Waart had captained, the orchestra discovered its capacities. Before his arrival, it had been demoralized by protracted labor battles and a music director who increasingly had his sights set elsewhere. De Waart's steadiness was an antidote. "Nothing good will come of not spending enough time with an orchestra," he said. He had endured the disapproval of those who thought progress was too slow. His strength, he maintained, came from the men and women on stage. Alert, eager, and flexible—these were the qualities he noted in the players. The *Christian Science Monitor* concurred, praising the orchestra in 1984 for its elegance and flexibility. As Edo de Waart prepared to take his leave of the San Francisco Symphony, it had become, as *Time* magazine proclaimed in 1983, a "West Coast success story."

x.

MANDATE FOR CHANGE
The Herbert Blomstedt Years (1985–1995)

THE MAN FOR THE JOB

At first the match seemed puzzling. Consider the San Francisco Symphony's music directors up to 1985. Henry Hadley and Alfred Hertz had been larger-than-life personalities, the one a dashing podium figure and composer, the other a bearded émigré who galvanized players with Romantic ideals and Old World discipline. Issay Dobrowen possessed a polish and charisma that initially counterbalanced a hands-off artistic attitude. Pierre Monteux's winning personality and consummate artistry enabled the orchestra to sculpt a national identity while establishing deep local roots. Enrique Jordá, who

began as a rising star, left exasperation in his wake. The commanding Josef Krips was a Maestro with a capital M, a man who represented the Viennese tradition. Seiji Ozawa captivated audiences with his love beads and thrilled them with electric conducting. Edo de Waart applied the ballast that helped an orchestra coalesce as it evolved into a great ensemble. Now came Herbert Blomstedt. San Francisco demanded a quotient of personal color from its celebrities, from Emperor Norton to the Beat poets, and if the color was not quite standard-issue, all the better. Herbert Blomstedt seemed

to make a point of deflecting attention from himself onto the music. His first San Francisco Symphony concerts in 1984 drew a committed response from the orchestra and made critics ask for more. "He was out to make a vibrant experience from a routine ritual," wrote Paul Hertelendy in the *San Jose Mercury News*, reporting on performances of Schubert's *Unfinished* Symphony and the Beethoven Fifth, "and the enthusiastic standing ovation at the end reflected his triumph." Beyond style or intrigue, Blomstedt possessed a more vital credential, the power to inspire. He was hired

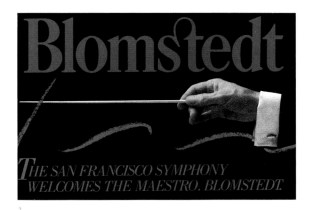

THE SAN FRANCISCO SYMPHONY
WELCOMES THE MAESTRO. BLOMSTEDT.

2

198

as music director a month after he first led the orchestra, his term to commence in September 1985.

In 1984 Herbert Blomstedt was all but a stranger to United States music lovers. Those familiar with his work knew it primarily from his recordings with the Swedish Radio Symphony, with which he had traversed the symphonies of Carl Nielsen. More blank stares. The Danish composer Nielsen, like his champion Herbert Blomstedt, was not a household name.

But European music lovers knew what this man was all about. He came to the San Francisco Symphony from the Dresden Staatskapelle, not only one of the world's oldest orchestras but one of the greatest. Its musicians had chosen him to be their conductor. His arrival in San Francisco was, in a roundabout way, a kind of homecoming. Herbert Blomstedt never claimed to be American, but he was a US native. He had been born in 1927 in Springfield, Massachusetts, about ninety miles west of the Boston suburb of Somerville, birthplace of Henry Hadley. Herbert Blomstedt's mother was American, his father Swedish. With his parents the boy moved to Sweden at the age of two, his father having been called back to his homeland by the Seventh-Day Adventist Church, which he served as a minister.

Blomstedt was drawn in his youth to theological as well as to musical studies, and although music won out, he would remain intensely devout. As a member of the Adventist Church, he abided by its principles, shunning meat, alcohol, caffeine, and tobacco, and refusing to rehearse on Saturdays, his church's Sabbath—although he did conduct concerts on that Sabbath because he viewed concerts as celebrations and spiritual communications, whereas rehearsals were strictly hard work.

He studied first at the Stockholm Conservatory and trained in musicology at the University of Uppsala. He continued to perfect his craft at the Royal College of Music in Stockholm, then studied conducting with Igor Markevitch in Salzburg, and Baroque and Renaissance music at the Basel Schola Cantorum. On a fellowship from the Swedish-American Foundation, he came to the New England Conservatory in Boston and went on to the Juilliard School in New York, where he sneaked into Arturo Toscanini's Carnegie Hall rehearsals. Leonard Bernstein arranged a Tanglewood Scholarship for him, and it was at Tanglewood that Blomstedt won the Koussevitzky Conducting Prize. He returned home an accomplished conductor, eventually taking posts as music director of the Oslo Philharmonic, Danish Radio Symphony, and Swedish Radio Symphony. In 1975 he assumed the directorship in Dresden. Among his recordings with the Staatskapelle was a set of the nine Beethoven symphonies still considered a benchmark among the recorded versions of those works.

He shunned flashiness for its own sake, whether in his personal life or in his art. He was unfailingly polite and ever the gentleman. Anyone

expecting to find a domineering European "maestro" struck from the Krips mold would be disappointed. Blomstedt understood human potentials and limits. If anything, his spiritual approach to the music, and his willingness to discuss that approach, seemed to make him the ideal artistic resident of a Northern California swept up in the tidal currents of the New Age. "Through music we can sometimes travel to that part of the human soul where we are closest to the finest aspects of ourselves," he said, and, "When I talk about playing good music, I refer to all the aspects of the musical experience. You want the music you produce . . . to reflect as deeply as it can the possibilities of the music as it echoes our souls and touches our feelings and fertilizes our thoughts. . . . As musicians, we all feel that music is, in a sense, the world in itself—not separate from the other world and also not mirroring it, but a world that derives its life from the total human experience."

Those who got to know Blomstedt even superficially soon discovered a rich store of humor behind a public persona easily misinterpreted as severe, given what many took to be the austerity of his lifestyle. His sharp wit could be punning (Ezra *Laderman*, he told a Symphony staffer who referred to that composer as *Laserman*, might be contemporary, but he was not *that* contemporary). His humor could also be obscure ("San Francisco too has had its Edo Period," he announced upon de Waart's departure to a baffled audience unfamiliar with Japanese history and Asian art). His jokes could even be amusingly barbed (a colleague's rehearsal technique, he once remarked to a third party, exemplified the concept of the iron fist inside the velvet glove, minus the iron fist).

Children adored Blomstedt and were drawn to him immediately. Early in his career, after all, Swedish television had presented him in a music-education program whose young viewers knew him as Uncle Baton.

But nothing brought out Blomstedt's seriousness as did the challenge to make good music. Hard work and single-minded intensity were his trademarks. "It is true that musicians in an orchestra really have the joy of their musical lives in the hands of one man in front of them. For those of us who have the privilege of making music as conductors with the musicians, it is a great challenge to try to do our best, to be prepared to the edge of our teeth, to be loaded with the music that we want to play, so that our mutual efforts are rewarding." For almost seventy-five years, San Franciscans had been entertained by music directors, sometimes in ways that went beyond the

music. *New York Times* critic John Rockwell advised board President Brayton Wilbur, Jr., that the two prerequisites for making a great orchestra were money and the right conductor. Shortly before his departure, Edo de Waart had claimed that his successor would be the one to lead the orchestra to a higher artistic plane. That was Herbert Blomstedt's mandate.

FULFILLING THE MANDATE

Herbert Blomstedt made his first mark as music director even before he assumed the post officially. Since 1980, a Beethoven Festival had occupied two weeks every June. Music lovers like to think of Beethoven as inexhaustible, and he is; yet so familiar have audiences and musicians become with him that he is susceptible to a kind of automatic, cruise-control playing and listening that ignores his radical ideas and

4

199

2

In his first Symphony season, Herbert Blomstedt was introduced simply as "The Maestro."

3

Symphony President Brayton Wilbur, Jr, prepares to hand the baton to Herbert Blomstedt at the opening of the Beethoven Festival in June 1985, Blomstedt's first appearance with the orchestra since his appointment as music director.

4

Less than a year after assuming his San Francisco post, Blomstedt led the orchestra in an acclaimed Carnegie Hall performance.

3

5

Charles Wuorinen, composer-in-residence from 1985 to 1989.

6

The Youth Orchestra's first tour of Europe came five years after the ensemble was founded.

7

The City of Vienna Prize, world's top honor for youth orchestras.

5

in-your-face confrontations. In June 1985, Blomstedt took on Beethoven, conducting the nine symphonies. Conductor and musicians fused their intensity in performances that revealed a myriad of detail, always in the context of the larger architecture. This was Beethoven heard anew. Blomstedt had left his calling card.

As Herbert Blomstedt's tenure began, the podium throughout September was occupied not by him but by Michael Tilson Thomas, who over the past eleven years had developed a close relationship with the orchestra and who ten years later would become Blomstedt's San Francisco successor. Tilson Thomas now saved the day by stepping in, Blomstedt's prior commitments making it impossible for him to open the San Francisco season.

When, in October, Blomstedt arrived to take command of the orchestra, he led two weeks of programs that would become entirely characteristic. The first week included Roger Sessions's Symphony No. 2, whose world premiere Pierre Monteux had led in San Francisco in 1947 and whose thick and thorny textures still challenged listeners almost forty years later. Also on Blomstedt's program was *Ein Heldenleben* by Richard Strauss, a composer with whom the conductor enjoyed special affinity, and whose music would appear on his programs nineteen times in the coming decade. Blomstedt's second week included Bruckner's Fourth, the *Romantic* Symphony. These two weeks were signs of things to come, for Blomstedt and the orchestra would go on to record each of these works together.

National touring, jump-started in the de Waart years, was a Blomstedt priority. In March 1986, he and the

orchestra embarked upon their first trip together, beginning with concerts in Sarasota and Orlando, Florida. This was analogous to a Broadway show opening in Philadelphia to work out the kinks. Concerts followed in Carnegie Hall, Chicago, and Ann Arbor. The music included two Blomstedt specialties, Nielsen's great *Inextinguishable* Symphony—audiences would come to know Nielsen better as they became more well-acquainted with Herbert Blomstedt—and Sibelius's *Tapiola*. "Conductor and players, in their first season together, already have settled into a productive rapport that exalts music over manner, substance over surface," announced the *Chicago Tribune*. "The impact was eloquent and stunning." Performances that could draw such a response were remarkable, considering the flu that accompanied the tour and which passed from musician to musician. Blomstedt himself remained impervious to illness and seemed blessed with unwavering good health. Alasdair Neale, named assistant conductor in 1989, recalled Mrs. Blomstedt's prediction that he would never be called upon to step in and conduct in her husband's place. She was right.

Repertory for this first tour with Herbert Blomstedt included *Movers and Shakers* by Charles Wuorinen, who had succeeded John Adams as composer-in-residence. Two artists more different than Adams and Wuorinen are hard to imagine, in their music and in their personalities. Each had his devoted followers. Each was an impassioned composer striving to communicate. Wuorinen was a dedicated modernist while Adams had an encompassing, willing-to-try anything approach. Adams was on a mission to bring back the audience he believed Schoenberg and his disciples had alienated, while Wuorinen, one of those disciples, gave the impression that the alienated audience simply needed a sure path into new works. Aggressive to the point of belligerence in his defense of new music ("Critics and journalists don't know anything," he once told *Newsweek*), he was happily ensconced in San Francisco, whose audiences he believed were the country's most open-minded and most inclined to give pioneering composers a chance.

Wuorinen had an undeniable sense of playfulness and grandeur in his music, too. Among the works he composed for the orchestra during his tenure as composer-in-residence were *The Golden Dance*, which launched the Symphony's seventy-fifth anniversary season in 1986 and which Blomstedt and the orchestra recorded for Nonesuch, and *Genesis*, a large-scale choral piece that compressed the creation story into forty minutes of brilliant and unexpected sounds, seeming to emerge from distant reaches of consciousness and communicating a sense of a world taking shape as the music unfolded. Both compositions were Symphony commissions, two of more than seventy-five works the Symphony has helped bring into being since 1961, when it performed its first commission, Charles Cushing's *Cereus*. Commissioning is essential to an orchestra's job description because an orchestra is a part of an evolving society, not merely a museum. Recognizing this fact, Peggy and Ralph Dorfman, the husband-and-wife philanthropist team who had supported new music at the San Francisco Symphony since 1971, celebrated the orchestra's seventy-fifth anniversary by establishing the Dr. Ralph I. Dorfman Commissioning Fund. To date, the Dorfmans and the fund

have helped underwrite almost thirty new works.

Touring, commissioning, recording. In some ways, Herbert Blomstedt was continuing on a trajectory that Edo de Waart had established. But Blomstedt was just getting started. One of the greatest of late-twentieth-century composers, Witold Lutosławski, was invited to write a work for the orchestra's seventy-fifth anniversary and conduct its world premiere in a week of concerts devoted to his music. *Chain III*, the result of the commission, was introduced in December 1986 under Lutosławski's direction, the first of his three San Francisco Symphony engagements.

6

Even before the seventy-fifth anniversary season opened—with a gala concert telecast on national TV, and featuring pianist Rudolf Serkin and soprano Leontyne Price in one of her final public appearances—the San Francisco Symphony Youth Orchestra had prepared European music lovers for artistry bred in the Bay Area. In July 1986, the Youth Orchestra embarked on a tour of Europe. In this first overseas journey, led by David Milnes, Jahja Ling's successor as Youth Orchestra music director, the young musicians headed the bill at the Fifteenth International Youth and Music Festival in Vienna, where they took the world's top honor for a youth orchestra, the City of Vienna Prize. The concert was broadcast, as was their Budapest performance. One press notice, from their Strasbourg concert, summed up the reaction: "These young people made music naturally, not in order to amaze the public, but above all to honor the works themselves."

In all ways, the Symphony seemed to be riding a crest. By June 1986,

7

the year-end deficit of $450,000 predicted in January had been converted to a $50,000 surplus. Although difficulties had been created by lower-than-expected grants from the city's Hotel Tax Fund and from the National Endowment for the Arts, total earned income at season's end was 2.4 percent over budget, total expenses were 2.2 percent under budget, and the budget was balanced for the eighth consecutive year.

The $23 million endowment campaign launched during de Waart's tenure and spearheaded by Brayton Wilbur received a major boost when Gordon Getty pledged to match $2 million of contributions, as long as those donations represented increased gifts or new gifts: the Getty Challenge, it was called. Board member Rhoda Goldman, in a campaign appeal, explained that the Symphony had never been so close to its goals—superb music-making, service to the community, and worldwide recognition—but that future annual deficits, major ones, were projected unless the Symphony's capital base increased. In only seven years, the budget had grown from $5.6 million to $18.6 million. And while the San Francisco Symphony enjoyed the most loyal audience of America's major orchestras, making it first in attendance, it was last in endowment strength among ensembles with comparable budgets. Within a year, the campaign would reach its goal, and efforts would continue to exceed the goal.

REASONS TO CELEBRATE
In early September 1986, shortly after the seventy-fifth anniversary season commenced, board members, Symphony staff, and eighteen members of the orchestra gathered to discuss long-range

8

Rehearsal at the Musikverein in Vienna, 1987.

9

Violinist Isaac Stern accompanied the orchestra on tour in 1987. In London, Blomstedt and Stern confer about Prokofiev's Violin Concerto No. 1.

9

203

plans. The pressing question was, *What was necessary for the future?* Among the answers: annual tours to Carnegie Hall, more opportunities for musicians to play chamber music, improved acoustics in the concert hall. The consensus was that "greatness" had been achieved, and the goal now should be to maintain and enhance it. Statements like these can seem grandiose, or just naïve. Greatness is not a plateau to reach, occupy, and defend. Even Beethoven had off days. As Michael Steinberg pointed out at that meeting, in an opinion seconded by board members Peter Platt and William Edwards, greatness is never truly "achieved" but is a permanent target.

Throughout its history, going back to its earliest days, the San Francisco Symphony had been preoccupied with the thing called greatness, which few seem able to define but which everyone seems to recognize.

Probably every major arts organization shares that preoccupation. What distinguished the talk of "greatness" in September 1986 is that this was one of the last times the term was so lightly used. As a word, it became less in evidence at the San Francisco Symphony. As a concept, it grew. The emphasis, unspoken but felt, was on showing rather than telling, on action rather than words. The Symphony's seventy-fifth anniversary provided a rationale for celebration. Hard work would bring reasons to celebrate.

Within several months, the Symphony embarked for Europe. Fourteen years had passed since the last tour of the continent. From February 11 to March 8, 1987, the orchestra gave eighteen concerts in seventeen cities, starting in New York and then continuing to London, Brussels—where Enrique Jordá was in the audience— Paris, Strasbourg, Vienna, Linz, Munich,

Berlin, Hannover, Geneva, Zurich, Milan, Florence, Turin, Stuttgart, and Frankfurt. The reviewer in Paris's *Figaro* expressed surprise that the orchestra could exhibit such brilliance in Berlioz's *Roman Carnival Overture* along with such mellowness in the Brahms First Symphony; and in playing the Brahms, he said, "San Francisco became a European city." The Vienna audience offered a prolonged and enthusiastic response to Bruckner's Symphony No. 6. Any American orchestra risks scorn in taking such a quintessential Viennese masterpiece to that city, for Vienna tends to dismiss outsiders' efforts to perform *its* music, but Blomstedt and the musicians cracked the code. Playing in a variety of halls on tour sharpens an orchestra's responses, each venue demanding that its acoustics be met on the hall's own terms. Vienna's legendary Musikverein, for instance, amplified the brass, and players had to translate *fortissimos*

NIELSEN
SYMPHONIES 4 & 5
SAN FRANCISCO SYMPHONY
HERBERT BLOMSTEDT

10

ORFF
CARMINA BURANA
LYNNE DAWSON · JOHN DANIECKI · KEVIN McMILLAN
SAN FRANCISCO SYMPHONY & CHORUS
HERBERT BLOMSTEDT

11

204

10

The Symphony's first Decca release captured France's Grand Prix du Disque award and inaugurated a cycle of the Nielsen symphonies.

11

The recording of Carmina burana *brought the Symphony its first Grammy.*

12

The San Francisco Symphony was featured in the 1988 Hong Kong Festival's San Francisco Week.

13

Nancy Bechtle, Symphony president from 1987 to 2001.

into *mezzo-fortes*. Blomstedt was delighted with what he heard. In Berlin he remarked that, while he always had good answers to the frequent question of why touring was important, he now had been given the best answer of all: the way it helped mold the orchestra's playing.

With that European tour, Blomstedt and the San Francisco Symphony opened a new chapter. They continued the story that spring, when negotiations were completed with Decca for a series of recordings. In those days Decca, among the world's most respected recording firms, marketed its products in the United States on the London label. Decca/London had achieved fame for legendary recordings that included the first stereo version of Wagner's complete *Ring* Cycle. The firm regularly recorded ensembles such as the Vienna Philharmonic, the London Symphony Orchestra, and the Chicago Symphony. Now Herbert Blomstedt and the San Francisco Symphony would join this roster.

The first recordings for Decca/London were made in the fall of 1987. Two CDs resulted, a Hindemith disk that included the *Mathis der Maler* Symphony, and a disk devoted to Carl Nielsen's Fourth and Fifth Symphonies, inaugurating a cycle of the composer's six symphonies. Blomstedt, among the world's foremost interpreters of Nielsen's music, took his share of grief from audiences who remained immune to its nobility, charms, and excitement, and Nielsen failed to find a place in the hearts of San Francisco audiences. But in their Nielsen cycle, the orchestra and its conductor created one of the great recorded documents of the late twentieth century. A year after its

release, the first Nielsen disk was awarded France's Grand Prix du Disque. Two years later their recording of the composer's Second and Third Symphonies won Britain's *Gramophone* award. The San Francisco Symphony had entered the world's music scene. The Bay Area had become an international music destination.

No one took any of this as a sign to rest. In February 1988 the orchestra visited Asia. The San Francisco Symphony was the featured attraction in the Hong Kong Festival's San Francisco Week. Concerts followed in Taipei, Fukuoka, Osaka, Nagoya, and Tokyo. Herbert Blomstedt, announced the *Hong Kong Standard*, "is able to get his players to present what amounts to a combined explanation and spiritual experience. There isn't anything better that can be done."

The tour was the Symphony's first visit to Asia since 1975. San Francisco had already reemerged across the Atlantic, and now it took new root across the Pacific as well. The sense of new beginnings was potent. In late 1987 Brayton Wilbur, Jr., stepped down as board president. Wilbur could be pleased with what had transpired in his seven years at the helm, years in which the Symphony had experienced its most rapid growth to date, with a new home, regular recording and touring, and an overall sense of newfound energy. Wilbur claimed that all this had brought him the most fun of his life. In 1985, the *San Francisco Chronicle* had named him Arts Man of the Year. He was, the *Chronicle* stated, an enemy of the status quo. Wilbur was not always known for his modesty, but he was genuine in his response to such praise. "If you only knew how unremarkable I am," he maintained. "This is a *we* deal, this Symphony business." He professed to be just one of eighty-four board members committed to the music and musicians. But Peter Pastreich was unequivocal and went on record, stating that, without Wilbur, the changes at the Symphony could not have happened. Wilbur was a San Francisco native who had come to the Symphony board in 1969, following the path of his father, who had joined in the 1930s. A gifted executive, Brayton Jr. was the latest in a long line of talented individuals dedicated to the community. Some board presidents were more in love with music than others. All shared a passion for the Bay Area and a belief in culture's power to rejuvenate mind and spirit: to be a pleasure, to bring people together, to be a force for good.

Succeeding Wilbur was Nancy Bechtle, the first woman to occupy the presidency since Leonora Wood Armsby and a descendant of one of the Symphony's founders, E. S. Heller. To her job, Nancy Bechtle brought Armsby-like enthusiasm. When a consulting firm suggested how effort and financial support together needed to bolster "vision" in long-range planning, her board colleague Sam Stewart summed up the consultants' recommendations as "Wisdom, Wealth, and Work." To those three W's, Bechtle added a fourth: Wit. In articulating what she hoped to do, she declined to use the word *great*, but everyone knew what she meant when she said, "I would like to arrive at a San Francisco Symphony concert in Vienna and find it as difficult to buy tickets to hear our orchestra as it is to get tickets when the Vienna Philharmonic comes to San Francisco." Nancy Bechtle spoke her mind, and spoke it clearly. That was part of her persona, along with a populist outlook and a democratic personal style. Her taste also extended past Beethoven. She loved country music.

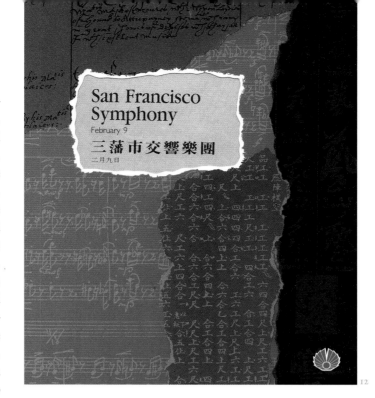

14

14

Children gather to hear an AIM ensemble.

IN CONCERT FOR THE COMMUNITY
While the San Francisco Symphony was establishing itself internationally, matters closer to home called for attention. Music programs had long been the victims of budget cuts in the city's public schools, and recent cuts had been brutal. In the early 1980s Yehudi Menuhin had made an eloquent plea on behalf of funding such programs, citing his own early experiences at Symphony concerts, where he was inspired to devote himself to studies that would transform him into one of the world's best-loved concert violinists. But every school music teacher and every arts organization in the city knew the struggle to maintain music programs would not be won. It was this realization that in 1988 led the Symphony to join forces with the San Francisco Unified School District and fight the battle on its own terms. With youth programs and Young People's Concerts

and Summer Music Workshops, the Symphony throughout its history had committed itself to Bay Area children. Its most intense effort yet would launch in 1988: Adventures in Music, AIM. With a grant from the National Endowment for the Arts, AIM targeted students in grades four and five in seventeen San Francisco public schools, reaching about six thousand students. By 2008, its twentieth year, it was serving more than twenty thousand students in grades one through five in all San Francisco public schools. AIM's genius was to coordinate core curriculum with music. These lessons were reinforced in classroom visits by small ensembles recruited from the Bay Area's music community—a mosaic of styles, from salsa to reggae to klezmer, all available through AIM. Years before, the Student Forum had proved how students could be transformed into Symphony patrons, even presidents. AIM started the

HERITAGE TRANSMISSION: GIVING CHILDREN ADVENTURES IN MUSIC

At San Francisco's Lakeshore Elementary School, a lesson in architectural basics is reinforced when the Bellavente Wind Quintet plays Elgar's *Pomp and Circumstance* March No. 1, the "graduation march." Bassoonist Beverly McChesney asks the other members of the group to line up. The musicians divide phrases of the music between them and play it—in the wrong order. McChesney asks the students to rearrange the musicians in the right order. Her colleagues move as directed by the kids and play their fragments again. Wrong. At last the students get the order right and the theme emerges in proper sequence. This lesson about structure is part of AIM—Adventures in Music, the San Francisco Symphony education program launched in 1988.

Since its founding, AIM has offered free music education to students in the San Francisco Unified School District, expanding eventually to reach every student in grades one through five. What began in 1988 as a test project in seventeen schools grew within its first year to encompass seventy-seven schools and more than nine thousand youngsters. AIM, the longest-running program of its kind among US orchestras, reaches an average of twenty-three thousand children annually.

AIM invites children into music by exploring music of all kinds. Along with Mozart and Beethoven, students are exposed to Afro-Cuban rhythms, Asian folk tunes, jazz, blues, hip-hop. While students are having a good time, they learn how music can play a role in other studies. AIM programs, created by the Symphony, offer musical experiences linked to instruction in subjects such as math, science, and writing. In-school performances by professional Bay Area musicians are a cornerstone

of the program. These AIM ensembles tie music to lessons in poetry, vocabulary, spelling, and more. Every year, students come to Davies Symphony Hall for a concert designed for them.

At the beginning of the academic year, AIM trains teachers to weave music into the school day. In 2008, Daniel Gelfand, a fifth-grade teacher at San Francisco's George Peabody Elementary School, described how AIM worked in his classroom. "Music applies to science, as we study the physics of sound. It's part of history when we learn the story of the music we hear. Then we talk and write about these things, and it becomes part of language arts."

When John Santos and his Afro-Latin band performed for them, fourth- and fifth-grade students at West Portal Elementary School were reminded that they had already encountered the *shekere*. The shekere, a beaded gourd-rattle, is part of Mexican composer Carlos Chávez's Toccata for Orchestra, which they had heard the San Francisco Symphony play. The shekere made the connection between concert hall and classroom. Students vied to be chosen to point out Cuba on the map. Two boys, curious to know how many classes of forty students can fit into Davies, worked on a division problem they devised.

"The business of creating an informed patron begins in the first grade," wrote the *Wall Street Journal* in 2008. "Here the San Francisco Symphony serves as the industry's benchmark." And that year, as AIM celebrated its twentieth anniversary, Dana Gioia, then completing his term as chairman of the National Endowment for the Arts, reflected on AIM and the future. "In the twenty-first century, the United States is competing in a global environment. If we succeed, it will be through innovation, creativity, and ingenuity. How can we believe this will happen if we remove the arts from the schools and from the communities?"

process earlier and its goals were at once less grand and more profound: to connect children with a cultural heritage they might otherwise never discover.

Just as revelations emerged in the classroom—those micro-encounters when a band or wind quartet played for students—larger encounters also led to discovery. In November 1988, when Blomstedt and the orchestra took Elliott Carter's Oboe Concerto (with soloist Heinz Holliger) to the East Coast shortly after giving the US premiere at home, the *Washington Post* concluded, "It may be time to add the name of San Francisco to the legendary list of America's 'Big Five' orchestras." To the superb US orchestras other than those of Boston, Chicago, Cleveland, New York, and Philadelphia, *Big Five* is a hated label. Now the San Francisco Symphony was helping turn it into an anachronism. And while the Symphony

was fashioning a national and international image, California itself was never forgotten. In the fall of 1989, Blomstedt and the orchestra took their music to Fresno, Sacramento, Chico, Santa Rosa, and Shasta County. No audiences were more appreciative than the audience in Weed, a logging town three hundred miles north of San Francisco, just off Interstate 5. Weed is not an affluent community and enjoys none of the cachet of its neighbor ten miles south, the city of Mount Shasta. Weed is, however, home to a community college, the College of the Siskiyous, and it was in the auditorium there that Blomstedt and the San Francisco Symphony performed for an audience who thrilled to Dvořák and Tchaikovsky. One listener summed up the occasion's significance. "This is the greatest thing that *has* ever happened in Weed," he said. "And it is probably the greatest thing that *will* ever happen in Weed."

The Northern California tour in early October 1989 (a Southern California counterpart would take place the following February) was prelude to a series of East Coast concerts a week later, including performances at Carnegie Hall and Avery Fisher Hall in New York. Short as the East Coast jaunt was, and as brilliant as the display of autumn reds and yellows outside Boston, everyone knew that such color was an omen of what the winter there would hold. As their plane headed west from Logan International Airport on a bright Saturday morning, the musicians were happy to return home, where the weather was constant. The baseball fans among them were especially eager to be back. Later that day the first-ever Bay Area World Series was set to begin, the San Francisco Giants and the Oakland A's having won their respective league championships.

15

A scene from Concerts for Kids.

15

ONE PLAYER TO A PART

The San Francisco Symphony plays 160 concerts a season, yet orchestra members don't stop there. They juggle their calendars to find slots between performances, practice, and teaching, all for chamber music.

Aurora Quartet, Caselli Quartet, Donatello Ensemble, Shostakovich Quartet, Stanford Quartet. Those are some of the many ensembles in which Symphony musicians of the past few decades have been active. Such groups give regular concerts. Other performances are organized as the opportunity arises or the occasion demands. For musicians, chamber music is a compulsion and a tonic—a revitalizing balance to their work in the orchestra, where a large group effort is what matters. Chamber music is one player to a part.

Preconcert chamber music, which the San Francisco Symphony began offering occasionally in the early 1990s, proved so popular that it led in 1993 to a five-concert Sunday afternoon chamber music series, featuring Symphony musicians. André Previn, Yo-Yo Ma, and Lang Lang have performed with Symphony chamber ensembles, and orchestra members who are also composers—such as violinists Mark Volkert and Sarn Oliver, and trumpet

player Mark Inouye—have had the opportunity to hear their music performed.

"Chamber music provides a chance to be heard and to be recognized as an individual," says Symphony violist Seth Mausner, whose efforts in the 1990s resulted in the preconcert chamber music performances that led to the regular series. The lessons learned and the skills developed in chamber music are translated back to the orchestra. Intonation and pitch skills, for example, are honed in a group with one string instrument on a part, when pitch has to be carefully matched, because even minor discrepancies are more immediately apparent than they would be in a large ensemble. Says Mausner: "You have to make a beautiful sound all the time in a chamber group."

Some benefits of chamber music are less quantifiable. Rapport can't be measured, but chamber music helps build an orchestra's cohesiveness as players get to know each other better and absorb music from different points of view. "Even if musicians don't have a lot of verbal input in orchestra rehearsals," Mausner explains, "we still rely on each other to play together. There has to be an understanding, a trust, an ability to listen."

17

16

In the aftermath of the Loma Prieta earthquake, October 17, 1989.

17

Five days after the Loma Prieta earthquake, Herbert Blomstedt led the orchestra and combined choruses of the Symphony and San Francisco Opera in Beethoven's Ninth Symphony. An audience of twenty thousand gathered in Golden Gate Park for this free concert, aimed at helping to heal a devastated Bay Area.

18

In December 1988, the month after the San Francisco Symphony introduced Elliot Carter's Oboe Concerto to North America, the orchestra took it on tour. At Carnegie Hall, Carter acknowledges applause. At extreme right is oboist Heinz Holliger, the concerto soloist.

Three days later, the Bay Area changed suddenly. At 5:04 on the afternoon of October 17, San Francisco felt the first waves of a magnitude 7.1 earthquake rocketing northward from the epicenter in the Santa Cruz Mountains, one of whose peaks, Loma Prieta, would lend the quake its name. The shaking began as many shakings do. Anyone accustomed to tremors paid little heed, until the tremors refused to subside but built into an agitation so massive that buildings rotated off their foundations, a freeway collapsed, and a section of the Bay Bridge's upper deck opened like a trap door, one vehicle plunging into the fissure and others, hitting their brakes, stopping at the edge of the chasm. At Candlestick Park, the Giants and the A's were warming up for game three of the World Series when the stadium began to move. The shaking was captured by TV cameras during the pregame show, and in moments the images made their way around the globe. Yet few in the city knew the extent of the damage. Phone service and electricity had been knocked out in most areas. Only as the evening progressed did those with battery-powered radios and televisions begin to comprehend what had taken place. They stared in disbelief at images of buildings destroyed in the Marina. They witnessed the heroic efforts of East Oakland residents working against the clock to free those trapped in their cars after the top deck of the Cypress Freeway had sent tons of concrete crashing onto vehicles. When the reckoning was taken, the most massive earthquake the Bay Area had experienced since 1906 had claimed the lives of sixty-three people, and almost thirty-eight hundred had been injured. Property damage stood at $6 billion. Davies Symphony Hall was relatively unharmed. The

Ruffatti organ received the brunt of the damage. Repairs to the instrument would cost twenty thousand dollars, most of it covered by the Federal Emergency Management Agency.

Herbert Blomstedt, having arrived in San Francisco from Boston with the orchestra, was set to return to Europe for a series of guest engagements. He rearranged his schedule immediately. Blomstedt understood music's healing power. Five days after the Loma Prieta earthquake, on a Sunday afternoon, an audience of twenty thousand gathered in Golden Gate Park to hear Blomstedt conduct the orchestra and the combined choruses of the San Francisco Symphony and San Francisco Opera in a free performance of Beethoven's Ninth Symphony. Donations were collected for those left in need by the quake. But more than anything, Beethoven's grand public statement made the day memorable. It was the composer's testament to the restorative power of music and *agape* and community, reaffirming continuity and inspiring the crowd with the conviction that a future existed. The event was called *In Concert for the Bay Area*. No title or slogan could have told the story more clearly.

TOGETHER, IN THE COMMUNITY

Community was on the mind of the Symphony board. In 1988, the city's largest arts organizations had been attacked for not including more nonwhite members on their boards and staffs. This attack came with a corollary: large arts groups focused on art created by white Europeans, and their largest audiences were those of white European heritage. Ronald Reagan's second term in office was ending, and to those who believed the wealthy had been offered unfair advantages over the past eight

years while those of more modest means had suffered, championship of nascent and struggling groups seemed urgent. Large arts organizations, it was claimed, were discriminatory in their hiring practices, and city money should therefore be shifted from support of large organizations to support smaller, ethnic, and multicultural organizations.

From its earliest days, the Symphony had been determined to be a good neighbor. On June 2, 1988, Nancy Bechtle and Peter Pastreich testified before the Board of Supervisors. Bechtle noted that 12.5 percent of the Symphony's fifty-six staff members were minority group members and 68 percent were women. As for service to the community, she pointed to the Youth Orchestra (with forty-seven minority members out of a total membership of ninety-five), Concerts for Kids (targeting urban schools), and the All San Francisco concert.

Pastreich explained that women had been part of the orchestra since the 1920s, also that 34 percent of the orchestra's current roster of 108 musicians were women, compared to 15 percent in Philadelphia, 17 percent in Boston and Chicago, 18 percent in New York. African-American and Asian conductors had been guests, works by black composers and by women had been performed. Pastreich acknowledged the applicant pool for orchestra membership included few minority candidates. Then he went to the heart of the issue. Any musician hoping to reach the playing standards of the Symphony would have to have begun music studies early—as early as age five or six, for a string player. Children had to be made familiar with concert music, and encouraged to study instruments. This argument also touched on the

corollary issue. Most of the Symphony's music might have been composed by white Europeans, but no ethnic group owns that music. Early exposure, regardless of background or race, could create a listener for life. Recognizing such a goal was one thing. Making good on it was no easy matter, especially given music cutbacks in the schools. But even as they spoke, work was proceeding on the Symphony's Adventures in Music program, which would soon bring music into the lives of schoolchildren of all races and ethnic backgrounds.

The source of municipal support for arts groups was Grants for the Arts (of the Hotel Tax Fund, made up from city hotel room taxes). GFTA rules mandated inversely proportional distributions to small and large arts organizations, smaller groups receiving a greater percentage of their annual budgets than large groups— although if viewed as simple *amounts* of funding, it was true that larger-budget organizations received larger grants. Within a year of the controversy over minority hiring, distribution of monies from Grants for the Arts was again called into question. The issue was that large arts organizations, presumably in less need of financial assistance than smaller organizations, received the bulk of city funding. It was proposed that GFTA

211

funding be awarded directly by a peer review process. The controversy led the Board of Supervisors to create a Cultural Affairs Task Force, a fifty-nine-member team to assess public arts funding. Along with Nancy Bechtle and board member Ellen Magnin Newman, Peter Pastreich was part of this team.

Pastreich has called Grants for the Arts "the most enlightened arts program in America," in that funding is based not on politics but on a formula determined by an organization's budget. It seemed to him that even smaller arts organizations were reluctant to disturb the objective apportionment guidelines, which did indeed remain in place. Then, in 1992, Pastreich helped the Cultural Affairs Task Force negotiate an arrangement that, rather than redistribute funding, enlarged it. A Cultural Equity Endowment was formed, financed with Hotel Tax money, and earmarked for multicultural arts groups. Small and large arts organizations share common needs, and forming the endowment acknowledged that fact. In San Francisco, arts funding is never a simple matter, although for the present a win-win resolution had been found.

CONSOLIDATING A REPUTATION

The Symphony's reputation for championing new music continued throughout the Blomstedt years with several high-profile commissions. In 1990, the orchestra performed the world premiere, with soloist Ole Böhn, of the Violin Concerto by one of America's foremost composers, Elliott Carter. Another distinguished American, George Perle, succeeded Charles Wuorinen as composer-in-residence in 1989, and in 1991 Blomstedt and orchestra performed new works by Perle and Peter Lieberson at home, in Carnegie Hall, and at Lincoln Center. In 1992, John Harbison's Oboe Concerto, commissioned for Principal Oboist William Bennett, was given its world premiere, and the following year Bennett, Blomstedt, and the orchestra introduced the work to Europe, then recorded it. French composer Henri Dutilleux was the focus of a series of concerts in early 1992.

"Every symphony concert has a weird, modern piece on the program," *Chronicle* columnist Steve Rubenstein had written in 1988, objecting to the programming of Elliott Carter's A Symphony of Three Orchestras. Two weeks later the *Chronicle* published a letter from Assistant Concertmaster Mark Volkert, himself a composer, in which he sided with Rubenstein. In response to such outcries, the *Chronicle*'s Robert Commanday, defending new-music programming, suggested that, since the Symphony appealed not only to those interested in exploring but also to those of less adventurous tastes, it should offer what he called a Coward's Series of only familiar works.

Things had gone too far. In January 1989, Volkert, Commanday, and Michael Steinberg were featured in a panel discussion on "Morning Concert," a radio call-in show (on KPFA-FM) hosted by composer and critic Charles Amirkhanian. For two hours they discussed an orchestra's responsibility to help create new music and, by performing it, to help listeners relate to what was transpiring in the music world. The Symphony had been housed in Davies Symphony Hall for eight years and during that time its sensitivity to such issues had increased, for in some ways music's future hinged on addressing them. Is all new music worth playing? What are the criteria for performance? Volkert objected to Carter's work because he found it lacked "human vitality," a point on which he and Steinberg differed. Music is often called timeless, but contemporary additions to the canon are clearly essential. If an orchestra performs only the familiar, is it abdicating responsibility to stimulate new thinking and expose listeners to other musical worlds? Does an orchestra have such a responsibility?

No simple answers were forthcoming, except for one. Any orchestra wishing to be taken seriously as part of the living culture must act as part of the living culture. In 1992 and 1993, efforts on behalf of contemporary music were focused in a festival called Wet Ink. British composer George Benjamin served as Wet Ink director in its first year, when sales for the two weeks of new-music concerts far exceeded budget, and Chinese-American composer Bright Sheng spearheaded Wet Ink in 1993.

Reputation was based on repertory and performance, but it was also built by introducing the orchestra to the world. The high point of touring in these years came in August 1990, when Blomstedt and the orchestra embarked on a sixteen-city, eighteen-concert tour of major European music festivals, including the first San Francisco Symphony appearances at festivals in Salzburg, Edinburgh, and Lucerne. The *London Times*, reviewing two Edinburgh performances, said that "Blomstedt's two San Francisco concerts were revelations, the undisputed critical hit of the music programme." In Salzburg, a single work—the Bruckner Fifth Symphony—was given a performance one reviewer described as the finest thing he had heard at the festival that summer. The Salzburg audience included Sir Georg Solti, who in the years since he had led the San Francisco Symphony in 1954 had become one of the world's most sought-after conductors. Sir Georg scribbled a note afterward and ensured it made its way to Blomstedt. It was a single exclamation and a single sentence—"Bravo!!! You and the orchestra are marvel-

lous!"—signed with a single name, "Solti." (The next day, invited to guest-conduct in San Francisco, Solti accepted. He would make good on the commitment in 1995.) A pair of concerts in Berlin took the orchestra to two different halls in what had been two different worlds: to the Philharmonie, home of the Berlin Philharmonic, in the erstwhile Western sector, and also to the ornate Schauspielhaus, in what had been the Eastern Zone. The Wall dividing the city since 1961 had come down less than a year before, and Berliners were still in celebration mode. Peter Pastreich proclaimed the tour the greatest he had experienced in his three decades of orchestra work. Trumpet player Laurie McGaw found an image to express something similar: "We knew we were there to hit the ball, and we knew we hit it."

21

19

Herbert Blomstedt, Composer John Harbison, and Principal Oboist William Bennett review the score of Harbison's Oboe Concerto, commissioned by the Symphony for Bennett and premiered in December 1992.

20

After performing Bruckner at the Salzburg Festival, Blomstedt and the orchestra won a new fan.

21

George Perle, composer-in-residence from 1989 to 1991.

22

Violinist Kum Mo Kim. Her father, John S. Kim, founded Seoul's National Philharmonic—Korea's first symphony orchestra—and at Tanglewood was a fellow conducting student with Herbert Blomstedt.

213

20

Sir Georg Solti KBE

Secretariat:
Charles Kaye
51 Elsworthy Road
London NW3 3BS

Telephone: 071-722 3365
Fax: 071-586 2433
Telex: 21344 Solti G
Cables: Soltisec LDN NW3 3BS

Bravo !!! 21. Aug. 90
You and the
Orchestra
are marvellous !

Solti

22

23

214

23

At ceremonies in Los Angeles in 1993, Chorus Director Vance George accepts the Symphony's first Grammy, for recording of Carmina burana. *Presenting the award is flutist James Galway.*

24

Backstage at the Brussels concert in 1990, Herbert Blomstedt met with an old friend of the San Francisco Symphony, Enrique Jordá.

25

In Leipzig, conductor Kurt Masur acted as tour guide for a group of Symphony musicians. Here they gather outside the church of St. Thomas, where Bach served as music director. Masur's audience (from left): Ezequiel Amador, Bruce Freifeld, David Krehbiel, Julie Giacobassi, and Mark Lawrence.

26

Cellist Mstislav Rostropovich, a surprise guest at Isaac Stern's seventieth birthday celebration, appeared in ballet dress. Here Slava cavorts with Stern and concert host Gregory Peck.

24

25

26

Earlier that summer, the Symphony celebrated the seventieth birthday of an artist with whom the organization had enjoyed a long friendship. Violinist Isaac Stern, one of San Francisco's favorite sons, was feted in a free concert at Stern Grove. Actor Gregory Peck hosted the event and headed the all-star cast, which also included violinist Gil Shaham, who would become a regular Symphony guest in years to come. Conductor David Zinman led the orchestra. The legendary cellist Mstislav Rostropovich made a surprise appearance in his first guest stint with the San Francisco Symphony since his Moscow concert in 1973. The audience required a moment to figure out what was happening, for Slava materialized dressed in a tutu, a sight that elicited the hoped-for gasps of shock followed by laughter, followed by delight as this odd ballerina picked up a cello, took a chair, and began

playing the Swan movement from Saint-Saëns's *Carnival of the Animals*. The next year, the Symphony would recognize another great San Franciscan, Yehudi Menuhin, with a seventieth-birthday performance.

The chemistry was good and the momentum continued. Recording proceeded at such a pace that, by the end of his decade-long San Francisco tenure, Blomstedt had led the orchestra in performances of sixty-two works that filled twenty-nine CDs. Among them were cycles of the Nielsen and Sibelius symphonies. In addition to the Grand Prix du Disque and *Gramophone* Award, the recordings were honored with Belgium's Caecilia Prize, Japan's Record Academy Award, and the Cannes Classical Award. And in 1993, the Symphony captured its first Grammy: for Orff's *Carmina burana*, named Best Choral Recording. Touring continued: back to Asia in the spring of

1992. Europe beckoned again in 1993, the same year as a tour of Southern California, the Midwest, and the East Coast; then another European journey in the spring of 1995, including concerts in Vienna, Budapest, Warsaw, London, Madrid, and Lisbon.

Blomstedt and the orchestra were capturing the world's attention. For consistently great concerts in San Francisco, another change was crucial.

SETTING THE SOUND STRAIGHT

"Great orchestras deserve great halls," Herbert Blomstedt told a press conference in 1990, shortly after the European festival tour, when he revealed plans for an acoustic renovation of Davies Symphony Hall. The time had come to face the facts. "The hall we came into in 1980 was seriously flawed, acoustically," Principal Bassoonist Stephen Paulson recalled. "And we all had to put a positive spin on it—not only for the public, but in our own minds." Spin may have been part of the strategy, but no one can be accused of reluctance to deal with the acoustic issues. Within six years of the hall's opening, acoustician Lawrence Kirkegaard began exploring modifications to help the musicians hear each other better on stage. At that point, in 1986, no major structural changes were envisioned. Their necessity was not equally apparent to all. Brayton Wilbur reported that his guest at a concert had pronounced the hall "acoustically perfect." And those words meant something, because Wilbur's guest was Ray Minshull of Decca Records. But from where Minshull would have sat, in Wilbur's box in a far loge, the sound had always been excellent. The same was not true everywhere else.

27

28

Acoustics is a strange mix of science and art. Those who built the great concert halls of the nineteenth and early twentieth centuries, venues such as Boston's Symphony Hall or Vienna's Musikverein, seem to have gotten everything right with a rudimentary grasp of physics, using little more than slide rules to work out their calculations. A Civil War–era meeting house like Mechanic's Hall in Worcester, Massachusetts, was not even designed as a concert hall, but to hear the San Francisco Symphony there was to be overwhelmed by a depth and burnish of sound that the ensemble's own home did not allow.

The space in which an orchestra plays defines and shapes the ensemble's sound. Musicians' ability to make music with the kind of polish and concentration it demands depends on what each of them hears from colleagues across the stage. In Davies, musicians strained to hear one another. As cellist Peter Shelton said, "Playing musically [was] an act of defiance." Blomstedt's contention that "great orchestras deserve great halls" was no slogan invented by the Symphony public relations department.

The plan Blomstedt revealed had evolved over five years. Larry Kirkegaard (of R. Lawrence Kirkegaard & Associates, based outside Chicago), one of the world's foremost acousticians, had devised the renovation strategy by analyzing the characteristics of Davies Symphony Hall and comparing them to those of halls the musicians had played in throughout the United States, Europe, and Asia. Accompanying the orchestra on tour, he measured sound levels not only in halls filled with people, but in empty halls, where he exploded rubber balloons, noted the decibel levels, and analyzed the

sound patterns of those reverberant bursts. Through interviews with orchestra members, Kirkegaard determined what they liked and disliked about various venues, and in his design for the San Francisco Symphony's home he tried to create an acoustic profile as close as possible to those favorite places.

Then, during 1991 and 1992, Davies Symphony Hall underwent an acoustic makeover carried out over two summers. Co-chairs Leonard Kingsley and Ray Dolby headed a renovation committee of board members, musicians, and members of the Symphony administration.

Phase One, in the summer of 1991, called for replacement of the nineteen acrylic dishes suspended over the stage. Originally designed as sonic reflectors, these discs were separated from each other by gaps through which the rising sound could escape like smoke up a chimney.

The dishes allowed for only limited tilt adjustment, and any such adjustment had to be performed manually. Height adjustment was electrical but not calibrated. In place of those went an acoustic canopy of fifty-nine Plexiglas panels—individual panels that, as a unit, made an all but continuous surface that drove sound back toward the stage. And each component of that surface could be adjusted at the touch of a control-panel switch, creating configurations tailored to the music and memorized by a microchip for future reference.

The more radical changes came in Phase Two the next year, when the auditorium was taken apart and reassembled. Working from Kirkegaard's design and with plans drawn up by architect Dave Larson and architectural supervisor Al Johansen, both

29

of Skidmore, Owings and Merrill, a team of two hundred builders labored from late April to early September. They demolished walls and removed all seats on the main floor. They dry-walled and plastered, installed new plumbing and electricity, and pre-fabricated structural steel. The new side walls above the stage presented designers with a special puzzle. The walls had to be prefabricated, light enough to be carried into the hall easily and lifted into position without a crane—which the stage would not support—yet dense enough to reflect sound. The solution: From a skeleton of structural steel erected on either side of the stage, between ceiling and terrace floor, construction crews hung interlocking modules, forty-four per side—great pods that, together, would give the illusion of one sweeping curve of masonry. In reality, those modules are made of fiberglass and are lined with steel tubing. Once the modules were hoisted

and welded into place, the tubes were filled with silica sand—thirty-three tons per side, blown in by compressed air—to give the walls the density and weight that acoustician Kirkegaard wanted. The paneling around the stage was removed and replaced with a heightened grillwork of cherry wood, hiding diffusers that would bounce sound back to the musicians in a way they had never experienced here. The previously flat stage was fitted with risers. In the audience, the floor of the orchestra level sloped upward from stage to rear of hall in a more pronounced gradient, en-suring the best sightlines. Aisle seat-ing replaced the former pattern of continental seating. Concrete was poured for the floors of the new boxes lining the sides and back of the orchestra level. Parquet was cemented to subfloor.

27

Davies Symphony Hall, just before the second and most extensive phase of acoustic renovation.

28

The renovated interior of Davies Symphony Hall.

29

Formal portrait in Davies Symphony Hall before its renovation, 1992.

30

31

30

To celebrate the Youth Orchestra's tenth anniversary, a CD compilation documented a decade's highlights.

31

Nancy Bechtle and Herbert Blomstedt take a sledgehammer to the stage bullnose, commencing Stage Two of the acoustic renovation.

When the dust cleared, the auditorium was smaller—seating capacity shrank from 3,063 to 2,743, volume from a million cubic feet to 950,000 cubic feet. The place was also more beautiful. The price tag for all this: $10 million, paid for by thousands of private gifts from subscribers and friends, and from the Symphony board, musicians, and staff. These gifts in turn helped earn major challenge grants from Gordon Getty, William Hewlett, and the Kresge Foundation.

The payoff was immediate, and long-term. Bassoonist Steve Paulson believed the orchestra's development began with the renovation, when he could hear his colleagues and even see them better, as though he were playing chamber music.

"Davies Symphony Hall is one of the friendliest halls in the world, in terms of feeling comfortable as a player on stage," said Alexander Barantschik, who became concertmaster in 2001 and is a veteran of the world's great concert halls. "In Davies, you can play really softly and still have the impression that the sound travels all over the hall, and you hear your sound. It returns to you. Some halls are a struggle. Davies Hall is not." Conductor Michael Tilson Thomas enjoyed the hall's new warmth, its participation, the way it sustained the sound, enabling the orchestra to concentrate on how a sound starts and ends. Some halls force musicians to think about each note's beginning, middle, and end, demanding attention that could more fruitfully be given to the music's essence.

Principal Percussionist Jack Van Geem summed up. "You develop your sound based on what you hear. Before 1992, we were the orchestra despite the hall. The hall has now become part of the orchestra."

After gala performances of Beethoven's Ninth Symphony to celebrate the hall's reopening that September, Herbert Blomstedt and the orchestra began the regular season with another epic work, Mahler's Symphony No. 2, the *Resurrection* Symphony. This music, with a dynamic from almost inaudible *pianissimos* to ear-shattering outbursts, demonstrated conclusively that Davies Symphony Hall was now a genuinely fine venue in which to encounter music.

On a Sunday in early October, the Symphony shared the good news with all. A Community Open House, free to everyone, welcomed the entire Bay Area to an afternoon of music—all kinds of music. Here was the opportunity to examine the new venue, and to hear it.

PASSAGES

Herbert Blomstedt still enjoyed the love of San Francisco audiences, but in November 1992, around the time that voters elected Bill Clinton as presidential successor to George H. W. Bush, Blomstedt announced that the Symphony also would undergo a transition of leadership. He would relinquish his post as music director in the fall of 1995, assuming the title Conductor Laureate.

Blomstedt, who had never spent much time in the United States before coming to San Francisco, was candid about how he believed the country had shaped him. "I think the American way of living—greater openness, more tolerance, especially in this liberal, open, and tolerant city—cannot help but influence a person in a good way. I think I am a more open, more spontaneous person than when I came here ten years ago. Europeans often say that America has been good for me"—and at that he laughed uproariously.

Blomstedt was convinced the orchestra had "found itself." It had, he believed, developed a personality whose brilliance he compared to that of a Nobel Prize winner, fixing on an analogy that might have been suggested by his native Sweden. The musicians always wanted to do their best. "They're offended if they are not allowed to."

By June 1993, a new music director had been hired: Michael Tilson Thomas, who had first conducted the orchestra in 1974 and who had often been mentioned as a future music director. Michael Tilson Thomas had long been referred to informally as MTT, but that monogram would soon become standard in talking about him in San Francisco. When he arrived to conduct a two-week festival of Russian music immediately after his appointment was announced, the concerts sold out immediately. A love affair had begun.

A sense of the future was concentrated into the denouement of Herbert Blomstedt's tenure, although no one could predict what that future would look like. In 1986, discussions of the "future" had looked toward visits to Carnegie Hall, acoustic improvements, and opportunities for Symphony musicians to play chamber music; and with the inauguration of a chamber music series in 1993, all those marks had been met. Not all the news was good. In December 1993, the orchestra went on strike for a week, holding fast especially on the issue of medical benefits, whose costs were escalating. No one was happy. A board summit called Vision 2000, looking toward the coming millennium, examined ways to increase income and control expenses. The deficit projected for the 1994–95 season would be the first in twenty years. Major expenses were increasing at almost twice the

cost of inflation. Contributing to the budget's structural problem was reduced government and corporate funding.

But in September 1995, as Michael Tilson Thomas was about to conduct his first performances as music director, subscription sales were $665,000 over the previous season, and single-ticket sales were $118,000 ahead of where they had stood in September 1994.

The Blomstedt Decade, as it was known, had catapulted the San Francisco Symphony out of the provinces and into the consciousness of the world. Herbert Blomstedt had fulfilled his mandate beyond anyone's expectations. The San Francisco Symphony, wrote Michael Steinberg, had been among music's best-kept secrets until Blomstedt's arrival—as Blomstedt himself had been, with little public name recognition. "It was a gamble on both sides, this marriage—bringing to San Francisco a man, one of whose most striking attributes was the studied avoidance of glamour and show; and, on Herbert Blomstedt's part, transplanting himself into a world in many ways vastly different from the one he knew. It worked, and it worked because on both sides there was inquisitiveness and trust, and because it was intrinsically good."

XI.

ON THE FUTURE'S FRONTIER

The Michael Tilson Thomas Years (1995–present)

WHAT'S COMING NEXT?

Suddenly the pace increased. The shift from an analog to a digital world had seemed gradual. Then, as though overnight, life filled with websites, blogs, hand-held devices, email, texting, downloads, apps. Innovations new in recent memory soon vanished, while those not yet invented were likely to be obsolete within a few years or a few hours of their release. As amazing as the technology itself was the speed with which it took hold. If Bay Area music lovers chose to mark this new period's onset, they could name a date: September 6, 1995, the day Michael Tilson Thomas led his first concert as San Francisco Symphony music director. The techno-transformation and the new tenure were coincidences. Yet anyone prone to find symbols in events would have an easy time with this pairing. In the history of the San Francisco Symphony as in the society at large, a new era had begun.

For years Michael Tilson Thomas had been called MTT—one of those acronyms that, like FDR or JFK, embodies a personality. When he first conducted the San Francisco Symphony, in January 1974, Michael Tilson Thomas was already one of the most visible conductors in America. In 1969 he had made national news when, as the twenty-four-year-old assistant conductor of the Boston Symphony, he took over from that orchestra's music director, William Steinberg, who was too ill to continue a Carnegie Hall performance. The legend of a young conductor saving the day, winning the acclaim of press and public after stepping in for an ailing older maestro, is a tale much overworked. Assistants often substitute, usually without fanfare. The persistent legend is based on two extraordinary instances. One was when Leonard Bernstein took

2

In the early years of the twentieth century MTT's paternal grandparents, Bessie and Boris Thomashefsky, were stars of New York's Yiddish theater, which they helped found.

3

Michael Tilson Thomas enjoyed a long and nurturing friendship with the dean of American composers, Aaron Copland.

over from Bruno Walter in 1943. The other came when Michael Tilson Thomas took over from Steinberg. Overnight, both Bernstein and MTT assumed a place in the American cultural consciousness. At only twenty-seven, MTT had become music director of the Buffalo Philharmonic and principal guest conductor of the Boston Symphony Orchestra. He had succeeded Leonard Bernstein as host of the New York Philharmonic Young People's Concerts on CBS-TV.

For his 1974 debut with the San Francisco Symphony, MTT had chosen the Mahler Ninth—paired, oddly enough, with a Mozart piano concerto in which John Browning was soloist. MTT appreciated the spirit he found among the players, made manifest not only in their playing but in a certain irreverence. Violinist Verne Sellin, who also served as the orchestra's personnel manager, went out of his way to welcome MTT and introduced the young conductor to his special brand of quirky humor. Should sections of Bruckner or Mahler bog down, Verne suggested, just insert the *Midsommarvaka*, a jaunty polka almost everyone knows even if they can't name it or its Swedish composer, Hugo Alfvén. While no one has acted on Sellin's advice, the music for *Midsommarvaka* always accompanies the orchestra on tour, a talismanic reminder that *gravitas* sometimes needs relief.

And the Mahler Ninth is serious business. MTT sensed the musicians' difficulty in hearing each other through the wooly sound on stage at the War Memorial Opera House. Despite that, he reveled in the drive with which the players gave themselves to the music. Everyone focused on creating a performance, by any and all means. Years later, he needed only four words to sum up the

spirit he encountered: *Let's go for it!* Conductor and orchestra joined in pursuit of the music. "The mystique that it takes a master (preferably old and European) conductor to find the mystique in Mahler went out the vents of the Opera House Wednesday," wrote the *Chronicle's* Robert Commanday.

Commanday made another telling point. Michael Tilson Thomas was an American. In 1974, he was one of only a handful of native-born American conductors who enjoyed recognition on the international music scene. He had grown up in Los Angeles. His father, Ted Thomas, had emigrated in the 1930s from New York City to the West Coast, where he worked as a script doctor and dialogue director in Hollywood. Ted Thomas's parents had been legends of New York's Yiddish Theater, Boris and Bessie Thomashefsky. They helped establish the Jewish theater scene in turn-of-the-twentieth-century New York. They acted and sang in plays they had written and, in some instances, directed and produced. They were consummate show people, and from them their grandson inherited a passion to communicate, a willingness to listen to his inner promptings, a fearless sense of drama, and a work ethic that drove him regularly forward into the small hours while others fell exhausted into their beds.

At the University of Southern California he was educated by a diverse group of teachers that included the pianist John Crown, Alice Ehlers (born while Brahms was still alive and a piano student of Theodor Leschetizky), and the composer Ingolf Dahl, a man whose breadth of musical interests were mirrored in his pupil. As a student MTT enjoyed contact with Stravinsky and served

THE EMINENT JEWISH ARTIST
BESSIE
THOMASHEFSKY

2

3

as accompanist for master classes led by two brilliant virtuosos, violinist Jascha Heifetz and cellist Gregor Piatigorsky. Later, he became close with Leonard Bernstein and Aaron Copland. From them he learned vital lessons he recalled when he was ready to share his own compositions with the world. He idolized the Godfather of Soul, James Brown, performed with Sarah Vaughan and Ella Fitzgerald, and championed works of the American musical theater. With tastes in literature and art that complemented his appetite for music of all varieties, it was no wonder, as Michael Steinberg wrote, that his frame of cultural reference and curiosity made him fundamentally different from most conductors.

He had been a regular guest with the San Francisco Symphony since his Opera House debut, and twice he planned and led the annual Beethoven Festival. After four seasons as principal guest conductor of the Los Angeles Philharmonic, he was named principal conductor of the London Symphony Orchestra. While in that post, he continued to guest-conduct, and he also founded the New World Symphony, a Miami Beach-based ensemble and training center to prepare young musicians for orchestra careers. When MTT arrived in San Francisco in 1995, he was a Californian coming home.

His mission in San Francisco, he said in a 1995 interview, would be to offer interesting music in committed performances. He did not program works as a physician prescribes medicine. He loved music that spoke urgently and with passion, music that had affected him and that he felt responsible for sharing with others. He believed compositions required context to illuminate their special qualities, and to establish that context a program should include works that reflected each other, some of them diverting, some challenging, some reaffirming. "The total result should be thought-provoking *and* fun." He spoke admiringly of the Bay Area, convinced it was a great musical community and, perched on the Pacific and facing Asia, geographically and sociologically primed for the twenty-first century, possessing all the possibilities for pioneering. To this equation, he brought adventure and excitement. "The key question should always be, what's coming next?"

SETTING THE PACE
AND CLEARING THE AIR

All the promotional materials announced that Michael Tilson Thomas and the San Francisco Symphony would deliver what MTT had promised: adventure and excitement. From the brochures that arrived in the mail to the billboards that rose

4

over the streets, MTT's image stared intensely into the viewer's eyes. The haircut and tailored jacket, the youthful and appealingly craggy features: they announced better than any slogan that the concert hall was a happening place, that to be absent was to be left behind—back in 1994, say, among those solitary diehards still committed to WordPerfect and Lotus 1-2-3, watching amber characters on black screens while the rest of the world had moved on to 1995, new software, and color monitors.

Promises are easy. MTT and the orchestra delivered. Unfamiliar music was often on the programs. During his first season, each of his concerts included music by an American composer, and among those works were John Adams's *Harmonielehre*, a suite MTT culled from Bernstein's opera *A Quiet Place*, Copland's Symphonic Ode, Henry Cowell's *Synchrony*, William Schuman's Symphony No. 8, and *Arcana* by Edgard Varèse. Rather than assume that listeners shared his passion for such music, he often introduced it with a few well-chosen words, inviting the audience into the experience. Trust built quickly, and listeners found themselves amazed at how much they enjoyed music they had meant to dislike. Nowhere was this illustrated as powerfully as in the festival that concluded the 1995–96 season. The June 1996 American Festival was announced in mid-December 1995 and a month later had already sold eighty-three thousand dollars in tickets, primarily to the two concerts that featured members of the iconic Bay Area rock group the

Grateful Dead, disbanded in fact but not in the hearts of its fans. That a classical musician could corral the Dead's musicians testified to Michael Tilson Thomas's showmanship and devotion to the cause. On the festival's opening night, Davies Symphony Hall was packed with Deadheads. Big-haired stoners sat side by side with balding men in suits and women dressed for a night on the town. Only at the Community Open House in 1992 had a Symphony event at Davies seen such a diverse group. Nor was MTT interested in any condescending crossover performance. Grateful Dead musicians Phil Lesh, Mickey Hart, and Bob Weir joined members of the San Francisco Symphony Youth Orchestra in John Cage's *Renga with Apartment House 1776*. That program also included the US premiere of John Adams's *Lollapalooza* and Ives's *Holidays* Symphony, each of its movements introduced by composer Lou Harrison, who read the prose prefaces Ives had written to establish the music's setting. The Deadheads loved the show. So did those in suits and gowns.

RCA Victor Red Seal also took an interest in the San Francisco Symphony and its new music director. The record label had enjoyed a long relationship with the organization dating to 1925 and Alfred Hertz's tenure, and throughout most of Pierre Monteux's San Francisco years. Now the collaboration revived. In the first weeks of Michael Tilson Thomas's tenure, engineers from RCA's parent company, BMG, recorded music Prokofiev had written for the ballet *Romeo and Juliet*. The trend in the industry was away from studio recordings in favor of those made in concert, the better to capitalize on the spontaneity of performances with an audience present. Changes were abreast in the record-

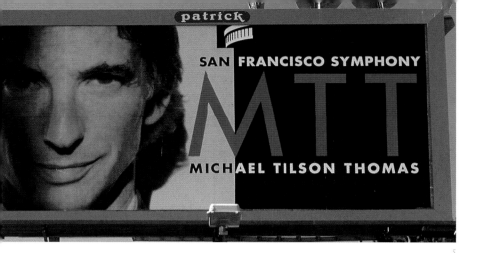

5

6

ing industry. Since CDs had become widely available in the mid-1980s, many well-loved older recordings were being digitally remastered for re-release, and these competed with new versions of the same music. At the same time, corporate mergers brought many recording firms under the blanket of just a few mega-corporations more interested in the bottom line than the merits of Toscanini's versus Klemperer's Beethoven. Add to this the expense of recording stateside, and it was clear that the Symphony was fortunate to have a contract to record. Few US orchestras did. As though to validate RCA's decision, its first San Francisco release captured the 1996 Grammy for Best Classical Recording.

"Everything was beautiful and nothing hurt," Kurt Vonnegut wrote in *Slaughterhouse-Five*. The temptation is to say the same of the Symphony around this time, but Vonnegut wrote with a sharpened pen, and to adopt his words would be to miss the complete picture. It is difficult, for instance, to imagine that a case still needed to be made for the arts. But in April 1996 Peter Pastreich found himself at Mayor Willie Brown's Economic Summit, where he, like Symphony leaders before him, reminded the city fathers that the arts remained vital to the municipal economy, attracting visitors and visitors' dollars. While the city has had a long history of arts support, the need to justify the arts seems constant. So much of art depends on economics. Again and again over the years, the Symphony was faced with the problem of budget, how to present great concerts and at the same time remain solvent. In 1934, economic problems had forced cancellation of the season. Now a campaign began to help ensure a measure of independence. The goal in the next thirty months would be to

4

First rehearsal in his new post: Michael Tilson Thomas greets Associate Principal Violist Yun Jie Liu and Principal Violist Geraldine Walther.

5

Preparing for a coming century: From the brochures that arrived in the mail to the billboards that rose over city streets, MTT's image stared intensely into the viewer's eyes.

6

Announcing the 1996 American Festival, culmination of MTT's first San Francisco Symphony season: from left, Phil Lesh (formerly of the Grateful Dead), MTT, and composers Lou Harrison and John Adams.

AN AUDITION (THE WAY IT IS)

Scott Pingel joined the San Francisco Symphony as principal bass in 2004. Here, he describes the intricate process through which jobs have come to be filled in a highly competitive profession, when hundreds of talented players may vie for a single post. (To learn how auditions were once conducted, see "An Audition (The Way It Was)," page 110.)

In the middle of my second season with the Charleston Symphony, I heard that the principal bass post in San Francisco was still open after four years. My resume was initially accepted, which meant I was spared the extra hassle of having to send a recording to qualify for the live audition.

I received a lengthy list of repertory from which excerpts would be chosen by the audition committee and disclosed just minutes before I went on stage. The list I got must have been one of the longest in bass audition history. It was most of a page, single-spaced. In some instances a specific movement of a piece was listed, but generally not even measure numbers were specified: "Beethoven Symphony No. 9: complete. *Ein Heldenleben:* complete." You could be asked to play anything from the entire piece. So I got all the parts together and made a book. I made an A, B, and C preparation list. The A list was what I needed to practice every day: the really hard stuff, like the Schoenberg Chamber Symphony No. 1 and *Heldenleben*. My B list I could practice every other day. The C list was my once- or twice-a-week stuff: things that were less technically demanding, or that I was more familiar with. I practiced four hours a day, for two months. That was in addition to my Charleston job. But I'd committed myself mentally to pursue the job in San Francisco. I knew I would just buckle down. The only blip came a few weeks before the audition, when I had an appendectomy and was off my bass for six days.

I'm told that, over the years the post was open, about 150 people had been heard, but when I came to audition there were only 20 or 25 of us. We'd been heavily vetted. Auditions are in three rounds: preliminaries, semifinals, and finals, although "final" really isn't the end. Every round is played behind a screen—it's completely anonymous. I didn't think I played that well in the preliminary round, but I moved into the semifinals.

You play for a twelve-member committee of musicians from the orchestra. In the preliminary round, you play for about ten minutes and show what you have to offer. The semifinals also last about ten minutes. The final round can be quite long. I think I was on stage twenty-five minutes. Michael Tilson Thomas

was asking me to try different things in different ways to get a sense of my versatility. It felt like an eternity.

Under our current contract, the audition committee presents a candidate to the music director. He does not vote initially. In the preliminary round, candidates are passed, or not passed, by democratic vote. No discussion is allowed. In the semifinal round, the committee can discuss the players they've heard. In the final round, the committee votes on whether a candidate is qualified for a tenure-track position. The music director ultimately decides whether a qualified candidate is offered a trial period or hired outright. But the music director cannot offer a trial week—or a job—if the committee's vote is negative.

After a trial week, the committee decides whether to recommend that the player be accepted into the orchestra for a year, which is called the *audition year*. If the music director does not agree, the candidate does not move on and the process is over. A new audition will have to be called. But if a musician plays an audition year, another vote must be taken on whether to offer a second, or *probationary year*. After two years, a tenure vote is taken. Candidates must receive the go-ahead both from the committee and the music director. If one party does not agree, the candidate does not advance.

You have to learn to trust yourself in an audition. You've prepared, and it's not as though you're suddenly going to forget everything—although people do freeze. I didn't think of my audition as an attempt to win a job. I wanted to play great music. There's a big difference. I believe that, if you play great music, people will want to hire you. When I got a bit nervous, I reminded myself I'd done my homework. And some nervous energy is good.

I flew to San Francisco on a Saturday afternoon for a Sunday evening audition. Candidates cover their own expenses, by the way. I stayed at the Holiday Inn near the airport. Often an orchestra will recommend local hotels. I never stay at those places. That's where all the other bass players are going to be. Once, I was auditioning for the Pittsburgh Symphony and heard a bass player practicing in the room next door. The night before an audition, that's the last thing you want.

Another candidate and I each got a trial week in San Francisco. My audition was in January. My trial week was in May. On June 18, the day before the cutoff date, MTT called to offer me the job.

227

*Left: Principal Bass Scott Pingel.
Above: Pingel stands with his bass
behind cellists Barbara Bogatin and
Barbara Andres. Positioned at the rear
of the stage, the bass section lays the
music's foundation.*

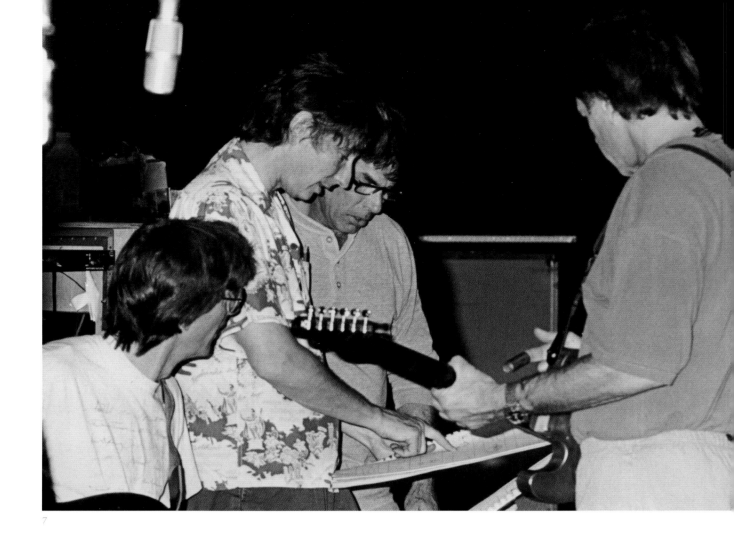

7

increase the Symphony's endowment by $40 million.

The budget proposed for the coming 1996–97 season estimated a loss of $1,444,450 as the gap between income and expenses widened, part of a national trend that the Endowment and Stabilization Campaign hoped to counteract. After fifteen years of balanced budgets, the Symphony for the past three years had operated in the red, with an accumulated deficit of $2.8 million. Staff had been cut. Yet the perception remained that the Symphony was in sound financial condition, especially with an endowment of $81 million.

This was the climate in which negotiating sessions for a new musicians' contract began in May 1996.

President Nancy Bechtle and the chair of the board's Labor Relations Committee, Leonard Kingsley, ex-

plained the situation in a visit with the musicians' attorney, Philip Sipser. Sipser had a long history of orchestra negotiations. In 1967, he had become the first legal counsel retained by the recently formed International Conference of Symphony and Opera Musicians. He had come to the group's attention when, after years of representing iron, dock, and brewery workers, he helped the New York Philharmonic settle a contract. Sipser was tough and unfazed by the prospect of battle. Bechtle and Kingsley told him that musicians' proposals called for what they believed were extraordinary costs. The board, they said, wanted to be fair, but with the endowment drive under way, potential donors had to know that increases were reasonable. Sipser suggested reducing deficits with funds from what appeared to be an already rich endowment. Kingsley told him that "would be like living on the income you got from selling your

house." Sipser said he had heard that kind of reasoning before. He thanked Bechtle and Kingsley for their visit.

By late fall, when the orchestra set out on its first European tour with MTT, subscription renewals for the season were at their strongest since the opening of Davies Symphony Hall. Yet a budget deficit had been posted, and management's first offer in contract negotiations had been rejected. The musicians had taken their case to the press and met with the mayor, and management had followed suit and presented its position to City Hall. Although the orchestra continued to play throughout the tour, beyond the contract's November 23 expiration, an impasse had been reached. The issues were the familiar ones, wages and pension, and these grew to include scheduling and something that would trouble the country as a whole in coming years, medical coverage.

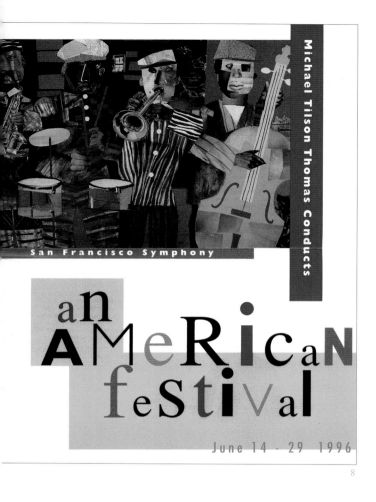

San Francisco Symphony

Michael Tilson Thomas Conducts

an AMeRIcaN feStIval

June 14 - 29 1996

8

7

Preparing a performance of John Cage's
Renga with Apartment House 1776,
a highlight of the 1996 American Festival.
Michael Tilson Thomas confers with members
of the former Grateful Dead. From left: Phil
Lesh, MTT, Mickey Hart, and Bob Weir.

8

An American orchestra and an American music
director teamed in An American Festival.

9

Program from concert in Düsseldorf, among
the stops in the European tour of 1996,
when MTT and the orchestra made their
first journey abroad together.

The San Francisco concerts that were to follow immediately upon return were canceled. The orchestra was on strike. The concert hall would be dark for nine weeks, until mid-February 1997.

No strike is happy while it continues. Hurt feelings and a sense of betrayal are the norm. While both parties are desperate not to be the loser in negotiations, neither party wants victory at the expense of the opponent's dignity, even if such an outcome may seem irrelevant or even appealing in the heat of battle. When a strike ends, healing can begin, especially if the parties recognize their common goals. As Nancy Bechtle wrote shortly after concerts resumed, disagreements, while part of a less than ideal world, can spur better communication. The proper roles of musicians and management, she said, were as members of the Symphony family. What had been learned through the strike would bring that family closer. Such words would have been too good to be true, had all parties not taken them seriously. Everyone understood that the new pace established before the strike had to be maintained. As music returned to Davies Symphony Hall, the air gradually could clear.

BACK UP TO SPEED

The artistic pace resumed quickly. Although a sizable deficit was anticipated for the current fiscal year, by June 1997 a small surplus was projected in the budget for the coming season. As the gap between revenues and expenses continued to spread, hopes were high for the endowment and stabilization campaign that aimed to end deficits once and for all—and in those days, when wild economic downturns still seemed relics of the Great Depression, such a goal appeared realistic.

Heinersdorff,
Konzerte
96/97
Dienstag, 19. November 1996, 20 Uhr
Tonhalle Düsseldorf
3. Konzert
im Abonnement
San Francisco
Symphony Orchestra
Leitung: **Michael Tilson Thomas**
Solistin: **Anne-Sophie Mutter,** Violine

Konzert Theater Kontor
René Heinersdorff jr.

9

A new relationship between orchestra and management offered reasons for optimism. With a grant from the William and Flora Hewlett Foundation, Symphony musicians, staff, and board members entered a series of workshops designed to educate them in the technique of conflict resolution. Nancy Bechtle's sense of a Symphony "family" was more than a word meant to deflect attention from an uncomfortable reality. By acknowledging differences, each party developed greater understanding of the other. Less than a year after frustrations had led to a long strike, musicians approached Leonard Kingsley and suggested that negotiations on the next contract begin early, and that a new contract might even extend beyond the customary three years. By September, a plan was outlined. Not only would negotiations begin immediately, but the goal would be to complete them within sixty days and settle upon

a contract to extend for six years. Robert Mnookin, a Harvard law professor and director of Harvard's Negotiation Research Project, was invited to participate and help arrive at a mutually agreeable conclusion. After lengthy preparations among all parties, negotiations began in November and were complete by December 19. A six-year contract was ratified by a wide margin, almost a year before the current contract was due to expire.

So singular an event was this in the history of American orchestras that, in retrospect, it seems almost to have been celebrated by an equally unusual artistic event that took place at around the same time. In April 1999, the San Francisco Symphony joined the heavy metal rock group Metallica—a band with Bay Area roots—in two evenings that could only be described as heavy metal symphonic rock—"a frappe of clas-

10

Three generations of executive directors meet in Davies Symphony Hall. From left, Peter Pastreich (who served from 1978 to 1999), Joseph A. Scafidi (a Symphony fixture from 1939 until 1978), and Brent Assink (executive director since 1999; general manager from 1990 until 1994).

11

In 1999, the San Francisco Symphony and Metallica met onstage in the Berkeley Community Theater for two evenings of heavy metal symphonic rock. The resulting album was titled S&M, *for* Symphony and Metallica.

10

sic orchestration and gut-punching rock 'n' roll," according to the *San Francisco Examiner*. The orchestra and the band played twenty Metallica songs. The decibels rose. The light show strobed in green and purple. An album and a video resulted. The title of both was *S&M*, for *Symphony and Metallica*.

Already subscription sales for the 1998–99 season exceeded $10 million, the first time that figure had been topped. Peter Pastreich, surveying this scene and looking back at his two decades as executive director, understood how much territory he and the Symphony had covered together. When he arrived in 1978, the orchestra had been a fine regional ensemble, but it lacked a national presence. He had found dedicated management, although its talents had been spread thin and its focus trained on the immediate moment, impairing strategic plans for the future. Pastreich was a catalyst who transformed management and made the Symphony a professional organization. He led it into the late twentieth century and ensured it would be poised to enter the new millennium. Having helped bring things to this point, Pastreich decided the time was right to turn leadership over to a successor. He announced his departure, set for April 1999.

MAVERICKS FOR A NEW MILLENNIUM

With a shock, the world realized how dependent it had become on technology. In retrospect, the "Y2K problem" was as much science fiction as problem, but it was a grave concern in the late 1990s. Because most computers had been designed for the twentieth century and were not programmed to move forward to 2000, their internal calendars at a second past midnight would revert to 1900, as an automobile speedometer at its limit turns over to zero. No computer would recognize the year 1900. Electricity grids would freeze. Planes would fall from the sky. Cottage industries grew up around Y2K as programmers raced to ensure that machines would not wreak havoc on the world at midnight 1999. The Symphony, which had been electronic since the early 1980s, was caught in the frenzy.

Because programmers worked so efficiently, or just because of luck, no global horrors took place as 1999 segued into the year 2000. But the widespread concern about the potential danger underlined how deeply the digital world had penetrated the general awareness. In 1995, the San Francisco Symphony launched a website. This initial foray into cyberspace was designed by a few staff members as a project for a

231

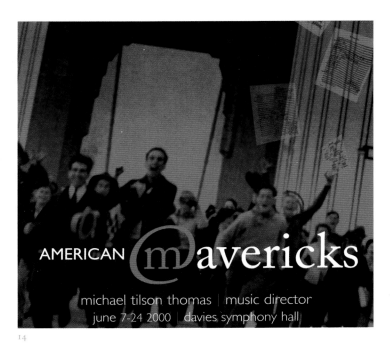

AMERICAN (m)avericks

michael tilson thomas | music director
june 7-24 2000 | davies symphony hall

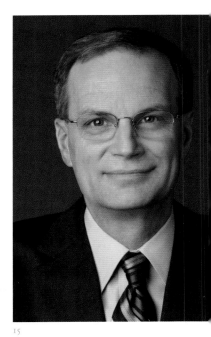

12

State of the art, circa 1980. Hewlett-Packard Foundation Executive Director Emery Rogers and Symphony President Brayton Wilbur, Jr., admire the Symphony's new HP3000 computer, probably the first major contribution the Symphony received from Silicon Valley. If anyone was thinking about Y2K back then, they did not share their foreboding with the national media.

13

American Mavericks reached audiences in new ways, including visual support projected on overhead screens. Beneath the screens, stage is set for Morton Feldman's Piece for Four Pianos (with a fifth piano converted to quartertone piano, for music of Charles Ives).

14

The American Mavericks festival of June 2000 spotlighted composers who were visionaries, pioneers, and iconoclasts. The plan was not calculated for success. The execution proved a hit.

15

Brent Assink, who joined the Symphony as executive director in 1999.

16

Phyllis Wattis, generous philanthropist and free spirit, helped bring American Mavericks to the Bay Area.

17

MTT and the orchestra play to a capacity audience of five thousand, opening the London Proms concerts in 2000.

course in online design. Within a year a new site launched, this one created by a professional designer and far beyond the first site in sophistication and depth. By late 1997, even this site was revamped. Visitors could learn about Symphony history, access artists' biographies, read program notes, and purchase tickets. From late 1996 until the end of 1997, 866 tickets were sold online; in the five months after the new site appeared, 1,255 tickets were sold via the Web. There was no looking back.

With the Symphony's new executive director, looking forward became an organizational mantra. Brent Assink was no stranger to the San Francisco Symphony. He had joined the organization as general manager in 1990, departing in 1994 to head the St. Paul Chamber Orchestra. From Howard Skinner to Joseph Scafidi to Peter Pastreich, the San Francisco Symphony had been fortunate in its chief executives. Each of them served a long term. Each loved music. Assink, a pianist and organist with degrees in musicology and also in business, would continue leading the Symphony

toward its artistic goals, building on the model Pastreich had established.

Brent Assink had come to his love of music through recordings, and in college he had worked as an announcer for a classical radio station. Long convinced of technology's power to carry music's messages far and wide, he was now a member of the most technologically advanced community on earth. Just as Northern California had given birth to a spiritual New Age, the Bay Area's techno-sector was remaking the world.

Michael Tilson Thomas also understood technology's power and had long used it to communicate. When he took over the New York Philharmonic Young People's Concerts on CBS-TV in the 1970s, he proved to be a natural for the television camera. Now new possibilities beckoned. As early as June 1999, even before the means to produce it were available, the seeds were sown for what five years later would become *Keeping Score*, a multimedia music-education program. "Cradle-to-grave" learning was one of MTT's passions—important, he maintained, to invite people into music and thus preserve the musical heritage, but also important because of where music could take an audience. For music could lead beyond itself to a kind of ethical sustenance, to visions of expanded possibilities. It had the power to change individuals and maybe, through them, to change societies. Video and the Internet would be enlisted on music's behalf.

By 2000, the San Francisco Symphony and Michael Tilson Thomas were a recognized team. They were onstage at Carnegie Hall when news came that their recording of three Stravinsky ballets—*The Firebird, The Rite of Spring,* and *Perséphone*—had won three Grammys, including the award for Best Classical Album. But along with emerging technologies and beyond tested technologies such as recordings, the live concert remained the surest way of touching and holding an audience. Concert-going was about to be remade. Michael Tilson Thomas had never been bashful in his programming. In American Mavericks, the festival the San Francisco Symphony presented in June 2000, he outdid even himself.

The festival was a risk. Music of the twentieth century was not a box-office draw, and much of the mavericks' music had been designed specifically to shock and surprise. To MTT, mavericks were American heroes. He described them as "composers who worked resolutely, aggressively, independently outside the mainstream, and their expressive goals were to explore unknown musical and psychological territories." Among the mavericks whose music was explored in that festival were Charles Ives (who liberated American music from European bondage), Henry Cowell (inventor of the tone

16

cluster), and John Cage (as much philosopher as musician). The Bay Area's Lou Harrison was represented, and Duke Ellington, and George Antheil—the Bad Boy of Music, whose *Ballet mécanique* had to wait almost eighty years, for the advent of computer and MIDI technology, to be heard as he conceived it. Aaron Copland, Morton Feldman, Steve Reich, John Adams, Steven Mackey. In their music, America's maverick composers reacted to the times in which they found themselves. They were part of US history. MTT believed listeners were ready to give them a hearing.

He was right. Through the generosity of Phyllis Wattis, one of San Francisco's most generous arts patrons and a woman more excited by the music of Stravinsky and Varèse than Mozart and Haydn, tickets were made affordable to "nontraditional" and younger listeners. More than eighteen thousand tickets were sold—compared to the fifteen thousand sold to the previous year's Stravinsky festival—and 27 percent of those who attended were new to the concert hall. Press from around the world focused on San Francisco. Years earlier, composer Charles Wuorinen had maintained that Bay Area audiences, more than any others in the country, were receptive to new music. MTT concurred, noting how San Francisco listeners responded, based on their own ears, without waiting for critics to tell them if they should or shouldn't like what they heard.

17

Later that summer, the orchestra toured Europe once again. What had seemed so extraordinary a feat just ten years earlier, when the Symphony had visited Europe's great music festivals, now came naturally, with a debut at the London Proms and a return to the Lucerne Festival, which already had surpassed the Salzburg

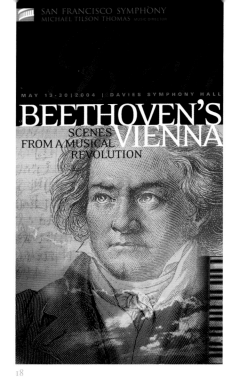

18

18
—

"Beethoven's Vienna," a 2004 festival, in-
troduced audiences to the artistic world and
musical rivalries that shaped the composer.

19
—

Among the Youth Orchestra's overseas jour-
neys was a 2001 tour to Russia and Eastern
Europe, including concerts in St. Petersburg
and Moscow.

20
—

The first Chinese New Year concert, 2000.
Author Amy Tan reads from her children's
book Sagwa, the Chinese Siamese Cat,
with musical accompaniment by the
orchestra and an ensemble playing Chinese
traditional instruments. Shown here, seated,
is erhu artist Jiebing Chen.

21
—

"Semi-staged" performances of opera
highlighted festivals in the MTT years. This
scene is from Beethoven's Fidelio, *presented*
in 2004.

Festival in prestige. The extraordinary but often reclusive pianist Martha Argerich, not an artist who typically toured with orchestras, joined MTT and the musicians in London and across the continent. That fall, as tickets for the new season went on sale online, website purchases of a hundred thousand dollars were realized in only twelve days. A year earlier, it took six weeks to reach that sum online.

For the Symphony and for the country, the future seemed secure.

WHAT THE FUTURE HELD

That all was not right with the world was apparent by late 2000, when a contested presidential election in the United States revealed how deep the country's political polarization had become. Some saw the election's eventual outcome, with the decision in favor of George W. Bush over Al Gore, as proof that providence controlled destiny, while others considered the decision a theft. Whichever side citizens took, the ground on which the camps might meet was dangerously circumscribed.

Against such a background, the San Francisco Symphony presented the North American premiere of a work filled with the promise of a new millennium, John Adams's "Nativity Oratorio," *El Niño.* The Symphony co-commissioned *El Niño* with Paris's Théâtre du Chatelet from its former composer-in-residence, who was by now a major figure on the international music scene. Staged by Adams's frequent collaborator, Peter Sellars, *El Niño* combined film and dance with vocal settings of texts from Latin American poets and the Gnostic gospels, all celebrating the ecstasies and pains of newborn arrival. To have been present as *El Niño* unfolded was to believe that the New Age might

have dawned, for here was music at once innovative and timeless and inclusive.

Inclusiveness also motivated a new kind of concert. In February, a special performance celebrating the Lunar New Year welcomed the Bay Area's extensive Asian community. Less than a century earlier, the Immigration Act of 1924 had banned Chinese immigrants from entering the country and denied citizenship to those already here. It was poor recompense for a people whose labors had helped build the rail system that joined the nation's two shores—to say nothing of enabling the San Francisco Symphony to take its music to the opposite coast in 1947. Ever since immigration restrictions were lifted in 1965, the Asian community had grown. And it had immersed itself in Western classical music, to the point that musicians of Asian heritage formed almost half the membership of the San Francisco Symphony Youth Orchestra. The Chinese New Year Concert fused Eastern and Western traditions, became an annual event, and in 2008 inspired an analogous concert reaching out to the Latino community, celebrating Día de los Muertos, the Day of the Dead.

In the dawn of the new millennium, the San Francisco Symphony Chorus made its first trip to Carnegie Hall, joining MTT and the orchestra in Stravinsky's *Perséphone* and Mahler's *Das klagende Lied.* After two years of searching, a new concertmaster was found to replace Raymond Kobler, who had left in 1999. Alexander Barantschik, leader of the London Symphony Orchestra during MTT's tenure there, assumed the duties in San Francisco in September 2001.

Never in its history had the San Francisco Symphony enjoyed such a national profile. The iconic CBS-TV news magazine *60 Minutes* profiled Michael Tilson Thomas in 2000 and repeated the segment in 2001. Ticket sales for the 2000–01 season exceeded the budgeted amount by almost $364,000, for a total income of $17.6 million, the highest ever. John Goldman, who would succeed Nancy Bechtle as president that December, cautioned against too optimistic a read on things to come, noting that fewer tickets to the 2001 Black & White Ball had been sold, and that donors were increasingly reluctant to contribute, citing as reasons the energy crisis and the dotcom meltdown that followed the bursting of the technology stock bubble in March 2000. Goldman issued his cautionary remarks on September 10, 2001, along with some good news. Despite the plummeting value of investments that had resulted in a loss of almost $5 million to the endowment, an operating surplus, combined with stabilization funds, would eliminate the accumulated deficit of $597,065. And everyone welcomed the new enterprise to be launched in two days. With the recording industry in disarray and its own RCA contract in limbo, the San Francisco Symphony had taken matters into its own hands and

created its own label, SFS Media. At the concert of September 12, MTT and the orchestra would begin recording a Mahler symphony cycle for the new label. They would start with a performance of the composer's Symphony No. 6, a work so pessimistic that it was often billed under an unofficial subtitle: *Tragic.*

Mahler believed in art's prophetic power, in the way it can reflect and shape history. Even he might have been stunned by the devastating coincidences of Symphony programming and world events. On the morning of September 11, 2001, hijackers linked to the Middle East terrorist group Al Qaeda commandeered four commercial jetliners for use as weapons. Wresting control of the aircraft, the hijackers aimed the first plane at the North Tower of the World Trade Center in New York City, and at 8:46 A.M. it found its mark. Seventeen minutes later the second plane hit the Trade Center's South Tower. Within two hours, both buildings collapsed. In the meantime, a third aircraft smashed into the Pentagon in Washington, DC.

Over rural Pennsylvania, passengers in the fourth plane seized the aircraft from their captors, but with

19

20

21

23

236

SAN FRANCISCO SYMPHONY
MICHAEL TILSON THOMAS

MAHLER

Symphony No. 6

24

22

A concert celebrating Día de los Muertos —the Day of the Dead—was introduced in 2008 and has been repeated annually, reaching out to the Bay Area Latino community.

23

Alexander Barantschik, named concert-master in 2001.

24

The recording of Mahler's Sixth Symphony inaugurated a cycle of the composer's orchestral music and went on to capture a 2002 Grammy for Best Orchestral Performance.

no one at the controls the plane crashed into the field below. In all, the day's death toll stood at nearly three thousand. Not since Pearl Harbor had the United States suffered such an attack on its soil.

The next evening, in San Francisco, the mood at the concert was somber. That the concert would go forward was essential, for at exactly such moments music could exert its power to focus emotions and unite listeners. Music, as MTT would say later in a different context, could offer certainty amid life's imponderables.

Events do not unfold according to a script or a score, but "within the music, we can be confident about how the F-sharp should resolve to the E-sharp." Now the music offered reassurance and catharsis. For if ever music had been created to voice feelings like the ones in Davies Symphony Hall that night, the Mahler Sixth Symphony was it. The performances captured by the microphones that week were filled with the passions of the moment. No one present could doubt that great art is anchored in reality.

Michael Tilson Thomas and many Symphony players began their combined histories years before they joined forces in San Francisco. Longtime cellist Margaret Tait and MTT attended the University of Southern California together. Associate Principal Bass Larry Epstein and he were colleagues at Tanglewood. Among the alumni of the New World Symphony, which MTT founded to help prepare gifted players for orchestra work: violinists Naomi Kazama and Chen Zhao, Principal Bass Scott Pingel, Associate Principal Oboist Jonathan Fischer, clarinetist Ben Freimuth, and timpanist David Herbert. At the Pacific Music Festival, MTT first encountered percussionist James Lee Wyatt III. All went on to share the same stage together.

They share more than a stage. Their camaraderie is based on what MTT has called a sense of shared musical understanding. His most poignant example of such understanding, and of how people can find one another inside music, is that of David Breeden.

David Breeden joined the orchestra in 1972 and from 1980 served as principal clarinetist until his death in 2005. David and MTT met as students at Tanglewood. They played chamber music, and David was in the orchestra. David had grown up in the Texas Bible Belt. MTT, who was from a secular household in Los Angeles, came from a show business heritage. Years after their student days, they encountered each other again in San Francisco. MTT tells the story: "In his life and his perspective, David came from such a different place than I did. He grew up in a small town. He was a very religious, conservative, God-fearing man. Yet within music, David and I had a beautiful understanding. We shared so much inspiring experience and were able, together, to take the music to really wonderful places. I so appreciated the arching, floating, aching quality of the sound he created. I'd compliment him on something or other, and his typical response was, 'Yeah—how 'bout that!' What we had was something you never could define, but it was essential to the mystery of music-making: that somehow, inside music, you are able to find a common cause and a common human understanding, and together you are able to make something wonderful happen, which can be shared by other people. That is the center of what it's all about, for those who make the music and those who listen to the music."

David Breeden. The shared musical understanding he and MTT enjoyed exemplifies how those of different backgrounds can unite through music.

Alexander Barantschik gives Agnes Albert a closeup look at the "David" Guarnerius violin, once the favorite instrument of Jascha Heifetz.

AGNES ALBERT AND THE HEIFETZ VIOLIN

In 2002, a subtle change was added to the orchestra's sound when Concertmaster Alexander Barantschik began playing the "David" Guarnerius violin, built in 1742. This is believed to be the instrument on which Ferdinand David introduced the Mendelssohn Violin Concerto in 1845. The great Jascha Heifetz purchased the violin in 1922 and in his will bequeathed it to the San Francisco Fine Arts Museums, stipulating that it be played only by musicians worthy of it and its legacy. When Heifetz died in 1987, the instrument fell silent and was put on display at the Palace of the Legion of Honor. Symphony board member

Agnes Albert was convinced that the "David" Guarnerius needed to be played in public, and played regularly. A fine instrument is in some ways a living organism and needs exercise to stay in shape. When Barantschik arrived at the Symphony as concertmaster in 2001, the time seemed right to realize Agnes Albert's dream. The Symphony and the Fine Arts Museums entered an agreement that gave Barantschik exclusive use of the instrument for three years—an agreement extended once that initial period ended. He would have the "David" at his disposal for all concerts in Davies Symphony Hall. Beginning in February 2003, he was featured with orchestra colleagues in what became a regular chamber music series at the California Palace of the Legion of Honor, offering the public the opportunity to hear the instrument in an intimate setting.

When Barantschik was growing up in Russia he listened to Heifetz recordings, becoming familiar with the sound of the violin he would one day play. "It is impossible to think part of [Heifetz's] soul is not inside it." Barantschik believes that, when he places his bow on the instrument's strings, something uncanny happens. "When you hit the right spot, suddenly it speaks with Heifetz's voice."

The Legion of Honor was the site of Barantschik's first public recital on the "David," on June 16, 2002. Agnes Albert was there. A musician herself, she had been a friend of every Symphony music director for the past fifty years and had known virtually every artist who had performed with the orchestra since the 1940s. Board presidents and Symphony management had sought her advice. She had been a childhood friend of Yehudi Menuhin, and an early champion of cellist Yo-Yo Ma and pianist Murray Perahia when those artists were barely out of their teens. She exerted a powerful force on music education, spurred the founding of the Symphony's Youth Orchestra, and she served on the board of the San Francisco Conservatory of Music. Of the many great concertgoing experiences Agnes Albert had had in her ninety-four years, Barantschik's recital ranked near the top. Those who saw her that evening have bittersweet memories. It was the last performance she attended. She suffered a massive stroke the next morning and died on June 19.

On a cool San Francisco morning later that month, in a memorial service at St. Agnes's Church, Alexander Barantschik lifted the "David" Guarnerius from its case and played one of Agnes Albert's favorite works, the Adagio from J. S. Bach's Sonata No. 1 in G minor for solo violin. This is music made to cut deep. Emerging from the Guarnerius, it was a tribute to a woman who had given many of her years to the San Francisco Symphony and had helped bring this remarkable instrument to the orchestra.

25

Among its many consequences, the shock of 9/11 eroded local economies. But even before the September tragedy, economic times had been unkind to the San Francisco Symphony's neighbors. In 2001 the San Jose Symphony declared bankruptcy. Like the Oakland Symphony, which closed its doors in 1986 before being reborn two years later as the Oakland East Bay Symphony, the San Jose orchestra was soon resurrected as the Symphony Silicon Valley. That these orchestras could regroup was a mark of how deeply the Bay Area valued music. Communities from Santa Rosa to Berkeley to Marin County and Stockton all supported fine local orchestras, yet the San Jose crisis emphasized again how precarious artistic undertakings could be.

The San Francisco Symphony felt its kinship with these orchestras. Along with its national and global prominence, it too remained a local

ensemble. That was underlined on September 11, 2002. At a free concert in Yerba Buena Gardens, Michael Tilson Thomas and the orchestra offered their community a musical remembrance of 9/11. American troops were now battling insurgents in Afghanistan, and the atmosphere in the country was bellicose, the hostile focus trained increasingly on Iraq. In San Francisco on that balmy evening, calm emerged from the music. The communal gathering, highlighted by a performance of Copland's *Lincoln Portrait*, narrated by the Reverend Cecil Williams of the city's Glide Memorial Church, displayed the best in the national character.

25

A year to the day after the terrorist attacks of September 11, 2001, MTT and the orchestra offered a free commemorative concert at Yerba Buena Gardens.

PRIVILEGE AND PATRONS

Nancy Bechtle had headed the San Francisco Symphony's Board of Governors for fourteen years, longer than any president except Leonora Wood Armsby, who served for seventeen years. Bechtle's tenure was marked by the greatest artistic and financial growth in Symphony history to that time, with tours and recordings, the acoustic renovation of Davies Symphony Hall, and an orchestra that played week after week for an audience larger than any in the country outside New York City. Among her proudest achievements had been landing MTT as music director. Fourteen years earlier, Bechtle had voiced the ambitious wish that, by the end of her term, tickets to hear the San Francisco Symphony perform in Vienna would be as difficult to buy as tickets to hear the Vienna Philharmonic play in San Francisco. "It happened!" she exclaimed in 2001. "We played two concerts in Vienna, and you couldn't get a ticket to get in!" Then she added a more serious comment. "It's not only audiences. I think musicians around the world know what our orchestra is like. Musicians are a discerning group, and they know how well we're playing. I'm a huge admirer of our orchestra. I can't imagine how they do what they do."

John Goldman, who succeeded Nancy Bechtle in December 2001, came from a long line of philanthropists. He was a descendant of Levi Strauss. His mother, Rhoda Haas Goldman, served on the Symphony board from 1983 until her death in 1996, and with her husband, Richard Goldman, she supported a broad range of community projects and established the Goldman Environmental Prize. John Goldman's grandmother, Elise Stern Haas (also a Symphony board member), established a series of young people's

concerts at the Symphony in the 1930s. Goldman took to heart the lessons he had learned from his family and absorbed through his 1960s social activism. He became a dedicated community servant—president of the San Francisco-based Jewish Community Federation, a trustee of the Richard and Rhoda Goldman Fund and the Goldman Environmental Foundation, and with commitments to a host of other organizations whose aim was to improve the quality of life. He was also a lover of what he called music's spirituality, believing that, "in many ways, music is the soul of who we are." A fan of the hard rock band Led Zeppelin since his youth, his concern was that many believed the symphonic world was elitist. "That's what we have to change. The Symphony should never seem to be the purview of the privileged."

Goldman was hearkening back to the San Francisco Symphony's basic principles. Yet the "privileged" will always play a role in the lives of great arts organizations. In fact, their support is vital to help ensure that the symphonic world is *not* exclusive. From the Renaissance to the present, patrons generous with both their time and money have been the crucial link between artists and a wider public. In San Francisco, they founded the Symphony and helped ensure its life. Now, early in the twenty-first century, they would make possible the SFS Media Mahler symphony cycle, which would carry the orchestra's sound around the world, reaching a cross-section of society.

On the heels of the first recording released by SFS Media came the launch of a new website dedicated to children and music education, sfskids.com. Technology was enabling

26

the Symphony to reach an ever-growing audience. The 1911 founders were the products of a world whose scientific fantasies were dominated by the fictions of Jules Verne and H. G. Wells, but not even those visionary authors could have foretold what was happening now. On the first day single tickets went on sale in the fall of 2002, sales via traditional channels such as phone and fax orders decreased by 13.5 percent from the year before while online sales were up by 61 percent.

Yet no amount of technological innovation could guarantee an orchestra's greatness. Audiences had marveled in 1919 as Alfred Hertz and the orchestra accompanied the Duo-Art player piano in a Saint-Saëns Concerto, but even then the real wonder was not so much the "playing" of pianist Harold Bauer as the feat that Hertz and the musicians executed, coordinating their efforts with a robotic soloist. Music would always demand more than ground-breaking technology. There was that essential representative of old technology, for instance: the musical instrument. The Symphony's new Cremona Fund, created to purchase great string instruments, took its name from the Italian city where craftsmen such as Antonio Stradivari and Giuseppe Antonio Guarneri had fashioned such masterpieces in the sixteenth and seventeenth centuries. The highest-profile of the Symphony's instrument acquisitions, however, was not technically an acquisition, but rather a loan. For years, Symphony patron and board member Agnes Albert had had her eyes on the great Guarnerius violin that the virtuoso Jascha Heifetz had willed to the Fine Arts Museums of San Francisco. When Alexander Barantschik was named concertmaster, Albert's lobbying resulted in an agreement that gave him use of the instrument in all concerts at Davies Symphony Hall.

KEEPING SCORE, AND OTHER TECHNOLOGIES

Michael Tilson Thomas and Agnes Albert had been especially close. For her ninetieth birthday, he conducted the orchestra in a work he had composed for the occasion, *Agnegram*. It was the first of his compositions he shared with San Francisco, and its success led to other performances of his music at the orchestra's concerts, including his Poems of Emily Dickinson, introduced in San Francisco in 2002 with soprano Renée Fleming, and *Urban Legend*, a witty concerto he wrote for Symphony contrabassoonist Steven Braunstein.

Anyone who imagined that MTT was a conductor content to confine his activities to the podium was not paying attention. In 2005 he introduced an evening-long entertainment, part documentary and part musical show. Originally titled *The Thomashefskys: Music and Memories from a Life in the Yiddish Theater*, this history of his grandparents'

27

241

26

John D. Goldman, who became Symphony president in 2001.

27

Jascha Heifetz as a young man, already a legend of the violin.

28

The website sfskids.com adopted whimsy to introduce children to music.

28

29

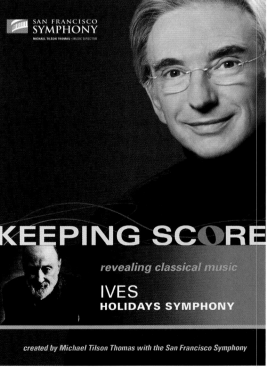

30

On location in Danbury, Connecticut, establishing a shot for the Ives episode of Keeping Score.

30

Keeping Score, *seen on nationwide TV, also reached viewers via DVD.*

31

In 2006, for an episode of The MTT Files *(radio component of* Keeping Score*), Michael Tilson Thomas interviewed one of his favorite artists, James Brown, the great Godfather of Soul.*

theatrical activities on New York's Lower East Side early in the twentieth century was a multimedia production re-creating an almost-forgotten world. That MTT wrote the script, made many of the orchestrations, performed at the piano, and (in a later version of the show) even sang one of the numbers was evidence of how far-reaching his creative energies went.

At the same time as this love letter to the past was born, the future of musical outreach was taking shape as *Keeping Score*. MTT and the Symphony had committed themselves to conveying music's messages to those who might not encounter them through any but technological avenues. A pilot TV episode of *Keeping Score* launched on PBS-TV's Great *Performances* in 2004. Produced with an award of $1.7 million for research and development from a local foundation, the Evelyn and Walter Haas, Jr. Fund, the program was devoted to Tchaikovsky's Fourth Symphony and established the *Keeping Score* format. Michael Tilson Thomas and Symphony musicians talked about the music, how the composer had come to write it, what a performance of it demanded, and how those demands could be met. The show was seen by millions.

The Haas, Jr. Fund in 2005 awarded the San Francisco Symphony an additional $8.3 million challenge grant specifically for *Keeping Score*, making its total $10 million contribution the largest in Symphony history to that date. In 2006, a series of three TV installments followed where the pilot had left off. The focus was on great musical communicators: Beethoven and his *Eroica* Symphony, Stravinsky and *The Rite of Spring*, and Aaron Copland and his uniquely "American" sound. Those who

missed the television shows could find them on DVD, and eventually as downloads. Visitors to a collateral website explored musical concepts and theories. Michael Tilson Thomas interviewed artists and colleagues in an eight-part radio series, *The MTT Files*, that brought the Symphony its second Peabody Award. (The first had come for *American Mavericks*, a 2001 radio series emerging from the Mavericks festival of 2000.) Another *Keeping Score* component, lower-tech but person-to-person, trained classroom teachers throughout the Western US— in Fresno, San Jose, Sonoma, Oklahoma City, and Flagstaff, Arizona—to integrate music into their core-subject lessons.

Keeping Score continued in 2009 with a second series. Final installments were scheduled for 2011. "As we move into the future," Michael Tilson Thomas said in 2003, a year after production on the *Keeping Score* pilot had begun, "TV, radio, and the Internet will help people stumble upon the San Francisco Symphony and discover how much we have to offer. It may also change their preconceptions about classical music." Once *Keeping Score* was underway, people did more than stumble upon the Symphony. A year after the 2006 series was released, *Keeping Score* had captured nearly 5 million viewers, and seventeen thousand DVDs had been sold.

SFS Media, meanwhile, had expanded its project of recording all the Mahler symphonies to include the composer's orchestral songs, including the great song cycle *Das Lied von der Erde*. The Mahler symphony recordings had garnered seven Grammy awards. Recognition came early, when the series' first installment, the Mahler Sixth Symphony recorded in the aftermath of 9/11, received the Grammy for Best Orchestral Performance. The

entire series, recorded in Super Audio CD surround sound—then the latest consumer-sound technology—received wide distribution through means undreamt of when the project commenced: digital downloads on home computers and portable music players.

By the second decade of the twenty-first century, technology had made strides unimaginable when the century began, and no end to its reach could be conceived. Already the Symphony owned a channel on the Internet video site YouTube. The YouTube Symphony Orchestra, which MTT conducted in the spring of 2009, was made up of musicians from around the world who had won membership through online auditions, which San Francisco Symphony musicians helped jury.

243

31

32

That same year, the Symphony became the first US orchestra to launch its own social networking site. Exactly a century earlier, ten civic leaders had gathered around a table at the Mercantile Trust Company of San Francisco, in the recently rebuilt Financial District, having answered the summons of a letter proposing that they help organize a permanent orchestra for the city. Imagine what T. B. Berry, E. S. Heller, and John Rothschild could have done with the electronic tools available to those who followed them.

THE GREAT AMERICAN ORCHESTRA

Beware the word *great* when describing yourself. Consider what you must do to elicit the word from others. The music-making is the thing itself. Even the music we know well, or think we know well, is about surprise and new ways of encountering the world. Words go only so far in describing the experience. That said, consider some of the complimentary words on record. In 2004, when MTT and the San Francisco Symphony performed in Cleveland, home to what many believe is an orchestra on a par with the world's best, the *Plain Dealer* wrote of "urgent and penetrating" performances, and of a concert that "will be remembered as one of the highlights of our musical season." The *Boston Globe* described a Mahler performance as "transcendent." The *New York Times*, summarizing a pair of Carnegie Hall concerts, wrote that "the players gave fiercely committed performances." In the days of Henry Hadley, civic boosters claimed they would soon have an orchestra equal to any in the country. The San Francisco Symphony survived its journey through the valley of the shadow of Issay Dobrowen, to emerge into the light of the Monteux years. It survived whatever triggered the wrath of George Szell, to blossom again under the stewardship of Josef Krips and the line of music directors who followed him, to say nothing of those behind the scenes.

In 2010 *New Yorker* critic Alex Ross recalled the legendary German conductor Wilhelm Furtwängler, who half a century earlier lamented "the dying out of improvisatory playing, by which he meant collective risk-taking, a sense of music unfolding in the here and now." As MTT often said, that sense of improvisation was what he and the orchestra pursued. In the spring of 2010, taking time out from a schedule that included San Francisco concerts, rehearsals, *Keeping Score* filming, and meetings with donors, he explained how the musicians and he sought to realize their ideal. The great strength of the San Francisco Symphony's playing, he said, is that it comes from the heart.

32

The recording of Mahler's Symphony No. 7 received two 2006 Grammys, for Best Classical Album and Best Orchestral Performance.

33

Michael Tilson Thomas and the San Francisco Symphony: the official portrait.

34

Violinist Mariko Smiley represents a family of Symphony music-makers. Her father, David, was a violist in the orchestra. Her husband, Sarn Oliver, is a Symphony violinist. Her brother Dan, the Symphony's principal second violinist, is married to Symphony violinist Suzanne Leon.

33

34

35

35

Three rows of wind musicians, from a conductor's-eye view: from bottom, oboist Pamela Smith, bassoonist Rob Weir, and Nicole Cash, associate principal horn.

36

MTT and baritone Thomas Hampson prepare one of Mahler's Wunderhorn *songs, part of an album of the composer's orchestral songs released in 2010, the final installment of the Mahler cycle launched by SFS Media in 2001.*

37

Reaching a new generation of artists: MTT coaches a Youth Orchestra rehearsal.

38, 39

By the early twenty-first century the San Francisco Symphony was a regular presence on the world's music scene. These posters announce performances in Greece and Spain.

36

For a conductor, part of the improvisatory process is to help players understand the parameters of a performance and allow them the independence to work within that space. Different players in each section contribute in their own ways to different aspects of the music. MTT explained: "Some are more aware of fugitive, delicate nuances. Some have a long, arching legato sound. Some are rhythmic wizards. Some have brilliant articulation. At different moments in the music these people take the lead and inspire one another to manifest—together—what the music is asking for."

His work with the orchestra concentrated on helping musicians feel comfortable with playing the subtlest music and, at the right moments, taking the necessary risks. Music-making is not a democracy, not a search for a middle ground. "An orchestral performance involves extremes, and requires people who are willing to become extremists." The conductor's job is to know how to encourage the kind of playing the music demands—especially if the music is by composers like Mahler or Stravinsky, who may ask some players to approach their parts as delicately as possible while others are running rampage.

Aware of who actually makes the music, MTT spoke of each musician's contribution as something to prize. "There are subtleties about orchestral performance which *cannot* be worked out from the conductor's beat. The real subtleties of ensemble come from the players listening to one another and watching *one another.*" Seeing new members of the orchestra observe him closely in performance, he would thank them for their attention, then suggest it could be more productively focused on Concertmaster Barantschik, or the leaders of their sections. What

37

he tried to do was work with musicians as a director works with great actors, offering perspective on how they could be most effective, with the most effect on the audience. No director, he pointed out, would tell an actor how to weight each word in a sentence, or how quickly or deliberately to speak the words. Louder, softer, faster, slower—those are the basics. "I'm happiest when I'm talking about the harmonies, the phrase shapes, the orchestration, what kinds of moods and feelings those are creating, and how players can work with these things. It pleases me when they find their own ways of doing this. An actor has to *become* the part. Musicians must feel the performance is theirs, because it is. *They're* the ones playing."

In many ways, the demands on an American orchestra's music director in the late twentieth and early twenty-first century have become extra-musical, growing into what might be expected of a corporate chief executive. Besides artistry, the job description today requires business and marketing savvy. For as expenses have increased beyond individual supporters' means to meet them, additional funding veins have to be uncovered and tapped. In such efforts, the music director plays an increasingly prominent role—as the face of the organization, and as advocate, solicitor, and ingratiatingly social host, whether speaking to an audience of neophytes and seasoned listeners, mingling glass-in-hand at parties with potential contributors, or making the Symphony's case to foundation executives. Such duties have been piled on top of rehearsing and conducting concerts, programming a season, keeping abreast of new talent among performers and composers, dealing with the countless personnel issues swarming in an orchestra of a hundred brilliant men and women who put themselves on the line week after week, and taking the heat along with the hoped-for praise. Fulfilling the ancillary tasks is not taught at conservatory.

Against that background, the music itself has got to remain paramount. And consider how much music is made: forty-plus weeks of concerts each year, each week a new program of about two hours, with about ten hours of rehearsal. Notes and more notes: thousands of them in (for example) just the second violin part of Mahler's Seventh Symphony. MTT points out that, for everyone on stage, "to stay on the learning curve of getting all that together, and then also allowing yourself to be vulnerable enough and involved enough in the musical message to make it work—this is a tremendous challenge."

The *spirit* of the music-making, MTT says, is a critical element. Guest conductors in San Francisco have been quick to compliment the orchestra's spirit, the willingness to entertain new and extreme approaches even to familiar music. Part of this spirit is the concept of *personal best*, which is ever-present among musicians. As a player becomes more experienced and more expert, the ultimate goal seems ever more elusive. Depending on a musician's viewpoint or frame of mind, the Sisyphean struggle for perfection can be discouraging, but it can also be exactly what makes the struggle itself worthwhile. Athletes will recognize MTT's reasoning. As surely as the San Francisco Giants

and Forty-Niners, an orchestra is a team—or a wolf pack, as MTT once characterized the San Francisco Symphony, going so far, at the end of especially fine performances, as to grit his teeth and utter appreciative growls.

Music lovers feast on the real-time playing a concert offers, on music unfolding in the here and now, and that is also among the reasons an orchestra tours: enabling distant audiences to hear the ensemble, live. In 2011, the San Francisco Symphony traveled to Europe again, this tour highlighted by Vienna concerts at a festival commemorating the centenary of Gustav Mahler's death. Packed along with scores and parts for the composer's Second, Sixth, and Ninth symphonies was the music for Hugo Alfvén's *Midsommarvaka*, homage to Verne Sellin, the old friend who almost forty years earlier had welcomed MTT to the San Francisco stage, when he first encountered the orchestra's brand of music-making. *Let's go for it!*

Touring confirms the continuing demand for live performance, despite technology that has made sound reproduction more immediate than ever. Executive Director Brent Assink found such demand heartening. Though a champion of technology, he urged audiences to embrace the live shared experience, in which attentive listeners energize the musicians, kindling musicians' responses that in turn draw listeners ever more deeply into the music. "This doesn't come from listening to a CD. It never can. It never will."

Music is about more than concerts, and concerts are about more than music. Thoughtful programming over time, Assink has said, enables listeners to familiarize themselves with a world outside their experience. "So

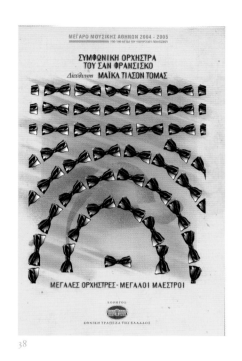

38

39

248

FESTIVALS WITH MTT (AND OTHERS)

Festivals have figured prominently throughout Michael Tilson Thomas's tenure. For two weeks, the focus is on a composer, or on a musical era or movement. Festival concepts arise from curiosity. "I'm always interested in exploring what I don't know and connecting the dots in a different way," MTT has said. "I try to encourage and provoke those same qualities in the audience." In these festivals, music has been heard in novel contexts. Thus Berlioz's oft-performed *Symphonie fanatastique* served as prelude to its sequel, the rarely performed *Lélio*. Beethoven appeared on programs alongside his contemporaries, famed in their day but since neglected. Stravinsky's sacred music became the subject of a concert performed in the kind of space for which it was meant, San Francisco's Grace Cathedral. The festivals presented during Michael Tilson Thomas's tenure suggest the breadth of special programming.

1996
An American Festival

1997
Celebrations of the Sacred and Profane (including music by J. S. Bach, Schubert, Berlioz, Scelsi, Berio)

1998
A Mahler Festival

1999
Stravinsky Festival

2000
American Mavericks

2001
Mozart Festival (conducted by Neville Marriner)

2002
Russian Festival

2003
Innocence Undone: Wagner, Weill, and the Weimar Years

2004
Beethoven's Vienna: Scenes from a Musical Revolution

2005
Of Thee I Sing: Yiddish Theater, Broadway, and the American Voice

2006
Romantic Visions: From Paradise to the Abyss (conducted by James Conlon; including music by Liszt, Schreker, Richard Strauss, Tchaikovsky, Verdi, Zemlinsky)

2007
Russian Firebrand, Russian Virtuoso: The Music of Prokofiev

2008
A Brahms Festival

2009
Dawn to Twilight: A Schubert/Berg Festival

2009
A Mahler Festival

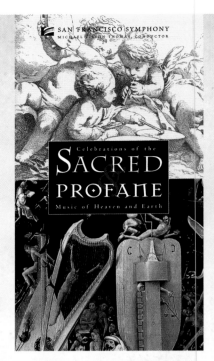

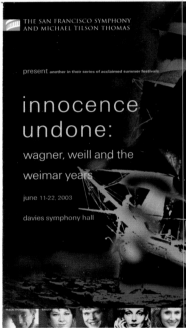

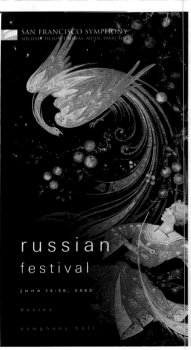

LUCERNE FESTIVAL
IM SOMMER

eros

Konzertprogramm 51 | Concert Program 51
Sinfoniekonzert 28 | Montag, 13. September 2010
Symphony Concert 28 | Monday 13 September 2010

San Francisco Symphony | Michael Tilson Thomas | Susan Graham

40

*Among the world's music festivals, that of
Lucerne had become one of the most acclaimed
by 2006, when the San Francisco Symphony
performed its first concerts in a multiyear
Lucerne residency that culminated in 2010.*

40

that the next time they encounter this music, it will be less scary." San Francisco's audience has always been receptive to the new and the unusual. Long before *diversity* became a word to describe the social fabric, the Bay Area was a place where many cultures lived side by side, a place where the risqué and the risky were prized. Ethnic groups once the targets of discrimination have become valued parts of the community without relinquishing their special qualities. As a cultural anchor in this community, the Symphony is a natural to offer music that mixes the new and the offbeat with more traditional fare. When listeners integrate the unfamiliar into their expectations, points of view expand. Whether a broader musical outlook can influence other parts of their lives is an open question. But if music challenges assumptions and enables its

participants to see beyond themselves, it can be part of a future that inches toward the ideal of tolerance and understanding Beethoven envisioned in his Ninth Symphony. And if technology can make music an ever-greater part of life, it is an ally in music's quest.

AN END AND A BEGINNING
In 1975, when Seiji Ozawa chose Boston over San Francisco, the decision seemed inevitable. Once again, East Coast had trumped West Coast, the beautiful older sister had seduced her blemished sibling's lover. But if all that seemed preordained, equally inevitable was the evening in 2010, when President Barack Obama awarded Michael Tilson Thomas the National Arts Medal and MTT spoke of the collaboration he and the Symphony enjoyed. The medal was awarded

to a man, not an institution, yet its bestowal on a West Coast native who led a West Coast orchestra was telling. During the past thirty years, since Davies Symphony Hall opened, the Symphony had reestablished its national and global presence, and in some ways the National Arts Medal symbolized how recognition was flowing from the country's power center toward the far side of the continent, where orchestras were reaffirming what they could do and be. In the music world, the scale's weights had become more evenly distributed.

"Here everything is more bohemian," Alfred Hertz had written of San Francisco in 1905. What Hertz found then is even more apparent as the world moves into the twenty-first century. San Francisco is a patchwork of many-colored and tightly knit pieces woven into a crazy quilt,

the sort of unity-in-diversity that is
the mark of America, just as Melville
had described in *Moby Dick*, in his
great symbols of the hodgepodge
counterpane and the white whale
itself, evoking a nation whose moral
sinew lay in understanding differences and assimilating them spiritually. Bay Area residents often imagine
themselves outside tradition, more
socially progressive than other parts
of the country, more inclined to ex-
periment. Trends have been born in
the Bay Area, without a doubt. Often
those innovations have become mainstream. Yet the spirit of San Francisco
is the spirit of American tradition.
The place was born in Gold Rush an-
archy and rearranged in seismic up-
heavals. It drew fortune-seekers from
across the country and emigrants
from other lands, and together that
population understood how music
could help root a new civilization.
The Bay Area's unruly mix of eth-
nicities and classes and opinions is
America in microcosm. From this microcosm the Symphony has absorbed
strength and formed character, and
its not-always-smoothly plotted history reflects the history of its hometown. Why should it be otherwise?
"To make an end is to make a beginning," T. S. Eliot wrote. So the story
continues, as does the music, which
leads not to conclusions, but to the
verge of what can be.

ENDNOTES

I. PRELIMINARIES:
ON CIVILIZATION'S FRONTIER

13   *"everything is more Bohemian"*: Alfred Hertz to "My Dear Brinkel," April 10, 1905. Alfred Hertz Collection, University of California Music Library.

14   *A night on a rooming-house cot*: Herbert Asbury, *The Barbary Coast* (New York: Thunder's Mouth Press, 1933), 13–14.

17   *Fifty years later he recalled*: J. B. Levison, *Memories for My Family* (San Francisco: John Henry Nash, 1933), 47.

17   *"His mere presence was exhausting"*: *Argonaut*, November 17, 1883.

17   *In her 1946 history*: Leonora Wood Armsby, "The San Francisco Symphony: First Decade," *California Historical Society Quarterly* 25, no. 3 (September 1946), 229.

18   *As historical geographer Gray Brechin writes*: Gray Brechin, *Imperial San Francisco* (Berkeley: University of California Press, 1999), 151–54.

18   *But historian Kevin Starr identified it in his story of Josiah Royce*: Josiah Royce, "Provincialism Based Upon a Study of Early Conditions in California," *Putnam's Magazine* 7 (1909), 233–35, 237. Quoted in Kevin Starr, *Americans and the California Dream, 1850–1915* (New York: Oxford University Press, 1973), 168.

II. A QUICK-START GUIDE TO
MAKING AN ORCHESTRA

20   *The Panama-Pacific International Exposition, whose scale*: William Lipsky, *San Francisco's Panama-Pacific International Exposition* (Charleston, SC: Arcadia Publishing Co., 2005), 7–8, 21, 23–24, 26.

22   *"The essential condition of such orchestras"*: Joseph Horowitz, *Classical Music in America* (New York: W. W. Norton & Company, 2005), 43–44.

22   *Heller, born in San Francisco, was an attorney*: Heller was also a great-uncle to Nancy Bechtle, who served as Symphony president from 1987 to 2001.

24   *the Musical Association of San Francisco was organized*: Musical Association of San Francisco, Minutes of a Meeting, December 20, 1909. Subsequent references to meeting minutes in this chapter are cited as "MASF minutes."

24   *Board member Frank Deering explained all this*: "Henry Hadley Is Luncheon Guest," *San Francisco Chronicle*, November 16, 1911.

25   *as the San Francisco Chronicle looked back on this recruitment*: "San Francisco's Symphony Orchestra," *San Francisco Chronicle*, July 25, 1915.

28   *Hadley was in top form, addressing a luncheon audience*: "Henry Hadley Is Luncheon Guest," *San Francisco Chronicle*, November 16, 1911.

28   *"I came here expecting to find good, capable musicians"*: Harvey Wickham, "Hadley Predicts Triumphs for Orchestra," *San Francisco Chronicle*, November 26, 1911.

28   *Packing the Cort Theatre that Friday afternoon*: "Society Appears in Its Richest Apparel," *San Francisco Chronicle*, December 9, 1911.

28   *The audience was there to listen, not just to be seen*: Harvey Wickham, "San Francisco Symphony Orchestra Wins Big Triumph," *San Francisco Chronicle*, December 9, 1911.

28   *Will L. Greenbaum, the orchestra's manager and a local impresario*: Will L. Greenbaum, "San Francisco Orchestra to Bring Music to the People," *San Francisco Chronicle*, December 8, 1911.

32   *At a Chamber of Commerce luncheon that afternoon, Joseph D. Redding*: "Advocates Plans for Opera-House," *San Francisco Chronicle*, April 18, 1912.

32   *"The orchestra, which was then [1911] a novelty"*: Harvey Wickham, "Local Symphony Season Has a Fine Beginning," *San Francisco Chronicle*, October 26, 1912.

32   *The resolution to build an opera house, entered into board minutes*: MASF minutes, November 6, 1912.

32   *"One can't think of what the old town would now do"*: Harvey Wickham, "Symphony Season Comes to an End," *San Francisco Chronicle*, March 10, 1913.

33   *"This matter [of inadequate musicians] was presented to your notice last April"*: MASF minutes, October 21, 1913.

33   *As early as March 1914, Bourn saw a way of surmounting such struggles*: MASF minutes, March 23, 1914.

33   *this was most evident in a concert to benefit the Belgian Relief Fund*: MASF minutes, November 5 1914.

34   *In a letter to the board, this band of players*: MASF minutes, December 2, 1914.

34   *Festival Hall was rebuilt*: *The Blue Book: A Comprehensive Official Souvenir View Book of The Panama-Pacific International Exposition at San Francisco 1915* (San Francisco: Robert A. Reid, 1915), 21, 118.

36   *but now he laid out the facts as he saw them*: Walter Anthony, "Music of France Captures Big Audience," *San Francisco Chronicle*, May 17, 1915.

36   *Association President Bourn tried to let Hadley down gently*: MASF minutes of Music Committee and Finance Committee, June 23, 1915.

36   *The temptation to accept Cecilia Casserly's offer*: MASF minutes, June 23, 1915; cf. Leta E. Miller, "'The Multitude Listens with the Heart': Orchestras, Urban Culture, and the Early Years of the San Francisco Symphony," in *Music, American Made: Essays in Honor of John Graziano*, edited by John Koegel (Sterling Heights, MI: Harmonie Park Press, forthcoming, 2011).

36   *"When the San Francisco Symphony occupies"*: Redfern Mason, "San Francisco Symphony Completes Fifth Season; What of the Future?" *San Francisco Examiner*, March 26, 1916.

36   *Here, Mason believed, was a man*: Redfern Mason, "Hertz May Head S.F. Orchestra," *San Francisco Examiner*, July 1, 1915.

CHAPTER 2 SIDEBARS
INTRODUCING HENRY HADLEY

Herbert R. Boardman, *Henry Hadley: Ambassador of Harmony* (Atlanta: Banner Press, Emory University, 1932).

New York Times, November 29, 1910; "Symphony Season Marked Success," *Seattle Times*, undated.

Alfred Metzger, "Henry K. Hadley, Our Symphony Leader," *Pacific Coast Musical Review*, September 2, 1911, 3.

Metzger, "Holiday Reflections," *Pacific Coast Musical Review*, December 16, 1911, 5.

Metzger, "The Symphony Concert," *Pacific Coast Musical Review*, December 16, 1911, 16.

Metzger, *Pacific Coast Musical Review*, February 24, 1912.

Harvey Wickham, "Conductor Hadley Arrives in Town," *San Francisco Chronicle*, October 19, 1911.

"Symphony Season Marked Success," *New York Times*, November 29, 1910.

"Leaders in Music to Honor Hadley," *New York Times*, September 8, 1937.

"Henry Hadley Will Direct Orchestra," *San Francisco Chronicle*, September 1, 1911.

"Birthday Honors to Henry Hadley," *San Francisco Chronicle*, December 21, 1912.

"Hadley Is Back from Europe," *San Francisco Chronicle*, September 23, 1913.

"Hadley Wins High Honors in New York," *San Francisco Chronicle*, July 18, 1920.

"Music," *The Seattle Times*, June 12, 1911.

SABOTEUR WITHIN, UNREASONABLE LADIES WITHOUT

MASF minutes, February 12, August 1, and October 8, 1912.

"Muse Breathless Over Art Crisis," *San Francisco Chronicle*, November 2, 1911.

III. PERSONAL STRUGGLES AND MUSICAL TRIUMPHS

40   *And so that August, a month after joining*: Leta E. Miller, "'The Multitude Listens with the Heart': Orchestras, Urban Culture, and the Early Years of the San Francisco Symphony," in *Music, American Made: Essays in Honor of John Graziano*, edited by John Koegel (Sterling Heights, MI: Harmonie Park Press, forthcoming, 2011).

40   *In July the San Francisco Chronicle reported*: "New Note Is Not an Ultimatum to Germany," *San Francisco Chronicle*, July 21, 1915.

40   *Alfred Hertz believed that the opening concert*: "Hadley's Friends, in Huff, Quit Music Association," *San Francisco Bulletin*, August 27, 1915.

40   *Joseph Guttman, claimed his boss had given "many evidences of his joy"*: "Weapons Are Sharpened for Symphony War," *San Francisco Chronicle*, April 5, 1916.

41   *Incredibly, the noise was still going on three years later*: Alfred Metzger, "S.F. Symphony Orchestra and Alfred Hertz Get Great Ovation," *Pacific Coast Musical Review*, October 18, 1919; E. M. B., "San Franciscans Hail Hertz Forces," *Musical America*, October 25, 1919.

43   *Manager Frank Healy estimated expenses for the coming season*: Musical Association of San Francisco, Minutes of a Meeting, August 2, September 24, September 30, 1915. Subsequent references to meeting minutes in this chapter are cited as "MASF minutes."

43   *"On one previous occasion only have I seen a symphony audience"*: Redfern Mason, "Hertz Leads Orchestra to Success," *San Francisco Examiner*, December 18, 1915.

43   *The Argonaut noted a new tonal beauty*: "The First Symphony Concert," *The Argonaut*, December 26, 1915.

43   *The Chronicle's Walter Anthony compared Hertz*: Walter Anthony, "Alfred Hertz Wins Triumph with Symphony Orchestra," *San Francisco Chronicle*, December 18, 1915.

44   *As late as the end of February 1916, board president W. B. Bourn*: MASF minutes of Music Committee, February 29, 1916.

44   *Through William H. Crocker, he had learned*: MASF minutes, March 17, 1916.

44   *"It was thought inadvisable to consider [Toscanini]"*: MASF minutes of Executive Committee, March 28, 1916.

44   *He detested manager Frank Healy*: Alfred Hertz to E. S. Heller, November 17, 1915. Alfred Hertz Papers, 1895–1937, San Francisco Public Library.

44 *The Executive Committee agreed, then passed a resolution:* MASF minutes of Executive Committee, March 21, 1916.

44 *Then there was Cecilia Casserly:* Leta E. Miller, *Music and Politics in San Francisco: From the 1906 Quake to the Second World War* (Berkeley: University of California Press, forthcoming, 2011); cf. "The Multitude Listens with the Heart."

46 *"I do not consider Hertz a good musician":* "Weapons Are Sharpened for Symphony War," *San Francisco Chronicle*, April 5, 1916.

46 *It was rumored that an overture had been made:* Jason Gibbs, "'The Best Music at the Lowest Price': People's Music in San Francisco," *MLA Northern California Newsletter* 17, no. 1 (Fall 2002): 5–8; cf. Thomas Nunan, "Invite Hadley to Become New Rival to Hertz," *Musical America*, April 15, 1916.

46 *The manager of the People's Philharmonic was Frank Healy:* "New Home for San Francisco Philharmonic," *Musical America*, June 17, 1916, 42.

46 *The Casserly version of the People's Philharmonic disbanded:* Gibbs, "'The Best Music at the Lowest Price.'"

46 *"The San Francisco Symphony is more important":* Redfern Mason, "Intrigue Over Conductors Hinders Development of Symphony Orchestra," *The Musical Leader*, April 27, 1916.

47 *Years later, Winthrop Sargeant:* Winthrop Sargeant, *Geniuses, Goddesses, and People* (New York: E. P. Dutton & Co., 1949), 11–12.

47 *It was proposed that the fund be doubled:* "S.F. Symphony Orchestra to Be Permanent Organization," *San Francisco Chronicle*, July 1, 1916.

47 *"We owe it to the community":* Redfern Mason, "San Francisco Symphony Completes Fifth Season; What of the Future?" *San Francisco Examiner*, March 26, 1916.

50 *Hertz was apt to aim withering comments:* Sargeant, *Geniuses*, 18-19.

50 *The formation in May 1917 of a Women's Auxiliary:* William Huck, "The San Francisco Symphony: Seventy-Five Years of Music," *Encore: The Archives for the Performing Arts Quarterly* 3, no. 3 (Summer 1986): 11.

51 *Autumn had seen a deadly resurgence of the "Spanish Flu":* "City Snapshots: San Francisco," *Influenza 1918*, American Experience, PBS.org.

51 *"I understand from some of my friends":* Howard Hanson to Alfred Hertz, November 4, 1919. Alfred Hertz Papers, 1895–1937, San Francisco Public Library.

51 *Writing to Hertz in October 1921, Roy Harris:* Roy Harris to Alfred Hertz, October 2, 1921; October 1, 1921. Hertz Papers, San Francisco Public Library.

52 *"The Orchestra must either progress or go back":* Alfred Hertz to John D. McKee, January 24, 1921. Hertz Papers, San Francisco Public Library.

52 *After intermission, Hertz and the musicians played:* Ray C. B. Brown, "S.F. Lovers of Music Give to Retain Hertz," *San Francisco Chronicle*, April 1, 1922. Cf. Robert Commanday, "The Musical Giant of San Francisco's 'Golden Age,'" *Sunday Examiner and Chronicle*, July 16, 1972. Leta Miller reports that the amount of pledges was reported differently in different sources, ranging from $10,000 to $11,000.

52 *Despite the audience's support, Hertz was not asked:* Alfred Hertz to Miss Z. W. Potter, April 11, 1922. Hertz Papers, San Francisco Public Library.

52 *in a confidential telegram to the orchestra there:* Alfred Hertz, telegram to J. Herman Thuman, May 9, 1922. Hertz Papers, San Francisco Public Library.

52 *Three days later he wrote to Mrs. Charles P. Taft:* Alfred Hertz to Mrs. Charles P. Taft, May 12, 1922. Hertz Papers, San Francisco Public Library.

52 *Hertz wrote a friend that he had considered rejecting:* Alfred Hertz to W. A. Clark, Jr., May 26, 1922. Hertz Papers, San Francisco Public Library.

53 *Hertz also established series of concerts in Oakland:* Miller, "The Multitude Listens with the Heart." Cf. Huck, "The San Francisco Symphony: Seventy-Five Years of Music," 14.

53 *The next year, violinist Mary Pasmore was hired:* William Huck, "Seventy-Five Years of the San Francisco Symphony," *California History* 65, no. 4 (December 1986): 252–53. Cf. Miller, "The Multitude Listens with the Heart."

55 *"Men of means would rehearse diligently":* Bruno David Ussher, "Music and Musical Activities," *Saturday Night*, April 5, 1924.

55 *Alfred Metzger maintained that never before in America:* Alfred Metzger, "Significance of Spring Music Festival," *Pacific Coast Musical Review*, March 17, 1924.

55 *This was an orchestra with traditions rooted:* Scott Foglesong, "Rain Comes to the Hertz Desert," Examiner.com, May 17, 2009.

55 *In September 1926, a plan was announced:* Arthur S. Garbett, "Symphony Broadcast Plan Meets Approval," *San Francisco News*, September 25, 1926.

59 *"Our future has never looked so bright as now":* Alexander Fried, "Alfred Hertz Tells of Symphony Plans," *San Francisco Chronicle*, October 16, 1927.

59 *what that city's press described as the country's first orchestra exchange:* "San Francisco Symphony Orchestra Arrives for First Exchange Concert," *Los Angeles Evening Express*, January 5, 1928.

59 *"I am now at my zenith":* "Hertz Gives Reasons for Resignation," *San Francisco Call*, October 9, 1929.

59 *"Not the least significant portion of these ovations":* "Glorious Work Alfred Hertz Has Done for San Francisco," *San Francisco Chronicle*, April 11, 1930.

CHAPTER 3 SIDEBARS
A LESSON WITH LOUIS PERSINGER

William Huck, "In Praise of Those Who Make the Music," San Francisco Symphony *Stagebill*, December 1986, 13–15.

THE PASMORE SISTERS: MAKE ROOM FOR WOMEN

"Pasmore, Henry Bickford," in *History of Music in San Francisco Series*, Vol. 6, *Early Master Teachers* (San Francisco: Works Progress Administration, Northern California, 1940), 50–69.

POLTERGEIST AT THE KEYBOARD

Harold Bauer to Alfred Hertz, January 30, 1919. Alfred Hertz Papers, 1895-1937, San Francisco Public Library.

Ray C. B. Brown, "Player Piano's Art Is Eerie," *San Francisco Examiner*, February 1, 1919.

Alfred Hertz to C. Arthur Longwell, January 30, 1919. Hertz Papers, San Francisco Public Library.

Alfred Hertz to W. V. Swords, April 10, 1919. Hertz Papers, San Francisco Public Library.

MASF minutes, August 21, 1918.

THE STANDARD HOUR: WHEN MUSIC AND TECHNOLOGY FUSED

Bill Bryson, *Made in America* (London: Secker & Warburg, 1994), 267. Regarding the 1921 Dempsey-Carpentier fight that brought radio into the national consciousness, Bryson has pointed out that a ringside account was to have been transmitted via radio to Times Square, where details would be relayed to those gathered outside the New York Times Building. Because of a malfunction, the news was instead relayed via ticker tape. Yet the thousands assembled in Times Square *believed* they were receiving their news through radio, and the thought that such instant communication was possible propelled the young medium's widespread popularity.

Joe Evans, "The 'Standard Hour' and SFS Radio Broadcast Timeline," unpublished paper, September 5, 2008. (San Francisco Symphony Archives.)

Alexander Fried, "Radio Creates Crisis in U.S. Music," *San Francisco Chronicle*, January 21, 1934.

Arthur S. Garbett, "Symphony Broadcast Plan Meets Approval," *San Francisco News*, September 25, 1926.

Bob Hall, "Standard Symphony Celebrates Tenth Year on Radio," *Call-Bulletin*, September 30, 1937.

William Huck, "The San Francisco Symphony: Seventy-Five Years of Music," in *Encore: The Archives of the Performing Arts Quarterly 3*, no. 3 (Summer 1986).

Redfern Mason, "Alfred Hertz Acclaimed in Radio Debut . . . Music Heard Through Entire West," *San Francisco Chronicle*, March 25, 1932.

Fred Krock, "KSMO and Successor Stations on 1550 kHz in San Francisco," *The Bay Area Radio Museum Presents: John Schneider's Voices Out of the Fog 25 August 2008*: www.sfradiomuseum.com.

Adrian Michaelis, "Still Music on the Western Air," *The Black Perspective in Music*, 3, no. 2 ("A Birthday Offering to William Grant Still," May 1975): 177–189.

IV. CRISIS AND RESCUE

60   *"we should not engage any one man for the full season"*: Musical Association of San Francisco, Minutes of a Meeting, April 24, 1930. Subsequent references to meeting minutes in this chapter are cited as "MASF minutes."

62   *He did, however, come with the recommendations*: MASF minutes, May 21, 1930.

62   *Issay Dobrowen, hired along with Cameron, would conduct the second half*: Jørn Fossheim, "Issay Dobrowen," translated by Andrew Smith, Simax Classics website, www.simax.no/artikkel.php?id=953.

62   *the Women's Auxiliary, who cited reports from abroad*: MASF minutes, February 4, 1931.

62   *In an interview three years later, he would admit, "shyly"*: Ernest Lenn, "Behind that Name: Dobrowen Loyal to But One Ruler—His Music," *San Francisco Examiner*, April 6, 1934.

63   *Youthful fire, however, came at a price*: Dobrowen details in this paragraph from MASF minutes, January 22, February 4, 1931.

63   *In June, J. B. Levison actually reported increased*: MASF minutes, June 5, 1931.

63   *In June 1931 he told his fellow board members*: MASF minutes, June 12, 1931.

64   *The Chronicle's Alexander Fried reported figures*: Alexander Fried, "Music Lovers Plan Drive for Symphony Aid," *San Francisco Chronicle*, January 20, 1932.

68   *It was chaired by Robert Watt Miller*: Frank Carmody to Robert Watt Miller, March 8, 1932.

68   *Mayor Angelo Rossi issued a statement*: "Symphony to Launch Appeal February 15," *San Francisco Examiner*, date unknown.

68   *"The San Francisco Symphony Orchestra is an institution"*: "Hayden Makes Strong Plea for Symphony," *San Francisco Examiner*, February 3, 1932.

68   *The Symphony Fund Campaign emphasized how much the Bay Area*: Irving R. Morrow to Ernest Born, June 24, 1950.

68   *Duke Ellington and his band*: "Duke Ellington to Aid Campaign," *San Francisco Examiner*, February 18, 1932.

68   *Dobrowen's divided loyalties were sanctioned by his contract*: MASF minutes, August 17, 1932.

68   *"the committee concurred that in view of the uncertainty"*: MASF minutes, May 12, 1932.

69   *They proposed a short season that would open*: Special Meeting with Orchestra Representatives, notes from July 15 and July 21, 1932.

69   *Molinari, whose relationship with musicians was by turns*: Leonora Wood Armsby, *Musicians Talk* (New York: The Dial Press, 1935), 51–52; Agnes Albert, oral history interview with Larry Rothe, August 2001. (San Francisco Symphony Archives.)

70   *Talk turned to bringing Dobrowen back*: MASF minutes, January 5 and 24, 1933.

70   *The answer seemed to be a 1933–34 season*: MASF minutes, February 20, 1933.

70   *"Mr. Dobrowen was here for so limited a period"*: Alexander Fried, "Symphony's Financial Deficit Near Artistic Shortage, Says Player," *San Francisco Chronicle*, no date.

71   *All present approved of Dobrowen's words*: MASF minutes, March 9, 1933.

71   *Some thought the board should be headed by two leaders*: MASF minutes, March 31, April 5, 1933.

74   *the alternatives were to engage a guest in his absence*: "Memoranda relating to engagements of Mr. Issay Dobrowen and Mr. Naoum Blinder for the coming season," MASF minutes, May 19, 1933.

74   *Tobin also proposed a reduction in Dobrowen's salary*: MASF minutes, May 26, 1933.

74   *Tobin agreed, on condition that the musicians*: MASF minutes, June 2, 1933.

74   *Association members agreed to underwrite any unlikely loss*: MASF minutes, July 11, 1933.

74   *Various proposals were floated*: MASF minutes, August 14, 1933.

74   *"an event in the musical history of San Francisco"*: Meeting with orchestra members, August 17, 1933.

74   *The union accepted the offer*: MASF minutes, August 31, 1933.

74   *In October 1933, Zirato proposed instead that Toscanini*: MASF minutes, October 23, October 26, 1933.

75   *"the great Italian maestro is as sorry about [the cancellation]"*: "Toscanini Will Not Come to S.F.," *San Francisco Chronicle*, March 18, 1934.

75   *It was early 1934 and the Depression*: MASF minutes, February 6, 1934.

75   *the nine-year-old piano prodigy Ruth Slenczynski*: In later years she was known as Ruth Slenczynska.

76   *Then, in a board meeting, in front of Tobin's colleagues*: MASF minutes, March 12, March 14, 1934.

76   *Tobin begged to differ*: Agnes Albert, oral history interview with Larry Rothe, August 2001. (San Francisco Symphony Archives.)

76 *He failed to see how promises could be made:* MASF minutes, March 14, 1934.

76 *McKee was convinced the Association's finances:* MASF minutes, April 25, 1934.

77 *A few days later, Tobin announced he would not continue:* MASF minutes, June 7, 1934.

77 *By October only half the funds for Tobin's:* MASF minutes, October 1, 1934.

77 *In December, he concluded that a season of even twelve weeks:* MASF minutes, December 5, December 6, December 13, 1934.

77 *Tobin went on record as stating that Dobrowen:* MASF minutes, January 3, 1935.

77 *"The season of 1934–35 must be abandoned":* MASF minutes, January 17, 1935.

79 *Hayden estimated this could raise thirty-five thousand:* J. Emmet Hayden to Executive Committee of the Musical Association of San Francisco, April 8, 1935.

79 *On March 28, the city-sponsored "Municipal Symphony Orchestra":* Marjory M. Fisher, "S.F. Chorus of 300 Sings Noted 'Ninth,'" *San Francisco News,* March 28, 1935.

79 *A story in one of the city's papers announced:* "Whole City in Campaign to Save Symphony," April 29, 1935, clipping from unidentified newspaper.

79 *When the polls closed on May 2 and the votes were tallied:* Marjory M. Fisher, "What Comes Next in Symphony Affairs?" *San Francisco News,* May 6, 1935.

79 *"City, Symphony Unite on Plan" was the title of the Examiner story:* "City, Symphony Unite on Plan," *San Francisco Examiner,* May 9, 1935.

79 *New Association officers were elected on July 22:* Alexander Fried, "Leaders Named for Symphony Sponsor Group," *San Francisco Examiner,* July 23, 1935.

CHAPTER 4 SIDEBARS
A HOME FOR MUSIC (*FINALMENTE!*)

Marjory M. Fisher, "Alfred Hertz Heads Concert at Opera House," *San Francisco News,* November 4, 1932.

Alexander Fried, "Opera House Passes in Test of Acoustics," *San Francisco Chronicle,* October 13, 1932.

William Huck, "The San Francisco Symphony: Seventy-Five Years of Music," *Encore: The Archives for the Performing Arts Quarterly* 3, no. 3 (Summer 1986): 11–14, 16: cf. Leonora Wood Armsby, "The San Francisco Symphony: First Decade," *California Historical Society Quarterly* 25, no. 3 (September 1946): 250.

MASF minutes of the Executive Committee, April 1, 1919.

MASF minutes of the Symphony Hall Committee, August 6, 1919.

ALL FOR THE SYMPHONY,
AND THEN SOME

Therese Zoski Dickman, "Ruth Slenczynska Biography," Southern Illinois University at Edwardsville website, http://www.siue.edu/lovejoylibrary/musiclistening/special_collections/title/slenczynska/slenczynska.shtml (2009).

Alexander Fried, "Girl Prodigy Arouses Ire of Molinari," *San Francisco Chronicle,* January 20, 1934.

Los Angeles Herald-Express, January 23, 1934.

"Prodigy Riles Molinari," *Los Angeles Times,* January 20, 1934.

BLOODY THURSDAY: CIVIL WAR
COMES TO SAN FRANCISCO

Clarence H. King, "Report of the Delegates of General Strike Committee," *The Musical News,* November 1934.

"'Bloody Thursday' Leaves S.F. Bitter Taste of Civil War: 2 Dead, Many Hurt," *The Daily News,* July 6, 1934.

"Police Battle Stevedore Mob, Arrest Many," *San Francisco News,* July 3, 1934.

V. SAN FRANCISCO'S
FAVORITE SPORT

82 *"That is very fine, and makes me think very highly":* Leonora Wood Armsby, *We Shall Have Music* (San Francisco: Pisani Printing and Publishing Co., 1960), 40.

82 *"You couldn't be fooled by his baton technique":* Detlev Olshausen, oral history interview with Allan Ulrich, 2005. (San Francisco Symphony Archives.)

82 *"He never cued entrances by jabbing his finger at a musician":* Joseph A. Scafidi, oral history interview with Larry Rothe, February 2003. (San Francisco Symphony Archives.)

83 *A month before Monteux was due in San Francisco:* "Heavy Advance Sale Augers [sic] Auspiciously for Symphony," *San Francisco Chronicle,* November 24, 1935.

83 *When Peter Conley reported on how harmonious negotiations:* Musical Association of San Francisco, Minutes of a Meeting, September 26, 1935. Subsequent references to meeting minutes in this chapter are cited as "MASF minutes."

84 *The music-making, she told her board:* MASF minutes, February 2, 1936.

85 *"With its head held high for the first time in years":* "San Francisco's Comeback," *Time,* April 27, 1936.

85 *In February, Joseph Thompson reminded the board:* MASF minutes, February 2, 1936.

85 *When Armsby announced that the coming season's budget:* MASF minutes, September 18, 1936.

86 *The board grew from sixty to seventy-five members:* MASF minutes, September 13, March 17, 1937.

86 *The season of 1938 was the best-selling year ever:* MASF minutes, January 10, 1940.

86 *Looking ahead to the season of 1938–39, the Finance Committee:* MASF minutes, January 26, 1938.

90 *"We are very eager to hear this orchestra":* Olin Downes to Leonora Wood Armsby, November 29, 1938. Entered into MASF minutes.

91 *Denied that increase because the Association:* MASF minutes, February 2, 1939.

91 *"I loved this city":* Doris Monteux, *It's All in the Music* (New York: Farrar, Straus and Giroux, 1965), 191.

91 *"I congratulate my colleague, M[onsieur] Monteux":* John Canarina, *Pierre Monteux: Maître* (Pompton Plains, NJ: Amadeus Press, 2003), 137.

92 *Looking back in 1973, Boone recalled Howard Skinner:* Philip S. Boone, *The San Francisco Symphony, 1940–1972,* an interview conducted by Harriet Nathan, the Bancroft Library, University of California

at Berkeley, Regional Oral History Office, the Arts and Community Oral History Project (1974), 17.

93   They adopted an official name: Boone, *The San Francisco Symphony*, 19, 31.

93   "That pleased me no end, as I did not want": Monteux, *It's All in the Music*, 191.

94   Armsby was happy to report: Report to Special Women's Committee, August 22, 1940.

94   "We travel a long road when we are identified with organizations": MASF minutes, September 4, 1940 (Annual Meeting); September 2, 1941 (Annual Meeting).

94   Hattie Sloss, a board member who: MASF minutes, September 4, 1941.

94   She spearheaded the development of three: MASF minutes, November 24, 1942.

94   Festivities, set for December 2, 1941, would be held: MASF minutes, October 6, 1941.

95   Joe Scafidi remembers the war years: Scafidi oral history.

98   "When the lights were dimmed for the first bars of music": Armsby, *We Shall Have Music*, 73.

98   "when a piece of music is finished, it no longer": MASF minutes, December 17, 1941.

98   "It may not be many days before it would be impossible": MASF minutes, April 3, 1942.

98   Sentiments such as these would enable Leonora Wood Armsby: MASF minutes, September 28, 1944.

98   On Christmas Eve 1942, Monteux and the orchestra: Canarina, *Pierre Monteux: Maître*, 144.

99   In 1944, in a concert supporting the sixth of eight: *The San Francisco Symphony Orchestra*, brochure, author unidentified (San Francisco: Boone, Sugg & Teves, 1945), 22.

99   From the Office of War Information in New York: MASF minutes, February 18, 1943; October 5, 1943 (Annual Meeting).

99   "We are two old fools who love music": Fifi Monteux [Doris Monteux], *Everyone Is Someone* (New York: Farrar, Straus & Cudahy, 1962), 73.

99   "Last year was an enjoyable season": MASF minutes, October 14, 1946.

100   In January 1946 Pierre Monteux proposed something: MASF minutes, January 23, 1946.

100   "Your Orchestra," Armsby said, "is carrying": MASF minutes, October 16, 1946.

102   Violinist David Schneider, on the other hand, described: David Schneider, *The San Francisco Symphony: Music, Maestros, and Musicians* (Novato, CA: Presidio Press, 1983), 65.

103   Nonetheless, the May 5 issue of Life devoted: "Pretty First Violinist," *Life*, May 5, 1947, 82 ff.

103   "The San Francisco Symphony orchestra . . . gave": James Williamson, "Symphony Well Received," *San Antonio Light*, March 25, 1947.

103   In Houston, a Sunday matinee brought out scarcely: Eleanor Wakefield, "Few Attend San Francisco Symphony's Fine Concert," *Houston Chronicle*, March 31, 1947.

103   Denton audiences cheered, the concert in Wichita Falls: "San Francisco Symphony Received Enthusiastically in TSCW Concert," *Denton Record-Chronicle*, March 26, 1947; "San Francisco Symphony Thrills Record Audience," *Wichita Falls Record-News*, March 27, 1947; E. Clyde Whitlock, "Monteux, at 72, Is Old-Style, but Technique Is Not Pedantic," undated and unidentified press clipping, Fort Worth, TX.

105   "We played in a lot of little towns": Paul Renzi, oral history interview with Larry Rothe, January 2003. (San Francisco Symphony Archives.)

105   "This was Jim Crow time": Olshausen oral history.

105   In Washington, DC, President Truman, who professed: Armsby, *We Shall Have Music*, 96.

105   Then came New York City and Carnegie Hall: Olshausen and Scafidi oral histories; Armsby, *We Shall Have Music*, 93.

105   "Out of the West came Pierre Monteux": Miles Kastendieck, "Recital Given by Monteux," *New York Journal-American*, April 12, 1947.

105   where the Globe's critic reported that the reserved: Cyrus Durgin, "San Francisco Orchestra," *Boston Globe*, April 14, 1947.

105   The train from Quebec, which was due to arrive in Jamestown: William J. Swank, "Pierre Monteux Receives Ovation," undated and unidentified press clipping, Jamestown Ohio.

105   The feared critic Claudia Cassidy: Claudia Cassidy, "On the Aisle," *Chicago Herald-American*, April 26, 1947.

106   during which the National Association of American Composers and Conductors: Hope Stoddard, *Symphony Conductors of the U.S.A.* (New York: Thomas Crowell, 1957), 272.

106   Board vice-president Charles Blyth pointed out: MASF minutes, February 10, 1948.

107   as late as 1951 the Association struggled to meet: MASF minutes, March 12, 1951.

107   The 1950 tombola was a celebration of Pierre Monteux's: Armsby, *We Shall Have Music*, 109-10.

108   "I feel I should have relinquished my post": Monteux, *It's All in the Music*, 89.

108   One more thing Monteux wanted to ensure: MASF minutes, February 9, December 26, 1950.

108   Attendance at Saturday concerts was decreasing: MASF minutes, September 28, October 19, 1950.

108   Throughout all this, Leonora Wood Armsby maintained: MASF minutes, October 19, 1950.

109   "I shall always cherish these past years of work": Pierre Monteux to Leonora Wood Armsby, April 25, 1951.

109   "I don't think Monteux was thinking too much about me": Agnes Albert to Larry Rothe in conversation, 1986.

109   "We'll leave all the fancy words about his greatness": "End of an Era," *Time*, April 21, 1952.

109   "It was impossible to think of the gold curtain": Armsby, *We Shall Have Music*, 119.

CHAPTER 5 SIDEBARS

LEONORA WOOD ARMSBY: LEADER FROM THE LAND OF LINCOLN

Leonora Wood Armsby, *Musicians Talk* (New York: The Dial Press, 1935).

Armsby, *We Shall Have Music* (San Francisco: Pisani Printing and Publishing Co., 1960). "Milestones," *Time*, April 7, 1930.

William Huck, "Leonora Wood Armsby: The Soul of the San Francisco Symphony," San Francisco Symphony *Stagebill*, November 1986, 13-15; 47–49.

Larry Rothe, oral history interview with Joseph A. Scafidi, February 2003. (San Francisco Symphony Archives.)

"Escaped 'Trustees' in New Gun Holdup—Eight Shots Fired at Mrs.George Armsby in Midnight Attempt to Stop Her Auto," *New York Times*, June 24, 1920.

"G. N. Armsby, Banker, to Wed Ex-Show Girl," *New York Times*, March 22, 1930.

"Peaches, Prunes & Bonds," *Time*, March 28, 1932.

RECORDING WITH MONTEUX

Paul Renzi, oral history interview with Larry Rothe, January 2003. (San Francisco Symphony Archives.)

Joseph A, Scafidi, oral history interview with Larry Rothe, February 2003. (San Francisco Symphony Archives.)

David Schneider, *The San Francisco Symphony: Music, Maestros, and Musicians* (Novato: Presidio Press, 1983), 36.

NAOUM BLINDER AND HIS MOST FAMOUS STUDENT

William Huck, "In Praise of Those Who Make the Music," San Francisco Symphony *Stagebill*, December 1986, 48–49.

Michael Steinberg, "Isaac Stern—on Music and Life," in *For the Love of Music* (with Larry Rothe) (New York: Oxford University Press, 2006), 200–01.

AN AUDITION (THE WAY IT WAS)

Detlev Olshausen, oral history interview with Allan Ulrich, 2005. (San Francisco Symphony Archives.)

VI. AN ENIGMA AND A TRAGEDY

116 *Marta Morgan, in the* San Jose Mercury News, *described him:* Marta Morgan, "Interest Generated in Symphony Post," *San Jose Mercury News,* August 25, 1953.

116 *"No guest conductor... has produced":* Marjory M. Fisher, *San Francisco News,* January 29, 1954.

116 *Few board members seemed excited about any:* San Francisco Symphony Association minutes, February 3, 1954. Subsequent references to meeting minutes in this chapter are cited as "SFSA minutes."

117 *Since Steinberg had removed himself from the running:* Joseph A. Scafidi, conversation with Larry Rothe, August 2, 2010.

117 *A motion was put forward to hire Jordá:* SFSA minutes, March 15, 1954.

118 *To read his words about music:* Hope Stoddard, *Symphony Conductors of the U.S.A.* (New York: Thomas Y. Crowell, 1957), 104–11.

118 *That was Joe Scafidi's recollection:* Comments by Paul Renzi, Joseph Scafidi, and Agnes Albert are from oral history interviews with Larry Rothe, conducted between August 2001 and February 2003. Comments from Detlev Olshausen are from an oral history interview with Allan Ulrich, conducted in 2005. (San Francisco Symphony Archives.)

119 *For those eager to know how firmly to apply a bow:* Renzi oral history.

119 *Often, not every work to be performed in concert:* Albert oral history; David Schneider, *The San Francisco Symphony: Music, Maestros, and Musicians* (Novato: Presidio Press, 1983), 101.

121 *In J. D. Zellerbach the Symphony had found:* SFSA minutes, July 12, 1961.

121 *The Foundation's ultimate purpose was to:* SFSA minutes, June 22, 1953.

122 *When the May T. Morrison Trust Estate pledged:* SFSA minutes, September 30, 1954.

122 *The orchestra, he said, was "the cultural heritage":* SFSA minutes, August 29, 1955.

122 *Acting on that belief, she organized what became:* SFSA minutes, May 28, September 11, October 10, 1956.

122 *He proposed approaching the Ford Foundation:* SFSA minutes, December 20, 1956.

122 *Ava Jean Pischel and Phil Boone submitted a reasonable:* SFSA minutes, February 28, 1956.

123 *"Little by little," Philip Boone recalled in 1973:* Philip S. Boone, *The San Francisco Symphony, 1940–*

1972, an interview conducted by Harriet Nathan, the Bancroft Library, University of California/ Berkeley, Regional Oral History Office, the Arts and Community Oral History Project (1974), 54.

123 *In May, Enrique Jordá's contract was once again:* SFSA minutes, May 26, 1958.

124 *Adler maintained that five years ago this could not:* SFSA minutes, October 11, 1960; Scafidi oral history.

124 *On the morning of February 16, 1961, the board's:* SFSA minutes, February 16, 1961.

124 *While praising Skinner for his commitment to the organization:* Boone, *The San Francisco Symphony,* 63.

125 *But Zellerbach did go on record for the first time:* SFSA minutes, March 3, 1961.

125 *Zellerbach was increasingly concerned:* SFSA minutes, June 28, 1961.

125 *Zellerbach, determined to erase the writing:* SFSA minutes, September 6, 1961.

125 *"I don't know what we can do":* Boone, *The San Francisco Symphony,* 60.

130 *Szell forwarded a copy of his letter:* Alexander Fried, "Why Szell Quit S.F.," *San Francisco Examiner,* March 28, 1962.

131 *Poet Kenneth Rexroth, then an Examiner columnist:* Kenneth Rexroth, "The Symphony in Trouble," *San Francisco Examiner,* April 8, 1962.

131 *"I think the man is emotionally immature":* Fried, "Why Szell Quit S.F."

131 *When* Time *reported in 1963 on an altercation:* Jonathan Cott, *Conversations with Glenn Gould* (Chicago: University of Chicago Press, 1984), 131–34; *Time,* "The Glorious Instrument," February 22, 1963.

131 *At the rehearsal the morning after Szell's letter:* Ross Parmenter, "Fur Flying in 'Frisco from Critic's Hint and Conductor's Criticism," *New York Times,* April 8, 1962; Boone, *The San Francisco Symphony,* 59; Albert oral history.

131 *Boone accused Fried of shirking responsibility:* SFSA minutes, April 4, 1962.

131 *Boone himself was the only person who could do:* Boone, *The San Francisco Symphony,* 61.

131 *A Conductor Selection Committee organized to search:* SFSA minutes, June 6 1962.

132 *The merger seemed to have some chance of success:* SFSA minutes, September 17, 1962.

CHAPTER 6 SIDEBARS
GLITTER AND DO GOOD: THE BLACK & WHITE BALL

Blanche Burnett, "Downtown Rocks at Black-White Symphony Hall," *San Francisco News*, April 20, 1956.

Herb Caen, "One Thing after Another," *San Francisco Chronicle*, March 18, 1969.

Caroline Drewes, "The Black & White Ball: S.F.'s Off-and-On Tradition," *San Francisco Examiner*, April 26, 1987.

The Duenna, "A Progressive Symphony in 'Black & White,'" *San Francisco Call-Bulletin*, April 19, 1956.

The Duenna, "All in Black & White!" *San Francisco Call-Bulletin*, April 20, 1956.

Frances Moffat, "'Black & White Ball' Is Sure to Be Repeated," *San Francisco Examiner*, April 29, 1956.

Frances Moffat, "Will It Really Be Black & White?" *San Francisco Chronicle*, January 26, 1969.

Alice Thibeau, "The Thirty-Year Bash," *San Francisco Focus*, April 1987, 8.

BREAKING THE COLOR BARRIER: CHARLES BURRELL JOINS THE SYMPHONY

Charles Burrell, personal communication to Larry Rothe, September 17, 2010.

"Charlie Burrell: A Denver Musical Legend," by Andrew Hudson and Purnell Steen (urbanspectrum.net).

VII. MUSICAL BODYBUILDING

137 *"Ladies and gentlemen, let us begin"*: Philip S. Boone, *The San Francisco Symphony, 1940–1972*, an interview conducted by Harriet Nathan, the Bancroft Library, University of California/Berkeley, Regional Oral History Office, the Arts and Community Oral History Project (1974), 76.

138 *Phil Boone accompanied Krips*: Boone, *The San Francisco Symphony*, 75.

139 *Within a few weeks of Krips's arrival, Alfred Frankenstein*: Alfred Frankenstein, "A Memorable Night of Music," *San Francisco Chronicle*, December 13, 1963.

139 *Krips believed he had been hired*: San Francisco Symphony Association minutes, November 20, 1963. Subsequent references to meeting minutes in this chapter are cited as "SFSA minutes."

140 *Flutist Paul Renzi appreciated his honesty*: Paul Renzi, oral history interview with Larry Rothe, January 2003 (San Francisco Symphony Archives); Josef Krips, *Ohne Liebe kann man keine Musik machen*, ed. Harrietta Krips (Vienna: Bohlau Verlag, 1994), 427.

140 *Krips worked on basics, critic Arthur Bloomfield*: Arthur Bloomfield, "The Sound that Seven Years Built," *San Francisco Sunday Examiner and Chronicle*, May 17, 1970.

141 *ICSOM opened the way for player involvement*: Julie Ayer, *More Than Meets the Ear: How Symphony Musicians Made Labor History* (Minneapolis: Syren Book Company, 2005), 59–63.

141 *Musicians in the fall of 1964 hoped to move*: SFSA minutes, September 10, 1964.

141 *Symphony violinist David Schneider took pride*: David Schneider, *The San Francisco Symphony: Music, Maestros, and Musicians* (Novato: Presidio Press, 1983), 154.

142 *Some believed Krachmalnick's high standards*: Joseph A. Scafidi, oral history interview with Larry Rothe, February 2003. (San Francisco Symphony Archives.)

142 *The orchestra despised him*: Paul Renzi, oral history interview with Larry Rothe, January 2003.

142 *Some players believed it arbitrary*: Schneider, *The San Francisco Symphony*, 147.

142 *The Association's representatives discovered dissatisfaction*: Detlev Olshausen, oral history interview with Allan Ulrich, 2005. (San Francisco Symphony Archives.)

142 *Boone, disturbed by the lack of communication*: SFSA minutes, December 17, 1965.

142 *"our violins began to have a Viennese sound"*: Krips, *Ohne Liebe*, 398.

143 *in April 1966, no less a national icon*: "Orchestras: The Elite Eleven," *Time*, April 8, 1966.

143 *The next month, the New York Times wrote*: Lawrence E. Davies, "A 'Miracle' Is Shrinking Deficit of Orchestra in San Francisco," *New York Times*, May 15, 1966.

143 *Boone and a handpicked committee met*: SFSA minutes, February 18, 1966.

145 *"you have a board which thinks you ought"*: Philip S. Boone, remarks to the orchestra, January 21, 1967.

146 *"a renaissance of compassion, awareness"*: *San Francisco Oracle* 1, no. 5, 1967.

146 *It was important, he stressed*: SFSA minutes, February 7, 1967, cf. December 26, 1967.

146 *Josef Krips had long admired the work*: Krips, *Ohne Liebe*, 406.

146 *He had a strong leader in place*: SFSA minutes, July 31, 1967; Philip Boone to Josef Krips, October 12, 1967.

147 *In a sense, the resolution was good all around*: Scafidi oral history.

148 *What Metcalf was describing, although he did not*: SFSA minutes, January 25, 1968.

148 *leading to a request for 206,000 additional troops*: Hedrick Smith, Neil Sheehan, Max Frankel, and Edwin L. Dale, Jr., "Westmoreland Requests 206,000 More Men, Stirring Debate in Administration," *New York Times*, March 10, 1968.

148 *Krips was dissuaded from scheduling*: Philip S. Boone, speech to the Bohemian Club, December 5, 1974.

148 *In his memoirs, he proudly quotes*: Krips, *Ohne Liebe*, 408, 412.

149 *The board's nominating committee was on the lookout*: SFSA minutes, August 13, September 17, 1968.

149 *Metcalf urged that his colleagues begin considering*: SFSA minutes, February 25, 1969.

149 *Metcalf distributed a series of graphs comparing*: SFSA minutes, April 30, June 17, 1969.

150 *"The tension broke that day"*: Joan Didion, "The White Album," in *The White Album* (New York: Farrar, Straus and Giroux, 1979), 47.

150 *Philip Boone, as Zellerbach had before him*: Details in this paragraph from SFSA minutes, October 27, November 6, 1969.

CHAPTER 7 SIDEBARS
FLIGHT FROM GRASS VALLEY

Philip S. Boone, *The San Francisco Symphony, 1940–1972,* an interview conducted by Harriet Nathan, the Bancroft Library, University of California/Berkeley, Regional Oral History Office, the Arts and Community Oral History Project (1974), 77–78.

Josef Krips, *Ohne Liebe kann man keine Musik machen,* ed. Harrietta Krips (Vienna: Bohlau Verlag, 1994), 388–89.

Joseph A. Scafidi, oral history interview with Larry Rothe, January 2003. (San Francisco Symphony Archives.)

RELAXING WITH JOSEF KRIPS

Joseph A. Scafidi, oral history interview with Larry Rothe, January 2003. (San Francisco Symphony Archives.)

For the Fog Cutter recipe, special thanks to Michelie Marshall, director of corporate operations at Trader Vic's, and Javier Del Campo, Trader Vic's beverage manager.

VIII. A NEW KIND OF GLAMOUR

154   *Even eighteen-year-old girls in miniskirts:* Author's personal recollection.

154   *Krips himself, never content:* Philip S. Boone, *The San Francisco Symphony, 1940–1972,* an interview conducted by Harriet Nathan, the Bancroft Library, University of California/Berkeley, Regional Oral History Office, the Arts and Community Oral History Project (1974), 102.

156   *He was born in 1935 in Manchuria:* Helena Matheopoulos, "Seiji Ozawa: The *Fantastic* Japanese," in *Maestro: Encounters with Conductors of Today* (New York: Harper and Row, 1982), 387–90.

156   *the "Now Generation Conductor," the press called him:* References to the "Now Generation Conductor" are found in *Coast FM & Fine Arts,* April 1970, and *Orchestra News,* March 1972.

157   *Violinist David Schneider recalled his intensity:* David Schneider, *The San Francisco Symphony: Music, Maestros, and Musicians* (Novato: Presidio Press, 1983), 176; Joseph A. Scafidi, oral history interview with Larry Rothe, February 2003.

157   *"You just went with it":* Detlev Olshausen, oral history interview with Allan Ulrich, 2005. (San Francisco Symphony Archives.)

158   *Stuart Canin, recalled a rehearsal of Messiaen's:* Stuart Canin, oral history interview with Allan Ulrich, 2008. (San Francisco Symphony Archives).

158   *Seiji Ozawa's first season:* San Francisco Symphony Association minutes, January 26, February 10, June 2, November 2, 1971. Subsequent references to meeting minutes in this chapter are cited as "SFSA minutes."

159   *Then, at the end of January 1972, Philip Boone:* SFSA minutes, January 26, 1972.

159   *"We started work together only last year":* Schneider, *The San Francisco Symphony,* 182–83.

162   *"If West Coasters are generally hung up":* Schneider, *The San Francisco Symphony,* 188.

163   *"an impossible situation," David Plant pointed out:* SFSA minutes, January 5, 1973.

163   *The concert was transmitted live to San Francisco:* KKHI-FM radio broadcast, May 15, 1973.

165   *One hot evening—this was now early June:* Ava Jean Brumbaum, oral history interview with Larry Rothe, 2005 (San Francisco Symphony Archives); Detlev Olshausen oral history.

166   *"The cellist played like a god":* Schneider, *The San Francisco Symphony,* 197, 200.

166   *When the flight from Moscow touched down:* Ava Jean Brumbaum oral history.

167   *After exchanging a few sentences with him:* Robin Sutherland, in conversation with Larry Rothe, January 6, 2010.

170   *The problem now was that he wanted to dismiss:* SFSA minutes, April 24 1974; Schneider, *The San Francisco Symphony,* 205.

170   *Concerns over musicians' reseating and tenure had been addressed:* "Report to the 1974 ICSOM Convention from the San Francisco Symphony Players' Committee."

170   *Jones, faulted for her intonation and rhythm:* Schneider, *The San Francisco Symphony,* 206–08.

170   *A group called Black Women Organized for Action:* Flyer, "Secrecy & the Symphony: A San Francisco Watergate??"

170   *Supervisor Terry Francois demanded a freeze:* Russ Cone, "Supervisors Eye Publicity Fund," undated article, clipping from unidentified newspaper.

170   *"I had to prove that music could be played":* Elayne Jones, interview with Dustin Harvey in the *Afro-American,* March 24, 1973, quoted in Jessie Carney Smith, *Notable Black Women,* Book II (Farmington Hills, MI: Gale Research, 1996), 351.

171   *While some believed the Jones issue:* "Report to the 1974 ICSOM Convention from the San Francisco Symphony Players' Committee"; notes from a meeting of May 15, 1974: Seiji Ozawa, members of the orchestra, and Joseph Scafidi, William Bernell, Verne Sellin, Carl Modell, Bruce Miller, and Miss Coty; SFSA minutes, March 3, 1977; Smith, *Notable Black Women,* 353.

174   *Years later, Symphony manager Joe Scafidi recalled asking:* Scafidi oral history.

174   *the national press also focused on the struggle:* See, for example, Donal Henahan, "About That Timpanist Who Got Drummed Out," *New York Times,* September 7, 1975.

174   *Metcalf could not promise happy times:* SFSA minutes, October 2, 1974.

174   *"At the end of the concert":* Edmund C. Wilkes, "San Franciscans: Ravel," *The Daily Yomiuri,* June 19, 1975.

174   *"Increasingly," Steinberg wrote, "San Francisco":* Michael Steinberg, "Observing Ozawa," *Boston Globe,* January 5, 1975.

175   *All he wanted to do, he said:* SFSA minutes, March 3, 1976; March 3, 1977.

175   *"the most important cultural step for the City":* SFSA minutes, March 3, 1977.

CHAPTER 8 SIDEBARS
A CHORAL JOURNEY, FROM *STAR TREK* TO STARDOM

Larry Rothe, "Premium Blend: The SFS Chorus at Twenty," San Francisco Symphony *Stagebill*, April-May 1993, 12ff.

Rothe, "A Sense of Flow: Meet Chorus Director Ragnar Bohlin," *Symphony* newsletter (Winter 2008): 2–3.

POPULAR AND SERIOUS, THIS MUSIC IS FOR EVERYONE

Robin Moore, *Fiedler, The Colorful Mr. Pops* (Boston: Little, Brown, 1968).

Carol Green Wilson, *Arthur Fiedler: Music for the Millions* (New York: Evans Publishing Co, 1968).

IX. A WEST COAST SUCCESS STORY

177 *Edo de Waart's goal for the San Francisco Symphony:* Unless otherwise referenced, quotations and paraphrases attributed to Edo de Waart in this chapter are from an interview with Larry Rothe, July 28, 2010.

178 *"I'm a stickler for playing the music":* Michael Muckian, "Edo de Waart, Milwaukee's New Maestro," www.expressmilwaukee.com, September 4, 2009.

178 *Having come up through the ranks of the orchestra:* David Schneider, *The San Francisco Symphony: Music, Maestros, and Musicians,* (Novato: Presidio Press, 1983), 232; David Landis, "Edo de Waart: Reflections and Reminiscences," *Encore, The Archives for the Performing Arts Quarterly* 2, nos. 1–2 (Winter-Spring 1985): 3.

178 *Canin's advice was simple:* Stuart Canin, oral history interview with Allan Ulrich, April 21, 2008. (San Francisco Symphony Archives.)

178 *It began with an overture from Joe Scafidi:* Peter Pastreich, interview with Joe Evans and Larry Rothe, April 30, 2010.

178 *"the top orchestra manager in the country":* San Francisco Symphony Association minutes, March 6, 1978. Subsequent references to Association minutes in this chapter are cited as "SFSA minutes."

178 *Among the reasons Pastreich was hired:* Schneider, *The San Francisco Symphony,* 233.

179 *He ramped up departments devoted to artistic administration:* SFSA minutes, September 27, 1979; January 24, 1980.

180 *Peters also mapped out tactics aimed at meeting:* SFSA minutes, January 24, 1980.

180 *by September 1979 they were 18 percent above:* SFSA minutes, September 27, 1979.

180 *The subscriber renewal rate stood at 87 percent:* Manager John Gidwitz, in San Francisco Symphony Board meeting of September 3, 1980.

181 *By September 1980, the two entities would merge:* San Francisco Symphony minutes, September 3, 1980. Subsequent references to Symphony Board minutes in this chapter are cited as "SFS minutes."

182 *Zellerbach reaffirmed the fact that the arts:* Harold L. Zellerbach: Art, Business and Public Life in San Francisco, an interview conducted by Harriet Nathan, The Bancroft Library, University of California/Berkeley, Regional Oral History Office, The Arts and Community Oral History Project (1978), 88.

182 *The Zellerbach Family Fund commissioned architects:* SFSA minutes, February 10, 1971.

182 *By 1973 it was decided that the Symphony itself:* Joseph A. Scafidi, oral history interview with Larry Rothe, February 2003.

183 *Within six months, only $5 million more:* SFSA minutes, June 15, 1977.

183 *At last, on February 24, 1978, ground was broken:* Jesse Hamlin, "S.F. Arts Center Gets Going," *San Francisco Chronicle,* February 25, 1978.

183 *Violinist Jorja Fleezanis would go on to become:* Jorja Fleezanis, interview with Larry Rothe, May 31, 2010.

185 *"The important thing to remember":* Walter Blum, "Taking the Temperature of the Symphony" (Part Two), *California Living,* April 12, 1981, 33.

185 *Twelve years after Davies opened:* Leonard Kingsley, oral history interview with Larry Rothe, July 2007. (San Francisco Symphony Archives.)

185 *Built by the Symphony, the hall is owned by:* SFS minutes, January 6, 1982.

186 *The Bay Area had long been home to:* Allan Ulrich, *The San Francisco Symphony and Contemporary Music: An Eight-Year Odyssey* (Washington, DC: American Symphony Orchestra League, 1985), 5; John Adams, *Hallelujah Junction* (New York: Farrar, Straus & Giroux, 2008), 108–09.

188 *As composers learned how receptive the Symphony:* Ulrich, *The San Francisco Symphony and Contemporary Music,* 4, 12.

191 *Negotiations were completed for ten discs:* SFS minutes, January 22, 1981; Schneider, *The San Francisco Symphony,* 251.

192 *And Roy Guenther in The Washington Post:* Landis, "Edo de Waart," 6.

192 *Now board president Brayton Wilbur suggested:* SFS minutes, July 14, 1983.

193 *By 1983, conductor Masur, not a man:* SFS minutes, March 17, 1983.

193 *By late fall 1980, $1.05 million had been:* SFS minutes, November 20, 1980.

194 *To help leap that hurdle, donor Pauline Chickering:* SFS minutes, January 20, 1983.

194 *Donations of every kind proved increasingly important:* SFS minutes, June 18, 1981.

194 *Even in the recessionary climate of 1982:* SFS minutes, September 23, 1982; September 22, 1983; September 25, 1984

X. MANDATE FOR CHANGE

194   *In 1984 a campaign was launched to raise:* SFS minutes, January 19, 1984; January 31, 1985.

195   *"Nothing good will come of not spending":* Landis, "Edo de Waart," 4.

195   *The Christian Science Monitor concurred:* Landis, "Edo de Waart," 4.

195   *as Time magazine proclaimed in 1983:* Michael Walsh, "Music: Which U.S. Orchestras are Best?" *Time*, April 25, 1983.

CHAPTER 9 SIDEBARS
POSTER MAN FOR MUSIC

Larry Rothe, "Bukovnik/SFS: Celebrating 25 Years," *Symphony* newsletter (Fall 2006), 7.

THEIR LOVE IS VOLUNTARY

Katherine Buchanan, interview with Larry Rothe, April 29, 2010.

Peter Pastreich, interview with Joseph Evans and Rothe, April 30, 2010.

Genelle Relfe, interview with Rothe, April 27, 2010.

Larry Rothe, "Philanthropists of Time," San Francisco Symphony *Stagebill*, January 1996, 12ff.

196   *"He was out to make a vibrant experience":* Paul Hertelendy, "Dashing Conductor Blomstedt Made the Violins Sing," *San Jose Mercury News*, February 10, 1984.

198   *As a member of the Adventist Church:* Mark Steinbrink, "San Francisco's New Conductor—A Man of Firm Beliefs," *New York Times*, March 9, 1986.

198   *"Through music we can sometimes travel":* Steinbrink, "San Francisco's New Conductor."

198   *"When I talk about playing good music":* Michael Steinberg, "A Conversation with the Maestro," *San Francisco Symphony Stagebill*, May 1985, 13.

199   *"It is true that musicians in an orchestra":* Steinberg, "A Conversation," 48.

199   New York Times *critic John Rockwell advised:* Richard Pontzious, "Arts Man of the Year: Brayton Wilbur Jr. has Orchestrated the Symphony's Recent Phenomenal Success," *California Living*, April 7, 1985, 12.

199   *Shortly before his departure, Edo de Waart:* San Francisco Symphony minutes, September 25, 1984. Subsequent references to Symphony minutes in this chapter are cited as "SFS minutes."

200   *"Conductor and players, in their first season together":* John von Rhein, "San Francisco Symphony Showcases its Potential," *Chicago Tribune*, March 14, 1986.

200   *Alasdair Neale, named assistant conductor in 1989:* Alasdair Neale, in conversation with Larry Rothe, October 1989.

201   *Recognizing this fact, Peggy and Ralph Dorfman:* SFS minutes, January 22, 1986.

201   *One press notice, from their Strasbourg concert:* "Enthusiastic Applause for San Francisco Symphony Youth Orchestra," *Dernieres Novelles D'Alsace*, July 23, 1986.

201   *In all ways, the Symphony seemed to be riding a crest:* SFS minutes, January 22, June 19, September 25, 1986.

202   *Board member Rhoda Goldman, in a campaign appeal:* Rhoda Goldman to Mr. and Mrs. William A. Smith, September 19, 1986; SFS minutes, April 16, 1987.

203   *The consensus was that "greatness":* SFS minutes, September 25, 1986.

204   *In Berlin he remarked that:* Michael Steinberg, "Diary of a European Tour," *San Francisco Symphony Stagebill*, April 1987, 42-43.

205   *But Peter Pastreich was unequivocal:* Pontzious, "Arts Man of the Year," 11, 13.

205   *When a consulting firm suggested:* SFS minutes, April 14, 1988.

211   *In 1988, the city's largest arts organizations:* Jeff J. Jones, "San Francisco's Prominent Arts Organizations: Why Aren't They Equal Opportunity Employers?" report of March 25, 1988.

211   *On June 2, 1988, Nancy Bechtle and Peter Pastreich:* Nancy Bechtle and Peter Pastreich, testimony to San Francisco Board of Supervisors, June 2, 1988.

212   *Within a year of the controversy over minority hiring:* Jeff Jones and Russell T. Cramer, "Institutionalized Discrimination in San Francisco's Arts Funding Patterns," report of April 20, 1989.

212   *Pastreich has called Grants for the Arts:* Peter Pastreich, interview with Joe Evans and Larry Rothe, April 30, 2010.

212   *A Cultural Equity Endowment was formed:* Dan Levy, "'Cultural Equity' Arts Fund OKd by S.F. Panel," *San Francisco Chronicle*, September 25, 1992.

212   *"Every symphony concert has a weird":* Steve Rubenstein, "The Real Challenge is to Stay Awake," *San Francisco Chronicle*, November 4, 1988.

212   *Two weeks later the* Chronicle *published:* Mark Volkert, "The New Music," *San Francisco Chronicle*, November 16, 1988.

212   *In response to such outcries, the* Chronicle's *Robert Commanday:* Robert Commanday, "Carter Requires Open Mind and Keen Ear," *San Francisco Sunday Examiner and Chronicle*, November 20, 1988, This World, 18.

212   *when sales for the two weeks of new-music concerts:* SFS minutes, April 2, 1992.

212   *The high point of touring in these years:* Larry Rothe, "The Symphony's Grand Tour: A Musical Odyssey of Europe," San Francisco Symphony *Stagebill*, November 1990, 54.

215   *"Great orchestras deserve great halls":* The section "Setting the Sound Straight" is based on Larry Rothe, "A Celebration of Sound," San Francisco Symphony *Stagebill*, September/October 1992, 12ff.

216   *Brayton Wilbur reported that his guest:* SFS minutes, September 25, 1986.

219   *"I think the American way of living":* Larry Rothe, "Herbert Blomstedt Talks about the Blomstedt Decade," San Francisco Symphony *Stagebill*, May 1995, 32, 34.

219   *A board summit called Vision 2000:* SFS minutes, June 13, 1995.

XI. ON THE FUTURE'S FRONTIER

219   *The San Francisco Symphony, wrote Michael Steinberg:* Michael Steinberg, "Celebrate the Blomstedt Decade" (brochure), 2.

CHAPTER 10 SIDEBARS
HERITAGE TRANSMISSION: GIVING CHILDREN ADVENTURES IN MUSIC

Richard Reynolds, "Hands on the Music (and off the Remote)," San Francisco Symphony *Playbill*, April 2005, 16ff.

ONE PLAYER TO A PART

Larry Rothe, "One Player to a Part," *Symphony* newsletter (Fall 1994): 2–3.

222   *Years later, he needed only four words:* Michael Tilson Thomas, interview with Larry Rothe, May 28, 2010.

222   *"The mystique that it takes a master":* Robert Commanday, "A Masterful Mahler," *San Francisco Chronicle*, January 4, 1974.

223   *"The key question should always be, what's coming next?"*: Michael Steinberg, "Looking Ahead with Michael Tilson Thomas," San Francisco Symphony *Stagebill*, April 1995, 47, 49.

225   *The goal in the next thirty months:* San Francisco Symphony minutes, January 11, 1996. Subsequent references to Symphony minutes in this chapter will be cited as "SFS minutes."

228   *The budget proposed for the coming 1996–97 season:* SFS minutes, June 25, October 17, 1996.

228   *Sipser had a long history of orchestra negotiations:* Julie Ayer, *More Than Meets the Ear: How Symphony Musicians Made Labor History* (Minneapolis: Syren Book Company, 2005), 72–73.

228   *Bechtle and Kingsley told him that musicians' proposals:* SFS minutes, June 25, 1996.

228   *By late fall, when the orchestra set out:* SFS minutes, September 24, October 17, 1996.

229   *As Nancy Bechtle wrote shortly after concerts:* Nancy Bechtle, "Here to Make Music," San Francisco Symphony *Stagebill*, February 1997, 3.

229   *Although a sizable deficit was anticipated:* Kathryn A. Koch, memorandum to Board of Governors, June 16, 1997.

230   *Less than a year after frustrations had led:* SFS minutes, June 23, 1997.

230   *A six-year contract was ratified:* SFS minutes, March 2, 1999. See also Robert Mnookin, *Bargaining with the Devil* (New York: Simon & Schuster, 2010), 177–208.

231   *"a frappe of classic orchestration":* Jane Ganahl, "Metal, with Strings Attached," *San Francisco Examiner*, April 22, 1999.

231   *Already subscription sales for the 1998–99 season:* SFS minutes, June 23, 1998.

232   *As early as June 1999:* SFS minutes, June 22, September 14, 1999.

233   *Through the generosity of Phyllis Wattis:* SFS minutes, March 27, 2000.

233   *MTT concurred, noting how San Francisco:* Michael Tilson Thomas, interview, May 28, 2010.

234   *A year earlier, it took six weeks to reach:* SFS minutes, September 25, 2000.

235   *Ticket sales for the 2000–01 season:* SFS minutes, September 10, December 3, 2001.

236   *"within the music, we can be confident":* Michael Tilson Thomas, interview, May 28, 2010.

240   *"It happened!" she exclaimed in 2001:* Larry Rothe, "Why We Love Nancy Bechtle," San Francisco Symphony *Playbill*, November 2001, 24.

240   *John Goldman, who succeeded Nancy Bechtle:* Larry Rothe, "The Evolution of John Goldman," San Francisco Symphony *Playbill*, January 2002, 16–17.

240   *On the first day single tickets went on sale:* Michele L. Prisk, memorandum to Board of Governors, September 12, 2002.

243   *"As we move into the future":* SFS minutes, September 22, 2003.

244   *the Plain Dealer wrote of "urgent and penetrating":* Donald Rosenberg, "Beloved Scores Emerge With New Energy," *The Plain Dealer*, March 19, 2004; Rosenberg, "A Night to Remember," *Plain Dealer*, March 22, 2004.

244   *The Boston Globe described a Mahler performance:* Richard Dyer, "Tilson Thomas Blends Mahler, N.H. Memories," *The Boston Globe*, March 24, 2004.

244   *the New York Times, summarizing a pair of Carnegie Hall concerts:* Jeremy Eichler, "Looking Homeward, with Mahler and Adams," *New York Times*, March 27, 2004.

244   *In 2010 New Yorker critic Alex Ross recalled:* Alex Ross, "Battle of the Bands," *The New Yorker*, March 22, 2010, 81.

247   *The spirit of the music-making, MTT said:* Michael Tilson Thomas, interview, May 28, 2010.

247   *Executive Director Brent Assink found such demand:* Brent Assink, "Quest for Excellence," interview with Larry Rothe, *Symphony* newsletter (Spring 2009), 2–3.

249   *But if all that seemed preordained:* Joshua Kosman, "National Medal of Arts for Symphony's Thomas," *San Francisco Chronicle*, February 25, 2010.

CHAPTER 11 SIDEBARS
AN AUDITION (THE WAY IT IS)

Scott Pingel, interview with Larry Rothe, April 28, 2010.

A SHARED UNDERSTANDING, THE CENTER OF THE MUSIC

Michael Tilson Thomas, interview with Larry Rothe, May 28, 2010.

AGNES ALBERT AND THE HEIFETZ VIOLIN

Ava Jean Brumbaum, "Agnes and the Heifetz Violin," unpublished paper, 2005.

Larry Rothe, "A Violin to Bring Us Full Circle," *Symphony* newsletter (Fall 2002): 3.

PHOTO CREDITS

ACADEMY OF MOTION PICTURE ARTS AND SCIENCES
Page 102/image 24

THE BANCROFT LIBRARY, UNIVERSITY OF CALIFORNIA, BERKELEY
Page 14/image 2, page 133/image 16

GARY BUKOVNIK
Page 187

CHARLES BURRELL
Page 135

CALIFORNIA HISTORICAL SOCIETY
Page 16/image 6, page 19/image 9, page 29/image 10, page 65/image 7

RUPERT GARCIA
Page 218/image 31

GERMAN FEDERAL ARCHIVES
Page 54/image 17

LIBRARY OF CONGRESS, PRINTS AND PHOTOGRAPHS DIVISION
Page 31/image 14, page 37/image 20, page 48, page 75/image 12, page 241/image 27

MUSEUM OF PERFORMANCE & DESIGN
Page 16/images 4 and 5, page 44/image 6, page 45, page 51/image 11, page 57, page 80/image 1, page 82/image 2, page 89, page 90/image 9, page 107/images 29 and 30

NORTHWESTERN UNIVERSITY
Page 52/image 12

THE SAN FRANCISCO HISTORY CENTER AT THE SAN FRANCISCO PUBLIC LIBRARY
Page 12/image 1, page 15/image 3, page 19/images 7 and 8, page 21/image 1, page 23/image 5, page 28/image 9, page 35/images 17 and 18, page 37/image 22, page 41/image 3, page 46/image 8, page 47/image 9, page 50/image 10, page 78, page 84/image 5, page 90/image 10, page 95/image 16, page 143/image 11, page 147/image 16, page 210/image 16

SAN FRANCISCO SYMPHONY
Photos by John Blaustein: Page 197/image 1, page 217/image 29
Photo by Russ Fischella: Page 205/image 13
Photo by Russ Langford: Page 225/image 5
Photos by Kristen Loken: Page 207, pages 208-209/image 15, page 213/image 22, page 220/image 1, page 235/image 20, page 237, page 238, page 244/image 32, page 246/image 36, page 251/image 41
Photos by Terrence McCarthy: Page 161, page 205/image 13, page 206/image 14, page 212/image 19, page 216/images 27 and 28, page 224/image 4, page 225/image 6, page 231/image 11, page 232/image 13, page235/image 21, page 236/image 23, page 239/image 25, page 240/image 26, page 246/image 38
Photo by Larry Merkle: Page 199/image 3
Photo by Ray "Scotty" Morris: Page 210/image 17

Photos by Eric Politzer: Page 227, page 245/image 34, page 246/image 35
Photo by Mary Robert: Page 203/image 9
Photo by Steve J. Sherman: Page 211/image 18
Photos by Oliver Theil: Page 230/image 10, page 233/image 17, page 241/image 28
Photos by Chris Wahlberg: Page 227, page 232/image 15, page 245/image 33

SFS MEDIA
Page 236/image 24, page 242/images 29 and 30

THOMASHEFSKY PROJECT/COLLECTION OF MICHAEL TILSON THOMAS
Page 223/image 2

UNIVERSITY OF WASHINGTON LIBRARIES, SPECIAL COLLECTIONS
Page 40/image 2 (UW29412z)

PHYLLIS C. WATTIS FOUNDATION
Page 233/image 16

Unless otherwise noted, all images courtesy of the San Francisco Symphony.

INDEX

Page numbers in italics indicate photographs.

A
Abalos, Señora, 14, 17, 18
Adams, Anne Everingham, *101*
Adams, John, 181, 188, 194, 195, 200, 224, *225*,
    233, 234
Adler, Kurt Herbert, 124, *130*
Aeolian Company, 48
Aherne, Brian, 86, 94
AIM (Adventures in Music), 153, *206–07*, 208,
    211
Albert, Agnes Clark, 70, 109, 118, 131, 142, *145*,
    146, 150, 152, 165, 184, *185*, 192, *238*, 241
Aldrich, Richard, 27
Alexander, Wallace, 67
Alfvén, Hugo, 222, 247
Alioto, Joseph, *147*, 148, 149, 151, 164, *165*, 166
Amador, Ezequiel, 214, *215*
Ameling, Elly, 191
American Festival, 224, *225*, *229*, 248
American Mavericks, 169, *232*, 233, 243, 248
Amirkhanian, Charles, 181, 212
Ampex Corporation, 116
Anderson, Marian, 86, *87*
Andres, Barbara, *227*
Andriessen, Louis, 188
Antheil, George, 233
Anthony, Walter, 34, 43
Antwerp Philharmonic, 118
Argerich, Martha, 234
Armsby, George Newell, 88
Armsby, Leonora Wood, 17, 55, 79, *80*, 81–86,
    88–89, 90, 93, 94, *95*, 98, 99, 103, *107*,
    108–9, 116, 122, 125, 137, 205, 240
Arrau, Claudio, 142
Arroyo, Martina, 187
Ashkenazy, Vladimir, 159
Ashley, Robert, 186
Assink, Brent, 10, *230*, *232*, 247, 249
Atkinson, Helen, 45, 53
Auber, Daniel-François-Esprit, 55
Augusteo Orchestra, 69
Aurora Quartet, 209
Avery Fisher Hall, 208
Ax, Emanuel, 193

B
Bach, Johann Sebastian, 73, 83, 161, 167, 186,
    187, 193, 214, 238, 248
Bach, P.D.Q., 169
Bank of America, 162, 182
Barantschik, Alexander, 10, 218, 234, *236*, *238*,
    241, 246
Barber, Samuel, 175
Barbirolli, John, 94
Barbour, Inez, 27
Barrymore, John, 27
Bass Training Program, 153
Bauer, Harold, *48*, 49, 240
Bay Region Symphony Orchestra, 86
The Beatles, 141
Bechtle, Nancy, 204, *205*, 211, 212, *218*, 228,
    229, 230, 235, 240
Beecham, Thomas, 62, 93, 94

Beethoven, Ludwig van, 25, 34, 40, *41*, 43, 55,
    56, 64, 71, 72, 73, 75, 79, 83, 86, 87, 99,
    100, 101, 109, 113, 140, 146, 151, 156, 160,
    161, 163, 167, 183, 193, 196, 198, 199–200,
    203, 205, 207, *210*, 211, 219, 223, 225, 226,
    234, 243, 248, 249
Beethoven Choir of New York, 39
Bellavente Wind Quintet, 207
Belluschi, Pietro, 182
Bem, Eugenia, 45, 53
Benjamin, George, 212
Bennett, Tony, 129
Bennett, William, *212*, 213
Benny, Jack, 121, *146*
Berg, Alban, 123, 188
Berio, Luciano, 124, 248
Berkeley Community Theater, 230, *231*
Berkshire Music Festival, 27
Berlin Philharmonic, 26, 42, 45, *54*, 62, 130, 213
Berlioz, Hector, 43, 86, 118, 119, 156, 160, 165,
    183, 203, 248
Bernell, William, 141, 156–57
Bernstein, Leonard, 156, 174, 178, 179, 198,
    221–22, 223
Berry, Tiernan Brien, 22, *23*, 24, 25, 29, 32, 244
Black & White Ball, 122, 125, *126–29*, 132, 190,
    192, 194, 235
Black Women Organized for Action, 170
Blinder, Naoum, 79, 86, *104*, 123, 174
Bloch, Ernest, *53*, 83, 186
Blomstedt, Herbert, 10, 194, *195*, 196, *197*, 198,
    199, 200–201, *202–03*, 204, 208, *210–11*,
    212, *213*, *214*, 215, 216, *218*, 219
Bloody Thursday, 77, *78*
Bloomfield, Arthur, 140
Blyth, Charles, 106, 122
BMG, 224
Bogatin, Barbara, *227*
Bohemian Club, 24, 32, 139, 144
Bohlin, Ragnar, *161*
Böhn, Ole, 212
Boone, Charles, 159
Boone, Philip, 92–93, *94*, 95, 107, 117, 121–25,
    131, 132, *136*, 137, *138*, 139, 141–43,
    145–48, *149*, 150, 151, 159, 162, 164, *165*
Borda, Deborah, 190
Boston Pops, 130, 168
Boston Symphony Orchestra, 22, 34, 35, *37*, 43,
    55, 64, 82, 92, 99, 156, 159, 162, 180, 221,
    222
Boulez, Pierre, 174, 181, 186
Bourn, W. B., 32, *33*, 36, 44, 46
Brahms, Johannes, 24, 26, 34, 43, 45, 71, 82, 86,
    99, 100, *101*, 102, 105, 138, 140, 146, 174,
    203, 222, 248
Brailowsky, Alexander, 121
Branca, Glenn, 181, 189
Braunstein, Steven, 241
Brechin, Gray, 18
Breeden, David, *237*
Brico, Antonia, *54*, 58
Bridges, Harry, 78
Brown, Arthur, Jr., 67
Brown, James, 169, 223, 242, *243*
Brown, Ray C. B., 49

Brown, Willie, 193, 225
Browning, John, 222
Bruch, Max, 24, 60
Bruckner, Anton, 140, 149, 200, 203, 213, 222
Brumbaum, Ava Jean Pischel, 10, 94, 122
Bryson, Peabo, 169
Bubb, Charles, 97
Buchanan, Katherine (Kathy), 10, 190
Buffalo Philharmonic, 139, 167, 222
Bukovnik, Gary, *187*
Burnham, Daniel, 18, *19*
Burrell, Charles, 10, 134, *135*
Bush, George H. W., 219
Bush, George W., 234

C

Caen, Herb, 129
Cage, John, 186, 224, 229, 233
California Arts Council, 153
California Pacific Exposition, 81
Cameron, Basil, *60, 62, 63,* 69
Candlestick Park, 210
Canin, Stuart, 10, *156,* 157, 158, 174, 178
Cape Town Symphony, 117
Carnegie Hall, 103, 105, 188, *189,* 191, 198, 199, 200, 203, 208, 210, 211, 212, 219, 221, 233, 234, 244
Carter, Elliott, 170, *171,* 188, 208, 210, *211,* 212
Carter, Jimmy, 194
Caruso, Enrico, 13, 18, *19,* 135
Casadesus, Henri, 110
Caselli Quartet, 209
Cash, Nicole, *246*
Casserly, Cecilia, 36, 37, 44, *46,* 50, 55, 58, 89
Casserly, John, 36, 46
Cassidy, Claudia, 106
Castillo, Javier, 152
Chadwick, George, 26
Chaliapin, Feodor, 62
chamber music, 26, 42, 45, 104, 203, 209, 218, 219, 237, 238
Charles, Ray, 169
Charleston Symphony, 226
Charter Amendment 3, 77, 78, 81, 85, 168
Chávez, Carlos, 207
Chen, Jiebing, 234, *235*
Chicago Symphony, 42, 106, 154, 156, 160, 204
Chickering, Pauline, 194
Chopin, Frédéric François, 30, 73
Cincinnati Symphony, 52
Civic Auditorium, *53,* 54, 55, 59, 67, 75, *78,* 79, 87, 94, 99, 107, 127, 169
Civic Center, 32, 67, 129, 185, 192
Claudio, Mary, 170
Cleveland Orchestra, 36, 130, 244
Cliburn, Van, 123, 130
Clinton, Bill, 219
Clooney, Rosemary, 169
Coghlan, Mabel, 94
Colors of Christmas holiday concerts, 169
Columbia Theatre, 181
Commanday, Robert, 212, 222
Community Arts and Education, 182
Community Open House, 219, 224
Concertgebouw Orchestra, 82, 142, 178

Concerts for Kids, 152, *208–9,* 211
Conley, Peter, 69, 81, 83
Copland, Aaron, 27, 147, 149, 175, 181, 222, *223,* 224, 233, 239, 243
Cortot, Alfred, 58, 72
Cort Theatre, 25, *28,* 29, *31,* 43, 181
Cowell, Henry, 224, 233
Cremona Fund, 240
CRI (Composers Recordings), 121
Crocker, William H., 32, 44, 50, 67
Crown, John, 222
Crumb, George, 174
Cultural Affairs Task Force, 212
Curran Theater, 181
Cushing, Charles, 121, 201

D

Dahl, Ingolf, 222
Damrosch, Walter, 17
Danish Radio Symphony, 198
David, Ferdinand, 238
"David" Guarnerius violin, *238, 241*
Davies, Louise M., 180, *181,* 183, *184, 185,* 190
Davies, Ralph K., 183
Davies Symphony Hall, 19, 67, 129, 152, 169, 177, 181, 182, *183,* 184, *185,* 186–88, *189,* 190–92, 193–95, 207, 210, 212, 215, *216–18,* 219, 224, 228, 229, *230,* 236, 238, 240, 241, 249
Debussy, Claude, 27, 82, 83, 191
Decca, 204, 216
Deck the Hall, 190
Deering, Frank, 24
de Leeuw, Reinbert, 181, 188
Del Tredici, David, 183
DeMars, Vincent, 182
DeMille, Cecil B., 89
Denver Symphony, 134, 135
de Pachmann, Vladimir, 30
de Sabata, Victor, 116
Detroit Symphony, 134
Deutsche Grammophon, 158, 159, 167
de Waart, Edo, 10, 170, 175, *176,* 177, *178–79,* 180, *181,* 183, 184, *185,* 186, 188, *189,* 191, *192,* 194, *195,* 196, 198–202
Dickinson, Emily, 241
d'Indy, Vincent, 96
Dixon, Dean, 159
Dobbs, Hugh Barrett, 68
Dobrowen, Issay, 60, *61,* 62, *63,* 64, 68, 69, *70,* 71, 74, 76, 77, 104, 123, 174, 196, 244
Dolby, Ray, 216
Dolores Park, 169
Donatello Ensemble, 209
Dorfman, Herman, 170
Dorfman, Peggy, 159, 201
Dorfman, Ralph, 159, 201
Dorfman Commissioning Fund, 201
Downes, Olin, 81, 90
Dresden Staatskapelle, 198
Dresher, Paul, 181
Duke, George, 135
Duncan, Isadora, 45
Dunham, Katherine, 98
Duo-Art reproducing piano, 48–49, 240

DuParc, Henri, 191
Dutilleux, Henri, 212
Dvořák, Antonín, 119, 165, 167, 208
Dyer, Joseph, Jr., 79
Dylan, Bob, 141

E

Easton, Sheena, 169
Edwards, Ninian, 88
Edwards, William, 203
Ehlers, Alice, 222
Ehrlich, Philip, 142
Elgar, Edward, 62, 207
Elizabeth II (Queen of England), 193
Elkus, Albert, 110
Ellington, Duke, 68, 169, 233
Ellis, Nancy, *111*
Elman, Mischa, 17, 58, 84
Enesco, Georges, 58
Epstein, Larry, 237
Eschenbach, Christoph, 159
Escovedo, Pete, 169

F

Faber, Mary, 131
Fairmont Hotel, 109, 127, 128
Falla, Manuel de, 119, 121, 133
Faulkner, William G., 98
Feinstein, Dianne, 188, *189*
Feldman, Morton, 186, 232, 233
Ferry Building, 106, 125, 169
festivals, 188, 192, 193, 213, 233, 234, 248, 249
Fiedler, Arthur, 107, 108, 130, *131,* 150, *168–69*
Fine, Vivian, 188
Firestone, Nathan, 110
Fischer, Jonathan, 237
Fisher, Marjory M., 84, 116
Fitzgerald, Ella, 169, 223
Fleezanis, Jorja, 10, 183
Fleisher, Leon, 86
Fleishhacker, Mortimer, 125
Fleming, Renée, 241
Ford Foundation, 122, 143, 149, 159
Franck, César Auguste, 71, 96, 97, 109
Francois, Terry, 170
Frankenstein, Alfred, 93, *96,* 116, 122, 123, 124, 130, 131, 132, *133,* 139
Free, Arthur M., 58
Freifeld, Bruce, 214, *215*
Freimuth, Ben, 237
Fricsay, Ferenc, 116, 117
Fried, Alexander, 59, 64, 67, 70–71, 73, 79, 116, 122, 123, 124, 130, 131, *132,* 133
Fritz Scheel's Orchestra, *16–17*
Furtseva, Ekaterina, 162
Furtwängler, Wilhelm, 244

G

Gabrieli, Giovanni, 161, 163
Gabrilowitsch, Ossip, 55
Galas, Diamanda, 181
Galway, James, *214*
Garcia, Jerry, 129
Garland, Judy, 103
Gelfand, Daniel, 207

George, Vance, 160, *214*
Germania Concert Society, 17
Gershwin, George, 86, 93, 169, 175
Gesin, Leonid, *111*
Getty, Gordon, 181, 202, 218
Getty Challenge, 202
Giacobassi, Julie, 214, *215*
Ginsberg, Allen, 121, 128
Gioia, Dana, 207
Giosi, Orlando, *101*
Glass, Philip, 181
Golden Gate Bridge, *84,* 85
Golden Gate International Exposition, *90,* 91, 93
Golden Gate Park, 40, *41,* 146, *157, 210,* 211
Golden Season, 125
Goldman, John, 10, 235, *240,* 241
Goldman, Rhoda, 202, 240
Goldman, Richard, 240
Gold Rush, 14, 144, 250
Gould, Glenn, 131
Grainger, Percy, 62
Grand Opera House, 18, 19
Grants for the Arts (GFTA), 211–12
Grateful Dead, 129, 224, 225, *228,* 229
Greenbaum, Will, 28, *29,* 152
Grofé, Ferde, *122,* 123
Guaraldi, Mafalda, *101*
Guenther, Roy, 192
Guillou, Jean, 192
Guttman, Joseph, 40

H
Haas, Elise Stern, 240
Haas, Jr. Fund, 243
Hadley, Henry, 24, *25, 26,* 27, 28, 29, 30, *31,* 32, 33, 34, 35, *36,* 37, 40, 43, 44, 46, 55, 64, 101, 102, 106, 168, 186, 196, 198, 244
Haitink, Bernard, 178
Halberstam, David, 121
Hampson, Thomas, *246*
Hampton, Lionel, 134
Handel, George Frideric, 14, 110, 161
Hanson, Howard, 51, *52,* 53, 58
Harbison, John, *212,* 213
Harding, Warren G., 53
Harris, Roy, 51–52, 118
Harrison, George, 141
Harrison, Lou, 181, 224, *225,* 233
Hart, Mickey, 224, *228,* 229
Haug, Julius, 57, *96,* 110
Hayden, J. Emmet, 54, 55, 68, 77, 79, 182
Haydn, Franz Joseph, 28, 149, 233
Healy, Frank, 29, 34, *35,* 43, 44, 46
Heavey, Jack, *100,* 101, 102
Heifetz, Jascha, 62, 64, 84, 174, 223, 238, *241*
Heller, Emanuel Siegfried, *22,* 23, 24, 67, 205, 244
Heller, Walter, 117
Henderson, Skitch, 169
Henze, Hans Werner, 118, 124
Herbert, David, 237
Herold, Rudolf, 17
Hertelendy, Paul, 196

Hertz, Alfred, 11, 13–14, 15, 18, *36,* 37, *38,* 39–42, *43,* 44–50, *51,* 52–60, 62, 67, 69, 71, 74, 76, 79, 86, 89, *92,* 103, 196, 224, 240, 249
Herz, Henri, 17
Hess, Myra, 84
Hewlett, William, 218
Hewlett Foundation, 230
Higginson, Henry Lee, 22, 34
Hillis, Margaret, 160
Hilton Hotel, 129
Hindemith, Paul, 83, 118, 124, 204
Hines, Earl "Fatha," 135
Hinrichs, Gustav, 17
Hinton, Milt, 134
Hofmann, Josef, 72
Holiday, Billie, 134
Holliger, Heinz, 208, 210, *211*
Hollywood Bowl, 41, 55, 89
Homeier, Louis, 17
Hope, Bob, 129
Horowitz, Vladimir, 58, 64, 174
Houser, Frank, 123, *125*
Hovhaness, Alan, 175
Howard Skinner Student Forum, 92–94, 142, *143,* 148, *175,* 190, 206
Hudson Hills Press, 187
Huntsville Symphony Orchestra, 73

I
IBM, 92
ICSOM (International Conference of Symphony and Opera Musicians), 141, 228
Imbrie, Andrew, 118, 186
Imperial Vienna Prater Orchestra, 17
Inouye, Mark, 209
Instrument Training and Support, 153
Iturbi, José, 84
Ives, Charles, 88, 161, 165, 175, 224, 232, 233, 242

J
Joachim, Joseph, 24, 60
Johansen, Al, 216
Johnson, Lyndon, 138, 149
Johnson, Van, 103
Jones, Elayne, 170, *171,* 174
Jones, Jim, 186
Joplin, Janis, 146
Jordá, Enrique, 91, 114, *115,* 116–19, *120,* 121, *122,* 123–25, 128, 130, *131,* 132, 140, 141, 146, 186, 196, 203, *214*
Jordan, Merrill, *101*
Judson, Arthur, 89
Justin Herman Plaza, 169

K
Kabuki Theatre, 189
Karp, Philip, 134
Kastendieck, Miles, 105
Kazama, Naomi, 237
Keeping Score, 232, 241, 242, 243, 244
Keilholz, Heinrich, 137
Keillor, Garrison, 169
Kendrick, Charles, 67
Kennedy, Charles "Pop," 142, *143*

Kennedy, John F., 124, 137–38
Kennedy, Robert, 149
Kennedy Center, 189
Kern, Jerome, 107
Kerouac, Jack, 100, 121
Khachaturian, Aram, 154
Kirkegaard, Lawrence, 216
Kim, John S., 213
Kim, Kum Mo, *213*
King, Martin Luther, Jr., 141, 148
Kingsley, Leonard, 216, 228, 230
Kirchner, Leon, 118, 124
Klatzkin, Benjamin, 97
Klemperer, Otto, 46
Kobler, Raymond, 181, *184,* 234
Kohloff, Roland, 174
Kostelanetz, André, 92, 122
Krachmalnick, Jacob, *140,* 141–42
Krehbiel, David, 214, *215*
Kresge Foundation, 218
Krips, Josef, 42, 131, *136,* 137, *138–39,* 140–41, *142–44,* 145, 146, 147, 148, *149,* 150, *151,* 154, 157, 162, *164,* 165, 178, 186, 196, 198, 244
Krips, Mitzi, 139, 144
Kubelík, Rafael, 106

L
Laderman, Ezra, 198
Lalo, Édouard, 30
lang, k. d., 129
Lang Lang, 209
Lansburgh, G. Albert, 67
Lapham, Roger, 106
Larson, Dave, 216
Lawrence, Mark, 214, *215*
Legassey, Oscar, 134
Lehmann, Lotte, 85
Leinsdorf, Erich, 116, 117
Leipzig Gewandhaus Orchestra, 62
Lennon, John, 141
Leon, Suzanne, 244
Leplin, Emanuel, 89
Leschetizky, Theodor, 222
Leschke, Hans, 54
Lesh, Phil, 224, *225, 228,* 229
Levison, J. B., 17, 60, 62, *63,* 64, 68, 69, 71, 74
Lhevinne, Josef, 27, 75
Lieberson, Peter, 212
Liebling, Joseph, 160
Ligeti, György, 159, 161, 174
Lincoln, Abraham, 88
Lincoln Center, 193, 212
Lindbergh, Charles, 58, 68
Ling, Jahja, *191,* 193, 201
Liszt, Franz, 28, 40, 49, 55, 73, 86
Liu, Yun Jie, *224,* 225
Loghner, Jack, 124
Loma Prieta earthquake (1989), *210,* 211
London Philharmonic, 62
London Proms, 232, *233,* 234
London Symphony Orchestra, 62, 82, 139, 204, 223, 234
Los Angeles Philharmonic, 56, 59, 81, 223
Losch, Tilly, 86

Los Lobos, 169
Lotta's Fountain, *12,* 13
Love, Eddie, 78
Lucchesi, Peggy Cunningham, *146*
Luce, Clare Boothe, 122
Lucerne Festival, 233, 249
Ludwig, Leopold, 123, 124
Lueth, Bill, 164, *165*
Lutosławski, Witold, 124, 201

M
Ma, Yo-Yo, 193, 209, 238
Mackey, Steven, 233
Maderna, Bruno, 181
Madrid National Orchestra, 117
Madrid Symphony Orchestra, 117
Magor, Louis, *160*
Mahler, Gustav, 41, 55, 101, 140, 161, 167, 188,
    191, 195, 219, 222, 234, 235, 236, 240, 243,
    244, 246, 247, 248
Mailliard, Charlotte, 129, 190, *192*
Mandyczewski, Eusebius, 138
Markevitch, Igor, 198
Mark Hopkins, 127
Marshall, Ingram, 181
Mason, Redfern, 36, 40, 43, 46, 47
Masur, Kurt, 193, 195, 214, *215*
Mausner, Seth, 209
Maybeck, Bernard, 67, 68
McCartney, Paul, 141
McChesney, Beverly, 207
McGaw, Laurie, 213
McKee, John D., *52,* 53, 76–77
McKenzie, Scott, 146
McKibbon, Al, 134
McKinsey & Co., 179
Mechanics Institute Pavilion, 17
Meet the Composer, 188
Mehta, Zubin, 188, *189*
Mellon Foundation, 194
Mendelssohn, Felix, 55, 86, 121, 183, 238
Menuhin, Yehudi, *42,* 46, 53–54, 75, *76,* 93,
    104, 159, 184, *185,* 206, 215, 238
Mercantile Trust Company, 20, *23,* 244
Merola, Gaetano, 67, 74, 92
Messiaen, Olivier, 158
Metallica, 230, *231*
Metcalf, Lawrence, 94, *148,* 149, 174, 175, 178,
    184, *185*
Metropolitan Opera, 13, 18, 36, 41, 187
Metzger, Alfred, 26–27, 41, 45, 55
Milhaud, Darius, *92,* 93, 118, 124, 152, 186
Milk, Harvey, 186
Miller, Leta E., 10, *44*
Miller, Robert Watt, 68
Mills College, 186
Milnes, David, 201
Milstein, Nathan, 58
Minshull, Ray, 216
Mnookin, Robert, 230
Molinari, Bernardino, 69, *70,* 71, 72, 73, 74
Monk, Meredith, 181, 188
Monteagle, Kenneth, 122, 123, *124,* 125
Monterey Pop Festival, 146
Monteux, Doris, 93, *105*

Monteux, Pierre, *80,* 81, *82, 83,* 84, *85,* 86, *87,*
    88, 89, *90, 91, 92,* 93, *94,* 95, *96,* 97, *98,*
    99, 100, 102, *103,* 104, *105,* 106–7, *108,*
    109, 110, *112–13,* 114, 116, 118, 122, 134,
    135, 137, 142, 151, 163, 174, 175, 186, 189,
    196, 200, 224, 244
Morgan, Marta, 116
Morgan, Virginia, *100,* 101
Morrison Trust, 122
Mortensen, Modesta, 45, 53
Moscone, George, 183, 186
Mozart, Leopold, 184
Mozart, Wolfgang Amadeus, 25, 130, 138, 139,
    140, 146, 162, 174, 186, 193, 207, 222, 233,
    248
The MTT Files, 242, 243
Muck, Karl, 34
Muir, John, 59
Munch, Charles, 156
Municipal Chorus, *53,* 54–55, 87
Municipal Concerts, 53, 54, 62, 64, 68, 84, 86,
    168
Municipal Symphony Orchestra, *78, 79*
Musical Association of San Francisco, 23, *24,* 25,
    27, 29, 30, 32, 33, 34, 36, 40–44, 46–48,
    50, 52, 53, 54, 60, 63, 64, 67, 71, 72, 74–77,
    78, 79, 81, 82, 83, 84, 85, 87, 88, 89, 90, 91,
    93, 94, 98, 100, 101, 106, 107, 108, 116, 121,
    122, 131, 142, 143, 145, 146, 147, 149
Musica Viva, 146–47
Music for Families, 153
Mussorgsky, Modest Petrovich, 154
Musto, Guido, 116

N
Nakagawa, Ryohei, 170, 171
National Association of American Composers
    and Conductors, 27, 106
National Endowment for the Arts, 141, 170, 179,
    194, 202, 206, 207
National Philharmonic (Seoul), 213
Neale, Alasdair, 200
Neighborhood Arts Program, 182
Netherlands Opera, 195
Netherlands Wind Ensemble, 178, 191
New and Unusual Music series, 181, 188–89
Newell, R. C., 76
Newman, Ellen Magnin, 10, 212
New World Symphony, 223, 237
New York Philharmonic, 27, 49, 55, 62, 64, 68,
    71, 74, 99, 104, 156, 174, 178, 179, 188, 222,
    228, 232
New York Symphony, 48
New York World's Fair, 90
Nielsen, Carl, 198, 200, 204, 215
Nimitz, Chester, 128
Nixon, Richard, 162, 174
Nonesuch, 201

O
Oakland East Bay Symphony, 239
Oakland Symphony, 132, 150, 160, 239
Obama, Barack, 249
Oesterreicher, Walter, 75
Oglesby, Richard, 88

Ohlsson, Garrick, 159
Oliver, Sarn, 209, 244
Oliveros, Pauline, 186
Olshausen, Detlev, 10, 105, 110, *111,* 118, 119,
    157
Opéra Comique, 90
Orchestra of Santa Cecilia, 69
Orchestre Symphonique de Paris, 82
Orff, Carl, 161, 215
Ormay, Gyula, 45
Osaka International Festival, 148
Oslo Philharmonic, 198
Ozawa, Seiji, 132, *145,* 146, 149, *154–55,* 156,
    157, 158, 159, 160, 162–63, *164,* 165, *166,
    167,* 170, *171, 172–73,* 174, *175,* 177, 178,
    186, 196, 249

P
Pacific Coast Musical Review, 26
Paderewski, Ignace Jan, 17
Page, Patti, 169
Palace Hotel, *12,* 13, 18, 32, 53
Palace of the Legion of Honor, 238
Palestine, Charlemagne, 181
Panama-Pacific International Exposition, 20, 32,
    34, *37,* 40, 43, 162
Parker, Horatio, 41
Pasmore, Dorothy, *45,* 53
Pasmore, Harriet, 45
Pasmore, Henry Bickford, 45
Pasmore, Mary, *45,* 53
Pasmore, Suzanne, *45*
Pasmore Trio, *45*
Pastreich, Peter, 10, 178–79, *180,* 181, 184, *185,*
    205, 211, 212, 213, 225, *230,* 231, 232
Patti, Adelina, 17
Paulson, Stephen, 10, 215, 218
Pearl Harbor, 95, 99
Peck, Gregory, 214, *215*
Perahia, Murray, 238
Perle, George, 186, 212, *213*
Perlet, Herman, *44*
Persinger, Louis, *42,* 46, 53–54
Persinger, Rolf, 42, 170
Peters, Bernadette, 169
Peters, Tom, 179, 180
Petri, Egon, 72
Philadelphia Chamber Orchestra, 142
Philadelphia Orchestra, 16, 17, 48, 55, 68, 71
Philharmonic Society of San Mateo County,
    55, 89
Philharmonie (Berlin), 213
Philips Records, 167, 188, 191, *192*
Phonogram, 191
pianos, reproducing, *See* Duo-Art reproducing
    Piano
Piastro, Mishel, *62,* 104
Piatigorsky, Gregor, 223
Picker, Tobias, 188
Pingel, Scott, 226, *227,* 237
Piston, Walter, 83
Pittsburgh Symphony Orchestra, 30, 226
Plant, David, 162, *163, 164, 165,* 174
Platt, Peter, 203
Polk, Willis, 19

Portland Symphony, 56
Portolá, Gaspar de, 20
Portolá Festival, 20, *21*
Preparedness Day, *47*
Presley, Elvis, 121, 128, 141
Previn, André, 195, 209
Price, Leontyne, 201
Price, Margaret, 191
Price, Thomas, 132
Pringsheim, Hans, 148
Procházka, Harrietta, 139, 144
Prokofiev, Sergei, 59, 203, 224
Puccini, Giacomo, 67

R

Rachmaninoff, Sergei, 27, 85, 121
Ravel, Maurice, 27, 58, 96, 174, 191
Ravinia Festival, 156
RCA, 54, 55, 96–97, 100, 121, 224–25, 235
Reagan, Nancy, *146*
Reagan, Patti, *146*
Reagan, Ronald, *146*, 194, 211
Redding, Joseph D., 32
Redding, Otis, 146
Reeves, Dianne, 135
Reger, Max, 27, 33
Reich, Steve, 186, 233
Reinberg, Donald, 170
Relfe, Genelle, 10, 190
Renzi, Paul, 10, 102, 105, 106, 118, 140, 157
Repeat Performance, 158, *159*, 162, 190
Respighi, Ottorino, 58, 83, 191
Rexroth, Kenneth, 130
Riley, Terry, 141, 186
Rimsky-Korsakov, Nikolai, 96
Roberts, Kathryn, 52
Rockwell, John, 199
Roden, Wayne, *111*
Rodrigo, Joaquín, 118
Rodzinski, Artur, 89
Rogers, Emery, *232*
Roncovieri, Alfred, 17
Roosevelt, Franklin, 60, 85, 99
Rosenbecker, Adolph, 27, *40*, 42
Ross, Alex, 244
Rossi, Angelo, 68, 78, 98
Rostropovich, Mstislav, 165, *166*, 167, 214, *215*
Rothschild, John, 22, *23*, 24, 25, 29, 32, 44
Rotterdam Philharmonic, 178, 191
Royce, Josiah, 18, 144
Rubenstein, Steve, 212
Rubinstein, Artur, 58, 121
Rudhyar, Dane, 181
Ruffatti organ, 192, *193*, 194, 211
Ruggles, Carl, 175
Rush, Loren, 152, 175
Russell, Henry, 15
Russo, William, 159, 167, 175

S

Saarinen, Eero, 182
Sabatini, William, *101*, 103
St. Francis Hotel, 127, 128, *129*
St. Louis Symphony, 178

Saint-Saëns, Camille, 48, 49, 82, 84, *85*, 86, 183, 192, 215, 240
Saito, Hideo, 156
Salkind, Milton, 188
Sample, James, 102
San Francisco
    character of, 250
    cityscapes, *14–15*, *19*
    earthquake (1906), 17–18, *19*, 20
    influenza epidemic (1918), *50*, 51
    Loma Prieta earthquake (1989), *210*, 211
    population of, 14, 20, 98, 121
San Francisco Arts Commission, 53, 79, 168, 169, 182
San Francisco Ballet, 98, 124, 182
San Francisco City Hall, *19*, *66*, 67, 98, 99, 129, 178, *179*, 186, 190, 228
San Francisco Conservatory of Flowers, *157*
San Francisco Fine Arts Museums, 238, 241
San Francisco Galleria, 189
San Francisco Mime Troupe, 183
San Francisco Municipal Chorus, 167
San Francisco Musical Institute, 17
San Francisco–Oakland Bay Bridge, 78, 85, 210
San Francisco Opera Association, 67
San Francisco Opera Orchestra, 42, 53, 67, 71, 124, 149, 151, 171, 181, 186
San Francisco People's Philharmonic, 44, 46, 50
San Francisco Philharmonic Society, *16*, 17
San Francisco Public Library, 182, 193
San Francisco Symphony
    auditioning for, 110, 226
    broadcasts of, 55, 56, *57*, 94, 99, 163–64, 183, 243
    education and, *152–53*, 206–7, 211, 232–33
    founding of, 18, 20, 22, 23, 24–25
    greatness and, 203, 205, 244
    on the Internet, 231–32, 243–44
    minorities in, 134–35, 170–71, 211
    in performance, *65*, *106*, *112–13*, *142*, *183*, *210*, *233*
    portraits of, *31*, *51*, *70*, *91*, *120*, *138*, *172–73*, *179*, *217*, *245*
    predecessors of, 17, 18
    recordings of, *54*, 55, *96–97*, 114, 116, 121, *133*, *158*, 159, 161, *167*, 188, *189*, 191, 192, *193*, *194*, 201, *204*, 215, 224–25, 233, 235, *236*, 242, 243
    in rehearsal, *202*, 203
    rivals of, 44, 46
    seasonal posters for, *187*
    on tour, 100, *101*, 102–3, *105*, 106, 148, 162, 163, *164–66*, *173*, 174, 188, *189*, 191, 192, 200, 203–4, 208, 210, *211*, 212–13, 215, 228–29, 233–34, 247
    women in, 45, 53, 211
San Francisco Symphony Association, 108, 116, 150, 174, 181
San Francisco Symphony Chorus, *160–61*, 167, 234
San Francisco Symphony Foundation, 117, 121, 123, 132, 162, 181, 190
San Francisco Symphony Youth Orchestra, 153, *191*, 192–93, 200, 201, 211, 218, 224, 234, 238, *246*

San Jose Symphony, 239
Santos, John, 207
Sargeant, Winthrop, 46–47
Sayre, Robert, 170
Scafidi, Joseph, 10, 82, 90, 95, 102, 118, 124, *140*, 141, 142, 144, *145*, 146, 150, 157, 174, 175, 178, *230*, 232,
Schauspielhaus, 213
Scheel, Fritz, *16*, 17
Schickele, Peter, 169
Schnabel, Artur, 72, *92*, 99
Schneider, David, 86, 102, 141–42, *152*, 157, 166
Schoenberg, Arnold, 124, 167, 200, 226
Schubert, Franz, 196
Schuller, Gunther, 159
Schuman, William, 224
Seal, 129
Season of Decision, 114, 116, 118
Season of Discovery, 114, 116
Seattle Symphony, 24, 26, 27, 56
Selfridge, Grant, 40
Sellars, Peter, 234
Sellin, Sandy, 160, 161
Sellin, Verne, 86, *153*, 160, 222, 247
September 11th attacks, 235–36, 239
Serkin, Peter, 174
Serkin, Rudolf, 121, 123, 146, 159, 201
Sessions, Roger, 83, 93, 141–42, 186, 188, 200
SFSKids.com, 153, *241*
SFS Media, 235, 240, 243, 246
Shaham, Gil, 215
Shakespeare, William, 86, 181
Sheinfeld, David, 159
Shelton, Peter, 10, 216
Sheng, Bright, 212
Sheraton-Palace, 127, 128
Sherman-Clay, 93
Shostakovich, Dmitri, 124
Shostakovich Quartet, 209
Sibelius, Jean, 62, 93, 200, 215
Siegel-Schwall Blues Band, 159
Simonsen, Frances, 45
Sinai, Joe, *101*
Sipser, Philip, 228
Skidmore, Owings, and Merrill, 182, 217
Skinner, Howard, 90, *91*, 93, 94, 103, *105*, 124, 141, 232
Slenczynski/Slenczynska, Ruth, *72*, 73, 75, *154*
Sloss, Hattie, 94
Smiley, Dan, 244
Smiley, David, 244
Smiley, Mariko, 244, *245*
Smith, Pamela, *246*
Snyder, Gary, 121
Sokoloff, Nikolai, 36, *37*, 44, 46, 55
Solti, Georg, 116, 117, *118*, 213
Solzhenitsyn, Aleksandr, 165
Sotomayor, Antonio, 107, 129
Sotoyama, Fuzo, 148
Spain, Jerry, 151
Sponsors of the Performing Arts Center, 182
Sproule, William, 44, 46
The Standard Hour (The Standard Symphony Hour), 55, 56, *57*, 67, 97, 114, 116, 122

Standard Oil Corporation of California, 55, 56–57, 100, 162
Stanford Chorus, 160, 167
Stanford Quartet, 209
Starr, Kevin, 18
Starr, Ringo, 141
Stein, Fritz, 24
Steinberg, Michael, 174, *180,* 203, 212, 219, 223
Steinberg, William, 116, 117, 221–22
Stern, Isaac, 86, *104,* 159, 193, *203,* 214, *215*
Stern, Rosalie Meyer, 68–69
Stern Grove, *65,* 68–69, 169, 215
Stewart, Samuel, 182, 184, *185,* 205
Stokowski, Leopold, 91, 94, 116
Strauss, Richard, 24, 27, 36, 51, 52, 56, 83, 97, 98, 100, 101, 102, 123, 128, 130, 138, 139, 140, 144, 187, 200, 248
Stravinsky, Igor, 27, 82, 84, *90,* 91, 93, 94, 123, 149, 157, 167, 188, 222, 233, 234, 243, 246, 248
Subotnick, Morton, 186
Summer & the Symphony series, 169
Summer in the City series, 169
Swedish Radio Symphony, 198
Swords, W. V., 48, 49
Symphony Perpetuation Day, 79
Symphony Silicon Valley, 239
Symphony Store, 190
Szell, George, 116, 117, 125, 130–31, 132, *133,* 244

T
Tack, Frank, 194
Taft, Mrs. Charles P., 52
Taft, William Howard, 20, 32
Tait, Margaret, 237
Tak, Eduard, 24, *28,* 29, 30, 42
Takemitsu, Tōru, 149
Tan, Amy, 234, *235*
Taneyev, Sergei, 62
Tanglewood Festival, 27
Tansman, Alexandre, 83
Taylor, Deems, 27
Taylor, Janice, 191
Tchaikovsky, Pyotr Ilich, 28, 30, 49, 64, 73, 86, 123, 130, 144, 149, 174, 208, 243, 248
Tcherepnin, Ivan, 188
Tenney, James, 181
Tetrazzini, Luisa, 17, 30, *31*
Théâtre des Champs-Elysées, 163, 164
Theodore Thomas Orchestra, 17, 42
Thomas, Theodore, 17, 28, 106, 222
Thomashefsky, Bessie, 222, *223*
Thomashefsky, Boris, 222
Thompson, C. W., 89
Thompson, Joseph S., *76,* 79, 84, 85
Thomson, Virgil, 123, 175
Tibbett, Lawrence, 27
TicketReach, 153
Tilson Thomas, Michael, 10, 26, 139, 161, 167, 169, 193, 200, 218, 219, *220,* 221–22, *223–25,* 226, *228,* 229, 232–33, 235, *236,* 237, *239,* 241, *242–46,* 248–49, *250–51*
Tippett, Michael, 188
Tircuit, Heuwell, 162

Tivoli Opera House, 64, *70,* 71, 181
Tjader, Cal, 128
Tobin, Richard, 25, 28, 29, 30, 34, 40, *71,* 73, 74, 75–77, 79, 85, 109, 121
Toronto Symphony, 156
Toscanini, Arturo, 44, 62, 74, *75,* 81, 104, 105, 198
Touzeau, Colette, 89
Trader Vic's, 150
Transamerica Pyramid, 182
Treasure Island, *90,* 91, 98–99
Truman, Harry, 105

U
University of California Berkeley, 160, 186
University of California San Francisco Symphony Forum, 92–94, 148
Upton, Anna-Logan, *122,* 123, 125, 127–29, 190
Urspruch, Anton, 55

V
Van Dyke, Marcia, *102,* 103
Van Dyke, W. S., 103
Van Geem, Jack, 10, *185,* 218
Varèse, Edgard, 224
Vaughan, Sarah, 169, 223
Vaughan Williams, Ralph, 83, 118
Verdi, Giuseppe, 160
Veterans Building, 129
Victor Talking Machine Company, 54, 55
Vienna Philharmonic, 45, 62, 139, 205, 240
Vienna State Opera, 139
Volkert, Mark, 209, 212
Volunteer Council, 181, 190
von Dohnányi, Ernst, 58
von Karajan, Herbert, 156
Vonnegut, Kurt, 225
von Rhein, John, 192

W
Wagner, Charley, 73
Wagner, Richard, 28, 36, 40, 41, 43, 50, 51, 55, 85, 100, 101, 102, 144, 204, 248
Wallenstein, Alfred, 116
Waller, Fats, 134
Walsh, Michael, 184
Walter, Bruno, 46, 92, *100,* 101, 116, 222
Walter, Edgar, 79
Walther, Geraldine, *111, 224,* 225
War Memorial Opera House, 64, *66,* 67, 69, 71, 72, *95,* 98, 100, 109, 129, 134, *135,* 137, *139,* 141, 154, 166, 174, 175, 181–83, 184, 185, 186, 192, 222, 223
Warwick, Dionne, 169
Waterman, Robert H., Jr., 179
Wattis, Phyllis, 232, *233*
Watts, André, 159, 163
Webern, Anton, 181
Weingartner, Felix, 24, 138
Weir, Bob, 224, *228,* 229, *246*
Wells, John, 182
Weston, Vic, 132
Wet Ink, 212
White, Al, 110
White, Dan, 186

The Who, 146
Wickham, Harvey, 26, 28, 32
Widenham, A. W., 48, 50, 54
Wilbur, Brayton, Jr., 129, 178, 180, *181,* 184, *185, 192, 199,* 202, 204–5, 216, *232*
Wilbur, Judy, *192*
Wilbur, Ray Lyman, *94,* 95
Wilford, Ronald, 146
Williams, Cecil, 239
Willson, Meredith, 85
Wilson, Olly, 175
Wilson, Woodrow, 32
Wolfrum, Philipp, 24
Wong, Victor, 175
Wood, Tingley Sylvanus, 88
Woodland Theatre, 64, 71, 89
Wuorinen, Charles, *200,* 201, 212, 233
Wyatt, James Lee, III, 237
Wyss, Niklaus, 160

Y
Yerba Buena Gardens, 169, *239*
YouTube Symphony Orchestra, 243
Ysaÿe, Eugène, 17, 42, 52

Z
Zamora, Florence, 86
Zech, Frederick, 17
Zellerbach, Harold, 182
Zellerbach, J. D., *116,* 117, 118, 121–23, 125, 127, 131, 132, 138, 150, 182
Zellerbach Family Fund, 182
Zhao, Chen, 237
Zimbalist, Efrem, 27, 30
Zinman, David, 215
Zirato, Bruno, 74
Zwilich, Ellen Taaffe, 188